PRAGMATISM

Pragmatism

A Contemporary Reader

Russell B. Goodman

ROUTLEDGE NEW YORK / LONDON

Published in 1995 by

Routledge
29 West 35th Street
New York, NY 10001-2299

Published in Great Britain by

Routledge
11 New Fetter Lane
London EC4P 4EE

Library of Congress Cataloging-in-Publication Data

Pragmatism : a contemporary reader / [edited by] Russell B. Goodman.
    p. cm.
    Includes bibliographic references and index.
    ISBN 0-415-90909-0—ISBN 0-415-90910-4 (pbk.)
    1. Pragmatism.   I. Goodman, Russell B.
B832.P755 1955
144 .3—dc20   95-8034
                                          CIP

CONTENTS

For my parents
and in memory of Jeffrey Thomas schneider

PREFACE

This book is meant for teachers and students of philosophy, literature, and political theory, and for those general readers interested in how our culture makes sense of itself. It consists of a set of statements mostly within but in some cases about pragmatism, focusing on contemporary developments. My introduction and headnotes will, I hope, serve as useful guides to the material, and I have appended a selected bibliography.

For valuable suggestions and discussion I wish to thank Thomas Alexander, David Dunaway, Anne Doughty Goodman, W. D. Hart, Susan Haack, Rupert Read, G. F. Schueler, and the readers for Routledge. (These people should not be held responsible, however, for any of the views expressed here.) Glenda Baxter, John McGraw, and Sandy Robbins helped prepare the manuscript for publication, and the College of Arts and Sciences of the University of New Mexico provided financial support. Special thanks to Maureen MacGrogan, philosophy editor at Routledge, for not only wanting the book but appreciating it.

Russell B. Goodman
Corrales, New Mexico
25 August, 1994

INTRODUCTION

"Each age," Emerson stated, "must write its own books."[1] Pragmatism may be, as William James suggested, "a new name for some old ways of thinking," found as much in Mill or Aristotle as in James or Peirce, but it nevertheless waxes and wanes in response to specific cultural and intellectual circumstances. Why does this age write its own pragmatic books? How is it that a philosophy so vibrant and promising at the turn of the twentieth century and so depleted at midcentury should revive now at century's end: after positivism, phenomenology, logical analysis, naturalized epistemology, and deconstruction?

To help answer these questions, consider the alternative reading of twentieth century philosophy offered by Hilary Putnam, a leading philosopher of logic, language, and mind who has taken a new turn towards pragmatism in his own work. According to Putnam, the first half of the twentieth century saw a series of attempts to construct metaphysical systems and the second, a series of attempts to overcome them. The systems of Carnap, Russell, and the early Wittgenstein were put forward as attacks on metaphysics, yet they were really, Putnam writes, "among the most ingenious, profound, and technically brilliant constructions of metaphysical systems ever achieved."[2] The "analytic philosophy" that these philosophers developed and that continued even as their original systems were overcome—stressing formal logic, careful attention to language, analysis, and argument more than overarching vision—now dominates the American and world philosophical scenes. Yet, Putnam writes, "at the very moment when analytic philosophy is recognized as the 'dominant movement' in world philosophy, it has come to the end of its own project—the dead end, not the completion."[3]

What brings pragmatism back again is neither the emergence of a new metaphysical system nor a technique for eliminating all systems, but rather the appreciation of a deep convergence of thought in twentieth century philosophy: in the writings of the classical pragmatists William James, Charles Sanders Peirce, and John Dewey, but also in the European philosophers Martin Heidegger and Ludwig Wittgenstein.[4] In Wittgenstein's *Philosophical Investigations,* James's *Pragmatism,* Dewey's *Experience and Nature,* and Heidegger's "Letter on Humanism" or "Building, Dwelling, Thinking," new ways of thinking about philosophical problems emerge in which *practice* and the *human* come to the fore. Contemporary pragmatists blend elements from all these writers and others: they know their Dewey but also their Derrida; their Peirce but also their Freud; James's "Stream of Thought" but also Wittgenstein's discussion of a necessarily private language. The new pragmatic consensus that emerged in the 1980s has its sources not only in philosophy but in literary criticism, legal theory, feminism, and political theory.

Pragmatism had originally announced itself in a lecture that Harvard professor William James gave at Berkeley in 1898, entitled "Philosophical Conceptions and Practical Results." Complicating the question of pragmatism's origins from the start, James credited his friend Charles Sanders Peirce with originating the "principle of pragmatism," which James stated as follows: "To attain perfect clearness in our thoughts of an object...we need only consider what effects of a conceivably practical kind the object may involve—what sensations we are to expect from it, and what reactions we must prepare."[5] Peirce and James stress results rather than origins in our understanding of ideas, and emphasize *our* sensations and *our* reactions. The world for a pragmatist is the world as we react to, or with, it—a scene of "transactions," as Dewey was to put it. James spoke of "the humanistic principle: you can't weed out the human contribution," from which it follows that we do not know things "in themselves," but only as intertwined with our contributions of organization, interest, and selection.[6] This "humanism" of the classical pragmatism of James and Dewey is an important source of its appeal to such neopragmatists as Putnam and Rorty.

Pragmatism has also had its important political and social side, exemplified most clearly in the career of John Dewey, and visible today in the work of Richard Rorty, Cornel West, and Nancy Fraser. Dewey developed theories of education and politics that are of a piece with his pragmatic theories of inquiry, truth, and meaning, and he states in his autobiography that *Democracy and Education*—a portion of which is reprinted below—contains what was for many years the fullest exposition of his philosophy. In pursuit of his belief that one learns by doing, Dewey (and his wife Alice) founded the Laboratory School at the University of Chicago. Dewey maintained a presence in the popular press for decades, discussing issues of war and peace, American foreign policy, poverty, and democracy. Angering both the radical and the Popular Front left, he traveled to Mexico (at the age of 77) to chair the 1937 Commission formed to investigate the charges made against Leon Trotsky in the Moscow Trials.[7]

Amid this welter of detail and tendency it is natural to try to define pragmatism or to seek its essence. The problem then becomes, however, one of proliferating rather than absent definitions. The pages of just one pragmatist work—James's *Pragmatism* (1907)—contain at least six accounts of what pragmatism is or contains: a theory of truth, a theory of meaning, a philosophical temperament, an epistemology/metaphysics stressing human interest and action, a method for dissolving philosophical disputes, and a skeptical anti-essentialism. No wonder that a year after James's book appeared Arthur Lovejoy was able to publish in *The Journal of Philosophy* a classic paper called "The Thirteen Pragmatisms," in which he claimed that not only did "pragmatism" stand for different doctrines, but that in some cases these doctrines conflicted.[8]

The relations of various pragmatists and pragmatisms to one another can best be understood, however, in terms of a metaphor James himself introduces when he attempts to define religion in *Varieties of Religious Experience*. Warning that "the theorizing mind tends always to the simplification of its materials," James admits at the outset "that we may very likely find no one essence, but many characters which may alternately be equally important in religion." So it is with pragmatism: there is no essence linking all pragmatist writers, but rather a series of "characters which may alternately be equally important." Two pragmatist writers may share a theory of truth and diverge on their theories of meaning; share a Romantic sense of fashioning the world but not a religious sensibility. The person who knows a subject best, James asserts, enjoys "an intimate acquaintance with all [its] particularities in turn," and would "naturally regard an abstract conception in which these were unified as a thing more misleading than enlightening."[9] Contemporary pragmatists take up one or another of the linked characters manifested by the classical pragmatists—as Putnam develops James's humanism, and Rorty Dewey's liberalism, for example—but they have half a century's worth of philosophical and historical developments behind them as they refashion pragmatic ideas in accordance with what Emerson called "their own sight of principles."[10]

The new turn in philosophy is displayed most vividly in the trajectory of Putnam's career. The Walter Beverly Pearson Professor of Mathematical Logic at Harvard, Putnam made his mark working in philosophy of language, philosophy of logic, and philosophy of mind, brilliantly extending the analytic line of philosophy running through Frege, Russell, Carnap, Ayer, and Quine. Beginning with his 1981 book *Reason, Truth and History*, and continuing with *The Many Faces of Realism* (1987), *Realism with a Human Face* (1990), and *Renewing Philosophy* (1992), Putnam turns towards the pragmatism of Peirce, Dewey, and especially James for new approaches to problems of language, knowledge, and value.

At the end of the nineteenth century, according to Putnam—in the work of such continental writers as Nietzsche and Husserl, but also in America in the work of James and Dewey—"Hume's project" began to be dismantled. This project was not simply Hume's "skeptical" account of causation but, Putnam writes, "the entire enterprise of dividing mundane 'reality' into the Furniture of the Universe and our 'projection.'" The late nineteenth century philosophers to whom Putnam calls attention—James, Dewey, Husserl, Heidegger—"have in common a rejection—a total root-and-branch rejection—of the enterprise mentioned, and a concern with the quotidian, with the *Lebenswelt*, with what a philosophy free of the search for a "true world" (Nietzsche's phrase!) might look like."[11]

Putnam finds this concern with the quotidian not only in the classical pragmatists and phenomenologists but also in the Oxford ordinary language philosopher J. L. Austin, the later Wittgenstein, and his Harvard colleague Stanley Cavell. He offers a version of pragmatism that combines what James called "the scientific loyalty to facts and willingness to take account of them" with "the old confidence in human values and the resultant spontaneity, whether of the religious or of the romantic type."[12] Putnam embraces science but not scientism (an overvaluation or overextension of scientific claims), "internal" or "pragmatic" realism but not relativism, morality but not fanaticism. Sailing between scientism and skepticism, he accepts "the position we are fated to occupy in any case, the position of beings who cannot have a view of the world that does not reflect our interests and values, but who are, for all that, committed to regarding some views of the world—and, for that matter, some interests and values—as better than others."[13]

Richard Rorty, the other great figure of contemporary pragmatism, also offers a blend of classical pragmatism, Wittgensteinian philosophy of language, and phenomenology. Writing in his groundbreaking *Philosophy and the Mirror of Nature* (1979) that Wittgenstein, Heidegger, and Dewey are "the three most important philosophers of our century," Rorty reads not only Wittgenstein's early philosophy but the early philosophy of Heidegger and Dewey as searches for foundations, for ways of "formulating an ultimate context for thought." Yet all three came to believe that this search was "self-deceptive, an attempt to retain a certain conception of philosophy after the notions needed to flesh out that conception (the seventeenth-century notions of knowledge and the mind) had been discarded."[14]

Rorty therefore attacks certain pictures of the mind, language, knowledge, and morality, and of philosophical problems concerning these subjects, but he does not reject the past altogether. "I hope," he writes, "that we never stop reading Plato, Aristotle, Kant, Hegel, Dewey, and Heidegger, but also hope that we may, sooner or later, stop trying to sucker the freshmen into taking an interest in 'the problem of the external world' and 'the problem of other minds.'"[15] In Rorty's long view of philosophical history, as in Putnam's, Kant plays a pivotal role in teaching that the shaping powers of the mind extend not just to our own isolated egoic experiences but to the very world in which that experience takes place. "About two hundred years ago," Rorty writes, "the idea that truth was made rather than found began to take hold of the imagination of Europe."[16] This idea of truth, suitably naturalized through pragmatism, undercuts "the problem of the external world" as traditionally conceived.

Rorty's pragmatism takes the form of an interdisciplinary or postdisciplinary conversation. Taking up issues in law, psychology, literary theory, and political theory, Rorty has become the most visible American philosopher since John Dewey. In "Feminism and

Pragmatism," for example (reprinted below), Rorty discusses the work of such feminist theorists as Catharine MacKinnon, Nancy Fraser, Eve Sedgwick, Marilyn Frye, and Sandra Harding, along with the views of Stanley Fish, Jonathan Culler, Dewey, Wittgenstein, and Habermas. Because Rorty sees pragmatism as redescribing both intellectual and moral progress "by substituting metaphors of evolutionary development for metaphors of progressively less distorted perception," he holds that "a pragmatist feminist will see herself as helping to create women rather than attempting to describe them more accurately."[17] Agreeing with this conception of the feminist pragmatist yet criticizing Rorty for offering an individualistic and aestheticized conception of abnormal discourse, Nancy Fraser (in a response reprinted below) contends nevertheless that Rorty's work on feminism marks a major new turn in his thought, in which "the oppositions between the public and the private, the community and the individual, the political and the aesthetic are exploded." The pragmatized feminism Fraser envisions growing from Rorty's work is "a discursive practice that involves far-reaching redescriptions of social life and thus has all the marks of the sublime, the abnormal, and the poetic, yet is simultaneously tied to the collective political enterprise of overcoming oppression and restructuring society."[18]

In achieving the interdisciplinary or extradisciplinary visibility that he has, Rorty follows his own advice in *Philosophy and the Mirror of Nature*: that philosophers no longer treat themselves as members of a privileged profession or subject who have "an overriding claim on the attention of the other participants in the conversation" because they practice "philosophical method" or have learned "philosophical analysis" in graduate school.[19] Rather, Rorty maintains, philosophy must admit its only provisional or partial authority and find its place along with literature, criticism, the sciences, politics, and history in the general "conversation of mankind."[20] In his latest book, *Contingency, Irony, and Solidarity*, Rorty blends substantial discussions of writers as diverse as Freud, Derrida, Orwell, Foucault, Habermas, and Proust in a defense of liberal democracy (albeit from the stance of the "liberal ironist"). Defining a liberal in part as someone who thinks that "cruelty is the worst thing we do,"[21] Rorty defends the critical role of novels—"books which help us become less cruel"[22]—in liberal democracies, in part through readings of Nabokov's *Pale Fire* and Orwell's *1984*. Like Dewey, Rorty calls for less attention to "the problems of philosophers," and more attention to "the problems of men."[23]

✳✳✳✳✳✳✳✳✳✳✳✳

Between Rorty and Putnam on the one hand and the classical pragmatists on the other stand two crucial developments in contemporary philosophy, each of which moved philosophers away from the idea that what we accept as true reflects the way the world is "in itself": W. V. O. Quine's attack on the "Two Dogmas of Empiricism" and Thomas Kuhn's historicizing of our conception of science.[24] Quine's 1953 paper showed the inadequacies of all extant definitions of a priori statements: those said to be "necessary," "analytic," or "true in virtue of their meaning." If no such statements exist then many traditional roles philosophers have allotted themselves—e.g., uncovering "transcendental presuppositions," practicing "conceptual analysis"—simply disappear. Quine wrote:

> Any statement can be held true come what may if we make drastic enough adjust-ments elsewhere in the system. Even a statement very close to the periphery can be held true in the face of recalcitrant experience by pleading hallucination or by amending certain statements of the kind called logical laws. Conversely, by the same token, no statement is immune to revision. Revision even of the logical law of the excluded middle has been proposed as a means of simplifying quantum mechanics; and what difference is there in principle between such a shift and a shift whereby Keppler superceded Ptolemy, or Einstein Newton, or Darwin Aristotle.[25]

Kuhn's *The Structure of Scientific Revolutions* showed how effectively a given scientific the-ory can maintain its dominance even in the face of contrary evidence. Rather than a straight line of development, in which facts are accumulated and added to one another, Kuhn found scientific progress to be a spiral, in which the great revolutions of Copernicus or Einstein remake the "paradigms" according to which "normal science" proceeds. Each scientific revolution, Kuhn wrote, requires

> the community's rejection of one time-honored scientific theory in favor of another incompatible with it. Each produced a consequent shift in the problems available for scientific scrutiny and in the standards by which the profession determined what should count as an admissible problem or as a legitimate problem-solution. And each transformed the scientific imagination in ways that we shall ultimately need to describe as a transformation of the world within which scientific work was done.[26]

Quine's paper accords with Kuhn's account because it highlights both the contingency of our theoretical schemes and their pragmatic support. Our world of physical objects is not less of a "myth," Quine writes, than the world of "Homer's Gods," and its superior-ity lies in its having proved "more efficacious than other myths as a device for working a manageable structure into the flux of experience."[27]

Quine's use of the term "myth" and his statement that the myth of physical objects is superior only "to most" other myths raise the issue of what Peirce called "fallibilism," our enduring capacity for mistakes; and this in turn raises an issue that divides pragma-tists from each other as well as from some of their opponents: the issue of truth. If our best theories of the world are going to be revised anyway, can we say any of them is true? More radically, is there any sense in speaking of truth at all?

This question serves as an entry into the heart of contemporary philosophical prag-matism, for Rorty and Putnam, like James and Dewey before them, want to sever the concept of truth from the idea of a preconstituted or absolute world to which our thoughts or propositions must correspond. Yet Putnam, like Peirce, feels the pull of something beyond any particular human scheme by which our schemes—whether moral, philosophical, aesthetic, or scientific—are measured or constrained. Rorty, in contrast, finds only "the conversation of mankind," and diagnoses Putnam's feeling as a trace of mistaken metaphysical theory from which Putnam would free himself if he were a more thoroughgoing pragmatist.

Rorty renews Dewey's attack on traditional metaphysics and epistemology (as in "Does Reality Possess Practical Character?", reprinted below). Epistemology, Rorty maintains, is the attempt to see "the patterns of justification within normal discourse as *more* than just such patterns...the attempt to see them as hooked on to something which demands moral commitment—Reality, Truth, Objectivity, Reason." Although he has no use for this "metaphysical" conception of Truth (one he finds even in Putnam), Rorty preserves a use for the term "truth" (with a small "t"). "'Objective truth,'" he writes in *Philosophy and the Mirror of Nature,* "is no more and no less than the best idea we currently have about how to explain what is going on."[28] Rorty puts the point a decade later in terms of the liberalism defended in *Contingency, Irony, and Solidarity*: "A liberal society is one which is content to call 'true' whatever the upshot of [free and open] encounters turns out to be."[29] Rorty's notion of "objective truth" has much of the flavor of James's view (his "pragmatist theory of truth") that the true idea is the one that allows us to get from one portion of our experience to another. Ideas become true, James states,

> just in so far as they help us to get into satisfactory relation with other parts of our experience.... Any idea upon which we can ride, so to speak; any idea that will carry us prosperously from any one part of our experience to any other part, linking things satisfactorily, working securely, simplifying, saving labor; is true for just so much, true in so far forth, true instrumentally.[30]

In *Reason, Truth and History,* Putnam retains allegiance to a more traditional view of truth, stressing the difference between rational acceptability at any given time and long-run or "ideal" acceptability. His view owes much to Peirce, who wrote, "The opinion which is fated to be ultimately agreed upon by all who investigate is what we mean by truth, and the object represented by this opinion is real."[31] This sentence expresses the key pragmatic (and Kantian) idea that truth is a human "opinion," an opinion of human inquirers rather than a property of things "as they are in themselves." Yet Peirce's statement contains two words important to Putnam's position but foreign to Rorty's view of things: "ultimately" and "fated." Both suggest a pull towards the final human opinion on the part of the world, a pull Putnam gets at when he writes that "the mind and the world jointly make up the mind and the world."[32]

Putnam and Rorty share the basic Wittgensteinian picture of language as an accretion of human practices; or, as Wittgenstein put it in *Philosophical Investigations,* "as an ancient city: a maze of little streets and squares, of old and new houses, and of houses with additions from various periods; and this surrounded by a multitude of new boroughs with straight regular streets and uniform houses."[33] But Rorty offers an account of language more deflationary than Putnam's and Wittgenstein's, in which not only is there no preestablished absolute set of meanings, but there is nothing more to language than "noises." Rorty calls this account "Darwinian": "a story about humans as animals with special organs and abilities: about how certain features of the human throat, hand, and brain enabled humans to start developing increasingly complex social practices, by batting increasingly complex noises back and forth."[34]

Putnam sees in Rorty's stance a form of "mental suicide" in which normative notions like rationality, right and wrong, and thinking have been eliminated in favor of a grim causal account of language as "noisemakings."[35] For Putnam, notions such as rationality are both "immanent (not to be found outside of concrete language games and institutions) and transcendent (a regulative idea that we use to criticize the conduct of all activities and institutions)."[36] Philosophers who lose sight of the immanence of reason are in the grip of fantasies of absolute knowledge, significance, or morality which, Putnam agrees with Rorty, are untenable. But philosophers who lose sight of the transcendence of reason, Putnam holds, fall into a deeply irrational "cultural relativism."[37] Putnam's complex position embracing immanence and transcendence is close to that expressed by Adorno and cited with approval by Habermas:

> The only philosophy we might responsibly engage in, after all that has happened, would no longer be free to credit itself with power over the absolute. It would indeed have to forbid itself to think the absolute, lest it betray the thought—and yet it must not allow itself to be gulled out of the emphatic concept of truth. This contradiction is its element.[38]

According to the logical positivism that formed the backdrop to Putnam's and Rorty's philosophical education,[39] all moral statements are "cognitively meaningless" "pseudo-statements" that are neither true nor false. One reason both philosophers turn towards pragmatism is the ease with which moral and political (and aesthetic) statements can be validated within pragmatic theory. To paraphrase Kant, the new pragmatists deny absolute truth in order to make room, along with humanized science, for humanized morality.[40]

The positivists were, according to Putnam and Rorty, in one way right: there are no absolute values waiting to be "discovered" by a humanity that must then find statements about them to be true. But since—as we have learned through the work of Quine, Nelson Goodman, Sellars, Kuhn, and others—there are no absolute scientific or observational truths either, no absolute foundations on which all legitimate disciplines depend, there is no way of ruling talk about morality altogether out of bounds. Trading on the humanly-constituted nature of all truth (with a small "t"), Rorty and Putnam each in his own way allows for and engages in substantial talk about morality. "I hold," Rorty writes, "that the distinction between true and false (the positivists' mark of 'cognitive status') is as applicable to statements like 'Yeats was a great poet', and 'Democracy is better than tyranny', as to statements like 'The earth goes around the sun'."[41]

Rorty defends liberal democracies not by comparing them to some a priori standard but by comparison with "other forms of social organization—those of the past and those envisaged by utopians."[42] "My hunch," he writes,

> is that Western social and political thought may have had the last conceptual revolu-
> tion it needs. J. S. Mill's suggestion that governments devote themselves to optimizing
> the balance between leaving people's private lives alone and preventing suffering
> seems to me pretty much the last word.[43]

Although Rorty sides with Habermas in supporting liberal democracy, he finds Habermas's project of grounding democracy in "domination-free communication" just one more metaphysical project, relying on an unrealizable ideal. Rorty praises Michel Foucault for his sensitivity to the ways domination may mask itself, especially in liberal democracies; but he faults him for giving insufficient weight to the "decrease in pain" these democracies bring about. Foucault, Rorty writes, is "an ironist who is unwilling to be a liberal," and Habermas "a liberal who is unwilling to be an ironist."[44]

Putnam also engages the thought of Foucault and Habermas. He shares with Foucault a sense for the historical determination of our concepts and values, but attacks Foucault's "relativism" and extreme "historicism." Although he applauds Habermas's idea that we can rationally assess better and worse ends rather than just the means to those ends, Putnam criticizes Habermas for retaining a strict distinction between the his-torical and the natural sciences, for failing to recognize that "interpretation, in a very wide sense of the term, and value are involved in our notion of rationality in every area."[45] In his Gifford Lectures, Putnam defends a claim that has both a Deweyan and a Habermasian ring: "Democracy is not just one form of social life among other workable forms of social life; it is the precondition for the full application of intelligence to the solution of social problems."[46] Democracy thus assumes not only a political but an intel-lectual role, a role in "the full application of intelligence."

Putnam—like Rorty—accords truth equally to scientific and to moral and aesthetic statements: "There *are* tables and chairs and ice cubes. There are also electrons and space–time regions and prime numbers and people who are a threat to world peace and moments of beauty and transcendence and many other things."[47] The variety of these statements indicates "the many faces" of the "pragmatic realism" that Putnam defends. (See the selections from *The Many Faces of Realism* reprinted below.)

Despite the widespread agreement between these two contemporary pragmatists, many readers (including Putnam, if not Rorty) have felt that there are profound differ-ences between their positions.[48] In "Putnam and the Relativist Menace," (1993) Rorty identifies five key statements of Putnam's with which he completely agrees, and then complains: "We seem, both to me and to philosophers who find both our views absurd, to be in much the same line of business. But Putnam sees us as doing something quite different, and I do not know why."[49]

William James has something useful to say about the nature of this difference in the first chapter of *Pragmatism*:

> The philosophy which is so important in each of us is not a technical matter; it is our more or less dumb sense of what life honestly and deeply means. It is only partly got from books; it is our individual way of just seeing and feeling the total push and pressure of the cosmos.... The history of philosophy is to a great extent that of a certain clash of human temperaments.[50]

Putnam and Rorty, I want to suggest, have radically different intellectual temperaments, evident not only in their divergences on such issues as truth, moral realism, or rationality, but in the differences of tone and tendency in their thought even in the many places where their views overlap. Their senses of the "total push and pressure of the cosmos" are at odds.

These temperamental differences can be clarified if we apply a distinction James introduces in *Pragmatism* to define pragmatism itself: that between the "tough-minded" and the "tender-minded" temperaments in philosophy. Although James presents the pragmatist—a "happy-go-lucky anarchistic sort of character"[51]— as a mediator between them, these two temperamental tendencies form a further division within pragmatism, exemplified today in Putnam and Rorty. James drew his distinction via two lists:

THE TENDER-MINDED	THE TOUGH-MINDED
Rationalistic (going by 'principles'),	Empiricist (going by 'facts'),
Intellectualistic,	Sensationalistic,
Idealistic,	Materialistic,
Optimistic,	Pessimistic,
Religious,	Irreligious,
Free-willist,	Fatalistic,
Monistic,	Pluralistic,
Dogmatical,	Sceptical[52]

Although Rorty and Putnam stand on the same side of some of these oppositions— for example, they are both "free-willist" and "pluralistic"— Putnam's "intellectualistic" emphasis on reason, sense of a "transcendent" rationality, moral realism, and essential cheerfulness place him on the tender-minded left side; whereas Rorty's eliminative materialism, stress on contingency ("going by 'facts'"), and generally skeptical character place him on the tough-minded right.

A further opposition within James's lists confirms this placement, for Putnam is in some sense a religious philosopher; and Rorty, with his project of "dedivinization" and his intense skepticism, determinedly irreligious. Putnam opens his 1990 Gifford Lectures, *Renewing Philosophy*, by stating that the Lectures' traditional concern with religion and more recent concern with science both "speak to me. As a practicing Jew, I am someone for whom the religious dimension of life has become increasingly important, although it is not a dimension I know how to philosophize about except by indirection."[53] *Renewing Philosophy* does include a chapter on Wittgenstein's "Lectures on Religious Belief," but Putnam's fundamental piety shows itself throughout his earlier pragmatic writing, especially in the tone and content of his discussions of what he calls "moral images" or "moral visions" of the world. Although Putnam has for years looked to Kant's epistemological theory as a predecessor of his "internal" or "pragmatic" realism, he now looks also to Kant's statements about the morally relevant noumenal domain (the domain, as Kant put it, of "God, Freedom, and Immortality"). The Kantian moral image, Putnam writes,

> includes the claim that a human being who has chosen not to think for himself about how to live, or has been coerced or "conditioned" into being unable to think for himself about how to live, has failed to live a fully human life. It contains also the vision of a community of individuals who respect one another for that capacity.[54]

William James thought of pragmatism as a philosophy that could allow one to "remain religious" while at the same time preserving "the richest intimacy with facts."[55] Dewey too had a religious streak, from his early reading of Coleridge through his late book *A Common Faith*.[56] Putnam's work falls into this religious pragmatist line (which also includes Cornel West, whose "Prophetic Pragmatism" is reprinted below). Rorty, in contrast, is as deeply irreligious as Albert Camus or Jean-Paul Sartre. He aims for "the point where we no longer worship anything, where we treat nothing as a quasi divinity, where we treat everything—our language, our conscience, our community—as a product of time and chance."[57]

****

If a great part of the current revival of pragmatism stems from forces internal to contemporary philosophy, another important part stems from a new appreciation, mostly outside professional philosophy, of a writer who has not until recently been taken to be a pragmatist at all: Ralph Waldo Emerson. Emerson's newly understood importance lies partly in his influence on Dewey and James, partly in the contemporaneity of some of his main ideas. For example, Emerson enunciates an anti-essentialism in regard to language as up to date as any proposed by Derrida or Rorty. "All symbols are fluxional," he writes in "The Poet," "all language is vehicular and transitive, and is good, as ferries and horses are, for conveyance, not as farms and houses are, for homestead."[58] Emerson thus portrays language not as a fixed mirror of the world's essence but as a tool for getting us from here to there, as something practical. James makes a similar point in *Pragmatism*: "if you follow the pragmatic method you cannot look on any ... word as closing your quest. You must bring out of each word its practical cash-value, set it at work within the stream of your experience. It appears less as a solution, then, than as a program for more work, and more particularly as an indication of the ways in which existing realities may be changed."[59]

Richard Poirier, Professor of English at Rutgers, finds in such continuities the basis for claiming that James owes an "enormous, and largely unadmitted, debt to Emerson."[60] In *The Renewal of Literature: Emersonian Reflections* (1987) and *Poetry and Pragmatism* (1992), Poirier traces an Emersonian pragmatist line running from Emerson through William James to Robert Frost and Wallace Stevens. Speaking of a pragmatist as "some version of Emerson," Poirier explains that a pragmatist might find a use for words like "God" or "Soul," but would suppose "that there was in fact really nothing outside to depend on and nothing inside either, nothing except the desire that there should be more than nothing."[61] Focusing on Emerson's use of a vocabulary of action, fact, and power, Poirier highlights the common emphases in Emerson and James "on transitions as a valuable form of action," and on "the need stressed by both of them for movement away from substantives or resting-places or settled texts."[62]

Poirier's many discussions of tone of voice in *Poetry and Pragmatism* raise the issue of temperament. "Emersonian pragmatists," he states, share much with such European writers as Nietzsche, Foucault and Derrida, but they have "a laid-back, rather quiet way... of imagining and responding to cultural crises."[63] Again, "Emersonian pragmatist writing" shares with T. S. Eliot and contemporary deconstructionists a skeptical attitude toward language; but "the tone of that writing hints at so few of the grim cultural prognoses heard not only in Eliot but in more recent complaints that language is a prison house, an instrument of repression that destroys individual identity even as it bestows it."[64] Emersonian pragmatists, this is to say, are optimistic and forward-looking even as they deny essential structures or foundations. The art of life, as Emerson says in "Experience," is to skate across its surfaces.

Tracing Emerson's "stress on the dynamic character of selves and structures, the malleability of tradition, and the transformative potential in human history,"[65] Cornel West argues in *The American Evasion of Philosophy: A Genealogy of Pragmatism* that these Emersonian preoccupations reach an important culmination in the thought of John Dewey. West, who is Professor of Religion at Harvard, highlights Dewey's 1903 essay "Ralph Waldo Emerson—Philosopher of Democracy," which reveals the considerable overlap Dewey found between his own projects and those of Emerson. Dewey writes that Emerson

> finds truth in the highway, in the untaught endeavor, the unexpected ideas.... His eyes are not fixed upon any Reality that is beyond or behind or in any way apart, and hence they do not have to be bent. They are versions of the Here and Now, and flow freely. The reputed transcendental worth of an overweening Beyond and Away,

Emerson, jealous for spiritual democracy, finds to be the possession of the unquestionable Present. [66]

West himself forges a new synthesis in the tradition of the "prophetic pragmatism" which he finds originally in Emerson, incorporating ideas of Karl Marx, W. E. B. Du Bois, Roberto Unger, Martin Luther King, Lionel Trilling, Richard Rorty, James, Dewey, Emerson, and others. In "Prophetic Pragmatism: Cultural Criticism and Political Engagement," the concluding chapter of *The American Evasion of Philosophy* (reprinted below), West writes: "Tradition can be both a smothering and a liberating affair, depending on which traditions are being invoked, internalized, and invented."[67] The tradition of American pragmatism that West seeks to continue "is less a philosophical tradition putting forward solutions to perennial problems in the Western philosophical conversation initiated by Plato, and more a continuous cultural commentary or set of interpretations that attempt to explain America to itself at a particular historical moment."[68]

A third contemporary important for our understanding of Emersonian pragmatism is Stanley Cavell, Professor of Aesthetics and the General Theory of Value at Harvard. Cavell is not concerned with setting Emerson within the pragmatist tradition at all, but with placing him in a line running from Kant and Wordsworth to Nietzsche, Heidegger, and Wittgenstein.[69] Nevertheless Cavell's work on Emerson's "epistemology of moods" (as in "Thinking of Emerson," reprinted below) helps us to understand Emerson's role in developing a pragmatic idealism in the tradition of Kant. His discussions of Emerson's (and Thoreau's) ideas about thinking and language are important touchstones for an understanding not only of Emerson but of such contemporary pragmatists as Poirier and Putnam.[70] Emerson shares with the pragmatists the crucial idea that truth is in the making rather than already established, and that it is made in some sense by humanity. William James stated in *Pragmatism*: "In our cognitive as well as in our active life we are creative....The world stands really malleable, waiting to receive its final touches at our hands." Yet James was preceded by Emerson, who wrote that "nature is thoroughly mediate.... It receives the dominion of man as meekly as the ass on which the Savior rode."[71] Emerson derived the idea of our role in constructing reality from his reading of Coleridge and Kant. Cavell's "Thinking of Emerson" first made the case for the claim that such Emersonian essays as "Experience" are saturated with Kantian ideas.

Emerson portrays himself as an experimenter: "No facts are to me sacred; none are profane; I simply experiment, an endless seeker, with no Past at my back."[72] Nowhere is his contemporary aspect clearer than in his description of experimentation as a form of revision or reinterpretation. In "Circles" (reprinted below) he writes: "Every ultimate fact is only the first of a new series. Every general law only a particular fact of some more general law presently to disclose itself."[73]

Even the virtues are experimental, Emerson asserts, liable to be replaced by newer, better ideals: "The... law of eternal procession, ranges all that we call the virtues, and extinguishes each in the light of a better."[74] Or as Dewey put it in a passage cited by Rorty in "Feminism and Pragmatism": "The worse or evil is a rejected good.... Until it is rejected it is a competing good. After rejection, it figures not as a lesser good, but as the bad of that situation."[75] The Romantic Emerson is a source for Harold Bloom's and Rorty's idea of the "strong poet," who "fills the sky" with his reinterpretation of others, only to yield to a further, no more final, interpretation of all past work. Rorty's goal of new and interesting conversation is itself an interpretation of what may be called the Emersonian sublime: a troping or turning or reinterpretation of previous statements.[76]

The emergence of contemporary literary pragmatism would no doubt have dismayed Peirce, who in 1905 was already distancing himself from James, and observing that his word "pragmatism" had begun "to be met with occasionally in the literary journals, where it gets abused in the merciless way that words have to expect when they fall into literary clutches."[77] Yet Peirce, as well as anyone who ever lived, knew that words' meanings are not under the control of a single speaker or writer, that they are instruments subject to continual reinterpretation. Pragmatism's antiessentialism, whether in regard to knowledge, language, morality, or the self, allows its practitioners to function in the world of postmodern theory, without however succumbing to what Rorty calls "the self-contradictory postmodernist rhetoric of unmasking," which presupposes that there is some underlying "true" or "theoretically validated" structure of oppression or disintegration, etc.[78]

Prominent among contemporary pragmatic critics is Stanley Fish, Professor of English at Duke, whose works include *Surprised by Sin: The Reader in "Paradise Lost"* (1967), *Self-Consuming Artifacts: The Experience of Seventeenth Century Literature* (1972), *Is There a Text in This Class?* (1980), *Doing What Comes Naturally: Change, Rhetoric and the Practice of Theory in Literary and Legal Studies* (1989), and *There's No Such Thing as Free Speech, and It's a Good Thing, Too* (1994). Central to Fish's pragmatic theory is a Peircean notion: that of an interpretive community. However, Fish retains little of Peirce's belief in objectivity. Whereas for Peirce truth is the opinion *fated* to be arrived at by the *final* community of inquirers, for Fish truth is what *any* interpretive community allows as true, a matter entirely *constituted* by that community. In "What Makes an Interpretation Acceptable?" reprinted below, Fish discusses various interpretations of William Blake's *The Tyger*, each of which claims to more perfectly accord with the text or facts of the poem than any other. Fish argues that all such facts exist only from the perspective of some interpretation that is itself grounded in an interpretive community, such as the community of scholars in this or that wing of contemporary American English departments. (Just as Kuhn had argued that the scientific "profession" sets the "standards" for what counts "as an admissible problem or as a legitimate problem-solution," so Fish argues that literary critics and literary historians set the standards for acceptable interpretations.) "Strictly speaking," Fish writes, "getting 'back-to-the-text' is not a move one can perform, because the text one gets back to will be the text demanded by some other interpretation and that interpretation will be presiding over its production.... it is only within the institution that the facts of literary study—texts, authors, periods, genres—become available."[79]

Fish's position is thus akin to Rorty's (and ultimately to James's): there is no text out-side of an interpretation, just as for Rorty "there is nothing beyond vocabularies which serves as a criterion of choice between them"[80] and for James "nothing outside the flux secures the issue of it."[81] For Fish, no interpretation of a work such as Faulkner's "A Rose for Emily" is impossible—not even the seemingly preposterous hypothesis that it is about Eskimos—just as for Rorty "anything [can] be made to look good or bad, impor-tant or unimportant, useful or useless, by being redescribed."[82] If Fish, like Rorty, tends towards an idealistic pragmatism—in which the world or the text threatens to drop out or collapse into a multitude of perspectives—then Poirier among the literary practi-tioners, like Putnam among the philosophical pragmatists, preserves a sense of encounter with a text (even as he stresses our interpretive powers over it). "Reading is nothing if it is not personal," Poirier writes. "It ought to get down ultimately to a struggle between what you want to make of a text and what it wants to make of itself and of you."[83]

This issue of objectivity or encounterability is also central to Ian Hacking's "Three Parables," which both explorers ways in which we make the world and records impor-tant ways in which we do not. "The Green Family" tells the story of a collection of Chinese green porcelain which, ignored for many years, nevertheless lay waiting to be appreciated by human eyes: "no matter what dark ages we endure, so long as cellars save for us an adequate body of work by the green family, there will be generations that redis-cover it. It will time and again show itself."[84] In his second parable, "Remaking the World" Hacking, who is Professor of History and Philosophy of Science and Technology at the University of Toronto, discusses ways in which new scientific theories change the world, for example, by allowing us to produce electric currents or new particles. But, he maintains, these ways of changing the world are evidence for scientific realism rather than for the relativism towards which Kuhn, Rorty, Fish, and others are inclined.

In his third parable, "Making Up People," Hacking argues that certain kinds of people are, as writers like Foucault have stressed, "constructed" or—as Hacking puts it—"made up." These people are essentially historical. A colonel in the United States army, for example, could not exist without the United States, and the United States could not exist without its history. In contrast to such scientific objects as electrons, Hacking con-cludes, "categories of people come into existence at the same time as kinds of people come into existence to fit those categories, and there is a two-way interaction between these processes."[85] Electrons, unlike colonels in the U.S. army, are not historical: they have always been available, even if the equipment to isolate and record them has not.

What then is pragmatism, and is it correct or even useful? These questions continue to be with us. If, as James stated, the person who knows a subject best enjoys "an intimate acquaintance with all [its] particularities in turn," then the best way to understand con-temporary pragmatism is to immerse oneself in these particularities rather than to search for a simple definition that will apply to them all. In this volume, I have therefore tried to select writings that illustrate the varieties of pragmatism in their most personal and pungent form, writings that will encourage and reward repeated readings. Selecting from an enormous outpouring of contemporary writing in many different fields, and from four of the the classical pragmatists, I have in the end settled on twelve of the strongest human voices I could find, in the hope that their contending visions might activate some reader's own vision of the current reconstruction of pragmatism and beyond. Since as Emerson stated "the one thing in the world of value, is, the active soul,"[86] the proper pragmatic response to pragmatism would be to take it up again and see what can be made of it.

Notes

1 Ralph Waldo Emerson, "The American Scholar." In *The Collected Works of Ralph Waldo Emerson*, ed. Robert E. Spiller et al.,vol.1 (Cambridge, MA: Harvard University Press, 1971); hereafter CW.

2 Hilary Putnam, *Realism with a Human Face* (Cambridge, MA: Harvard University Press, 1990), p. 51; hereafter RHF.

3 RHF, p. 52.

4 For reevaluations of these philosophers see Mark Okrent, *Heidegger's Pragmatism* (Ithaca: Cornell University Press, 1988); Putnam's forthcoming book on Wittgenstein and Pragmatism (Blackwell); and Russell B. Goodman, "What Wittgenstein Learned from William James," *History of Philosophy Quarterly* , July 1994, pp. 339–54.

5 William James, *Pragmatism* (Cambridge, MA: Harvard University Press, 1975), p. 259; hereafter P.

6 P, p. 122.

7 See the account in Robert B. Westbrook, *John Dewey and American Democracy* (Ithaca and London: Cornell University Press, 1991), pp. 280 ff.

8 Arthur Lovejoy, "The Thirteen Pragmatisms," *Journal of Philosophy* 5 (1908), pp. 5–12, 29–39. Reprinted in Arthur Lovejoy, *The Thirteen Pragmatisms* (Baltimore: Johns Hopkins University Press, 1963), pp. 1–29.

9 William James, *Varieties of Religious Experience* In William James, *Writings 1902–1910* (New York: The Library of America, 1987), p. 32.

10 Emerson, "The American Scholar," Penguin, p. 88.

11 RHF, p. 52.

12 P, p. 17.

13 RHF, p. 178.

14 Richard Rorty, *Philosophy and the Mirror of Nature* (Princeton: Princeton University Press, 1979), p. 5; hereafter PMN.

15 Richard Rorty, "Putnam and the Relativist Menace," *Journal of Philosophy* 90:9 (1993), p. 447 fn. 8; hereafter PRM.

16 Richard Rorty, *Contingency, Irony, and Solidarity* (Cambridge: Cambridge University Press, 1989), p. 3; hereafter CIS.

17 Rorty, "Feminism and Pragmatism," pp. 234, 238.

18 For other work on feminism and pragmatism see the special issue of *Hypatia* (vol. 8, no. 2, Spring 1993) edited by Charlene Haddock Seigfried. For critical discussion of Rorty's public/private distinction see

Giles Gunn, *Thinking Across the American Grain: Idealogy, Intellect, and the New Pragmatism* (Chicago: University of Chicago Press, 1992), pp. 106 ff.

19 Rorty, PMN, p. 392.

20 The phrase is Michael Oakeshott's. See PMN, p. 389.

21 CIS, p. xv. I say "in part" because of his use of Mill's liberalism, CIS, p. 63.

22 CIS, p. 141.

23 John Dewey, "The Need for a Recovery of Philosophy," *The Middle Works of John Dewey*, vol. 10 (Carbondale and Edwardsville: Southern Illinois University Press), p. 47.

24 Willard Van Orman Quine, "Two Dogmas of Empiricism" In *From a Logical Point of View* (Cambridge, MA: Harvard University Press), 1953, pp. 20–46; hereafter TDE; Thomas S. Kuhn, *The Structure of Scientific Revolutions* (Chicago and London: University of Chicago Press, 1962).

25 Quine, TDE, p. 40 ; as quoted in Putnam, "'Two Dogmas' Revisited," in *Realism and Reason* (Cambridge: Cambridge University Press, 1983), p. 90.

26 Kuhn, p. 4.

27 TDE, p. 44.

28 PMN, p. 385.

29 CIS, p. 52.

30 P, p. 34.

31 *Collected Papers of Charles Sanders Peirce*, ed. Charles Hartshorne and Paul Weiss (Cambridge, MA: The Belknap Press of Harvard University Press, 1965), p. 268.

32 Hilary Putnam, *Reason, Truth, and History* (Cambridge: Cambridge University Press, 1981), p11; hereafter RTH. Later he states that truth "is expected to be stable or 'convergent'; if both a statement and its negation could be 'justified,' even if conditions were as ideal as one could hope to make them, there is no sense in thinking of the statement as *having* a truth-value" (p. 56). However, see his more recent attack on convergence as "incoherent" in RHF, p. 171, and the discussion in Rorty, PRM, pp. 443-61.

33 Ludwig Wittgenstein, *Philosophical Investigations*, trans. G. E. M. Anscombe (New York: Macmillan, 1953), para. 18.

34 PRM, p. 448. At times, as here, Rorty seems to stand outside of the complex social practices in which he claims we are all immersed. These practices then flatten out: a production of *A Midsummer Night's Dream*, the sounds of one's local pop station, and a torture victim's screams become equally "noises." (There is some irony in Rorty's offering this account of language and at the same time insisting on the value of literature.) But Rorty's current "Darwinism" squares with nothing so much as his earlier, prepragmatic, writings on "eliminative materialism," in which he defended the view not that mental terms can be *reduced* to physical terms but that, like "witch" or "phlogiston," they will eventually *disappear* and so be *eliminated* from our language. Taking a stance that owes as much to the logical positivist Rudolf Carnap as to Nietzsche, Rorty maintains that the vocabulary of "truth," "meaning," "reason," and "philosophy" will and ought to disappear from the intelligent conversation of humankind. Not only God, but any form of metaphysics, is dead. See Richard Rorty, "Mind-Body Identity, Privacy, and Categories," in *Review of Metaphysics* 19:1 (September 1965), pp.24-54. See also "In Defense of Eliminative Materialism," in *Review of Metaphysics* 24:1 (September 1970), pp.112-21.

35 Hilary Putnam, "Why Reason Can't Be Naturalised." In *Realism and Reason: Philosophical Papers,* vol. 3 (Cambridge: Cambridge University Press, 1983), p. 246; hereafter RR.

36 RR, p. 234.

37 RR, p. 235. For criticism of Rorty on the issue of truth, see Susan Haack, "Vulgar Pragmatism: An Unedifying Prospect," in her *Evidence and Inquiry: Towards Reconstruction in Epistemology* (Oxford, UK and Cambridge, MA: Blackwell, 1993), pp. 182–202. See also her "'We Pragmatists...': Peirce and Rorty in Conversation," *Synthese* (forthcoming); and "Pragmatism," in *Companion to Philosophy,* ed. N. Bunnin and E. James (Oxford: Blackwell, forthcoming).

38 Cited in Thomas McCarthy, *The Critical Theory of Jurgen Habermas* (Cambridge, MA, and London, UK: MIT Press, 1981), p. 105.

39 See for example A. J. Ayer, *Language, Truth, and Logic* (London: Gollanz, 1936).

40 Kant wrote that he had found it "necessary to deny *knowledge,* in order to make room for *faith.*" *Immanuel Kant's Critique of Pure Reason,* trans. Norman Kemp Smith (London: Macmillan, 1963), p. 29.

41 CIS, p. 54n.

42 CIS, p. 53.

43 CIS, p. 63.

44 CIS, pp. 63, 61.

45 Putnam, "Beyond Historicism," in RR, p. 300.

46 Hilary Putnam, *Renewing Philosophy* (Cambridge, MA: Harvard University Press, 1992), p. 180. Richard Bernstein is another important contemporary philosopher with roots in American pragmatism and substantial work in the tradition of the Frankfurt School. See his *John Dewey* (New York: Washington Square Press, 1966); *Praxis and Action: Contemporary Philosophies of Human Activity* (Philadelphia: University of Pennsylvania Press, 1971); *The Restructuring of Social and Political Theoory* (New York: Harcourt Brace Jovanovich, 1976); *Beyond Objectivism and Relativism: Science, Hermeneutics, and Praxis* (Philadelphia: University of Pennsylvania Press, 1983); "Dewey, Democracy: The Task Before Us," in *Post-Analytic Philosophy,* ed. John Rajchman and Cornel West (New York: Columbia University Press, 1985); pp. 48–59; "One Step Forward, Two Steps Backward: Richard Rorty on Liberal Democracy and Philosophy," *Political Theory 15* (1987), pp. 538–63.

47 Hilary Putnam, *The Many Faces of Realism* (LaSalle, IL: Open Court, 1987), p. 16; hereafter MFR..

48 See for example, Putnam, RHF, pp. 19 ff.

49 PRM, p. 458.

50 P, pp. 9, 11.

51 p. 124.

52 p. 13.

53 Putnam, *Renewing Philosophy,* p. 1.

54 Putnam, MFR, p. 62.

55 P, p. 23.

56 See Russell B. Goodman, *American Philosophy and the Romantic Tradition* (Cambridge; Cambridge University Press, 1990), chapters 3 and 4.

57 CIS, p. 22.

58 Goodman, *American Philosophy* p. 54.

59 P, p. 28.

60 Richard Poirier, *The Renewal of Literature: Emersonian Reflections* (New York: Random House, 1987), p. 47; hereafter RL.

61 RL, p. 14.

62 RL, pp. 16, 17.

63 Richard Poirier, *Poetry and Pragmatism* (Cambridge, MA: Harvard University Press, 1992), p. 155.

64 Ibid, p. 134.

65 Cornel West, *The American Evasion of Philosophy: A Genealogy of Pragmatism* (Madison, WI: University of Wisconsin Press, 1987), p. 10.

66 John Dewey, *The Middle Works of John Dewey*, vol.3 (Carbondale and Edwardsville: Southern Illinois University Press, 1976), pp. 189-90.

67 West, p. 228.

68 Ibid, p. 5.

69 See Stanley Cavell, *The Senses of Walden: An Expanded Edition* (San Francisco: North Point Press, 1979), *In Quest of the Ordinary* (Chicago: University of Chicago Press, 1988), and *This New Yet Unapproachable America* (Albuquerque, NM: Living Batch Books,1979). In his most recent writing, Cavell contests the application to Emerson of the term "pragmatist," and explains his own sense of distance from Dewey: "Dewey was remembering something philosophy should mostly be, but ... the world he was responding to missed the worlds I seemed to live in, missing the heights of modernism in the arts, the depths of psychoanalytic discovery, the ravages of the century's politics, the wild intelligence of American popular culture. Above all, missing the question, and the irony in philosophy's questioning, whether philosophy, however reconstructed, was any longer possible, and necessary, in this world" (*Conditions Handsome and Unhandsome*, Chicago: University of Chicago Press, 1979, p. 13). In *A Pitch of Philosophy* (Cambridge, MA: Harvard University Press, 1994, p. 168), Cavell suggests that Emerson is "one whose writing [Dewey] misses in his own," and associates Dewey's alleged failure as a writer with a continued "repression of Emerson's words." These charges, whatever their merits as applied to Dewey, would be considerably less plausible directed against William James, a pragmatist about whom Cavell is silent, or against such neopragmatists as Putnam and Poirier. (For the claim that it is precisely Emerson's writing that one can find in James's [albeit in largely unacknowledged form], see the Poirier section below.)

70 On Putnam's relationship to Cavell, see James Conant's introduction to *Realism with a Human Face*.

71 James, P ,p. 123;CW,vol. 1, p. 25.

72 CW vol. 2, p. 236.

73 CW vol. 2, pp. 227-8.

74 CW vol. 2, p. 234.

75 Rorty, "Feminism and Pragmatism." See below, p. 136.

76 Cf. Poirier and Julie Ellison, *Emerson's Romantic Style* (Princeton: Princeton University Press, 1984. Rorty states: "people will still read Plato, Aristotle, Descartes, Kant, Hegel, Wittgenstein, and Heidegger. What roles these men will play in our descendants' conversation, no one knows" (PMN, p. 394). For Rorty's evaluation of Emerson's importance for Dewey's pragmatism see his "Just One More Species Doing Its Best," *London Review of Books*, 13:4 (25 July,1991), pp. 3-7.

77 Peirce, "What Pragmatism Is," *Collected Papers*, vol. 5, p. 276.

78 Rorty, "Feminism and Pragmatism," p. 237.

79 Stanley Fish, *Is There a Text in This Class?* (Cambridge, MA: Harvard University Press, 1978), pp. 354–355.

80 Rorty, CIS, p. 80.

81 See James's "Pragmatism and Humanism," reprinted below, p.76.

82 CIS, p. 7. Cf. Jean Bethke Elshtain, "Don't Be Cruel: Reflections on Rortyan Liberalism," in Daniel W. Conway and John E. Seary, eds., *Irony: Essays in Self Betrayal* (New York: St. Martin's Press, 1992), pp. 199–218; and Rorty's reply, pp. 219–24.

83 PP, p. 167.

84 Ian Hacking, "*Five Parables*," Philosophy and History, ed. Richard Porty, J.B. Schneewind, and Quentin Skinner (Cambridge: Cambridge University Press, 1984), p. 105.

85 Ibid, p. 122.

86 Emerson, "The American Scholar," CW vol. 1, p. 56.

CLASSICAL
PRAGMATISM

RALPH WALDO EMERSON
(1803–1882)

Long ignored not only by students of pragmatism but by professional philosophers, Emerson's writing received new and inspired attention in the 1980s from such philosophical writers as Stanley Cavell, Richard Poirier, and Cornel West. Emerson now appears not only as a formidable thinker in his own right but also as a source for Nietzsche and Heidegger and, in America, for James and Dewey. Emerson's pragmatic side can be seen in those parts of "The American Scholar" (1837) where he stresses the role of action in scholarship or thought: "The preamble of thought, the transition through which it passes from the unconscious to the conscious, is action. Only so much do I know, as I have lived." The emphasis on "results" or "consequences," on the "new" and the future, is characteristic of Emerson's entire philosophy, according to which we are alive only in our transitions, and dead if confined to our routines.

"Circles," reprinted below from Emerson's first series of essays of 1841, expresses his metaphysics of flux and expansion, and his idea—so important for John Dewey—that morality, no less than science or art, is experimental. No virtue is final, Emerson states, "all are initial"; and we must learn to abandon not only our vices but our virtues in the light of better ones. The universe Emerson depicts is, like James's, radically open: "there is no outside, no enclosing wall," and "every ultimate fact is only the first of a new series." The series of expanding circles brings us surprises and changes of mood so radical that from one moment to the next "our moods do not believe in each other." Yet, Emerson states, there is no hope for us without the growth these unsettling changes brings about. "We do not guess today the mood, the pleasure, the power of tomorrow, when we are building up our being."

Crucial for Emerson's relation to later pragmatists is what we may call— borrowing a word from William James—his *humanism,* his idea that the world comes to us through the human lenses of our temperaments and moods. "Life," Emerson wrote in his great essay "Experience" (1844), "is a train of moods like a string of beads, and, as we pass through them they prove to be many-colored lenses which paint the world their own hue, and each shows only what lies in its focus." Our changing moods and individual temperaments lie behind Emerson's depiction of an ungrounded world of "sliding surfaces." Yet Emerson seeks a way of "skating" across these surfaces of life, a balance between what we cannot avoid and what our own powers of imposition and reception allow us to do.

CIRCLES

RALPH WALDO EMERSON

NATURE centres into balls,
And her proud ephemerals,
Fast to surface and outside,
Scan the profile of the sphere;
Knew they what that signified,
A new genesis were here.

The eye is the first circle; the horizon which it forms is the second; and throughout nature this primary figure is repeated without end. It is the highest emblem in the cipher of the world. St. Augustine described the nature of God as a circle whose centre was everywhere and its circumference nowhere. We are all our lifetime reading the copious sense of this first of forms. One moral we have already deduced in considering the circular or compensatory character of every human action. Another analogy we shall now trace, that every action admits of being outdone. Our life is an apprenticeship to the truth that around every circle another can be drawn; that there is no end in nature, but every end is a beginning; that there is always another dawn risen on mid-noon, and under every deep a lower deep opens.

This fact, as far as it symbolizes the moral fact of the Unattainable, the flying Perfect, around which the hands of man can never meet, at once the inspirer and the condemner of every success, may conveniently serve us to connect many illustrations of human power in every department.

There are no fixtures in nature. The universe is fluid and volatile. Permanence is but a word of degrees. Our globe seen by God is a transparent law, not a mass of facts. The law dissolves the fact and holds it fluid. Our culture is the predominance of an idea which draws after it this train of cities and institutions. Let us rise into another idea; they will disappear. The Greek sculpture is all melted away, as if it had been statues of ice; here and there a solitary figure or fragment remaining, as we see flecks and scraps of snow left in cold dells and mountain clefts in June and July. For the genius that created it creates now somewhat else. The Greek letters last a little longer, but are already passing under the same sentence and tumbling into the inevitable pit which the creation of new thought opens for all that is old. The new continents are built out of the ruins of an old planet; the new races fed out of the decomposition of the foregoing. New arts destroy the old. See the investment of capital in aqueducts, made useless by hydraulics; fortifications, by gunpowder; roads and canals, by railways; sails, by steam; steam by electricity.

You admire this tower of granite, weathering the hurts of so many ages. Yet a little waving hand built this huge wall, and that which builds is better than that which is built. The hand that built can topple it down much faster. Better than the hand and nimbler was the invisible thought which wrought through it; and thus ever, behind the coarse effect, is a fine cause, which, being narrowly seen, is itself the effect of a finer cause. Everything looks permanent until its secret is known. A rich estate appears to women a firm and lasting fact; to a merchant, one easily created out of any materials, and easily lost. An orchard, good tillage, good grounds, seem a fixture, like a gold mine, or a river, to a citizen; but to a large farmer, not much more fixed than the state of the crop. Nature looks provokingly stable and secular, but it has a cause like all the rest; and when once I comprehend that, will these fields stretch so immovably wide, these leaves hang so individually considerable? Permanence is a word of degrees. Every thing is medial. Moons are no more bounds to spiritual power than bat-balls.

The key to every man is his thought. Sturdy and defying though he look, he has a helm which he obeys, which is the idea after which all his facts are classified. He can only be reformed by showing him a new idea which commands his own. The life of man is a self-evolving circle, which, from a ring imperceptibly small, rushes on all sides outwards to new and larger circles, and that without end. The extent to which this generation of circles, wheel without wheel, will go, depends on the force or truth of the individual soul. For it is the inert effort of each thought, having formed itself into a circular wave of circumstance,—as for instance an empire, rules of an art, a local usage, a religious rite,—to heap itself on that ridge and to solidify and hem in the life. But if the soul is quick and strong it bursts over that boundary on all sides and expands another orbit on the great deep, which also runs up into a high wave, with attempt again to stop and to bind. But the heart refuses to be imprisoned; in its first and narrowest pulses it already tends outward with a vast force and to immense and innumerable expansions.

Every ultimate fact is only the first of a new series. Every general law only a particular fact of some more general law presently to disclose itself. There is no outside, no enclosing wall, no circumference to us. The man finishes his story,—how good! how final! how it puts a new face on all things! He fills the sky. Lo! on the other side rises also a man and draws a circle around the circle we had just pronounced the outline of the sphere. Then already is our first speaker not man, but only a first speaker. His only redress is forthwith to draw a circle outside of his antagonist. And so men do by themselves. The result of to-day, which haunts the mind and cannot be escaped, will presently be abridged into a word, and the principle that seemed to explain nature will itself be included as one example of a bolder generalization. In the thought of to-morrow there is a power to upheave all thy creed, all the creeds, all the literatures of the nations, and marshal thee to a heaven which no epic dream has yet depicted. Every man is not so much a workman in the world as he is a suggestion of that he should be. Men walk as prophecies of the next age.

Step by step we scale this mysterious ladder; the steps are actions, the new prospect is power. Every several result is threatened and judged by that which follows. Every one seems to be contradicted by the new; it is only limited by the new. The new statement is always hated by the old, and, to those dwelling in the old, comes like an abyss of skepticism. But the eye soon gets wonted to it, for the eye and it are effects of one cause; then its innocency and benefit appear, and presently, all its energy spent, it pales and dwindles before the revelation of the new hour.

Fear not the new generalization. Does the fact look crass and material, threatening to degrade thy theory of spirit? Resist it not; it goes to refine and raise thy theory of matter just as much.

There are no fixtures to men, if we appeal to consciousness. Every man supposes himself not to be fully understood; and if there is any truth in him, if he rests at last on the divine soul, I see not how it can be otherwise. The last chamber, the last closet, he must feel was never opened; there is always a residuum unknown, unanalyzable. That is, every man believes that he has a greater possibility.

Our moods do not believe in each other. To-day I am full of thoughts and can write what I please. I see no reason why I should not have the same thought, the same power of expression, to-morrow. What I write, whilst I write it, seems the most natural thing in the world; but yesterday I saw a dreary vacuity in this direction in which now I see so much; and a month hence, I doubt not, I shall wonder who he was that wrote so many continuous pages. Alas for this infirm faith, this will not strenuous, this vast ebb of a vast flow! I am God in nature; I am a weed by the wall.

The continual effort to raise himself above himself, to work a pitch above his last height, betrays itself in a man's relations. We thirst for approbation, yet cannot forgive the approver. The sweet of nature is love; yet if I have a friend I am tormented by my imperfections. The love of me accuses the other party. If he were high enough to slight me, then could I love him, and rise by my affection to new heights. A man's growth is seen in the successive choirs of his friends. For every friend whom he loses for truth, he gains a better. I thought as I walked in the woods and mused on my friends, why should I play with them this game of idolatry? I know and see too well, when not voluntarily blind, the speedy limits of persons called high and worthy. Rich, noble and great they are by the liberality of our speech, but truth is sad. O blessed Spirit, whom I forsake for these, they are not thou! Every personal consideration that we allow costs us heavenly state. We sell the thrones of angels for a short and turbulent pleasure.

How often must we learn this lesson? Men cease to interest us when we find their limitations. The only sin is limitation. As soon as you once come up with a man's limitations, it is all over with him. Has he talents? has he enterprise? has he knowledge?

It boots not. Infinitely alluring and attractive was he to you yesterday, a great hope, a sea to swim in; now, you have found his shores, found it a pond, and you care not if you never see it again.

Each new step we take in thought reconciles twenty seemingly discordant facts, as expressions of one law. Aristotle and Plato are reckoned the respective heads of two schools. A wise man will see that Aristotle platonizes. By going one step farther back in thought, discordant opinions are reconciled by being seen to be two extremes of one principle, and we can never go so far back as to preclude a still higher vision.

Beware when the great God lets loose a thinker on this planet. Then all things are at risk. It is as when a conflagration has broken out in a great city, and no man knows what is safe, or where it will end. There is not a piece of science but its flank may be turned to-morrow; there is not any literary reputation, not the so-called eternal names of fame, that may not be revised and condemned. The very hopes of man, the thoughts of his heart, the religion of nations, the manners and morals of mankind are all at the mercy of a new generalization. Generalization is always a new influx of the divinity into the mind. Hence the thrill that attends it.

Valor consists in the power of self-recovery, so that a man cannot have his flank turned, cannot be out-generalled, but put him where you will, he stands. This can only be by his preferring truth to his past apprehension of truth, and his alert acceptance of it from whatever quarter; the intrepid conviction that his laws, his relations to society, his Christianity, his world, may at any time be superseded and decease.

There are degrees in idealism. We learn first to play with it academically, as the magnet was once a toy. Then we see in the heyday of youth and poetry that it may be true, that it is true in gleams and fragments. Then its countenance waxes stern and grand, and we see that it must be true. It now shows itself ethical and practical. We learn that God IS; that he is in me; and that all things are shadows of him. The idealism of Berkeley is only a crude statement of the idealism of Jesus, and that again is a crude statement of the fact that all nature is the rapid efflux of goodness executing and organizing itself. Much more obviously is history and the state of the world at any one time directly dependent on the intellectual classification then existing in the minds of men. The things which are dear to men at this hour are so on account of the ideas which have emerged on their mental horizon, and which cause the present order of things, as a tree bears its apples. A new degree of culture would instantly revolutionize the entire system of human pursuits.

Conversation is a game of circles. In conversation we pluck up the *termini* which bound the common of silence on every side. The parties are not to be judged by the spirit they partake and even express under this Pentecost. To-morrow they will have receded from this high-water mark. To-morrow you shall find them stooping under the old pack-saddles. Yet let us enjoy the cloven flame whilst it glows on our walls. When each new speaker strikes a new light, emancipates us from the oppression of the last speaker to oppress us with the greatness and exclusiveness of his own thought, then yields us to another redeemer, we seem to recover our rights, to become men. O, what truths profound and executable only in ages and orbs, are supposed in the announcement of every truth! In common hours, society sits cold and statuesque. We all stand waiting, empty,—knowing, possibly, that we can be full, surrounded by mighty symbols which are not symbols to us, but prose and trivial toys. Then cometh the god and converts the statues into fiery men, and by a flash of his eye burns up the veil which shrouded all things, and the meaning of the very furniture, of cup and saucer, of chair and clock and tester, is manifest. The facts which loomed so large in the fogs of yesterday,—property, climate, breeding, personal beauty and the like, have strangely changed their proportions. All that we reckoned settled shakes and rattles; and literatures, cities, climates, religions, leave their foundations and dance before our eyes. And yet here again seethe swift circumscription! Good as is discourse, silence is better, and shames it. The length of the discourse indicates the distance of thought betwixt the speaker and the hearer. If they were at a perfect understanding in any part, no words would be necessary thereon. If at one in all parts, no words would be suffered.

Literature is a point outside of our hodiernal circle through which a new one may be described. The use of literature is to afford us a platform whence we may command a view of our present life, a purchase by which we may move it. We fill ourselves with ancient learning, install ourselves the best we can in Greek, in Punic, in Roman houses, only that we may wiselier see French, English and American houses and modes of living. In like manner we see literature best from the midst of wild nature, or from the din of affairs, or from a high religion. The field cannot be well seen from within the field. The astronomer must have his diameter of the earth's orbit as a base to find the parallax of any star.

Therefore we value the poet. All the argument and all the wisdom is not in the encyclopedia, or the treatise on metaphysics, or the Body of Divinity, but in the sonnet or the play. In my daily work I incline to repeat my old steps, and do not believe in remedial force, in the power of change and reform. But some Petrarch or Ariosto, filled with the new wine of his imagination, writes me an ode or a brisk romance, full of daring thought and action. He smites and arouses me with his shrill tones, breaks up my whole chain of habits, and I open my eye on my own possibilities. He claps wings to the sides of all the solid old lumber of the world, and I am capable once more of choosing a straight path in theory and practice.

We have the same need to command a view of the religion of the world. We can never see Christianity from the catechism: —from the pastures, from a boat in the pond, from amidst the songs of wood-birds we possibly may. Cleansed by the elemental light and wind, steeped in the sea of beautiful forms which the field offers us, we may chance to cast a right glance back upon biography. Christianity is rightly dear to the best of mankind; yet was there never a young philosopher whose breeding had fallen into the Christian church by whom that brave text of Paul's was not specially prized: "Then shall also the Son be subject unto Him who put all things under him, that God may be all in all." Let the claims and virtues of persons be never so great and welcome, the instinct of man presses eagerly onward to the impersonal and illimitable, and gladly arms itself against the dogmatism of bigots with this generous word out of the book itself.

The natural world may be conceived of as a system of concentric circles, and we now and then detect in nature slight dislocations which apprise us that this surface on which we now stand is not fixed, but sliding. These manifold tenacious qualities, this chemistry and vegetation, these metals and animals, which seem to stand there for their own sake, are means and methods only,—are words of God, and as fugitive as other words. Has the naturalist or chemist learned his craft, who has explored the gravity of atoms and the elective affinities, who has not yet discerned the deeper law whereof this is only a partial or approximate statement, namely that like draws to like, and that the goods which belong to you gravitate to you and need not be pursued with pains and cost? Yet is that statement approximate also, and not final. Omnipresence is a higher fact. Not through subtle subterranean channels need friend and fact be drawn to their counterpart, but, rightly considered, these things proceed from the eternal generation of the soul. Cause and effect are two sides of one fact.

The same law of eternal procession ranges all that we call the virtues, and extinguishes each in the light of a better. The great man will not be prudent in the popular sense; all his prudence will be so much deduction from his grandeur.

But it behooves each to see, when he sacrifices prudence, to what god he devotes it; if to ease and pleasure, he had better be prudent still; if to a great trust, he can well spare his mule and panniers who has a winged chariot instead. Geoffrey draws on his boots to go through the woods, that his feet may be safer from the bite of snakes; Aaron never thinks of such a peril. In many years neither is harmed by such an accident. Yet it seems to me that with every precaution you take against such an evil you put yourself into the power of the evil. I suppose that the highest prudence is the lowest prudence. Is this too sudden a rushing from the centre to the verge of our orbit? Think how many times we shall fall back into pitiful calculations before we take up our rest in the great sentiment, or make the verge of to-day the new centre. Besides, your bravest sentiment is familiar to the humblest men. The poor and the low have their way of expressing the last facts of philosophy as well as you. "Blessed be nothing" and "The worse things are, the better they are" are proverbs which express the transcendentalism of common life.

One man's justice is another's injustice; one man's beauty another's ugliness; one man's wisdom another's folly; as one beholds the same objects from a higher point. One man thinks justice consists in paying debts, and has no measure in his abhorrence of another who is very remiss in this duty and makes the creditor wait tediously. But that second man has his own way of looking at things; asks himself Which debt must I pay first, the debt to the rich, or the debt to the poor? the debt of money, or the debt of thought to mankind, of genius to nature? For you, O broker, there is no other principle but arithmetic. For me, commerce is of trivial import: love, faith, truth of character, the aspiration of man, these are sacred; nor can I detach one duty, like you, from all other duties, and concentrate my forces mechanically on the payment of moneys. Let me live onward; you shall find that, though slower, the progress of my character will liquidate all these debts without injustice to higher claims. If a man should dedicate himself to the payment of notes, would not this be injustice? Does he owe no debt but money? And are all claims on him to be postponed to a landlord's or a banker's?

There is no virtue which is final; all are initial. The virtues of society are vices of the saint. The terror of reform is the discovery that we must cast away our virtues, or what we have always esteemed such, into the same pit that has consumed our grosser vices:

> Forgive his crimes, forgive his virtues too,
> Those smaller faults, half converts to the right.

It is the highest power of divine moments that they abolish our contritions also. I accuse myself of sloth and unprofitableness day by day; but when these waves of God flow into me I no longer reckon lost time. I no longer poorly compute my possible achievement by what remains to me of the month or the year; for these moments confer a sort of omnipresence and omnipotence which asks nothing of duration, but sees that the energy of the mind is commensurate with the work to be done, without time.

And thus, O circular philosopher, I hear some reader exclaim, you have arrived at a fine Pyrrhonism, at an equivalence and indifferency of all actions, and would fain teach us that *if we are true,* forsooth, our crimes may be lively stones out of which we shall construct the temple of the true God!

I am not careful to justify myself. I own I am gladdened by seeing the predominance of the saccharine principle throughout vegetable nature, and not less by beholding in morals that unrestrained inundation of the principle of good into every chink and hole that selfishness has left open, yea into selfishness and sin itself; so that no evil is pure, nor hell itself without its extreme satisfactions. But lest I should mislead any when I have my own head and obey my whims, let me remind the reader that I am only an experimenter. Do not set the least value on what I do, or the least discredit on what I do not, as if I pretended to settle any thing as true or false. I unsettle all things. No facts are to me sacred; none are profane; I simply experiment, an endless seeker with no Past at my back.

Yet this incessant movement and progression which all things partake could never become sensible to us but by contrast to some principle of fixture or stability in the soul. Whilst the eternal generation of circles proceeds, the eternal generator abides. That central life is somewhat superior to creation, superior to knowledge and thought, and contains all its circles. Forever it labors to create a life and thought as large and excellent as itself, but in vain, for that which is made instructs how to make a better.

Thus there is no sleep, no pause, no preservation, but all things renew, germinate and spring. Why should we import rags and relics into the new hour? Nature abhors the old, and old age seems the only disease; all others run into this one. We call it by many names,—fever, intemperance, insanity, stupidity and crime; they are all forms of old age; they are rest, conservatism, appropriation, inertia; not newness, not the way onward. We grizzle every day. I see no need of it. Whilst we converse with what is above us, we do not grow old, but grow young. Infancy, youth, receptive, aspiring, with religious eye looking upward, counts itself nothing and abandons itself to the instruction flowing from all sides. But the man and woman of seventy assume to know all, they have outlived their hope, they renounce aspiration, accept the actual for the necessary and talk down to the young. Let them then become organs of the Holy Ghost; let them be lovers; let them behold truth; and their eyes are uplifted, their wrinkles smoothed, they are perfumed again with hope and power. This old age ought not to creep on a human mind. In nature every moment is new; the past is always swallowed and forgotten; the coming only is sacred. Nothing is secure but life, transition, the energizing spirit. No love can be bound by oath or covenant to secure it against a higher love. No truth so sublime but it may be trivial to-morrow in the light of new thoughts. People wish to be settled; only as far as they are unsettled is there any hope for them.

Life is a series of surprises. We do not guess to-day the mood, the pleasure, the power of tomorrow, when we are building up our being. Of lower states, of acts of routine and sense, we can tell somewhat; but the masterpieces of God, the total growths and universal movements of the soul, he hideth; they are incalculable. I can know that truth is divine and helpful; but how it shall help me I can have no guess, for *so to be* is the sole inlet of *so to know*. The new position of the advancing man has all the powers of the old, yet has them all new. It carries in its bosom all the energies of the past, yet is itself an exhalation of the morning. I cast away in this new moment all my once hoarded knowledge, as vacant and vain. Now for the first time seem I to know any thing rightly. The simplest words,—we do not know what they mean except when we love and aspire.

The difference between talents and character is adroitness to keep the old and trodden round, and power and courage to make a new road to new and better goals. Character makes an overpowering present; a cheerful, determined hour, which fortifies all the company by making them see that much is possible and excellent that was not thought of. Character dulls the impression of particular events. When we see the conqueror we do not think much of any one battle or success. We see that we had exaggerated the difficulty. It was easy to him. The great man is not convulsible or tormentable; events pass over him without much impression. People say sometimes, 'See what I have overcome; see how cheerful I am; see how completely I have triumphed over these black events.' Not if they still remind me of the black event. True conquest is the causing the calamity to fade and disappear as an early cloud of insignificant result in a history so large and advancing.

The one thing which we seek with insatiable desire is to forget ourselves, to be surprised out of our propriety, to lose our sempiternal memory and to do something without knowing how or why; in short to draw a new circle. Nothing great was ever achieved without enthusiasm. The way of life is wonderful; it is by abandonment. The great moments of history are the facilities of performance through the strength of ideas, as the works of genius and religion. "A man," said Oliver Cromwell, "never rises so high as when he knows not whither he is going." Dreams and drunkenness, the use of opium and alcohol are the semblance and counterfeit of this oracular genius, and hence their dangerous attraction for men. For the like reason they ask the aid of wild passions, as in gaming and war, to ape in some manner these flames and generosities of the heart.

CHARLES SANDERS PEIRCE
(1839–1914)

A brilliant and quirky mathematician, physicist and philosopher, Peirce's "How to Make Our Ideas Clear," published in 1878, is acknowledged to be pragmatism's original written statement—even though the term "pragmatism" does not occur in it. It contains the definitive sentence James quotes in *Pragmatism*: "Consider what effects, which might conceivably have practical bearings, we conceive the object of our conception to have. Then, our conception of these effects is the whole of our conception of the object." From this sentence flows pragmatism as a theory of meaning, and as a theory about states of belief. A slightly different statement from Peirce's paper introduces the key pragmatic idea of action or practice into his definition: "There is no distinction of meaning so fine as to consist in anything but a possible difference of practice." Pragmatism's debunking aspect can be observed in Peirce's use of this idea to attack as "senseless jargon" the Catholic idea that something "having all the sensible characters of wine [is] in reality blood."

Behind Peirce's pragmatist principle lies his analysis of inquiry. In "The Fixation of Belief" (1877) Peirce distinguishes four main methods by which human beings come to have the beliefs that they do—four ways of fixing beliefs. The method of tenacity operates simply by one's continuing to believe whatever it is one has come to believe in the first place, a method Peirce likens to an ostrich with its head in the sand. The "method of authority," arises because of the clashes between individuals practicing the method of tenacity. It consists in believing what the authorities decree, and it is enforced, Peirce tells us, by "institutions," "priesthoods," and "massacres." The third method, the a priori method of the philosophers, consists in believing that which is, or seems, agreeable to reason. Peirce worries that this method is arbitrary, like matters of taste, and subject to the control of "accidental" factors. So he embraces a fourth method—the "method of science"—in which belief is determined by "some external permanency—by something upon which our thinking has no effect." The beliefs of greatest integrity, Peirce states, are those which would be arrived at by "every man... if inquiry were sufficiently persisted in."

"We may define the real," Peirce writes in "How to Make Our Ideas Clear," "as that whose characters are independent of whatever anybody may think them to be." Along with this stress on objectivity, however, is a human-centered vision that is so characteristic of later pragmatisms. "Thought is an action," he writes, and "the action of thought is excited by the irritation of doubt." Our intellectual progress is ordained not by independent reality but by our interactions with it. Peirce's expression both of the human determination of our picture of the world and of the world as something "independent" is an important touchstone for such contemporary writers as Hilary Putnam and Ian Hacking.

Thought, Peirce states in one of his memorable metaphors, is like an air or melody, and our sensations like the notes. Belief is a pause or resting place in this melody, a "demi-cadence which closes a musical phrase in the symphony of our intellectual life." No such closure is final: "who can be sure," Peirce asks, "of what we shall not know in a few hundred years?"

HOW TO MAKE OUR IDEAS CLEAR

CHARLES SANDERS PEIRCE

I

Whoever has looked into a modern treatise on logic of the common sort, will doubt-less remember the two distinctions between *clear* and *obscure* conceptions, and between *distinct* and *confused* conceptions. They have lain in the books now for nigh two centuries, unimproved and unmodified, and are generally reckoned by logicians as among the gems of their doctrine.

A clear idea is defined as one which is so apprehended that it will be recognized wher-ever it is met with, and so that no other will be mistaken for it. If it fails of this clearness, it is said to be obscure.

This is rather a neat bit of philosophical terminology; yet, since it is clearness that they were defining, I wish the logicians had made their definition a little more plain. Never to fail to recognize an idea, and under no circumstances to mistake another for it, let it come in how recondite a form it may, would indeed imply such prodigious force and clearness of intellect as is seldom met with in this world. On the other hand, merely to have such an acquaintance with the idea as to have become familiar with it, and to have lost all hesitancy in recognizing it in ordinary cases, hardly seems to deserve the name of clearness of apprehension, since after all it only amounts to a subjective feeling of mastery which may be entirely mistaken. I take it, however, that when the logicians speak of "clearness," they mean nothing more than such a familiarity with an idea, since they regard the quality as but a small merit, which needs to be supplemented by another, which they call *distinctness.*

A distinct idea is defined as one which contains nothing which is not clear. This is tech-nical language; by the *contents* of an idea logicians understand whatever is contained in its definition. So that an idea is *distinctly* apprehended, according to them, when we can give a precise definition of it, in abstract terms. Here the professional logicians leave the subject; and I would not have troubled the reader with what they have to say, if it were not such a striking example of how they have been slumbering through ages of intellectual activity, listlessly disregarding the enginery of modern thought, and never dreaming of applying its lessons to the improvement of logic. It is easy to show that the doctrine that familiar use and abstract distinctness make the perfection of apprehension has its only true place in philosophies which have long been extinct; and it is now time to formulate the method of attaining to a more perfect clearness of thought, such as we see and admire in the thinkers of our own time.

When Descartes set about the reconstruction of philosophy, his first step was to (theoretically) permit skepticism and to discard the practice of the schoolmen of looking to authority as the ultimate source of truth. That done, he sought a more natural fountain of true principles, and professed to find it in the human mind; thus passing, in the directest way, from the method of authority to that of apriority, as described in my first paper.[1] Self-consciousness was to furnish us with our fundamental truths, and to decide what was agreeable to reason. But since, evidently, not all ideas are true, he was led to note, as the first condition of infallibility, that they must be clear. The distinction between an idea *seeming* clear and really being so, never occurred to him. Trusting to introspection, as he did, even a knowledge of external things, why should he question its testimony in respect to the contents of our own minds? But then, I suppose, seeing men, who seemed to be quite clear and positive, holding opposite opinions upon fundamental principles, he was further led to say that clearness of ideas is not sufficient, but that they need also to be distinct, i.e., to have nothing unclear about them. What he probably meant by this (for he did not explain himself with precision) was, that they must sustain the test of dialectical examination; that they must not only seem clear at the outset, but that discussion must never be able to bring to light points of obscurity connected with them.

Such was the distinction of Descartes, and one sees that it was precisely on the level of his philosophy. It was somewhat developed by Leibnitz. This great and singular genius was as remarkable for what he failed to see as for what he saw. That a piece of mechanism could not do work perpetually without being fed with power in some form, was a thing perfectly apparent to him; yet he did not understand that the machinery of the mind can only transform knowledge, but never originate it, unless it be fed with facts of observation. He thus missed the most essential point of the Cartesian philosophy, which is, that to accept propositions which seem perfectly evident to us is a thing which, whether it be logical or illogical, we cannot help doing. Instead of regarding the matter in this way, he sought to reduce the first principles of science to formulas which cannot be denied without self-contradiction, and was apparently unaware of the great difference between his position and that of Descartes. So he reverted to the old formalities of logic, and, above all, abstract definitions played a great part in his philosophy. It was quite natural, therefore, that on observing that the method of Descartes labored under the difficulty that we may seem to ourselves to have clear apprehensions of ideas which in truth are very hazy, no better remedy occurred to him than to require an abstract definition of every important term. Accordingly, in adopting the distinction of *clear* and *distinct* notions, he described the latter quality as the clear apprehension of everything contained in the definition; and the books have ever since copied his words. There is no danger that his chimerical scheme will ever again be overvalued. Nothing new can ever be learned by analyzing definitions. Nevertheless, our existing beliefs can be set in order by this process, and order is an essential element of intellectual economy, as of every other. It may be acknowledged, therefore, that the books are right in making familiarity with a notion the first step toward clearness of apprehension, and the defining of it the second. But in omitting all mention of any higher perspicuity of thought, they simply mirror a philosophy which was exploded a hundred years ago. That much-admired "ornament of logic"—the doctrine of clearness and distinctness—may be pretty enough, but it is high time to relegate to our cabinet of curiosities the antique *bijou,* and to wear about us something better adapted to modern uses.

The very first lesson that we have a right to demand that logic shall teach us is, how to make our ideas clear; and a most important one it is, depreciated only by minds who stand in need of it. To know what we think, to be masters of our own meaning, will make a solid foundation for great and weighty thought. It is most easily learned by those whose ideas are meagre and restricted; and far happier they than such as wallow helplessly in a rich mud of conceptions. A nation, it is true, may, in the course of generations, overcome the disadvantage of an excessive wealth of language and its natural concomitant, a vast, unfathomable deep of ideas. We may see it in history, slowly perfecting its literary forms, sloughing at length its metaphysics, and, by virtue of the untirable patience which is often a compensation, attaining great excellence in every branch of mental acquirement. The page of history is not yet unrolled which is to tell us whether such a people will or will not in the long-run prevail over one whose ideas (like the words of their language) are few, but which possesses a wonderful mastery over those which it has. For an individual, however, there can be no question that a few clear ideas are worth more than many confused ones. A young man would hardly be persuaded to sacrifice the greater part of his thoughts to save the rest; and the muddled head is the least apt to see the necessity of such a sacrifice. Him we can usually only commiserate, as a person with a congenital defect. Time will help him, but intellectual maturity with regard to clearness comes rather late, an unfortunate arrangement of Nature, inasmuch as clearness is of less use to a man settled in life, whose errors have in great measure had their effect, than it would be to one whose path lies before him. It is terrible to see how a single unclear idea, a single formula without meaning, lurking in a young man's head, will sometimes act like an obstruction of inert matter in an artery, hindering the nutrition of the brain, and condemning its victim to pine away in the fullness of his intellectual vigor and in the midst of intellectual plenty. Many a man has cherished for years as his hobby some vague shadow of an idea, too meaningless to be positively false; he has, nevertheless, passionately loved it, has made it his companion by day and by night, and has given to it his strength and his life, leaving all other occupations for its sake, and in short has lived with it and for it, until it has become, as it were, flesh of his flesh and bone of his bone; and then he has waked up some bright morning to find it gone, clean vanished away like the beautiful Melusina of the fable, and the essence of his life gone with it. I have myself known such a man; and who can tell how many histories of circle-squarers, metaphysicians, astrologers, and what not, may not be told in the old German story?

II

The principles set forth in the first of these papers lead, at once, to a method of reaching a clearness of thought of a far higher grade than the "distinctness" of the logicians. We have there found that the action of thought is excited by the irritation of doubt, and ceases when belief is attained; so that the production of belief is the sole function of thought. All these words, however, are too strong for my purpose. It is as if I had described the phenomena as they appear under a mental microscope. Doubt and Belief, as the words are commonly employed, relate to religious or other grave discussions. But here I use them to designate the starting of any question, no matter how small or how great, and the resolution of it. If, for instance, in a horse-car, I pull out my purse and find a five-cent nickel and five coppers, I decide, while my hand is going to the purse, in which way I will pay my fare. To call such a question Doubt, and my decision Belief, is certainly to use words very disproportionate to the occasion. To speak of such a doubt as causing an irritation which needs to be appeased, suggests a temper which is uncomfortable to the verge of insanity. Yet, looking at the matter minutely, it must be admitted that, if there is the least hesitation as to whether I shall pay the five coppers or the nickel (as there will be sure to be, unless I act from some previously contracted habit in the matter), though irritation is too strong a word, yet I am excited to such small mental activities as may be necessary to deciding how I shall act. Most frequently doubts arise from some indecision, however momentary, in our action. Sometimes it is not so. I have, for example, to wait in a railway station, and to pass the time I read the advertisements on the walls, I compare the advantages of different trains and different routes which I never expect to take, merely fancying myself to be in a state of hesitancy, because I am bored with having nothing to trouble me. Feigned hesitancy, whether feigned for mere amusement or with a lofty purpose, plays a great part in the production of scientific inquiry. However the doubt may originate, it stimulates the mind to an activity which may be slight or energetic, calm or turbulent. Images pass rapidly through consciousness, one incessantly melting into another, until at last, when all is over—it may be in a fraction of a second, in an hour, or after long years—we find ourselves decided as to how we should act under such circumstances as those which occasioned our hesitation. In other words, we have attained belief.

In this process we observe two sorts of elements of consciousness, the distinction between which may best be made clear by means of an illustration. In a piece of music there are the separate notes, and there is the air. A single tone may be prolonged for an hour or a day, and it exists as perfectly in each second of that time as in the whole taken together; so that, as long as it is sounding, it might be present to a sense from which everything in the past was as completely absent as the future itself. But it is different with the air, the performance of which occupies a certain time, during the portions of which only portions of it are played. It consists in an orderliness in the succession of sounds which strike the ear at different times; and to perceive it there must be some continuity of consciousness which makes the events of a lapse of time present to us. We certainly only perceive the air by hearing the separate notes; yet we cannot be said to directly hear it, for we hear only what is present at the instant, and an orderliness of succession cannot exist in an instant. These two sorts of objects, what we are *immediately* conscious of and what we are *mediately* conscious of, are found in all consciousness. Some elements (the sensations) are completely present at every instant so long as they last, while others (like thought) are actions having beginning, middle, and end, and consist in a congruence in the succession of sensations which flow through the mind. They cannot be immediately present to us, but must cover some portion of the past or future. Thought is a thread of melody running through the succession of our sensations.

We may add that just as a piece of music may be written in parts, each part having its own air, so various systems of relationship of succession subsist together between the same sensations. These different systems are distinguished by having different motives, ideas, or functions. Thought is only one such system, for its sole motive, idea, and function, is to produce belief, and whatever does not concern that purpose belongs to some other system of relations. The action of thinking may incidentally have other results; it may serve to amuse us, for example, and among *dilettanti* it is not rare to find those who have so perverted thought to the purposes of pleasure that it seems to vex them to think that the questions upon which they delight to exercise it may ever get finally settled; and a positive discovery which takes a favorite subject out of the arena of literary debate is met with ill-concealed dislike. This disposition is the very debauchery of thought. But the soul and meaning of thought, abstracted from the other elements which accompany it, though it may be voluntarily thwarted, can never be made to direct itself toward anything but the production of belief. Thought in action has for its only possible motive the attainment of thought at rest; and whatever does not refer to belief is no part of the thought itself.

And what, then, is belief? It is the demi-cadence which closes a musical phrase in the symphony of our intellectual life. We have seen that it has just three properties: First, it is something that we are aware of; second, it appeases the irritation of doubt; and, third, it involves the establishment in our nature of a rule of action, or, say for short, a *habit*. As it appeases the irritation of doubt, which is the motive for thinking, thought relaxes, and comes to rest for a moment when belief is reached. But, since belief is a rule for action, the application of which involves further doubt and further thought, at the same time that it is a stopping-place, it is also a new starting place for thought. That is why I have permitted myself to call it thought at rest, although thought is essentially an action. The *final* upshot of thinking is the exercise of volition, and of this thought no longer forms a part; but belief is only a stadium of mental action, an effect upon our nature due to thought, which will influence future thinking.

The essence of belief is the establishment of a habit, and different beliefs are distinguished by the different modes of action to which they give rise. If beliefs do not differ in this respect, if they appease the same doubt by producing the same rule of action, then no mere differences in the manner of consciousness of them can make them different beliefs, any more than playing a tune in different keys is playing different tunes. Imaginary distinctions are often drawn between beliefs which differ only in their mode of expression;—the wrangling which ensues is real enough, however. To believe that any objects are arranged as in Fig. 1, and to believe that they are arranged in Fig. 2, are

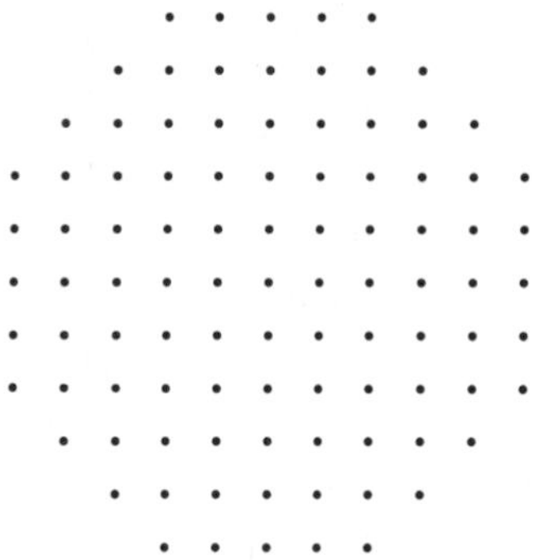

Fig. 1 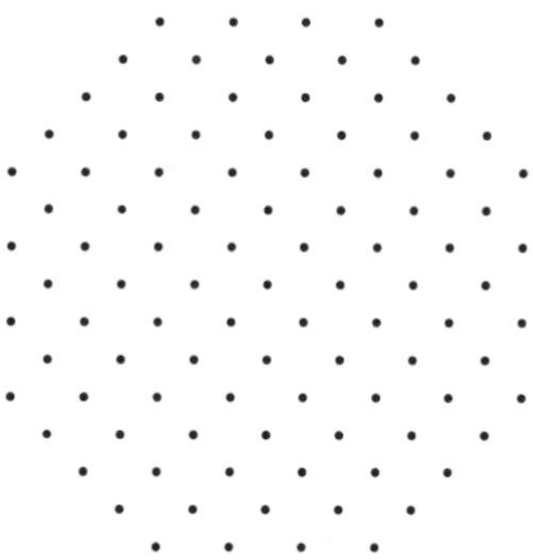   Fig. 2

one and the same belief; yet it is conceivable that a man should assert one proposition and deny the other. Such false distinctions do as much harm as the confusion of beliefs really different, and are among the pitfalls of which we ought constantly to beware, especially when we are upon metaphysical ground. One singular deception of this sort, which often occurs, is to mistake the sensation produced by our own unclearness of thought for a character of the object we are thinking. Instead of perceiving that the obscurity is purely subjective, we fancy that we contemplate a quality of the object which is essentially mysterious; and if our conception be afterward presented to us in a clear form we do not recognize it as the same, owing to the absence of the feeling of unintelligibility. So long as this deception lasts, it obviously puts an impassable barrier in the way of perspicuous thinking; so that it equally interests the opponents of rational thought to perpetuate it, and its adherents to guard against it.

Another such deception is to mistake a mere difference in the grammatical construction of two words for a distinction between the ideas they express. In this pedantic age, when the general mob of writers attend so much more to words than to things, this error is common enough. When I just said that thought is an action, and that it consists in a relation, although a person performs an action but not a relation, which can only be the result of an action, yet there was no inconsistency in what I said, but only a grammatical vagueness.

From all these sophisms we shall be perfectly safe so long as we reflect that the whole function of thought is to produce habits of action; and that whatever there is connected with a thought, but irrelevant to its purpose, is an accretion to it, but no part of it. If there be a unity among our sensations which has no reference to how we shall act on a given occasion, as when we listen to a piece of music, why we do not call that thinking. To develop its meaning, we have, therefore, simply to determine what habits it produces, for what a thing means is simply what habits it involves. Now, the identity of a habit depends on how it might lead us to act, not merely under such circumstances as are likely to arise, but under such as might possibly occur, no matter how improbable they may be. What the habit is depends on when and *how* it causes us to act. As for the *when*, every stimulus to action is derived from perception; as for the *how*, every purpose of action is to produce some sensible result. Thus, we come down to what is tangible and practical, as the root of every real distinction of thought, no matter how subtle it may be; and there is no distinction of meaning so fine as to consist in anything but a possible difference of practice.

To see what this principle leads to, consider in the light of it such a doctrine as that of transubstantiation. The Protestant churches generally hold that the elements of the sacrament are flesh and blood only in a tropical sense; they nourish our souls as meat and the juice of it would our bodies. But the Catholics maintain that they are literally just that; although they possess all the sensible qualities of wafer-cakes and diluted wine. But we can have no conception of wine except what may enter into a belief, either—

1. That this, that, or the other, is wine; or,
2. That wine possesses certain properties.

Such beliefs are nothing but self-notifications that we should, upon occasion, act in regard to such things as we believe to be wine according to the qualities which we believe wine to possess. The occasion of such action would be some sensible perception, the motive of it to produce some sensible result. Thus our action has exclusive reference to what affects the senses, our habit has the same bearing as our action, our belief the same as our habit, our conception the same as our belief; and we can consequently mean nothing by wine but what has certain effects, direct or indirect, upon our senses; and to talk of something as having all the sensible characters of wine, yet being in reality blood, is senseless jargon. Now, it is not my object to pursue the theological question; and having used it as a logical example I drop it, without caring to anticipate the theologian's reply. I only desire to point out how impossible it is that we should have an idea in our minds which relates to anything but conceived sensible effects of things. Our idea of anything is our idea of its sensible effects; and if we fancy that we have any other we deceive ourselves, and mistake a mere sensation accompanying the thought for a part of the thought itself. It is absurd to say that thought has any meaning unrelated to its only function. It is foolish for Catholics and Protestants to fancy themselves in disagreement about the elements of the sacrament, if they agree in regard to all their sensible effects, here or hereafter.

It appears, then, that the rule for attaining the third grade of clearness of apprehension is as follows: Consider what effects, which might conceivably have practical bearings, we conceive the object of our conception to have. Then, our conception of these effects is the whole of our conception of the object.

III

Let us illustrate this rule by some examples; and, to begin with the simplest one possible, let us ask what we mean by calling a thing *hard*. Evidently that it will not be scratched by many other substances. The whole conception of this quality, as of every other, lies in its conceived effects. There is absolutely no difference between a hard thing and a soft thing so long as they are not brought to the test. Suppose, then, that a diamond could be crystallized in the midst of a cushion of soft cotton, and should remain there until it was finally burned up. Would it be false to say that that diamond was soft? This seems a foolish question, and would be so, in fact, except in the realm of logic. There such questions are often of the greatest utility as serving to bring logical principles into sharper relief than real discussions ever could. In studying logic we must not put them aside with hasty answers, but must consider them with attentive care, in order to make out the principles involved. We may, in the present ease, modify our question, and ask what prevents us from saying that all hard bodies remain perfectly soft until they are touched, when their hardness increases with the pressure until they are scratched. Reflection will show that the reply is this: there would be no *falsity* in such modes of speech. They would involve a modification of our present usage of speech with regard to the words hard and soft, but not of their meanings. For they represent no fact to be different from what it is; only they involve arrangements of facts which would be exceedingly maladroit. This leads us to remark that the question of what would occur under circumstances which do not actually arise is not a question of fact, but only of the most perspicuous arrangement of them. For example, the question of free-will and fate in its simplest form, stripped of verbiage, is something like this: I have done something of which I am ashamed; could I, by an effort of the will, have resisted the temptation, and done otherwise? The philosophical reply is, that this is not a question of fact, but only of the arrangement of facts. Arranging them so as to exhibit what is particularly pertinent to my question—namely, that I ought to blame myself for having done wrong—it is perfectly true to say that, if I had willed to do otherwise than I did, I should have done otherwise. On the other hand, arranging the facts so as to exhibit another important consideration, it is equally true that, when a temptation has once been allowed to work, it will, if it has a certain force, produce its effect, let me struggle how I may. There is no objection to a contradiction in what would result from a false supposition. The *reductio ad absurdum* consists in showing that contradictory results would follow from a hypothesis which is consequently judged to be false. Many questions are involved in the free-will discussion, and I am far from desiring to say that both sides are equally right. On the contrary, I am of opinion that one side denies important facts, and that the other does not. But what I do say is, that the above single question was the origin of the whole doubt; that, had it not been for this question, the controversy would never have arisen; and that this question is perfectly solved in the manner which I have indicated....

IV

Let us now approach the subject of logic, and consider a conception which particularly concerns it, that of *reality*. Taking clearness in the sense of familiarity, no idea could be clearer than this. Every child uses it with perfect confidence, never dreaming that he does not understand it. As for clearness in its second grade, however, it would probably puzzle most men, even among those of a reflective turn of mind, to give an abstract definition of the real. Yet such a definition may perhaps be reached by considering the points of difference between reality and its opposite, fiction. A figment is a product of somebody's imagination; it has such characters as his thought impresses upon it. That those characters are independent of how you or I think is an external reality. There are, however, phenomena within our own minds, dependent upon our thought, which are at the same time real in the sense that we really think them. But though their characters depend on how we think, they do not depend on what we think those characters to be. Thus, a dream has a real existence as a mental phenomenon, if somebody has really dreamt it; that he dreamt so and so, does not depend on what anybody thinks was dreamt, but is completely independent of all opinion on the subject. On the other hand, considering, not the fact of dreaming, but the thing dreamt, it retains its peculiarities by virtue of no other fact than that it was dreamt to possess them. Thus we may define the real as that whose characters are independent of what anybody may think them to be.

But, however satisfactory such a definition may be found, it would be a great mistake to suppose that it makes the idea of reality perfectly clear. Here, then, let us apply our rules. According to them, reality, like every other quality, consists in the peculiar sensible effects which things partaking of it produce. The only effect which real things have is to cause belief, for all the sensations which they excite emerge into consciousness in the form of beliefs. The question therefore is, how is true belief (or belief in the real) distinguished from false belief (or belief in fiction). Now, as we have seen in the former paper, the ideas of truth and falsehood, in their full development, appertain exclusively to the scientific method of settling opinion. A person who arbitrarily chooses the propositions which he will adopt can use the word truth only to emphasize the expression of his determination to hold on to his choice. Of course, the method of tenacity never prevailed exclusively; reason is too natural to men for that. But in the literature of the dark ages we find some fine examples of it. When Scotus Erigena is commenting upon a poetical passage in which hellebore is spoken of as having caused the death of Socrates, he does not hesitate to inform the inquiring reader that Helleborus and Socrates were two eminent Greek philosophers, and that the latter having been overcome in argument by the former took the matter to heart and died of it! What sort of an idea of truth could a man have who could adopt and teach, without the qualification of a perhaps, an opinion taken so entirely at random? The real spirit of Socrates, who I hope would have been delighted to have been "overcome in argument," because he would have learned something by it, is in curious contrast with the naive idea of the glossist, for whom discussion would seem to have been simply a struggle. When philosophy began to awake from its long slumber, and before theology completely dominated it, the practice seems to have been for each professor to seize upon any philosophical position he found unoccupied and which seemed a strong one, to intrench himself in it, and to sally forth from time to time to give battle to the others. Thus, even the scanty records we possess of those disputes enable us to make out a dozen or more opinions held by different teachers at one time concerning the question of nominalism and realism. Read the opening part of the "Historia Calamitatum" of Abelard, who was certainly as philosophical as any of his contemporaries, and see the spirit of combat which it breathes. For him, the truth is simply his particular stronghold. When the method of authority prevailed, the truth meant little more than the Catholic faith. All the efforts of the scholastic doctors are directed toward harmonizing their faith in Aristotle and their faith in the Church, and one may search their ponderous folios through without finding an argument which goes any further. It is noticeable that where different faiths flourish side by side, renegades are looked upon with contempt even by the party whose belief they adopt; so completely has the idea of loyalty replaced that of truth-seeking. Since the time of Descartes, the defect in the conception of truth has been less apparent. Still, it will sometimes strike a scientific man that the philosophers have been less intent on finding out what the facts are, than on inquiring what belief is most in harmony with their system. It is hard to convince a follower of the *a priori* method by adducing facts; but show him that an opinion he is defending is inconsistent with what he has laid down elsewhere, and he will be very apt to retract it. These minds do not seem to believe that disputation is ever to cease; they seem to think that the opinion which is natural for one man is not so for another, and that belief will, consequently, never be settled. In contenting themselves with fixing their own opinions by a method which would lead another man to a different result, they betray their feeble hold of the conception of what truth is.

On the other hand, all the followers of science are fully persuaded that the processes of investigation, if only pushed far enough, will give one certain solution to every question to which they can be applied. One man may investigate the velocity of light by studying the transits of Venus and the aberration of the stars; another by the oppositions of Mars and the eclipses of Jupiter's satellites; a third by the method of Fizeau; a fourth by that of Foucault; a fifth by the motions of the curves of Lissajoux; a sixth, a seventh, an eighth, and a ninth, may follow the different methods of comparing the measures of statical and dynamical electricity. They may at first obtain different results, but, as each perfects his method and his processes, the results will move steadily together toward a destined centre. So with all scientific research. Different minds may set out with the most antagonistic views, but the progress of investigation carries them by a force outside of themselves to one and the same conclusion. This activity of thought by which we are carried, not where we wish, but to a foreordained goal, is like the operation of destiny. No modification of the point of view taken, no selection of other facts for study, no natural bent of mind even, can enable a man to escape the predestinate opinion. This great law is embodied in the conception of truth and reality. The opinion which is fated[2] to be ultimately agreed to by all who investigate, is what we mean by the truth, and the object represented in this opinion is the real. That is the way I would explain reality.

But it may be said that this view is directly opposed to the abstract definition which we have given of reality, inasmuch as it makes the characters of the real to depend on what is ultimately thought about them. But the answer to this is that, on the one hand, reality is independent, not necessarily of thought in general, but only of what you or I or any finite number of men may think about it; and that, on the other hand, though the object of the final opinion depends on what that opinion is, yet what that opinion is does not depend on what you or I or any man thinks. Our perversity and that of others may indefinitely postpone the settlement of opinion; it might even conceivably cause an arbitrary proposition to be universally accepted as long as the human race should last. Yet even that would not change the nature of the belief, which alone could be the result of investigation carried sufficiently far; and if, after the extinction of our race, another should arise with faculties and disposition for investigation, that true opinion must be the one which they would ultimately come to. "Truth crushed to earth shall rise again," and the opinion which would finally result from investigation does not depend on how anybody may actually think. But the reality of that which is real does depend on the real fact that investigation is destined to lead, at last, if continued long enough, to a belief in it.

But I may be asked what I have to say to all the minute facts of history, forgotten never to be recovered, to the lost books of the ancients, to the buried secrets.

> Full many a gem of purest ray serene
>> The dark, unfathomed caves of ocean bear;
> Full many a flower is born to blush unseen,
>> And waste its sweetness on the desert air.

Do these things not really exist because they are hopelessly beyond the reach of our knowledge? And then, after the universe is dead (according to the prediction of some scientists), and all life has ceased forever, will not the shock of atoms continue though there will be no mind to know it? To this I reply that, though in no possible state of knowledge can any number be great enough to express the relation between the amount of what rests unknown to the amount of the known, yet it is unphilosophical to suppose that, with regard to any given question (which has any clear meaning), investigation would not bring forth a solution of it, if it were carried far enough. Who would have said, a few years ago, that we could ever know of what substances stars are made whose light may have been longer in reaching us than the human race has existed? Who can be sure of what we shall not know in a few hundred years? Who can guess what would be the result of continuing the pursuit of science for ten thousand years, with the activity of the last hundred? And if it were to go on for a million, or a billion, or any number of years you please, how is it possible to say that there is any question which might not ultimately be solved?

But it may be objected, "Why make so much of these remote considerations, especially when it is your principle that only practical distinctions have a meaning?" Well, I must confess that it makes very little difference whether we say that a stone on the bottom of the ocean, in complete darkness, is brilliant or not—that is to say, that it *probably* makes no difference, remembering always that that stone *may* be fished up to-morrow. But that there are gems at the bottom of the sea, flowers in the untraveled desert, etc., are propositions which, like that about a diamond being hard when it is not pressed, concern much more the arrangement of our language than they do the meaning of our ideas.

It seems to me, however, that we have, by the application of our rule, reached so clear an apprehension of what we mean by reality, and of the fact which the idea rests on, that we should not, perhaps, be making a pretension so presumptuous as it would be singular, if we were to offer a metaphysical theory of existence for universal acceptance among those who employ the scientific method of fixing belief. However, as metaphysics is a subject much more curious than useful, the knowledge of which, like that of a sunken reef, serves chiefly to enable us to keep clear of it, I will not trouble the reader with any more Ontology at this moment. I have already been led much further into that path than I should have desired; and I have given the reader such a dose of mathematics, psychology, and all that is most abstruse, that I fear he may already have left me, and that what I am now writing is for the compositor and proof-reader exclusively. I trusted to the importance of the subject. There is no royal road to logic, and really valuable ideas can only be had at the price of close attention. But I know that in the matter of ideas the public prefer the cheap and nasty; and in my next paper I am going to return to the easily intelligible, and not wander from it again. The reader who has been at the pains of wading through this month's paper, shall be rewarded in the next one by seeing how beautifully what has been developed in this tedious way can be applied to the ascertainment of the rules of scientific reasoning.

We have, hitherto, not crossed the threshold of scientific logic. It is certainly important to know how to make our ideas clear, but they may be ever so clear without being true. How to make them so, we have next to study. How to give birth to those vital and procreative ideas which multiply into a thousand forms and diffuse themselves everywhere, advancing civilization and making the dignity of man, is an art not yet reduced to rules, but of the secret of which the history of science affords some hints.

Notes

1 Editor's note: Peirce published "The Fixation of Belief" in the *Popular Sicence Monthly* in 1877, a year before "How to Make Our Ideas Clear." See the *Collected Papers of Charles Sanders Peirce*, vol. 5, ed. Charles Hartshorne and Paul Weiss (Cambridge, MA: The Belknap Press of Harvard University Press, 1965), pp. 223-47. For a brief account of this paper, see pp. 36-37 above.

2 Fate means merely that which is sure to come true, and can nohow be avoided. It is a superstition to suppose that a certain sort of events are ever fated, and it is another to suppose that the word fate can never be freed from its superstitious taint. We are all fated to die.

WILLIAM JAMES
(1842–1910)

The older brother of the novelist Henry James, William James introduced experimental psychology into the American university and published the monumental *Principles of Psychology* in 1890. In subsequent years he turned from psychology towards philosophy and religion, publishing *The Will to Believe* in 1896 and *Varieties of Religious Experience* in 1902, and in the final decade of his life developing positions he called "pluralism," "radical empiricism," and "pragmatism."

The two chapters reprinted below from James's 1907 book *Pragmatism* forcefully express the main ideas and tendencies of his and subsequent pragmatisms. "What Pragmatism Means" begins with one of James's most memorable (if not most intelligible) stories: of a dispute about whether a man chasing a squirrel around a tree goes around the squirrel too. James takes this story as emblematic of philosophy's tendency to get stuck in interminable disputes, and his own intervention to settle the dispute as a model of pragmatist method. That method is, according to James, based on Peirce's pragmatic account of meaning, according to which our conception of a thing is the "conceivable effects of a practical kind the object may involve."

In addition to a theory of meaning and a method for settling metaphysical disputes, pragmatism is also for James a theory of truth. Ideas, James holds, are themselves parts of experience, and they "become true just in so far as they help us to get into satisfactory relation with other parts of our experience." Or as he also states it, true ideas are those on which we can "ride." Such formulations express James's rejection of the idea that truth corresponds to some nonexperienced, preconstituted reality, and his commitment to an account that takes truth to be a set of relations within human experience. Truth,

James writes, is "a species of the good"; truths carry us "prosperously" towards or allow us to "get into satisfactory relation" with other parts of experience.

Reinforcing this experiential view of truth is a general epistemological and metaphysical view that James, following the Oxford pragmatist F. C. S. Schiller, called "humanism." "What Pragmatism Means" contains the statement, so important for Hilary Putnam's contemporary version of pragmatism, that "the trail of the human serpent is over everything." "Pragmatism and Humanism," the second chapter of *Pragmatism* reprinted here, contains James's most considered explication of this doctrine. Although James emphasizes the human determination of the world, he at the same time offers a nuanced contrary account of the world's facticity or resistance. "We carve out everything," James states, "just as we carve out constellations, to serve our human purposes." Nevertheless, there are "resisting factors in every experience of truth-making," including not only our present sensations or experiences but the whole body of our prior beliefs. We modify the "ancient mass" of our beliefs, but on the whole "we patch and tinker more than we renew." James holds neither that we create our truths out of nothing, nor that truth is entirely independent of humanity. He embraces "the humanistic principle: you can't weed out the human contribution."

PRAGMATISM

WILLIAM JAMES

What Pragmatism Means

Some years ago, being with a camping party in the mountains, I returned from a solitary ramble to find every one engaged in a ferocious metaphysical dispute. The *corpus* of the dispute was a squirrel—a live squirrel supposed to be clinging to one side of a tree-trunk; while over against the tree's opposite side a human being was imagined to stand. This human witness tries to get sight of the squirrel by moving rapidly round the tree, but no matter how fast he goes, the squirrel moves as fast in the opposite direction, and always keeps the tree between himself and the man, so that never a glimpse of him is caught. The resultant metaphysical problem now is this: *Does the man go round the squirrel or not?* He goes round the tree, sure enough, and the squirrel is on the tree; but does he go round the squirrel? In the unlimited leisure of the wilderness, discussion had been worn threadbare. Every one had taken sides, and was obstinate; and the numbers on both sides were even. Each side, when I appeared therefore appealed to me to make it a majority. Mindful of the scholastic adage that whenever you meet a contradiction you must make a distinction, I immediately sought and found one, as follows: "Which party is right," I said, "depends on what you *practically mean* by 'going round' the squirrel. If you mean passing from the north of him to the east, then to the south, then to the west, and then to the north of him again, obviously the man does go round him, for he occupies these successive positions. But if on the contrary you mean being first in front of him, then on the right of him, then behind him, then on his left, and finally in front again, it is quite as obvious that the man fails to go round him, for by the compensating movements the squirrel makes, he keeps his belly turned towards the man all the time, and his back turned away. Make the distinction, and there is no occasion for any farther dispute. You are both right and both wrong according as you conceive the verb 'to go round' in one practical fashion or the other."

Although one or two of the hotter disputants called my speech a shuffling evasion, saying they wanted no quibbling or scholastic hair-splitting, but meant just plain honest English "round," the majority seemed to think that the distinction had assuaged the dispute.

I tell this trivial anecdote because it is a peculiarly simple example of what I wish now to speak of as *the pragmatic method.* The pragmatic method is primarily a method of settling metaphysical disputes that otherwise might be interminable. Is the world one or many?—fated or free?—material or spiritual?—here are notions either of which may or may not hold good of the world; and disputes over such notions are unending. The pragmatic method in such cases is to try to interpret each notion by tracing its respective practical consequences. What difference would it practically make to any one if this notion rather than that notion were true? If no practical difference whatever can be traced, then the alternatives mean practically the same thing, and all dispute is idle. Whenever a dispute is serious, we ought to be able to show some practical difference that must follow from one side or the other's being right.

A glance at the history of the idea will show you still better what pragmatism means. The term is derived from the same Greek word πρᾶγμα meaning action, from which our words "practice" and "practical" come. It was first introduced into philosophy by Mr. Charles Peirce in 1878. In an article entitled "How to Make Our Ideas Clear" in the "Popular Science Monthly" for January of that year.[1] Mr. Peirce, after pointing out that our beliefs are really rules for action, said that, to develop a thought's meaning, we need only determine what conduct it is fitted to produce: that conduct is for us its sole significance. And the tangible fact at the root of all our thought distinctions, however subtle, is that there is no one of them so fine as to consist in anything but a possible difference of practice. To attain perfect clearness in our thoughts of an object, then, we need only consider what conceivable effects of a practical kind the object may involve—what sensations we are to expect from it, and what reactions we must prepare. Our conception of these effects, whether immediate or remote, is then for us the whole of our conception of the object, so far as that conception has positive significance at all.

This is the principle of Peirce, the principle of pragmatism. It lay entirely unnoticed by any one for twenty years, until I, in an address before Professor Howison's philosophical union at the university of California, brought it forward again and made a special application of it to religion. By that date (1898) the times seemed ripe for its reception. The word "pragmatism" spread, and at present it fairly spots the pages of the philosophic journals. On all hands we find the "pragmatic movement" spoken of, sometimes with respect, sometimes with contumely, seldom with clear understanding. It is evident that the term applies itself conveniently to a number of tendencies that hitherto have lacked a collective name, and that it has "come to stay."

To take in the importance of Peirce's principle, one must get accustomed to applying it to concrete cases. I found a few years ago that Ostwald, the illustrious Leipzig chemist, had been making perfectly distinct use of the principle of pragmatism in his lectures on the philosophy of science, though he had not called it by that name.

"All realities influence our practice," he wrote me, "and that influence is their meaning for us. I am accustomed to put questions to my classes in this way: In what respects would the world be different if this alternative or that were true? If I can find nothing that would become different, then the alternative has no sense."

That is, the rival views mean practically the same thing, and meaning, other than practical, there is for us none. Ostwald in a published lecture gives this example of what he means. Chemists have long wrangled over the inner constitution of certain bodies called "tautomerous." Their properties seemed equally consistent with the notion that an instable hydrogen atom oscillates inside of them, or that they are instable mixtures of two bodies. Controversy raged, but never was decided. "It would never have begun," says Ostwald, " if the combatants had asked themselves what particular experimental fact could have been made different by one or the other view being correct. For it would then have appeared that no difference of fact could possibly ensue; and the quarrel was as unreal as if, theorizing in primitive times about the raising of dough by yeast, one party should have invoked a "brownie," while another insisted on an "elf" as the true cause of the phenomenon."[2]

It is astonishing to see how many philosophical disputes collapse into insignificance the moment you subject them to this simple test of tracing a concrete consequence. There can *be* no difference anywhere that doesn't *make* a difference elsewhere—no difference in abstract truth that doesn't express itself in a difference in concrete fact and in conduct consequent upon that fact, imposed on somebody, somehow, somewhere, and somewhen. The whole function of philosophy ought to be to find out what definite difference it will make to you and me, at definite instants of our life, if this world-formula or that world-formula be the true one.

There is absolutely nothing new in the pragmatic method. Socrates was an adept at it. Aristotle used it methodically. Locke, Berkeley, and Hume made momentous contributions to truth by its means. Shadworth Hodgson keeps insisting that realities are only what they are "known as." But these forerunners of pragmatism used it in fragments: they were a prelude only. Not until in our time has it generalized itself, become conscious of a universal mission, pretended to a conquering destiny. I believe in that destiny, and I hope I may end by inspiring you with my belief.

Pragmatism represents a perfectly familiar attitude in philosophy, the empiricist attitude, but it represents it, as it seems to me, both in a more radical and in a less objectionable form than it has ever yet assumed. A pragmatist turns his back resolutely and once for all upon a lot of inveterate habits dear to professional philosophers. He turns away from abstraction and insufficiency, from verbal solutions, from bad *a priori* reasons, from fixed principles, closed systems, and pretended absolutes and origins. He turns towards concreteness and adequacy, towards facts, towards action and towards power. That means the empiricist temper regnant and the rationalist temper sincerely given up. It means the open air and possibilities of nature, as against dogma, artificiality, and the pretence of finality in truth.

At the same time it does not stand for any special results. It is a method only. But the general triumph of that method would mean an enormous change in what I called in my last lecture the "temperament"of philosophy. Teachers of the ultra-rationalistic type would be frozen out, much as the courtier type is frozen out in republics, as the ultramontane type of priest is frozen out in protestant lands. Science and metaphysics would come much nearer together, would in fact work absolutely hand in hand.

Metaphysics has usually followed a very primitive kind of quest. You know how men have always hankered after unlawful magic, and you know what a great part in magic *words* have always played. If you have his name, or the formula of incantation that binds him, you can control the spirit, genie, afrite, or whatever the power may be. Solomon knew the names of all the spirits, and having their names, he held them subject to his will. So the universe has always appeared to the natural mind as a kind of enigma, of which the key must be sought in the shape of some illuminating or power-bringing word or name. That word names the universe's *principle,* and to possess it is after a fashion to possess the universe itself. "God," "Matter," "Reason," "the Absolute," "Energy," are so many solving names. You can rest when you have them. You are at the end of your metaphysical quest.

But if you follow the pragmatic method, you cannot look on any such word as closing your quest. You must bring out of each word its practical cash-value, set it at work within the stream of your experience. It appears less as a solution, then, than as a program for more work, and more particularly as an indication of the ways in which existing realities may be *changed.*

Theories thus become instruments, not answers to enigmas, in which we can rest. We don't lie back upon them, we move forward, and, on occasion, make nature over again by their aid. Pragmatism unstiffens all our theories, limbers them up and sets each one at work. Being nothing essentially new, it harmonizes with many ancient philosophic tendencies. It agrees with nominalism for instance, in always appealing to particulars; with utilitarianism in emphasizing practical aspects; with positivism in its disdain for verbal solutions, useless questions and metaphysical abstractions.

All these, you see, are *anti-intellectualist* tendencies. Against rationalism as a pretension and a method pragmatism is fully armed and militant. But, at the outset, at least, it stands for no particular results. It has no dogmas, and no doctrines save its method. As the young Italian pragmatist Papini has well said, it lies in the midst of our theories, like a corridor in a hotel. Innumerable chambers open out of it. In one you may find a man writing an atheistic volume; in the next some one on his knees praying for faith and strength; in a third a chemist investigating a body's properties. In a fourth a system of idealistic metaphysics is being excogitated; in a fifth the impossibility of metaphysics is being shown. But they all own the corridor, and all must pass through it if they want a practicable way of getting into or out of their respective rooms.

No particular results then, so far, but only an attitude of orientation, is what the pragmatic method means. *The attitude of looking away from first things, principles, "categories," supposed necessities; and of looking towards last things, fruits, consequences, facts.*

So much for the pragmatic method! You may say that I have been praising it rather than explaining it to you, but I shall presently explain it abundantly enough by showing how it works on some familiar problems. Meanwhile the word pragmatism has come to be used in a still wider sense, as meaning also a certain *theory of truth.* I mean to give a whole lecture to the statement of that theory, after first paving the way, so I can be very brief now. But brevity is hard to follow, so I ask for your redoubled attention for a quarter of an hour. If much remains obscure, I hope to make it clearer in the later lectures.

One of the most successfully cultivated branches of philosophy in our time is what is called inductive logic, the study of the conditions under which our sciences have evolved. Writers on this subject have begun to show a singular unanimity as to what the laws of nature and elements of fact mean, when formulated by mathematicians, physicists and chemists. When the first mathematical, logical, and natural uniformities, the first *laws,* were discovered, men were so carried away by the clearness, beauty and simplification that resulted, that they believed themselves to have deciphered authentically the eternal thoughts of the Almighty. His mind also thundered and reverberated in syllogisms. He also thought in conic sections, squares and roots and ratios, and geometrized like Euclid. He made Kepler's laws for the planets to follow; he made velocity increase proportionally to the time in falling bodies; he made the law of the sines for light to obey when refracted; he established the classes, orders, families and genera of plants and animals, and fixed the distances between them. He thought the archetypes of all things, and devised their variations; and when we rediscover any one of these his wondrous institutions, we seize his mind in its very literal intention.

But as the sciences have developed farther, the notion has gained ground that most, perhaps all, of our laws are only approximations. The laws themselves, moreover, have grown so numerous that there is no counting them; and so many rival formulations are proposed in all the branches of science that investigators have become accustomed to the notion that no theory is absolutely a transcript of reality, but that any one of them may from some point of view be useful. Their great use is to summarize old facts and to lead to new ones. They are only a man-made language, a conceptual shorthand, as some one calls them, in which we write our reports of nature; and languages, as is well known, tolerate much choice of expression and many dialects.

Thus human arbitrariness has driven divine necessity from scientific logic. If I mention the names of Sigwart, Mach, Ostwald, Pearson, Milhaud, Poincaré, Duhem, Ruyssen, those of you who are students will easily identify the tendency I speak of, and will think of additional names.

Riding now on the front of this wave of scientific logic Messrs. Schiller and Dewey appear with their pragmatistic account of what truth everywhere signifies. Everywhere, these teachers say, "truth" in our ideas and beliefs means the same thing that it means in science. It means, they say, nothing but this, *that ideas (which themselves are but parts of our experience) become true just in so far as they help us to get into satisfactory relation with other parts of our experience,* to summarize them and get about among them by conceptual short-cuts instead of following the interminable succession of particular phenomena. Any idea upon which we can ride, so to speak; any idea that will carry us prosperously from any one part of our experience to any other part, linking things satisfactorily, working securely, simplifying, saving labor; is true for just so much, true in so far forth, true *instrumentally.* This is the 'instrumental' view of truth taught so successfully at Chicago, the view that truth in our ideas means their power to 'work,' promulgated so brilliantly at Oxford.

Messrs. Dewey, Schiller and their allies, in reaching this general conception of all truth, have only followed the example of geologists, biologists and philologists. In the establishment of these other sciences, the successful stroke was always to take some simple process actually observable in operation—as denudation by weather, say, or variation from parental type, or change of dialect by incorporation of new words and pronunciations—and then to generalize it, making it apply to all times, and produce great results by summating its effects through the ages.

The observable process which Schiller and Dewey particularly singled out for generalization is the familiar one by which any individual settles into *new opinions.* The process here is always the same. The individual has a stock of old opinions already, but he meets a new experience that puts them to a strain. Somebody contradicts them; or in a reflective moment he discovers that they contradict each other; or he hears of facts with which they are incompatible; or desires arise in him which they cease to satisfy. The result is an inward trouble to which his mind till then had been a stranger, and from which he seeks to escape by modifying his previous mass of opinions. He saves as much of it as he can, for in this matter of belief we are all extreme conservatives. So he tries to change first this opinion, and then that (for they resist change very variously), until at last some new idea comes up which he can graft upon the ancient stock with a minimum of disturbance of the latter, some idea that mediates between the stock and the new experience and runs them into one another most felicitously and expediently.

This new idea is then adopted as the true one. It preserves the older stock of truths with a minimum of modification, stretching them just enough to make them admit the novelty, but conceiving that in ways as familiar as the case leaves possible. An *outrée* explanation, violating all our preconceptions, would never pass for a true account of a novelty. We should scratch round industriously till we found something less eccentric. The most violent revolutions in an individual's beliefs leave most of his old order standing. Time and space, cause and effect, nature and history, and one's own biography remain untouched. New truth is always a go-between, a smoother-over of transitions. It marries old opinion to new fact so as ever to show a minimum of jolt, a maximum of continuity. We hold a theory true just in proportion to its success in solving this "problem of maxima and minima." But success in solving this problem is eminently a matter of approximation. We say this theory solves it on the whole more satisfactorily than that theory; but that means more satisfactorily to ourselves, and individuals will emphasize their points of satisfaction differently. To a certain degree, therefore, everything here is plastic.

The point I now urge you to observe particularly is the part played by the older truths. Failure to take account of it is the source of much of the unjust criticism leveled against pragmatism. Their influence is absolutely controlling. Loyalty to them is the first principle—in most cases it is the only principle; for by far the most usual way of handling phenomena so novel that they would make for a serious rearrangement of our preconception is to ignore them altogether, or to abuse those who bear witness for them.

You doubtless wish examples of this process of truth's growth, and the only trouble is their superabundance. The simplest case of new truth is of course the mere numerical addition of new kinds of facts, or of new single facts of old kinds, to our experience—an addition that involves no alteration in the old beliefs. Day follows day, and its contents are simply added. The new contents themselves are not true, they simply *come* and *are*. Truth is *what we say about* them, and when we say that they have come, truth is satisfied by the plain additive formula.

But often the day's contents oblige a rearrangement. If I should now utter piercing shrieks and act like a maniac on this platform, it would make many of you revise your ideas as to the probable worth of my philosophy. "Radium" came the other day as part of the day's content, and seemed for a moment to contradict our ideas of the whole order of nature, that order having come to be identified with what is called the conservation of energy. The mere sight of radium paying heat away indefinitely out of its own pocket seemed to violate that conservation. What to think? If the radiations from it were nothing but an escape of unsuspected "potential" energy, pre-existent inside of the atoms, the principle of conservation would be saved. The discovery of "helium" as the radiation's outcome, opened a way to this belief. So Ramsay's view is generally held to be true, because, although it extends our old ideas of energy, it causes a minimum of alteration in their nature.

I need not multiply instances. A new opinion counts as "true" just in proportion as it gratifies the individual's desire to assimilate the novel in his experience to his beliefs in stock. It must both lean on old truth and grasp new fact; and its success (as I said a moment ago) in doing this, is a matter for the individual's appreciation. When old truth grows, then, by new truth's addition, it is for subjective reasons. We are in the process and obey the reasons. That new idea is truest which performs most felicitously its function of satisfying our double urgency. It makes itself true, gets itself classed as true, by the way it works; grafting itself then upon the ancient body of truth, which thus grows much as a tree grows by the activity of a new layer of cambium.

Now Dewey and Schiller proceed to generalize this observation and to apply it to the most ancient parts of truth. They also once were plastic. They also were called true for human reasons. They also mediated between still earlier truths and what in those days were novel observations. Purely objective truth, truth in whose establishment the function of giving human satisfaction in marrying previous parts of experience with newer parts played no role whatever, is nowhere to be found. The reasons why we call things true is the reason why they *are* true, for "to be true" *means* only to perform this marriage-function.

The trail of the human serpent is thus over everything. Truth independent; truth that we *find* merely; truth no longer malleable to human need; truth incorrigible, in a word; such truth exists indeed superabundantly—or is supposed to exist by rationalistically minded thinkers; but then it means only the dead heart of the living tree, and its being there means only that truth also has its paleontology, and its "prescription," and may grow stiff with years of veteran service and petrified in men's regard by sheer antiquity. But how plastic even the oldest truths nevertheless really are has been vividly shown in our day by the transformation of logical and mathematical ideas, a transformation which seems even to be invading physics. The ancient formulas are reinterpreted as special expressions of much wider principles, principles that our ancestors never got a glimpse of in their present shape and formulation.

Mr. Schiller still gives to all this view of truth the name of "Humanism," but, for this doctrine too, the name of pragmatism seems fairly to be in the ascendant, so I will treat it under the name of pragmatism in these lectures.

Such then would be the scope of pragmatism—first, a method; and second, a genetic theory of what is meant by truth. And these two things must be our future topics.

What I have said of the theory of truth will, I am sure, have appeared obscure and unsatisfactory to most of you by reason of its brevity. I shall make amends for that hereafter. In a lecture on "common sense" I shall try to show what I mean by truths grown petrified by antiquity. In another lecture I shall expatiate on the idea that our thoughts become true in proportion as they successfully exert their go-between function. In a third I shall show how hard it is to discriminate subjective from objective factors in Truth's development. You may not follow me wholly in these lectures; and if you do, you may not wholly agree with me. But you will, I know, regard me at least as serious, and treat my effort with respectful consideration.

You will probably be surprised to learn, then, that Messrs. Schiller's and Dewey's theories have suffered a hailstorm of contempt and ridicule. All rationalism has risen against them. In influential quarters Mr. Schiller, in particular, has been treated like an impudent schoolboy who deserves a spanking. I should not mention this, but for the fact that it throws so much sidelight upon that rationalistic temper to which I have opposed the temper of pragmatism. Pragmatism is uncomfortable away from facts. Rationalism is comfortable only in the presence of abstractions. This pragmatist talk about truths in the plural, about their utility and satisfactoriness, about the success with which they "work," etc., suggests to the typical intellectualist mind a sort of coarse lame second-rate makeshift article of truth. Such truths are not real truth. Such tests are merely subjective. As against this, objective truth must be something non-utilitarian, haughty, refined, remote, august, exalted. It must be an absolute correspondence of our thoughts with an equally absolute reality. It must be what we *ought* to think unconditionally. The conditioned ways in which we *do* think are so much irrelevance and matter for psychology. Down with psychology, up with logic, in all this question!

See the exquisite contrast of the types of mind! The pragmatist clings to facts and concreteness, observes truth at its work in particular cases, and generalizes. Truth, for him, becomes a class-name for all sorts of definite working-values in experience. For the rationalist it remains a pure abstraction, to the bare name of which we must defer. When the pragmatist undertakes to show in detail just *why* we must defer, the rationalist is unable to recognize the concretes from which his own abstraction is taken. He accuses us of *denying* truth; whereas we have only sought to trace exactly why people follow it and always ought to follow it. Your typical ultra-abstractionist fairly shudders at concreteness: other things equal, he positively prefers the pale and spectral. If the two universes were offered, he would always choose the skinny outline rather than the rich thicket of reality. It is so much purer, clearer, nobler.

I hope that as these lectures go on, the concreteness and closeness to facts of the pragmatism which they advocate maybe what approves itself to you as its most satisfactory peculiarity. It only follows here the example of the sister-sciences, interpreting the unobserved by the observed. It brings old and new harmoniously together. It converts the absolutely empty notion of a static relation of "correspondence" (what that may mean we must ask later) between our minds and reality, into that of a rich and active commerce (that any one may follow in detail and understand) between particular thoughts of ours, and the great universe of other experiences in which they play their parts and have their uses.

But enough of this at present? The justification of what I say must be postponed. I wish now to add a word in further explanation of the claim I made at our last meeting, that pragmatism may be a happy harmonizer of empiricist ways of thinking with the more religious demands of human beings.

Men who are strongly of the fact-loving temperament, you may remember me to have said, are liable to be kept at a distance by the small sympathy with facts which that philosophy from the present-day fashion of idealism offers them. It is far too intellectualistic. Old fashioned theism was bad enough, with its notion of God as an exalted monarch, made up of a lot of unintelligible or preposterous "attributes"; but, so long as it held strongly by the argument from design, it kept some touch with concrete realities. Since, however, darwinism has once for all displaced design from the minds of the "scientific," theism has lost that foothold; and some kind of an immanent or pantheistic deity working *in* things rather than above them is, if any, the kind recommended to our contemporary imagination. Aspirants to a philosophic religion turn, as a rule, more hopefully nowadays towards idealistic pantheism than towards the older dualistic theism, in spite of the fact that the latter still counts able defenders.

But, as I said in my first lecture, the brand of pantheism offered is hard for them to assimilate if they are lovers of facts, or empirically minded. It is the absolutistic brand, spurning the dust and reared upon pure logic. It keeps no connexion whatever with concreteness. Affirming the Absolute Mind, which is its substitute for God, to be the rational presupposition of all particulars of fact, whatever they may be, it remains supremely indifferent to what the particular facts in our world actually are. Be they what they may, the Absolute will father them. Like the sick lion in Esop's fable, all footprints lead into his den, but *nulla vestigia retrorsum.* You cannot redescend into the world of particulars by the Absolute's aid, or deduce any necessary consequences of detail important for your life from your idea of his nature. He gives you indeed the assurance that all is well with *Him,* and for his eternal way of thinking; but thereupon he leaves you to be finitely saved by your own temporal devices.

Far be it from me to deny the majesty of this conception, or its capacity to yield religious comfort to a most respectable class of minds. But from the human point of view, no one can pretend that it doesn't suffer from the faults of remoteness and abstractness. It is eminently a product of what I have ventured to call the rationalistic temper. It disdains empiricism's needs. It substitutes a pallid outline for the real world's richness. It is dapper, it is noble in the bad sense, in the sense in which to be noble is to be inapt for humble service. In this real world of sweat and dirt, it seems to me that when a view of things is "noble," that ought to count as a presumption against its truth, and as a philosophic disqualification. The prince of darkness may be a gentleman, as we are told he is, but whatever the God of earth and heaven is, he can surely be no gentleman. His menial services are needed in the dust of our human trials, even more than his dignity is needed in the empyrean.

Now pragmatism, devoted though she be to facts, has no such materialistic bias as ordinary empiricism labors under. Moreover, she has no objection whatever to the realizing of abstractions, so long as you get about among particulars with their aid and they actually carry you somewhere. Interested in no conclusions but those which our minds and our experiences work out together, she has no *a priori* prejudices against theology. *If theological ideas prove to have a value for concrete life, they will be true, for pragmatism, in the sense of being good for so much. For how much more they are true, will depend entirely on their relations to the other truths that also have to be acknowledged.*

What I said just now about the Absolute, of transcendental idealism, is a case in point. First, I called it majestic and said it yielded religious comfort to a class of minds, and then I accused it of remoteness and sterility. But so far as it affords such comfort, it surely is not sterile; it has that amount of value; it performs a concrete function. As a good pragmatist, I myself ought to call the Absolute true "in so far forth," then; and I unhesitatingly now do so.

But what does *true in so far forth* mean in this case? To answer, we need only apply the pragmatic method. What do believers in the Absolute mean by saying that their belief affords them comfort? They mean that since, in the Absolute finite evil is "overruled" already, we may, therefore, whenever we wish, treat the temporal as if it were potentially the eternal, be sure that we can trust its outcome, and, without sin, dismiss our fear and drop the worry of our finite responsibility. In short, they mean that we have a right ever and anon to take a moral holiday, to let the world wag in its own way, feeling that its issues are in better hands than ours and are none of our business.

The universe is a system of which the individual members may relax their anxieties occasionally, in which the don't-care mood is also right for men, and moral holidays in order,—that, if I mistake not, is part, at least, of what the Absolute is "known-as," that is the great difference in our particular experiences which his being true makes, for us, that is his cash-value when he is pragmatically interpreted. Farther than that the ordinary lay-reader in philosophy who thinks favorably of absolute idealism does not venture to sharpen his conceptions. He can use the Absolute for so much, and so much is very precious. He is pained at hearing you speak incredulously of the Absolute, therefore, and disregards your criticisms because they deal with aspects of the conception that he fails to follow.

If the Absolute means this, and means no more than this, who can possibly deny the truth of it? To deny it would be to insist that men should never relax, and that holidays are never in order.

I am well aware how odd it must seem to some of you to hear me say that an idea is "true" so long as to believe it is profitable to our lives. That it is good, for as much as it profits, you will gladly admit. If what we do by its aid is good, you will allow the idea itself to be good in so far forth, for we are the better for possessing it. But is it not a strange misuse of the word "truth," you will say, to call ideas also "true" for this reason?

To answer this difficulty fully is impossible at this stage of my account. You touch here upon the very central point of Messrs. Schiller's, Dewey's and my own doctrine of truth, which I can not discuss with detail until my sixth lecture. Let me now say only this, that truth is one *species of good,* and not, as is usually supposed, a category distinct from good, and co-ordinate with it. *The true is the name of whatever proves itself to be good in the way of belief, and good, too, for definite, assignable reasons.* Surely you must admit this, that if there were *no* good for life in true ideas, or if the knowledge of them were positively disadvantageous and false ideas the only useful ones, then the current notion that truth is divine and precious, and its pursuit a duty, could never have grown up or become a dogma. In a world like that, our duty would be to *shun* truth, rather. But in this world, just as certain foods are not only agreeable to our taste, but good for our teeth, our stomach, and our tissues; so certain ideas are not only agreeable to think about, or agreeable as supporting other ideas that we are fond of, but they are also helpful in life's practical struggles. If there be any life that it is really better we should lead, and if there be any idea which, if believed in, would help us to lead that life, then it would be really *better for us* to believe in that idea, *unless, indeed, belief in it incidentally clashed with other greater vital benefits.*

"What would be better for us to believe"! This sounds very like a definition of truth. It comes very near to saying what we ought to believe: and in that definition none of you would find any oddity. Ought we ever not to believe what it is *better for us* to believe? And can we then keep the notion of what is better for us, and what is true for us, permanently apart?

Pragmatism says no, and I fully agree with her. Probably you also agree, so far as the abstract statement goes, but with a suspicion that if we practically did believe everything that made for good in our own personal lives, we should be found indulging all kinds of fancies about this world's affairs, and all kinds of sentimental superstitions about a world hereafter. Your suspicion here is undoubtedly well founded, and it is evident that something happens when you pass from the abstract to the concrete that complicates the situation.

I said just now that what is better for us to believe is true *unless the belief incidentally clashes with some other vital benefit.* Now in real life what vital benefits is any particular belief of ours most liable to clash with? What indeed except the vital benefits yielded by *other beliefs* when these prove incompatible with the first ones? In other words, the greatest enemy of any one of our truths may be the rest of our truths. Truths have once for all this desperate instinct of self-preservation and of desire to extinguish whatever contradicts them. My belief in the Absolute, based on the good it does me, must run the gauntlet of all my other beliefs. Grant that it may be true in giving me a moral holiday. Nevertheless, as I conceive it,—and let me speak now confidentially, as it were, and merely in my own private person,—it clashes with other truths of mine whose benefits I hate to give up on its account. It happens to be associated with a kind of logic of which I am the enemy, I find that it entangles me in metaphysical paradoxes that are inacceptable, etc., etc. But as I have enough trouble in life already without adding the trouble of carrying these intellectual inconsistencies, I personally just give up the Absolute. I just *take* my moral holidays; or else as a professional philosopher, I try to justify them by some other principle.

If I could restrict my notion of the Absolute to its bare holiday-giving value, it wouldn't clash with my other truths. But we can not easily thus restrict our hypotheses. They carry supernumerary features, and these it is that clash so. My disbelief in the Absolute means then disbelief in those other supernumerary features, for I fully believe in the legitimacy of taking moral holidays.

You see by this what I meant when I called pragmatism a mediator and reconciler and said, borrowing the word from Papini, that she "unstiffens" our theories. She has in fact no prejudices whatever, no obstructive dogmas, no rigid canons of what shall count as proof. She is completely genial. She will entertain any hypothesis, she will consider any evidence. It follows that in the religious field she is at a great advantage both over positivistic empiricism, with its anti-theological bias, and over religious rationalism, with its exclusive interest in the remote, the noble, the simple, and the abstract in the way of conception.

In short, she widens the field of search for God. Rationalism sticks to logic and the empyrean. Empiricism sticks to the external senses. Pragmatism is willing to take anything, to follow either logic or the senses and to count the humblest and most personal experiences. She will count mystical experiences if they have practical consequences. She will take a God who lives in the very dirt of private fact—if that should seem a likely place to find him.

Her only test of probable truth is what works best in the way of leading us, what fits every part of life best and combines with the collectivity of experience's demands, nothing being omitted. If theological ideas should do this, if the notion of God, in particular, should prove to do it, how could pragmatism possibly deny God's existence? She could see no meaning in treating as "not true" a notion that was pragmatically so successful. What other kind of truth could there be, for her, than all this agreement with concrete reality?

In my last lecture I shall return again to the relations of pragmatism with religion. But you see already how democratic she is. Her manners are as various and flexible, her resources as rich and endless, and her conclusions as friendly as those of mother nature.

Pragmatism And Humanism

What hardens the heart of every one I approach with the view of truth sketched in my last lecture is that typical idol of the tribe, the notion of *the* Truth, conceived as the one answer, determinate and complete, to the one fixed enigma which the world is believed to propound. For popular tradition, it is all the better if the answer be oracular, so as itself to awaken wonder as an enigma of the second order, veiling rather than revealing what its profundities are supposed to contain. All the great single-word answers to the world's riddle, such as God, the One, Reason, Law, Spirit, Matter, Nature, Polarity, the Dialectic Process, the Idea, the Self, the Oversoul, draw the admiration that men have lavished on them from this oracular role. By amateurs in philosophy and professionals alike, the universe is represented as a queer sort of petrified sphinx whose appeal to men consists in a monotonous challenge to his divining powers. The Truth: what a perfect idol of the rationalistic mind! I read in an old letter—from a gifted friend who died too young—these words: "In everything, in science, art, morals and religion, there *must* be one system that is right and *every* other wrong." How characteristic of the enthusiasm of a certain stage of youth! At twenty-one we rise to such a challenge and expect to find the system. It never occurs to most of us even later that the question "what is *the* truth?" is no real question (being irrelative to all conditions) and that the whole notion of *the* truth is an abstraction from the fact of truths in the plural, a mere useful summarizing phrase like *the* Latin Language or *the* Law.

Common-law judges sometimes talk about the law, and schoolmasters talk about the latin tongue, in a way to make their hearers think they mean entities pre-existent to the decisions or to the words and syntax, determining them unequivocally and requiring them to obey. But the slightest exercise of reflexion makes us see that, instead of being principles of this kind, both law and latin are results. Distinctions between the lawful and the unlawful in conduct, or between the correct and incorrect in speech, have grown up incidentally among the interactions of men's experiences in detail; and in no other way do distinctions between the true and the false in belief ever grow up. Truth grafts itself on previous truth, modifying it in the process, just as idiom grafts itself on previous idiom, and law on previous law. Given previous law and a novel case, and the judge will twist them into fresh law. Previous idiom; new slang or metaphor or oddity that hits the public taste;—and presto, a new idiom is made. Previous truth; fresh facts:—and our mind finds a new truth.

All the while, however, we pretend that the eternal is unrolling, that the one previous justice, grammar or truth are simply fulgurating and not being made. But imagine a youth in the courtroom trying cases with his abstract notion of "the" law, or a censor of speech let loose among the theatres with his idea of "the" mother-tongue, or a professor setting up to lecture on the actual universe with his rationalistic notion of "the Truth" with a big T, and what progress do they make? Truth, law, and language fairly boil away from them at the least touch of novel fact. These things *make themselves* as we go. Our rights, wrongs, prohibitions, penalties, words, forms, idioms, beliefs, are so many new creations that add themselves as fast as history proceeds. Far from being antecedent principles that animate the process, law, language, truth are but abstract names for its results.

Laws and languages at any rate are thus seen to be man-made things. Mr. Schiller applies the analogy to beliefs, and proposes the name of "Humanism" for the doctrine that to an unascertainable extent our truths are man-made products too. Human motives sharpen all our questions, human satisfactions lurk in all our answers, all our formulas have a human twist. This element is so inextricable in the products that Mr. Schiller sometimes seems almost to leave it an open question whether there be anything else. "The world," he says, "is essentially ΤΛη, it is what we make it. It is fruitless to define it by what it originally was or by what it is apart from us ; it *is* what is made of it. Hence . . . the world is plastic."[3] He adds that we can learn the limits of the plasticity only by trying, and that we ought to start as if it were wholly plastic, acting methodically on that assumption, and stopping only when we are decisively rebuked.

This is Mr. Schiller's butt-end-foremost statement of the humanist position, and it has exposed him to severe attack. I mean to defend the humanist position in this lecture, so I will insinuate a few remarks at this point.

Mr. Schiller admits as emphatically as any one the presence of resisting factors in every actual experience of truth-making, of which the new-made special truth must take account, and with which it has perforce to "agree." All our truths are beliefs about "Reality"; and in any particular belief the reality acts as something independent, as a thing *found*, not manufactured. Let me here recall a bit of my last lecture.

"Reality" is in general what truths have to take account of;[4] and the *first* part of reality from this point of view is the flux of our sensations. Sensations are forced upon us, coming we know not whence. Over their nature, order and quantity we have as good as no control. *They* are neither true nor false; they simply *are.* It is only what we say about them, only the

names we give them, our theories of their source and nature and remote relations, that may be true or not.

The *second* part of reality, as something that our beliefs must also obediently take account of is the *relations* that obtain between our sensations or between their copies in our minds. This part falls into two sub-parts: 1) the relations that are mutable and accidental, as those of date and place; and 2) those that are fixed and essential because they are grounded on the inner natures of their terms. Both sorts of relation are matters of immediate perception. Both are "facts." But it is the latter kind of fact that forms the more important sub-part of reality for our theories of knowledge. Inner relations namely are "eternal," are perceived whenever their sensible terms are compared; and of them our thought—mathematical and logical thought so-called—must eternally take account.

The *third* part of reality, additional to these perceptions (tho largely based upon them), is the *previous truths* of which every new inquiry takes account. This third part is a much less obdurately resisting factor: it often ends by giving way. In speaking of these three portions of reality as at all times controlling our belief's formation, I am only reminding you of what we heard in our last hour.

Now however fixed these elements of reality may be, we still have a certain freedom in our dealings with them. Take our sensations. *That* they are is undoubtedly beyond our control; but *which* we attend to, note, and make emphatic in our conclusions depends on our own interests; and, according as we lay the emphasis here or there, quite different formulations of truth result. We read the same facts differently. "Waterloo," with the same fixed details, spells a "victory" for an Englishman; for a Frenchman it spells a "defeat." So, for an optimist philosopher the universe spells victory, for a pessimist, defeat.

What we say about reality thus depends on the perspective into which we throw it. The *that* of it is its own; but the *what* depends on the *which;* and the which depends on *us.* Both the sensational and the relational parts of reality are dumb; they say absolutely nothing about themselves. We it is who have to speak for them. This dumbness of sensations has led such intellectualists as T. H. Green and Edward Caird to shove them almost beyond the pale of philosophic recognition, but pragmatists refuse to go so far. A sensation is rather like a client who has given his case to a lawyer and then has passively to listen in the courtroom to whatever account of his affairs, pleasant or unpleasant, the lawyer finds it most expedient to give. Hence, even in the field of sensation, our minds exert a certain arbitrary choice. By our inclusions and omissions we trace the field's extent; by our emphasis we mark its foreground and its background; by our order we read it in this direction or in that. We receive in short the block of marble, but we carve the statue ourselves.

This applies to the "eternal" parts of reality as well: we shuffle our perceptions of intrinsic relation and arrange them just as freely. We read them in one serial order or another, class them in this way or in that, treat one or the other as more fundamental, until our beliefs about them form those bodies of truth known as logics, geometrics, or arithmetics, in each and all of which the form and order in which the whole is cast is flagrantly man-made.

Thus, to say nothing of the new *facts* which men add to the matter of reality by the acts of their own lives, they have already impressed their mental forms on that whole third of reality which I have called "previous truths." Every hour brings its new percepts, its own facts of sensation and relation, to be truly taken account of; but the whole of our past dealings with such facts is already funded in the previous truths. It is therefore only the smallest and recentest fraction of the first two parts of reality that comes to us without the human touch, and that fraction has immediately to become humanized in the sense of being squared, assimilated, or in some way adapted, to the humanized mass already there. As a matter of fact we can hardly take in an impression at all, in the absence of a preconception of what impressions there may possibly be.

When we talk of reality "independent" of human thinking, then, it seems a thing very hard to find. It reduces to the notion of what is just entering into experience and yet to be named, or else to some imagined aboriginal presence in experience, before any belief about the presence had arisen, before any human conception had been applied. It is what is absolutely dumb and evanescent, the merely ideal limit of our minds. We may glimpse it, but we never grasp it; what we grasp is always some substitute for it which previous human thinking has peptonized and cooked for our consumption. If so vulgar an expression were allowed us, we might say that wherever we find it, it has been already *faked*. This is what Mr. Schiller has in mind when he calls independent reality a mere unresisting τλη, which *is* only to be made over by us.

That is Mr. Schiller's belief about the sensible core of reality. We "encounter" it (in Mr. Bradley's words) but don't possess it. Superficially this sounds like Kant's view; but between categories fulminated before nature began, and categories gradually forming themselves in nature's presence, the whole chasm between rationalism and empiricism yawns. To the genuine "Kantianer" Schiller will always be to Kant as a satyr to Hyperion.

Other pragmatists may reach more positive beliefs about the sensible core of reality. They may think to get at it in its independent nature, by peeling off the successive man-made wrappings. They may make theories that tell us where it comes from and all about it; and *if these theories work satisfactorily they will be true.* The transcendental idealists say there is no core, the finally completed wrapping being reality and truth in one. Scholasticism still teaches that the core is "matter." Professor Bergson, Heymans, Strong, and others believe in the core and bravely try to define it. Messrs. Dewey and Schiller treat it as a "limit." Which is the truer of all these diverse accounts, or of others comparable with them, unless it be the one that finally proves the most satisfactory? On the one hand there will stand reality, on the other an account of it which it proves impossible to better or to alter. If the impossibility prove permanent, the truth of the account will be absolute. Other content of truth than this I can find nowhere. If the anti-pragmatists have any other meaning, let them for heaven's sake reveal it, let them grant us access to it!

Not *being* reality, but only our belief *about* reality, it will contain human elements, but these will *know* the non-human element, in the only sense in which there can be knowledge of anything. Does the river make its banks, or do the banks make the river? Does a man walk with his right leg or with his left leg more essentially? Just as impossible may it be to separate the real from the human factors in the growth of our cognitive experience.

Let this stand as a first brief indication of the humanistic position. Does it seem paradoxical? If so, I will try to make it plausible by a few illustrations, which will lead to a fuller acquaintance with the subject.

In many familiar objects every one will recognize the human element. We conceive a given reality in this way or in that, to suit our purpose, and the reality passively submits to the conception. You can take the number 27 as the cube of 3, or as the product of 3 and 9, or as 26 *plus* 1, or 100 *minus* 73, or in countless other ways, of which one will be just as true as another. You can take a chess-board as black squares on a white ground, or as white squares on a black ground, and neither conception is a false one.

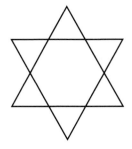 You can treat the adjoined figure as a star, as two big triangles crossing each other, as a hexagon with legs set up on its angles, as six equal triangles hanging together by their tips, etc. All these treatments are true treatments—the sensible *that* upon the paper resists no one of them. You can say of a line that it runs east, or you can say that it runs west, and the line *per se* accepts both descriptions without rebelling at the inconsistency.

We carve out groups of stars in the heavens, and call them constellations, and the stars patiently suffer us to do so,—though if they knew what we were doing, some of them might feel much surprised at the partners we had given them. We name the same constellation diversely, as Charles's Wain, the Great Bear, or the Dipper. None of the names will be false, and one will be as true as another, for all are applicable.

In all these cases we humanly make an *addition* to some sensible reality, and that reality tolerates the addition. All the additions "agree" with the reality; they fit it, while they build it out. No one of them is false. Which may be treated as the *more* true, depends altogether on the human use of it. If the 27 is a number of dollars which I find in a drawer where I had left 28, it is 28 minus 1. If it is the number of inches in a board which I wish to insert as a shelf into a cupboard 26 inches wide, it is 26 plus 1. If I wish to ennoble the heavens by the constellations I see there, "Charles's Wain" would be more true than "Dipper." My friend Frederick Myers was humorously indignant that that prodigious star-group should remind us Americans of nothing but a culinary utensil.

What shall we call a *thing* anyhow? It seems quite arbitrary, for we carve out everything, just as we carve out constellations, to suit our human purposes. For me, this whole "audience" is one thing, which grows now restless, now attentive. I have no use at present for its individual units, so I don't consider them. So of an "army," of a "nation." But in your own eyes, ladies and gentlemen, to call you "audience" is an accidental way of taking you. The permanently real things for you are your individual persons. To an anatomist, again, those persons are but organisms, and the real things are the organs. Not the organs, so much as their constituent cells, say the histologists; not the cells, but their molecules, say in turn the chemists.

We break the flux of sensible reality into things, then, at our will. We create the subjects of our true as well as of our false propositions.

We create the predicates also. Many of the predicates of things express only the relations of the things to us and to our feelings. Such predicates of course are human additions. Cæsar crossed the Rubicon, and was a menace to Rome's freedom. He is also an American schoolroom pest, made into one by the reaction of our schoolboys on his writings. The added predicate is as true of him as the earlier ones.

You see how naturally one comes to the humanistic principle: you can't weed out the human contribution. Our nouns and adjectives are all humanized heirlooms, and in the theories we build them into, the inner order and arrangement is wholly dictated by human considerations, intellectual consistency being one of them. Mathematics and logic themselves are fermenting with human rearrangements; physics, astronomy and biology follow massive cues of preference. We plunge forward into the field of fresh experience with the beliefs our ancestors and we have made already; these determine what we notice; what we notice determines what we do; what we do again determines what we experience; so from one thing to another, altho the stubborn fact remains that there *is* a sensible flux, what is *true of it* seems from first to last to be largely a matter of our own creation.

We build the flux out inevitably. The great question is: does it, with our additions, *rise or fall in value?* Are the additions *worthy or unworthy?* Suppose a universe composed of seven stars, and nothing else but three human witnesses and their critic. One witness names the stars "Great Bear"; one calls them "Charles's Wain"; one calls them the "Dipper." Which human addition has made the best universe of the given stellar material? If Frederick Myers were the critic, he would have no hesitation in "turning down" the American witness.

Lotze has in several places made a deep suggestion. We naïvely assume, he says, a relation between reality and our minds which may be just the opposite of the true one. Reality, we naturally think, stands ready-made and complete, and our intellects supervene with the one simple duty of describing it as it is already. But may not our descriptions, Lotze asks, be themselves important additions to reality? And may not previous reality itself be there, far less for the purpose of reappearing unaltered in our knowledge, than for the very purpose of stimulating our minds to such additions as shall enhance the universe's total value. "*Die erhöhung des vorgefundenen daseins*" is a phrase used by Professor Eucken somewhere, which reminds one of this suggestion by the great Lotze.

It is identically our pragmatistic conception. In our cognitive as well as in our active life we are creative. We *add,* both to the subject and to the predicate part of reality. The world stands really malleable, waiting to receive its final touches at our hands. Like the kingdom of heaven, it suffers human violence willingly. Man *engenders* truths upon it.

No one can deny that such a role would add both to our dignity and to our responsibility as thinkers. To some of us it proves a most inspiring notion. Signore Papini, the leader of Italian pragmatism, grows fairly dithyrambic over the view that it opens of man's divinely-creative functions.

The import of the difference between pragmatism and rationalism is now in sight throughout its whole extent. The essential contrast is that *for rationalism reality is ready-made and complete from all eternity, while for pragmatism it is still in the making, and awaits part of its complexion from the future.* On the one side the universe is absolutely secure, on the other it is still pursuing its adventures.

We have got into rather deep water with this humanistic view, and it is no wonder that misunderstanding gathers round it. It is accused of being a doctrine of caprice. Mr. Bradley, for example, says that a humanist, if he understood his own doctrine, would have to "hold any end, however perverted, to be rational, if I insist on it personally, and any idea, however mad, to be the truth if only some one is resolved that he will have it so." The humanist view of "reality," as something resisting, yet malleable, which controls our thinking as an energy that must be taken "account" of incessantly (tho not necessarily merely *copied*) is evidently a difficult one to introduce to novices. The situation reminds me of one that I have personally gone through. I once wrote an essay on our right to believe, which I unluckily called the Will to Believe. All the critics, neglecting the essay, pounced upon the title. Psychologically it was impossible, morally it was iniquitous. The "will to deceive," the "will to make-believe," were wittily proposed as substitutes for it.

The alternative between pragmatism and rationalism, in the shape in which we now have it before us, is no longer a question in the theory of knowledge, it concerns the structure of the universe itself.

On the pragmatist side we have only one edition of the universe, unfinished, growing in all sorts of places, especially in the places where thinking beings are at work.

On the rationalist side we have a universe in many editions, one real one, the infinite folio, or *édition de luxe,* eternally complete; and then the various finite editions, full of false readings, distorted and mutilated each in its own way.

So the rival metaphysical hypotheses of pluralism and monism here come back upon us. I will develop their differences during the remainder of our hour.

And first let me say that it is impossible not to see a temperamental difference at work in the choice of sides. The rationalist mind, radically taken, is of a doctrinaire and authoritative complexion: the phrase "must be" is ever on its lips. The bellyband of its universe must be tight. A radical pragmatist on the other hand is a happy-go-lucky anarchistic sort of creature. If he had to live in a tub like Diogenes he wouldn't mind at all if the hoops were loose and the staves let in the sun.

Now the idea of this loose universe affects your typical rationalists in much the same way as "freedom of the press" might affect a veteran official in the Russian bureau of censorship; or as "simplified spelling" might affect an elderly schoolmistress. It affects him as the swarm of protestant sects affects a papist onlooker. It appears as backboneless and devoid of principle as "opportunism" in politics appears to an old-fashioned French legitimist, or to a fanatical believer in the divine right of the people.

For pluralistic pragmatism, truth grows up inside of all the finite experiences. They lean on each other, but the whole of them, if such a whole there be, leans on nothing. All "homes" are in finite experience; finite experience as such is homeless. Nothing outside of the flux secures the issue of it. It can hope salvation only from its own intrinsic promises and potencies.

To rationalists this describes a tramp and vagrant world, adrift in space, with neither elephant nor tortoise to plant the sole of its foot upon. It is a set of stars hurled into heaven without even a centre of gravity to pull against. In other spheres of life it is true that we have got used to living in a state of relative insecurity. The authority of "the State," and that of an absolute "moral law," have resolved themselves into expediencies, and holy church has resolved itself into "meeting-houses." Not so as yet within the philosophic classrooms. A universe with such as *us* contributing to create its truth, a world delivered to *our* opportunisms and our private judgments! Home-rule for Ireland would be a millennium in comparison. We're no more fit for such a part than the Filipinos are "fit for self-government." Such a world would not be *respectable* philosophically. It is a trunk without a tag, a dog without a collar in the eyes of most professors of philosophy?

What then would tighten this loose universe, according to the professors?

Something to support the finite many, to tie it to, to unify and anchor it. Something *un*exposed to accident, something eternal and unalterable. The mutable in experience must be rounded on immutability. Behind our *de facto* world, our world in act, there must be a *de jure* duplicate fixed and previous, with all that can happen here already there *in posse,* every drop of blood, every smallest item, appointed and provided, stamped and branded, without chance of variation. The negatives that haunt our ideals here below must be themselves negated in the absolutely Real. This alone makes the universe solid. This is the resting deep. We live upon the stormy surface; but with this our anchor holds, for it grapples rocky bottom. This is Wordsworth's "eternal peace abiding at the heart of endless agitation." This is Vivekananda's mystic One of which I read to you. This is Reality with the big R, reality that makes the timeless claim, reality to which defeat can't happen. This is what the men of principles, and in general all the men whom I called tender-minded in my first lecture, think themselves obliged to postulate.

And this, exactly this, is what the tough-minded of that lecture find themselves moved to call a piece of perverse abstraction-worship. The tough-minded are the men whose alpha and omega are *facts.* Behind the bare phenomenal facts, as my tough-minded old friend Chauncey Wright, the great Harvard empiricist of my youth, used to say, there is *nothing.* When a rationalist insists that behind the facts there is the *ground* of the facts, the *possibility* of the facts, the tougher empiricists accuse him of taking the mere name and nature of a fact and clapping it behind the fact as a duplicate entity to make it possible. That such sham grounds are often invoked is notorious. At a surgical operation I once heard a bystander ask a doctor why the patient breathed so deeply. "Because ether is a respiratory stimulant," the doctor answered. "Ah!" said the questioner, as if that were a good explanation. But this is like saying that cyanide of potassium kills because it is a "poison," or that it is so cold to-night because it is "winter," or that we have five fingers because we are "pentadactyls." These are but names for the facts, taken from the facts, and then treated as previous and explanatory. The tender-minded notion of an absolute reality is, according to the radically tough-minded, framed on just this pattern. It is but our summarizing name for the whole spread-out and strung-along mass of phenomena, treated as if it were a different entity, both one and previous.

You see how differently people take things. The world we live in exists diffused and distributed, in the form of an indefinitely numerous lot of *eaches,* coherent in all sorts of ways and degrees; and the tough-minded are perfectly willing to keep them at that valuation. They can *stand* that kind of world, their temper being well adapted to its insecurity. Not so the tender-minded party. They must back the world we find ourselves born into by "another and a better" world in which the eaches form an All and the All a One that logically presupposes, co-implicates, and secures each *each* without exception.

Must we as pragmatists be radically tough-minded? or can we treat the absolute edition of the world as a legitimate hypothesis? It is certainly legitimate, for it is thinkable, whether we take it in its abstract or in its concrete shape.

By taking it abstractly I mean placing it behind our finite life as we place the word "winter" behind to-night's cold weather. "Winter" is only the name for a certain number of days which we find generally characterized by cold weather, but it guarantees nothing in that line, for our thermometer to-morrow may soar into the 70s. Nevertheless the word is a useful one to plunge forward with into the stream of our experience. It cuts off certain probabilities and sets up others. You can put away your straw hats; you can unpack your arctics. It is a summary of things to look for. It names a part of nature's habits, and gets you ready for their continuation. It is a definite instrument abstracted from experience, a conceptual reality that you must take account of, and which reflects you totally back into sensible realities. The pragmatist is the last person to deny the reality of such abstractions. They are so much past experience funded.

But taking the absolute edition of the world concretely means a different hypothesis. Rationalists take it concretely and *oppose* it to the world's finite editions. They give it a particular nature. It is perfect, finished. Everything known there is known along with everything else; here, where ignorance reigns, far otherwise. If there is want there, there also is the satisfaction provided. Here all is process; that world is timeless. Possibilities obtain in our world; in the absolute world, where all that is *not* is from eternity impossible, and all that *is* is necessary, the category of possibility has no application. In this world crimes and horrors are regretable. In that totalized world regret obtains not, for "the existence of ill in the temporal order is the very condition of the perfection of the eternal order."

Once more, either hypothesis is legitimate in pragmatist eyes, for either has its uses. Abstractly, or taken like the word winter, as a memorandum of past experience that orients us towards the future, the notion of the absolute world is indispensable. Concretely taken, it is also indispensable, at least to certain minds, for it determines them religiously, being often a thing to change their lives by, and by changing their lives, to change whatever in the outer order depends on them.

We can not therefore methodically join the tough minds in their rejection of the whole notion of a world beyond our finite experience. One misunderstanding of pragmatism is to identify it with positivistic tough-mindedness, to suppose that it scorns every rationalistic notion as so much jabber and gesticulation, that it loves intellectual anarchy as such and prefers a sort of wolf-world absolutely unpent and wild and without a master or a collar to any philosophic classroom product whatsoever. I have said so much in these lectures against the over-tender forms of rationalism, that I am prepared for some misunderstanding here, but I confess that the amount of it that I have found in this very audience surprises me, for I have simultaneously defended rationalistic hypotheses, so far as these re-direct you fruitfully into experience.

For instance I receive this morning this question on a post-card: "Is a pragmatist necessarily a complete materialist and agnostic?" One of my oldest friends, who ought to know me better, writes me a letter that accuses the pragmatism I am recommending of shutting out all wider metaphysical views and condemning us to the most *terre-à-terre* naturalism. Let me read you some extracts from it.

"It seems to me," my friend writes, "that the pragmatic objection to pragmatism lies in the fact that it might accentuate the narrowness of narrow minds.

"Your call to the rejection of the namby-pamby and the wishy-washy is of course inspiring. But altho it is salutary and stimulating to be told that one should be responsible for the immediate issues and bearings of his words and thoughts, I decline to be deprived of the pleasure and profit of dwelling also on remoter bearings and issues, and it is the *tendency* of pragmatism to refuse this privilege.

"In short, it seems to me that the limitations, or rather the dangers, of the pragmatic tendency, are analogous to those which beset the unwary followers of the "natural sciences." Chemistry and physics are eminently pragmatic; and many of their devotees, smugly content with the data that their weights and measures furnish, feel an infinite pity and disdain for all students of philosophy and metaphysics whomsoever. And of course everything can be expressed,—after a fashion, and "theoretically,"—in terms of chemistry and physics, that is, *everything except the vital principle of the whole,* and that, they say, there is no pragmatic use in trying to express; it has no bearings—for *them.* I for my part refuse to be persuaded that we can not look beyond the obvious pluralism of the naturalist and the pragmatist to a logical unity in which they take no interest."

How is such a conception of the pragmatism I am advocating possible, after my first and second lectures? I have all along been offering it expressly as a mediator between tough-mindedness and tender-mindedness. If the notion of a world *ante rem,* whether taken abstractly like the word winter, or concretely as the hypothesis of an Absolute, can be shown to have any consequences whatever for our life, it has a meaning. If the meaning works, it will have *some* truth that ought to be held to through all possible reformulations, for pragmatism.

The absolutistic hypothesis, that perfection is eternal, aboriginal, and most real, has a perfectly definite meaning, and it works religiously. To examine how, will be the subject of my next and final lecture.

Notes

1 Translated in the *Revue Philosophique* for January, 1879 (vol. vii).

2 "Theorie und Praxis," *Zeitsch. des Oesterreichischen Ingenieur u. Architecten-Vereines,* 1905, Nr. 4 u. 6. I find a still more radical pragmatism than Ostwald's in an address by Professor W. S. Franklin: "I think that the sickliest notion of physics, even if a student gets it, is that it is 'the science of masses, molecules, and the ether.' And I think that the healthiest notion, even if a student does not wholly get it, is that physics is the science of the ways of taking hold of bodies and pushing them!" *(Science,* January 2, 1903.)

3 *Personal Idealism,* p. 60.

4 Mr. Taylor in his *Elements of Metaphysics* uses this excellent pragmatic definition.

JOHN DEWEY
(1859-1952)

Although his most famous books—*Reconstruction in Philosophy* (1920), *Experience and Nature* (1925), *The Quest for Certainty* (1929), and *Art as Experience* (1934)—lay ahead of him when Dewey published "Does Reality Possess Practical Character?" in 1908, he was then almost fifty, his career at Michigan and Chicago over and his new life at Columbia University well underway. Dewey had made a name for himself as an educational theorist who stressed interest and action, and as a neo-Hegelian who became a pragmatist. Here he defines pragmatism as "the doctrine that reality possesses practical character and that this character is most efficaciously expressed in the function of intelligence."

Under the influence of James and Peirce, Dewey spurned the pre-established character of Hegel's tripartite logic, developing a naturalized logic of inquiry based on Peirce's model of problem situation/action/belief. Dewey's emphatic naturalism—a source for Rorty's contemporary "Darwinism"—can be seen here in his statement that "the rational function seems to be intercalcated in a scheme of practical adjustments," our hands, legs, eyes, and brain all "part of the same practical machinery for bringing about adaptation of the environment to the life requirements of the organism."

Dewey sees traditional epistemology as suffering from "intellectual lock-jaw." Like James and Husserl, he offers an anti-Cartesian psychology in which the subjective self of Descartes is distributed over a set of projects and experiential interactions. "Awareness," Dewey writes, "is itself a blanket term, covering, in the same bed, delusion, doubt, confusion, ambiguity, and definition, organization, logical conclusiveness assured by evidence and reason. Any naturalistic or realistic theory is committed to the idea that all of these terms bear impartially the same relation to things"

Traditional epistemology takes our knowledge—whether propositions or states of knowing—to be a mirror of the world. Dewey asserts, in contrast, that our knowing participates in forming or altering the world. In this sense "reality possesses practical character." "We have to do a doctrine," Dewey states in one of the surprisingly pungent remarks scattered throughout his writings, "in order to know its truth." This thought lies at the heart of Dewey's educational philosophy.

In the brief autobiography "From Absolutism to Experimentalism," which hepublished in 1930, Dewey spoke of *Democracy and Education* (1916) as the place "in which my philosophy, such as it is, was most fully expounded." Dewey's theory of education is wedded to his pragmatism because of its stress on action; and because it contests traditional distinctions between value and fact, experience and thinking, the outcome and the process of knowing, the child and the environment. In "Education as Growth," reprinted below from *Democracy and Education,* Dewey states: "Adaptation is quite as much adaptation *of* the environment to our own activities as of our activities *to* the environment." The adaptations Dewey seeks, whether in the schools or without, are those that organize "the powers that ensure growth." "Life means growth," Dewey writes, and growth is "adequacy of life, irrespective of age." Life may be "superficial" and slack, or it may be deep and powerful. Dewey ends "Education as Growth" with Emerson's call to "arm" the child's nature "with knowledge in the very direction in which it points," and with the thought, absent from standard caricatures of Dewey, that the growing power of the child requires "immense claims on the time, the thought, on the life of the teacher."

DOES REALITY POSSESS PRACTICAL CHARACTER?

JOHN DEWEY

I

Recently I have had an experience which, insignificant in itself, seems to mean something as an index-figure of the present philosophic situation. In a criticism of the neo-Kantian conception that *a priori* functions of thought are necessary to constitute knowledge, it became relevant to deny its underlying postulate: viz., the existence of anything properly called mental states or subjective impressions precedent to all objective recognitions, and requiring accordingly some transcendental function to order them into a world of stable and consistent reference. It was argued that such so-called original mental data are in truth turning points of the readjustment, or making over, through a state of incompatibility and shock, of objective affairs. This doctrine was met by the cry of "subjectivism"! It had seemed to its author to be a criticism, on grounds at once naturalistic and ethical, of the ground proposition of subjectivism. Why this diversity of interpretations? So far as the writer can judge, it is due to the fact that certain things characteristic of practical life, such things as lack and need, conflict and clash, desire and effort, loss and satisfaction, had been frankly referred to reality; and to the further fact that the function and structure of knowing were systematically connected with these practical features. These conceptions are doubtless radical enough; the latter was perhaps more or less revolutionary. The probability, the antecedent probability, was that hostile critics would have easy work in pointing out specific errors of fact and interpretation. But no: the simpler, the more effective method, was to dismiss the whole thing as anarchic subjectivism.

This was and remains food for thought. I have been able to find but one explanation: In current philosophy, everything of a practical nature is regarded as "merely" personal, and the "merely" has the force of denying legitimate standing in the court of cosmic jurisdiction. This conception seems to me the great and the ignored assumption in contemporary philosophy: many who might shrink from the doctrine if expressly formulated hang desperately to its implications. Yet surely as an underlying assumption, it is sheer prejudice, a culture-survival. If we suppose the traditions of philosophic discussion wiped out and philosophy starting afresh from the most active tendencies of to-day,—those striving in social life, in science, in literature, and art,—one can hardly imagine any philosophic view springing up and gaining credence, which did not give large place, in its scheme of things, to the practical and personal, and to them without employing disparaging terms, such as phenomenal, merely subjective, and so on. Why, putting it mildly, should what gives tragedy, comedy, and poignancy to life, be excluded from things? Doubtless, what we call life, what we take to be genuinely vital, is not all of things, but it is a part of things; and is that part which counts most with the philosopher—unless he has quite parted with his ancient dignity of lover of wisdom. What becomes of philosophy so far as humane and liberal interests are concerned, if, in an age when the person and the personal loom large in politics, industry, religion, art, and science, it contents itself with this parrot cry of phenomenalism, whenever the personal comes into view? When science is carried by the idea of evolution into introducing into the world the principles of initiative, variation, struggle, and selection; and when social forces have driven into bankruptcy absolutistic and static dogmas as authorities for the conduct of life, it is trifling for philosophy to decline to look the situation in the face. The relegation, as matter of course, of need, of stress and strain, strife and satisfaction, to the merely personal and the merely personal to the limbo of something which is neither flesh, fowl, nor good red herring, seems the thoughtless rehearsal of ancestral prejudice.

When we get beyond the echoing of tradition, the sticking point seems to be the relation of knowledge to the practical function of things. Let reality be in itself as "practical" as you please, but let not this practical character lay profane hands on the ark of truth. Every new mode of interpreting life—every new gospel—is met with the charge of antinomianism. An imagination bound by custom apprehends the restrictions that are relaxed and the checks that are removed, but not the inevitable responsibilities and tests that the new idea brings in. And so the conception that knowledge makes a difference in and to things looks licentious to those who fail to see that the necessity of doing well this business, of making the right difference puts intelligence under bonds it never yet has known: most of all in philosophy, the most gayly irresponsible of the procedures, and the most irresponsively sullen, of the historic fruits of intelligence.

Why should the idea that knowledge makes a difference to and in things be antecedently objectionable ? If one is already committed to a belief that Reality is neatly and finally tied up in a packet without loose ends, unfinished issues or new departures, one would object to knowledge making a difference just as one would object to any other impertinent obtruder. But if one believes that the world itself is in transformation, why should the notion that knowledge is the most important mode of its modification and the only organ of its guidance be *a priori* obnoxious ?

There is, I think, no answer save that the theory of knowledge has been systematically built up on the notion of a static universe, so that even those who are perfectly free in accepting the lessons of physics and biology concerning moving energy and evolution, and of history concerning the constant transformation of man's affairs (science included), retain an unquestioning belief in a theory of knowledge which is out of any possible harmony with their own theory of the matters to be known. Modern episte-mology, having created the idea that the way to frame right conceptions is to analyze knowledge, has strengthened this view. For it at once leads to the view that realities must themselves have a theoretic and intellectual complexion—not a practical one. This view is naturally congenial to idealists; but that realists should so readily play into the hands of idealists by asserting what, on the basis of a formal theory of knowledge, realities must be, instead of accepting the guidance of things in divining what knowledge *is,* is an anomaly so striking as to support the view that the notion of static reality has taken its last stand in ideas about knowledge. Take, for example, the most striking, because the extreme case—knowledge of a past event. It is absurd to suppose that knowledge makes a difference to the final or appropriate content of knowledge: to the subject-matter which fulfils the requirements of knowing. In this case, it would get in its own way and trip itself up in endless regress. But it seems the very superstition of intellectualism to suppose that this fact about knowledge can decide what is the nature of that reference to the past which when rightly made is final. No doctrine about knowledge can hinder the belief—if there be sufficient specific evidence for it—that what we know as past may be something which has *irretrievably* undergone just the difference which knowledge makes.

Now arguments against pragmatism—by which I mean the doctrine that reality pos-sesses practical character and that this character is most efficaciously expressed in the function of intelligence[1]—seem to fall blandly into this fallacy. They assume that to hold that knowledge makes a difference in existences is equivalent to holding that it makes a difference in the object *to be* known, thus defeating its own purpose; witless that the reality which is the appropriate object of knowledge in a given case may be precisely a reality in which knowing has succeeded in making the needed difference. This ques-tion is not one to be settled by manipulation of the concept of knowledge, nor by dialectic discussion of its essence or nature. It is a question of facts, a question of what knowing exists as in the scheme of existence. If things undergo change without thereby ceasing to be real, there can be no *formal* bar to knowing being one specific kind of change in things, nor to its test being found in the successful carrying into effect of the kind of change intended. If knowing be a change in a reality, then the more knowing reveals this change, the more transparent, the more adequate, it is. And if all existences are in tran-sition, then the knowledge which treats them as if they were something of which knowledge is a kodak fixation is just the kind of knowledge which refracts and perverts them. And by the same token a knowing which actively participates in a change in the way to effect it in the needed fashion would be the type of knowing which is valid. If reality be itself in transition—and this doctrine originated not with the objectionable pragmatist but with the physicist and naturalist and moral historian—then the doctrine that knowledge is reality making a particular and specified sort of change in itself seems to have the best chance at maintaining a theory of knowing which itself is in wholesome touch with the genuine and valid.

II

If the ground be cleared of *a priori* objections, and if it be evident that pragmatism cannot be disposed of by any formal or dialectic manipulations of "knowledge" or "truth," but only by showing that some specific things are not of the sort claimed, we may consider some common sense affiliations of pragmatism. Common sense regards intelligence as having a purpose and knowledge as amounting to something. I once heard a physicist, quite innocent of the pragmatic controversy, remark that the knowledge of a mechanic or farmer was what the Yankee calls gumption—acknowledgment of things in their belongings and uses, and that to his mind natural science was only gumption on a larger scale: the convenient cataloguing and arranging of a whole lot of things with reference to their most efficacious services. Popularly, good judgment is judgment as to the relative values of things: good sense is horse sense, ability to take hold of things right end up, to fit an instrument to an obstacle, to select resources apt for a task. To be reasonable is to recognize things in their offices as obstacles and as resources. Intelligence, in its ordinary use, is a practical term; ability to size up matters with respect to the needs and possibilities of the various situations in which one is called to do something; capacity to envisage things in terms of the adjustments and adaptations they make possible or hinder. Our objective test of the presence or absence of intelligence is influence upon behavior. No capacity to make adjustments means no intelligence; conduct evincing management of complex and novel conditions means a high degree of reason. Such conditions at least suggest that a reality-to-be-known, a reality which is the appropriate subject-matter of knowledge is reality-of-use-and-in-use, direct or indirect, and that a reality which is not in any sort of use, or bearing upon use, may go hang, *so far as knowledge is concerned.*

No one, I suppose, would deny that all knowledge issues in some action which changes things to some extent—be the action only a more deliberate maintenance of a course of conduct already instinctively entered upon. When I see a sign on the street corner I can turn or go on, knowing what I am about. The perceptions of the scientist need have no such overt or "utilitarian" uses, but surely after them he behaves differently, as an inquirer if in no other way; and the cumulative effect of such changes finally modifies the overt action of the ordinary man. That knowing, *after the event,* makes a difference of this sort, few I suppose would deny: if that were all pragmatism means, it would perhaps be accepted as a harmless truism. But there is a further question of fact: just how is the "consequent" action related to the "precedent" knowledge? When is "after the event"? What degree of continuity exists? Is the difference between knowing and acting intelligently one of kind or simply one of dominant quality? How does a thing, if it is not already in change in the knowing, manage to issue at its term in action? Moreover, do not the changes actively effected constitute the whole *import* of the knowledge, and hence its final measure and test of validity? If it merely *happens* that knowing when it is done with passes into some action, by what miracle is the subsequent action so pat to the situation? Is it not rather true that the "knowledge" is instituted and framed in anticipation of the consequent issue, and, in the degree in which it is wise and prudent, is held open to revision during it? Certainly the moralist (one might quote, for example, Goethe, Carlyle, and Mazzini) and the common man often agree that full knowledge, adequate assurance, of reality is found only in the issue which fulfils ideas; that we have to do a doctrine to *know* its truth; otherwise it is only dogma or doctrinaire programme. Experimental science is a recognition that no idea is entitled to be termed knowledge till it has passed into such overt manipulation of physical conditions as constructs the object to which the idea refers. If one could get rid of his traditional logical theories and set to work afresh to frame a theory of knowledge on the basis of the procedure of the common man, the moralist and the experimentalist, would it be the forced or the natural procedure to say that the realities which we *know,* which we are sure of, are precisely those realities that have taken shape in and through the procedures of knowing?

I turn to another type of consideration. Certainly one of the most genuine problems of modern life is the reconciliation of the scientific view of the universe with the claims of the moral life. Are judgments in terms of the redistribution of matter in motion (or some other closed formula) alone valid? Or are accounts of the universe in terms of possibility and desirability, of initiative and responsibility, also valid? There is no occasion to expatiate on the importance of the moral life, nor upon the supreme importance of intelligence within the moral life. But there does seem to be occasion for asking how moral judgments—judgments of the would and should—relate themselves to the world of scientific knowledge. To frame a theory of knowledge which makes it necessary to deny the validity of moral ideas, or else to refer them to some other and separate kind of universe from that of common sense and science, is both provincial and arbitrary. The pragmatist has at least tried to face, and not to dodge, the question of how it is that moral and scientific "knowledge" can both hold of one and the same world. And whatever the difficulties in his proffered solution, the conception that scientific judgments are to be assimilated to moral is closer to common sense than is the theory that validity is to be denied of moral judgments because they do not square with a preconceived theory of the nature of the world to which scientific judgments must refer. And all moral judgments are about changes to be made.

III

I turn to one affiliation of the pragmatic theory with the results of recent science. The necessity for the occurrence of an event in the way of knowledge, of an organism which reacts or behaves in a specific way, would seem to be as well established as any scientific proposition. It is a peculiar fact, a fact fit to stir curiosity, that the rational function seems to be intercalated in a scheme of practical adjustments. The parts and members of the organism are certainly not there primarily for pure intellection or for theoretic contemplation. The brain, the last physical organ of thought, is a part of the same practical machinery for bringing about adaptation of the environment to the life requirements of the organism, to which belong legs and hand and eye. That the brain frees organic behavior from complete servitude to immediate physical conditions, that it makes possible the liberation of energy for remote and ever expanding ends is, indeed, a precious fact, but not one which removes the brain from the category of organic devices of behavior.[2] That the organ of thinking, of knowledge, was at least originally an organ of conduct, few, I imagine, will deny. And even if we try to believe that the cognitive function has supervened as a different operation, it is difficult to believe that the transfiguration has been so radical that knowing has lost all traces of its connection with vital impulse. But unless we so assume, have we any alternatives except to hold that this continual presence of vital impulse is a disturbing and refracting factor which forever prevents knowledge from reaching its own aim; or else that a certain promoting, a certain carrying forward of the vital impulse, importing certain differences in things, *is* the aim of knowledge?

The problem cannot be evaded—save ostrich wise—by saying that such considerations are "merely genetic," or "psychological," having to do only with the origin and natural history of knowing. For the point is that the organic reaction, the behavior of the organism, affects the *content* of awareness. The subject-matter of all awareness is thing-related-to-organism—related as stimulus direct or indirect or as material of response, present or remote, ulterior or achieved. No one—so far as I know—denies this with respect to the perceptual field of awareness. Pains, pleasures, hunger, and thirst, all "secondary" qualities, involve inextricably the "interaction" of organism and environment. The perceptual field is distributed and arranged as the possible field of selective reactions of the organism at its centre. Up and down, far and near, before and behind, right and left, hard and soft (as well as white and black, bass and alto), involve reference to a centre of behavior.

This material has so long been the stock in trade of both idealistic arguments and proclamations of the agnostic "relativity" of knowledge that philosophers have grown aweary of listening. But even this lethargy might be quickened by a moderate hospitality to the pragmatic interpretation. That red, or far and near, or hard and soft, or big and little, involve a relation between organism and environment, is no more an argument for idealism than is the fact that water involves a relation between hydrogen and oxygen.[3] It is, however, an argument for the ultimately practical value of these distinctions—that they are *differences* made in what things would have been without organic behavior—differences made not by "consciousness" or "mind," but by the organism as the active centre of a system of activities. Moreover, the whole agnostic sting of the doctrine of "relativity" lies in the assumption that the ideal or aim of knowledge is to repeat or copy a prior existence—in which case, of course, the making of contemporaneous differences by the organism in the very fact of awareness would get in the way and forever hinder the knowledge function from the fulfilment of its proper end. Knowledge, awareness, in this case suffers from an impediment which no surgery can better. But if the aim of knowing be precisely to make *certain* differences in an environment, to carry on to *favorable* issue, by the readjustment of the organism, certain changes going on indifferently in the environment, then the fact that the changes of the organism enter pervasively into the subject-matter of awareness is no restriction or perversion of knowledge, but part of the fulfilment of its end.

The only question would then be whether the *proper* reactions take place. The whole agnostic, positivistic controversy is flanked by a single move. The issue is no longer an ideally necessary but actually impossible copying, *versus* an improper but unavoidable modification of reality through organic inhibitions and stimulations: but it is the right, the economical, the effective, and, if one may venture, the useful and satisfactory reaction versus the wasteful, the enslaving, the misleading, and the confusing reaction. The presence of organic responses, influencing and modifying every content, every subject-matter of awareness, is the undoubted fact. But the significant thing is the *way* organic behavior enters in—the *way* it influences and modifies. We assign very different values to different types of "knowledge,"—or subject-matters involving organic attitudes and operations. Some are only guesses, opinions, suspicious characters; others are "knowledge" in the honorific and eulogistic sense—science; some turn out mistakes, blunders, errors. Whence and how this discrimination of character in what is taken at its own time to be good knowledge? Why and how is the matter of some "knowledge" genuine-knowing and of other mis-knowing? Awareness is itself a blanket term, covering, in the same bed, delusion, doubt, confusion, ambiguity, and definition, organization, logical conclusiveness assured by evidence and reason. Any naturalistic or realistic theory is committed to the idea that all of these terms bear impartially the same relation to things considered as sheer existences. What we must have in any case is the same existences— the same in kind—only differently arranged or linked up. But why then the tremendous difference in value? And if the unnaturalist, the non-realist, says the difference is one of existential kind, made by the working here malign, there benign, of "consciousness," "psychical" operations and states, upon the existences which are the direct subject-matter of knowledge, there is still the problem of discriminating the conditions and nature of the respective beneficent and malicious interventions of the peculiar "existence" labelled consciousness.[4] The realness of error, ambiguity, doubt and guess poses a problem. It is a problem which has perplexed philosophy so long and has led to so many speculative adventures, that it would seem worth while, were it only for the sake of variety, to listen to the pragmatic solution. It is the business of that organic adaptation involved in all knowing to make a *certain* difference in reality, but *not* to make any old difference, any casual difference. The right, the true and good, difference is that which carries out satisfactorily the specific purpose for the sake of which knowing occurs. All manufactures are the product of an activity, but it does not follow that all manufactures are equally good. And so all "knowledges" are differences made in things by knowing, but some differences are not calculated or wanted in the knowing, and hence are disturbers and interlopers when they come—while others fulfil the intent of the knowing, being in such harmony with the consistent behavior of the organism as to reinforce and enlarge its functioning. A mistake is literally a mishandling; a doubt is a temporary suspense and vacillation of reactions; an ambiguity is the tension of alternative but incompatible modes of responsive treatment; an inquiry is a tentative and retrievable (because intra-organic) mode of activity entered upon prior to launching upon a knowledge which is public, ineluctable—without anchors to windward—*because* it has taken physical effect through overt action.

It is practically all one to say that the norm of honorable knowing is to make no difference in *its* object, and that its aim is to attain and buttress a specific kind of difference in reality. Knowing fails in its business if it makes a change in its *own* object—that is a mistake; but its own object is none the less a prior existence changed in a certain way. Nor is this a play upon the two senses—end and subject-matter—of "object." The organism has its appropriate functions. To maintain, to expand adequate functioning is its business. This functioning does not occur *in vacuo*. It involves co-operative and readjusted changes in the cosmic medium. Hence the appropriate subject-matter of awareness is not reality at large, a metaphysical heaven to be mimeographed at many removes upon a badly constructed mental carbon paper which yields at best only fragmentary, blurred, and erroneous copies. Its proper and legitimate object is that relationship of organism and environment in which functioning is most amply and effectively attained; or by which, in case of obstruction and consequent needed experimentation, its later eventual free course is most facilitated. As for the other reality, metaphysical reality at large, it may, so far as awareness is concerned, go to its own place.

For ordinary purposes, that is for practical purposes, the truth and the realness of things are synonymous. We are all children who say "really and truly." A reality which is so taken in organic response as to lead to subsequent reactions that are off the track and aside from the mark, while it is, existentially speaking, perfectly real, is not *good* reality. It lacks the hallmark of value. Since it is a certain *kind* of object which we want, that which will be as favorable as possible to a consistent and liberal or growing functioning, it is this kind, the *true* kind, which for us monopolizes the title of reality. Pragmatically, teleologically, this identification of truth and "reality" is sound and reasonable: rationalistically, it leads to the notion of the duplicate versions of reality, one absolute and static because exhausted; the other phenomenal and kept continually on the jump because otherwise its own inherent nothingness would lead to its total annihilation. Since it is only genuine or sincere things, things which are good for what they pretend to in the way of consequences, that we want or are after, *morally* they alone are "real."

IV

So far we have been dealing with awareness as a fact—a fact there like any fact—and have been concerned to show that the subject-matter of awareness is, in any case, things in process of change; and in such change that the knowing function takes a hand in trying to guide it or steer it, so that *some* (and *not* other) differences accrue. But what about the awareness itself? What happens when it is made the subject-matter of awareness? What sort of a thing is it? It is, I submit, mere sophistication (futile at that), to argue either that we cannot become aware of awareness without involving ourselves in an endless regress, or that whenever we are aware of anything we are thereby necessarily aware of awareness once for all, so that it has no character save this purely formal and empty one. Taken concretely, awareness is an event with certain specifiable conditions. We may indeed be aware of it formally, as a bare fact, just as we may be cognizant of an explosion without knowing anything of its nature. But we may also be aware of it in a curious and analytic spirit, undertaking to study it in detail. This inquiry, like any other inquiry, proceeds by determining conditions and consequences. Here awareness is a characteristic fact, presenting to inquiry its own characteristic ear-marks; and a valid knowledge of awareness is the same sort of thing as valid knowledge of the spectrum or of a trotting horse; it proceeds generically in the same way and must satisfy the same generic tests.

What, then, is awareness found to be? The following answer, dogmatically summary in form, involves positive difficulties, and glides over many points where our ignorance is still too great. But it represents a general trend of scientific inquiry, carried on, I hardly need say, on its own merits without respect to the pragmatic controversy. Awareness means *attention,* and attention means a crisis of some sort in an existent situation; a forking of the roads of some material, a tendency to go this way and that. It represents something the matter, something out of gear, or in some way menaced, insecure, problematical and strained. This state of tension, of ambiguous indications, projects and tendencies, is not merely in the "mind," it is nothing merely emotional. It is in the facts of the situation as transitive facts; the emotional or "subjective" disturbance is just a part of the larger disturbance. And if, employing the *language* of psychology, we say that attention is a phenomenon of conflicting habits, being the process of resolving this conflict by finding an act which functions all the factors concerned, this language does not make the facts "merely psychological"—whatever that means.[5] The habits are as biologic as they are "personal," and as cosmic as they are biologic. They are the total order of things expressed in one way; just as a physical or chemical phenomenon is the same order expressed in another way. The statement in terms of conflict and readjustment of habits is at most one way of locating the disturbance in *things;* it furnishes no substitute for, or rival of, reality, and no "psychical" duplication.

If this be true, then awareness, even in its most perplexed and confused state, a state of maximum doubt and precariousness of subject-matter, means things entering, *via* the particular thing known as organism, into a peculiar condition of differential—or additive—change. How can we refuse to raise and consider the question of how things in this condition are related to the prior state which emerges into it, and to the subsequent state of things into which it issues?[6]

Suppose the case to be awareness of a chair. Suppose that this awareness comes only when there is some problematic affair with which the chair is in some way—in whatever degree of remoteness—concerned. It may be a wonder whether that is a chair at all; or whether it is strong enough to stand on; or where I shall put it; or whether it is worth what I paid for it; or, as not infrequently happens, the situation involved in uncertainty may be some philosophic matter in which the perception of the chair is cited as evidence or illustration. (Humorously enough, the awareness of it may even be cited in the course of a philosophic argument intended to show that awareness has nothing to do with situations of incompleteness and ambiguity.) Now what of the change the chair undergoes in entering this way into a situation of perplexed inquiry? Is this any part of the genuineness of that chair with which we are concerned? If not, where is the change found? In something totally different called "consciousness"? In that case how can the operations of inquiry, of observation and memory and reflection, ever have any assurance of getting referred back to the *right* object? Positively the presumption is that the *chair-of-which-we-are-speaking,* is the chair *of-which-we-are-speaking;* it is the *same* thing that is out there which is involved also in the doubtful situation. Moreover, the reference to "consciousness" as the exclusive locus of the doubt only repeats the problem, for "consciousness," by the theory under consideration, means, after all, only the chair as concerned in the problematical situation. The *physical* chair remains unchanged, you say. Surely, if as is altogether likely, what is *meant* by physical is precisely *that part* of the chair as object of total awareness which remains unaffected, for certain possible purposes, by entering for certain other actual purposes into the situation of awareness. But how can we segregate, *antecedently* to experimental inquiry, the "physical" chair from the chair which is now the object to be known; into what contradictions do we fall when we attempt to define the object of one awareness not in its own terms, but in terms of a selected type of object which is the appropriate subject-matter of some other cognizance!

But awareness means inquiry as well as doubt—these are the negative and positive, the retrospective and the prospective relationships of the thing. This means a genuinely *additive* quale—one of readjustment in prior things.[7] I know the dialectic argument that nothing can assume a new relation, because in order to do so it must already be completely related—when it comes from an absolutist I can understand why he holds it, even if I cannot understand the idea itself. But apart from this conceptual reasoning we must follow the lead of our subject-matter; and when we find a thing assuming new relations in the process of inquiry, must accept the fact and frame our theory of things and of knowing to include it, not assert that it is impossible because we already have a theory of knowledge which precludes it. In inquiry, the existence which has become doubtful always undergoes experimental reconstruction. This may be largely imaginative or "speculative." We may view certain things *as if* placed under varying conditions, and consider what then happens to them. But such differences are really transformative so far as they go,—and besides, such inquiries never reach conclusions finally justifiable. In important and persistent inquiry, we insist upon something in the way of actual physical making—be it only a diagram. In other words, *science,* or knowing in its honorific sense, is experimental, involving physical construction. We insist upon something being *done about* it, that we may see how the idea when carried into effect comports with the other things through which our activities are hedged in and released. To avoid this conclusion by saying that knowing makes no difference in the "truth," but merely is the preliminary exercise which discovers it, is that old friend whose acquaintance we have repeatedly made in this discussion: the fallacy of confusing an existence anteceding knowing with the object which terminates and fulfils it. For knowing to make a difference in its own final term is gross self-stultification; it is none the less so when the aim of knowing is precisely to guide things straight up to this term. When "truth" means the accomplished introduction of certain new differences into conditions, why be foolish enough to make other and more differences, which are not wanted since they are irrelevant and misleading?

Were it not for the teachings of sad experience, it would not be necessary to add that the change in environment made by knowing is not a total or miraculous change. Transformation, readjustment, reconstruction all imply prior existences: existences which have characters and behaviors of their own which must be accepted, consulted, humored, manipulated or made light of, in all kinds of differing ways in the different contexts of different problems. Making a difference in reality does not mean making any more difference than we find by experimentation can be made under the given conditions—even though we may still hope for different fortune another time under other circumstances. Still less does it mean making a thing into an unreality, though the pragmatist is sometimes criticised as if any change in reality must be a change into non-reality. There are difficulties indeed, both dialectic, and real or practical, in the fact of change—in the fact that only a permanent can change and that change is alteration of a permanent. But till we enjoin botanists and chemists from referring to changes and transformations in their subject-matter on the ground that for anything to change means for it to part with its reality, we may as well permit the logician to make similar references.

V

Sub specie aeternitatis? or *sub specie generationis?* I am susceptible to the aesthetic charm of the former ideal—who is not? There are moments of relaxation: there are moments when the demand for peace, to be let alone and relieved from the continual claim of the world in which we live that we be up and doing something about it, seems irresistible; when the responsibilities imposed by living in a moving universe seem intolerable. We contemplate with equal mind the thought of the eternal sleep. But, after all, this is a matter in which reality and not the philosopher is the court of final jurisdiction. Outside of philosophy, the question seems fairly settled; in science, in poetry, in social organization, in religion—wherever religion is not hopelessly at the mercy of a Frankenstein philosophy which it originally called into being as its own slave. Under such circumstances there is danger that the philosophy which tries to escape the form of generation by taking refuge under the form of eternity will only come under the form of a by-gone generation. To try to escape from the snares and pitfalls of time by recourse to traditional problems and interests—rather than that let the dead bury their own dead. Better it is for philosophy to err in active participation in the living struggles and issues of its own age and times than to maintain an immune monastic impeccability, without relevancy and bearing in the generating ideas of its contemporary present. In the one case, it will be respected, as we respect all virtue that attests its sincerity by sharing in the perplexities and failures, as well as in the joys and triumphs, of endeavor. In the other case, it bids fair to share the fate of whatever preserves its gentility, but not its activity, in descent from better days; namely, to be snugly ensconced in the consciousness of its own respectability.

Notes

1　This definition, in the present state of discussion, is an arbitrary or personal one. The text does not mean that "pragmatism" is currently used exclusively in this sense; obviously there are other senses. It does not mean it is the sense in which it *ought* to be used. I have no wish to legislate either for language or for philosophy. But it marks the sense in which it *is* used in this paper; and the pragmatic movement is still so loose and variable that I judge one has a right to fix his own meaning, provided he serves notice and adheres to it.

2　It is interesting to note how the metaphysical puzzles regarding "parallelism," "interaction," "automatism," the relation of "consciousness" to "body," evaporate when one ceases isolating the brain into a peculiar physical substrate of mind at large, and treats it simply as one portion of the body as the instrumentality of adaptive behavior.

3　I owe this illustration to my colleague, Dr. Montague.

4　Of course on the theory I am interested in expounding, the so-called action of "consciousness" means simply the organic releases in the way of behavior which are the conditions of awareness, and which also modify its content.

5 What does it mean? Does the objectivity of fact disappear when the biologist gives it a biological statement? Why not object to his conclusions on the ground that they are "merely" biological?

6 It is this question *of the relation to one other of different successive states of things* which the pragmatic method substitutes for the epistemological inquiry of how one sort of existence, purely mental, temporal but not spatial, immaterial, made up of sublimated gaseous consciousness, can get beyond itself and have valid reference to a totally different kind of existence—spatial and extended; and how it can receive impressions from the latter, etc.,—all the questions which constitute that species of confirmed intellectual lock-jaw called epistemology.

7 We have arrived here, upon a more analytic platform, at the point made earlier concerning the fact that knowing *issues* in action which changes things.

EDUCATION AS GROWTH

JOHN DEWEY

1. The Conditions of Growth.—In directing the activities of the young, society determines its own future in determining that of the young. Since the young at a given time will at some later date compose the society of that period, the latter's nature will largely turn upon the direction children's activities were given at an earlier period. This cumulative movement of action toward a later result is what is meant by growth.

The primary condition of growth is immaturity. This may seem to be a mere truism—saying that a being can develop only in some point in which he is undeveloped. But the prefix "im" of the word immaturity means something positive, not a mere void or lack. It is noteworthy that the terms "capacity" and "potentiality" have a double meaning, one sense being negative, the other positive. Capacity may denote mere receptivity, like the capacity of a quart measure. We may mean by "potentiality" a merely dormant or quiescent state—a capacity to become something different under external influences. But we also mean by capacity an ability, a power; and by potentiality potency, force. Now when we say that immaturity means the possibility of growth, we are not referring to absence of powers which may exist at a later time; we express a force positively present—the *ability* to develop.

Our tendency to take immaturity as mere lack, and growth as something which fills up the gap between the immature and the mature is due to regarding childhood *comparatively,* instead of intrinsically. We treat it simply as a privation because we are measuring it by adulthood as a fixed standard. This fixes attention upon what the child has not, and will not have till he becomes a man. This comparative standpoint is legitimate enough for some purposes, but if we make it final, the question arises whether we are not guilty of an overweening presumption. Children, if they could express themselves articulately and sincerely, would tell a different tale; and there is excellent adult authority for the conviction that for certain moral and intellectual purposes adults must become as little children.

The seriousness of the assumption of the negative quality of the possibilities of immaturity is apparent when we reflect that it sets up as an ideal and standard a static end. The fulfillment of growing is taken to mean an *accomplished* growth: that is to say, an Ungrowth, something which is no longer growing. The futility of the assumption is seen in the fact that every adult resents the imputation of having no further possibilities of growth; and so far as he finds that they are closed to him mourns the fact as evidence of loss, instead of falling back on the achieved as adequate manifestation of power. Why an unequal measure for child and man?

Taken absolutely, instead of comparatively, immaturity designates a positive force or ability,—the *power* to grow. We do not have to draw out or educe positive activities from a child, as some educational doctrines would have it. Where there is life, there are already eager and impassioned activities. Growth is not something done to them; it is something they do. The positive and constructive aspect of possibility gives the key to understanding the two chief traits of immaturity, dependence and plasticity. (1) It sounds absurd to hear dependence spoken of as something positive, still more absurd as a power. Yet if helplessness were all there were in dependence, no development could ever take place. A merely impotent being has to be carried, forever, by others. The fact that dependence is accompanied by growth in ability, not by an ever increasing lapse into parasitism, suggests that it is already something constructive. Being merely sheltered by others would not promote growth. For (2) it would only build a wall around impotence. With reference to the physical world, the child is helpless. He lacks at birth and for a long time thereafter power to make his way physically, to make his own living. If he had to do that by himself, he would hardly survive an hour. On this side his helplessness is almost complete. The young of the brutes are immeasurably his superiors. He is physically weak and not able to turn the strength which he possesses to coping with the physical environment.

1. The thoroughgoing character of this helplessness suggests, however, some compensating power. The relative ability of the young of brute animals to adapt themselves fairly well to physical conditions from an early period suggests the fact that their life is not intimately bound up with the life of those about them. They are compelled, so to speak, to have physical gifts because they are lacking in social gifts. Human infants, on the other hand, can get along with physical incapacity just because of their social capacity. We sometimes talk and think as if they simply happened to be *physically* in a social environment; as if social forces exclusively existed in the adults who take care of them, they being passive recipients. If it were said that children are themselves marvelously endowed with *power* to enlist the cooperative attention of others, this would be thought to be a backhanded way of saying that others are marvelously attentive to the needs of

children. But observation shows that children are gifted with an equipment of the first order for social intercourse. Few grown-up persons retain all of the flexible and sensitive ability of children to vibrate sympathetically with the attitudes and doings of those about them. Inattention to physical things (going with incapacity to control them) is accompanied by a corresponding intensification of interest and attention as to the doings of people. The native mechanism of the child and his impulses all tend to facile social responsiveness. The statement that children, before adolescence, are egotistically self-centered, even if it were true, would not contradict the truth of this statement. It would simply indicate that their social responsiveness is employed on their own behalf, not that it does not exist. But the statement is not true as matter of fact. The facts which are cited in support of the alleged pure egoism of children really show the intensity and directness with which they go to their mark. If the ends which form the mark seem narrow and selfish to adults, it is only because adults (by means of a similar engrossment in their day) have mastered these ends, which have consequently ceased to interest them. Most of the remainder of children's alleged native egoism is simply an egoism which runs counter to an adult's egoism. To a grown-up person who is too absorbed in his own affairs to take an interest in children's affairs, children doubtless seem unreasonably engrossed in *their* own affairs.

From a social standpoint, dependence denotes a power rather than a weakness; it involves interdependence. There is always a danger that increased personal independence will decrease the social capacity of an individual. In making him more self-reliant, it may make him more self-sufficient; it may lead to aloofness and indifference. It often makes an individual so insensitive in his relations to others as to develop an illusion of being really able to stand and act alone—an unnamed form of insanity which is responsible for a large part of the remediable suffering of the world.

2. The specific adaptability of an immature creature for growth constitutes his plasticity. This is something quite different from the *plasticity* of putty or wax. It is not a capacity to take on change of form in accord with external pressure. It lies near the pliable elasticity by which some persons take on the color of their surroundings while retaining their own bent. But it is something deeper than this. It is essentially the ability to learn from experience; the power to retain from one experience something which is of avail in coping with the difficulties of a later situation. This means power to modify actions on the basis of the results of prior experiences, the power to *develop dispositions.* Without it, the acquisition of habits is impossible.

It is a familiar fact that the young of the higher animals, and especially the human young, have to *learn* to utilize their instinctive reactions. The human being is born with a greater number of instinctive tendencies than other animals. But the instincts of the lower animals perfect themselves for appropriate action at an early period after birth, while most of those of the human infant are of little account just as they stand. An original specialized power of adjustment secures immediate efficiency, but, like a railway ticket, it is good for one route only. A being who, in order to use his eyes, ears, hands, and legs, has to experiment in making varied combinations of their reactions, achieves a control that is flexible and varied. A chick, for example, pecks accurately at a bit of food in a few hours after hatching. This means that definite coordinations of activities of the eyes in seeing and of the body and head in striking are perfected in a few trials. An infant requires about six months to be able to gauge with approximate accuracy the action in reaching which will coordinate with his visual activities; to be able, that is, to tell whether he can reach a seen object and just how to execute the reaching. As a result, the chick is limited by the relative perfection of its original endowment. The infant has the advantage of the *multitude* of instinctive tentative reactions and of the experiences that accompany them, even though he is at a temporary disadvantage because they cross one another. In learning an action, instead of having it given ready-made, one of necessity learns to vary its factors, to make varied combinations of them, according to change of circumstances. A possibility of continuing progress is opened up by the fact that in learning one act, methods are developed good for use in other situations. Still more important is the fact that the human being acquires a habit of learning. He learns to learn.

The importance for human life of the two facts of dependence and variable control has been summed up in the doctrine of the significance of prolonged infancy.[1] This prolongation is significant from the standpoint of the adult members of the group as well as from that of the young. The presence of dependent and learning beings is a stimulus to nurture and affection. The need for constant continued care was probably a chief means in transforming temporary cohabitations into permanent unions. It certainly was a chief influence in forming habits of affectionate and sympathetic watchfulness; that constructive interest in the well-being of others which is essential to associated life. Intellectually, this moral development meant the introduction of many new objects of attention; it stimulated foresight and planning for the future. Thus there is a reciprocal influence. Increasing complexity of social life requires a longer period of infancy in which to acquire the needed powers; this prolongation of dependence means prolongation of plasticity, or power of acquiring variable and novel modes of control. Hence it provides a further push to social progress.

2. Habits as Expressions of Growth.—We have already noted that plasticity is the capacity to retain and carry over from prior experience factors which modify subsequent activities. This signifies the capacity to acquire habits, or develop definite dispositions. We have now to consider the salient features of habits. In the first place, a habit is a form of executive skill, of efficiency in doing. A habit means an ability to use natural conditions as means to ends. It is an active control of the environment through control of the organs of action. We are perhaps apt to emphasize the control of the body at the expense of control of the environment. We think of walking, talking, playing the piano, the specialized skills characteristic of the etcher, the surgeon, the bridge-builder, as if they were simply ease, deftness, and accuracy on the part of the organism. They are that, of course; but the measure of the value of these qualities lies in the economical and effective control of the environment which they secure. To be able to walk is to have certain properties of nature at our disposal—and so with all other habits.

Education is not infrequently defined as consisting in the acquisition of those habits that effect an adjustment of an individual and his environment. The definition expresses an essential phase of growth. But it is essential that adjustment be understood in its active sense of *control* of means for achieving ends. If we think of a habit simply as a change wrought in the organism, ignoring the fact that this change consists in ability to effect subsequent changes in the environment, we shall be lead to think of "adjustment" as a conformity to environment as wax conforms to the seal which impresses it. The environment is thought of as something fixed, providing in its fixity the end and standard of changes taking place in the organism; adjustment is just fitting ourselves to this fixity of external conditions.[2] Habit as *habituation* is indeed something *relatively* passive; we get used to our surroundings—to our clothing, our shoes, and gloves; to the atmosphere as long as it is fairly equable; to our daily associates, etc. Conformity to the environment, a change wrought in the organism without reference to ability to modify surroundings, is a marked trait of such habituations. Aside from the fact that we are not entitled to carry over the traits of such adjustments (which might well be called *accommodations*, to mark them off from active adjustments) into habits of active use of our surroundings, two features of habituations are worth notice. In the first place, we get used to things by *first* using them.

Consider getting used to a strange city. At first, there is excessive stimulation and excessive and ill-adapted response. Gradually certain stimuli are selected because of their relevancy, and others are degraded. We can say either that we do not respond to them any longer, or more truly that we have effected a persistent response to them—an equilibrium of adjustment. This means, in the second place, that this enduring adjustment supplies the background upon which are made specific adjustments, as occasion arises. We are never interested in changing the *whole* environment; there is much that we take for granted and accept just as it already is. Upon this background our activities focus at certain points in an endeavor to introduce needed changes. Habituation is thus our adjustment to an environment which at the time we are not concerned with modifying, and which supplies a leverage to our active habits.

Adaptation, in fine, is quite as much adaptation *of* the environment to our own activities as of our activities *to* the environment. A savage tribe manages to live on a desert plain. It adapts itself. But its adaptation involves a maximum of accepting, tolerating, putting up with things as they are, a maximum of passive acquiescence, and a minimum of active control, of subjection to use. A civilized people enters upon the scene. It also adapts itself. It introduces irrigation; it searches the world for plants and animals that will flourish under such conditions; it improves, by careful selection, those which are growing there. As a consequence, the wilderness blossoms as a rose. The savage is merely habituated; the civilized man has habits which transform the environment.

The significance of habit is not exhausted, however, in its executive and motor phase.

It means formation of intellectual and emotional disposition as well as an increase in ease, economy, and efficiency of action. Any habit marks an *inclination*—an active preference and choice for the conditions involved in its exercise. A habit does not wait, Micawber-like, for a stimulus to turn up so that it may get busy; it actively seeks for occasions to pass into full operation. If its expression is unduly blocked, inclination shows itself in uneasiness and intense craving. A habit also marks an intellectual disposition. Where there is a habit, there is acquaintance with the materials and equipment to which action is applied. There is a definite way of understanding the situations in which the habit operates. Modes of thought, of observation and reflection, enter as forms of skill and of desire into the habits that make a man an engineer, an architect, a physician, or a merchant. In unskilled forms of labor, the intellectual factors are at minimum precisely because the habits involved are not of a high grade. But there are habits of judging and reasoning as truly as of handling a tool, painting a picture, or conducting an experiment.

Such statements are, however, understatements. The habits of mind involved in habits of the eye and hand supply the latter with their significance. Above all, the intellectual element in a habit fixes the relation of the habit to varied and elastic use, and hence to continued growth. We speak of *fixed* habits. Well, the phrase may mean powers so well established that their possessor always has them as resources when needed. But the phrase is also used to mean ruts, routine ways, with loss of freshness, openmindedness, and originality. Fixity of habit may mean that something has a fixed hold upon us, instead of our having a free hold upon things. This fact explains two points in a common notion about habits: their identification with mechanical and external modes of action to the neglect of mental and moral attitudes, and the tendency to give them a bad meaning, an identification with "bad habits." Many a person would feel surprised to have his aptitude in his chosen profession called a habit, and would naturally think of his use of tobacco, liquor, or profane language as typical of the meaning of habit. A habit is to him something which has a hold on him, something not easily thrown off even though judgment condemn it.

Habits reduce themselves to routine ways of acting, or degenerate into ways of action to which we are enslaved just in the degree in which intelligence is disconnected from them. Routine habits are unthinking habits; "bad" habits are habits so severed from reason that they are opposed to the conclusions of conscious deliberation and decision. As we have seen, the acquiring of habits is due to an original plasticity of our natures: to our ability to vary responses till we find an appropriate and efficient way of acting. Routine habits, and habits that possess us instead of our possessing them, are habits which put an end to plasticity. They mark the close of power to vary. There can be no doubt of the tendency of organic plasticity, of the physiological basis, to lessen with growing years. The instinctively mobile and eagerly varying action of childhood, the love of new stimuli and new developments, too easily passes into a "settling down," which means aversion to change and a resting on past achievements. Only an environment which secures the full use of intelligence in the process of forming habits can counteract this tendency. Of course, the same hardening of the organic conditions affects the physiological structures which are involved in thinking. But this fact only indicates the need of persistent care to see to it that the function of intelligence is invoked to its maximum possibility. The short-sighted method which falls back on mechanical routine and repetition to secure external efficiency of habit, motor skill without accompanying thought, marks a deliberate closing in of surroundings upon growth.

3. The Educational Bearings of the Conception of Development.—We have had so far but little to say in this chapter about education. We have been occupied with the conditions and implications of growth. If our conclusions are justified, they carry with them, however, definite educational consequences. When it is said that education is development, everything depends upon *how* development is conceived. Our net conclusion is that life is development, and that developing, growing, is life. Translated into its educational equivalents, this means *(i)* that the educational process has no end beyond itself; it is its own end; and that *(ii)* the educational process is one of continual reorganizing, reconstructing, transforming.

1. Development when it is interpreted in *comparative* terms, that is, with respect to the special traits of child and adult life, means the direction of power into special channels: the formation of habits involving executive skill, definiteness of interest, and specific objects of observation and thought. But the comparative view is not final. The child has specific powers; to ignore that fact is to stunt or distort the organs upon which his growth depends. The adult uses his powers to transform his environment, thereby occasioning new stimuli which redirect his powers and keep them developing. Ignoring this fact means arrested development, a passive accommodation. Normal child and normal adult alike, in other words, are engaged in growing. The difference between them is not the difference between growth and no growth, but between the modes of growth appropriate to different conditions. With respect to the development of powers devoted to coping with specific scientific and economic problems we may say the child should be growing in manhood. With respect to sympathetic curiosity, unbiased responsiveness, and openness of mind, we may say that the adult should be growing in childlikeness. One statement is as true as the other.

Three ideas which have been criticized, namely, the merely privative nature of immaturity, static adjustment to a fixed environment, and rigidity of habit, are all connected with a false idea of growth or development,—that it is a movement toward a fixed goal. Growth is regarded as *having* an end, instead of *being* an end. The educational counterparts of the three fallacious ideas are first, failure to take account of the instinctive or native powers of the young; secondly, failure to develop initiative in coping with novel situations; thirdly, an undue emphasis upon drill and other devices which secure automatic skill at the expense of personal perception. In all cases, the adult environment is accepted as a standard for the child. He is to be brought up *to* it.

Natural instincts are either disregarded or treated as nuisances—as obnoxious traits to be suppressed, or at all events to be brought into conformity with external standards. Since conformity is the aim, what is distinctively individual in a young person is brushed aside, or regarded as a source of mischief or anarchy. Conformity is made equivalent to uniformity. Consequently, there are induced lack of interest in the novel, aversion to progress, and dread of the uncertain and the unknown. Since the end of growth is outside of and beyond the process of growing, external agents have to be resorted to to induce movement towards it. Whenever a method of education is stigmatized as mechanical, we may be sure that external pressure is brought to bear to reach an external end.

2. Since in reality there is nothing to which growth is relative save more growth, there is nothing to which education is subordinate save more education. It is a commonplace to say that education should not cease when one leaves school. The point of this commonplace is that the purpose of school education is to insure the continuance of education by organizing the powers that insure growth. The inclination to learn from life itself and to make the conditions of life such that all will learn in the process of living is the finest product of schooling.

When we abandon the attempt to define immaturity by means of fixed comparison with adult accomplishments, we are compelled to give up thinking of it as denoting lack of desired traits. Abandoning this notion, we are also forced to surrender our habit of thinking of instruction as a method of supplying this lack by pouring knowledge into a mental and moral hole which awaits filling. Since life means growth, a living creature lives as truly and positively at one stage as at another, with the same intrinsic fullness and the same absolute claims. Hence education means the enterprise of supplying the conditions which insure growth, or adequacy of life, irrespective of age. We first look with impatience upon immaturity, regarding it as something to be got over as rapidly as possible. Then the adult formed by such educative methods looks back with impatient regret upon childhood and youth as a scene of lost opportunities and wasted powers. This ironical situation will endure till it is recognized that living has its own intrinsic quality and that the business of education is with that quality.

Realization that life is growth protects us from that so-called idealizing of childhood which in effect is nothing but lazy indulgence. Life is not to be identified with every superficial act and interest. Even though it is not always easy to tell whether what appears to be mere surface fooling is a sign of some nascent as yet untrained power, we must remember that manifestations are not to be accepted as ends in themselves. They are signs of possible growth. They are to be turned into means of development, of carrying power forward, not indulged or cultivated for their own sake. Excessive attention to surface phenomena (even in the way of rebuke as well as of encouragement) may lead to their fixation and thus to arrested development. What impulses are moving toward, not what they have been, is the important thing for parent and teacher. The true principle of respect for immaturity cannot be better put than in the words of Emerson:

"Respect the child. Be not too much his parent. Trespass not on his solitude. But I hear the outcry which replies to this suggestion: Would you verily throw up the reins of public and private discipline; would you leave the young child to the mad career of his own passions and whimsies, and call this anarchy a respect for the child's nature? I answer,— Respect the child, respect him to the end, but also respect yourself... The two points in a boy's training are, to keep his *naturel* and train off all but that; to keep his *naturel,* but stop off his uproar, fooling, and horseplay; keep his nature *and arm it with knowledge in the very direction in which it points."* And as Emerson goes on to show, this reverence for childhood and youth instead of opening up an easy and easy-going path to the instructors, "involves at once, immense claims on the time, the thought, on the life of the teacher. It requires time, use, insight, event, all the great lessons and assistances of God; and only to think of using it implies character and profoundness."[3]

Notes

1 Intimations of its significance are found in a number of writers, but John Fiske, in his "Excursions of an Evolutionist," is accredited with its first systematic exposition.

2 This conception is, of course, a logical correlate of the conceptions of the external relation of stimulus and response, considered in the last chapter, and of the negative conceptions of immaturity and plasticity noted in this chapter.

3 Ralph Waldo Emerson, "Education," in Ralph Waldo Emerson, *Lectures and Biographical Sketches* (Boston and New York: Houghton, Mifflin and Company, 1883), pp. 144, 154 [ed.].

CONTEMPORARY PRAGMATISM

RICHARD RORTY
(B. 1931)

The first of the following selections, "The Contingency of Language," opens Rorty's *Contingency, Irony, and Solidarity* (1989), a work that blends accounts of Wittgenstein, Heidegger, Dewey, Freud, Davidson, Bloom, and Mill in discussions of language, self, politics, and literature. Like Dewey, Rorty seeks to naturalize (or, as he puts it, "dedivinize") our account of the world: to replace the idea of purpose by the laws of evolution, the isolated Cartesian self by an evolving Freudian, Deweyan, "body-mind," and the language of God or Plato's ideas by a set of "increasingly complex noises batted back and forth" by human animals. Rorty looks to Wittgenstein and Davidson in supporting the pragmatic idea that "alternative vocabularies [are] more like alternative tools than like bits of a jigsaw puzzle." Our language, he maintains, is a set of practices for making our way in the world, a product of evolution no less than "the anteater's snout or the bower-bird's skill at weaving." Once we understand the practical character of language there is reason neither to take it as representing the world nor as expressing ourselves—any more than the snout of the anteater or the weaving of the bower-bird represents "the intrinsic nature of things."

If language is to be understood more as a way to cope than as a "mirror of nature," if truth is not "waiting out there to be discovered" but fashioned by us, what accounts for the progress, or at least the succession, of our inquiries, whether scientific, aesthetic, political, or moral? Drawing on sources as diverse as Wittgenstein's *On Certainty*, Kuhn's *Structure of Scientific Revolutions*, Harold Bloom's *The Anxiety of Influence* and *Agon*, and Heidegger's *Being and Time*, Rorty credits the poet—"one who makes things new"—with the great advances of human belief and culture. Yet he cautions that this does not mean that we can or should simply decide to believe anything: "Europe did not *decide* to accept the idiom of Romantic poetry, or of socialist politics, or of Galilean mechanics. That sort of shift was no more an act of will than it was a result of argument. Rather, Europe gradually lost the habit of using certain words and gradually acquired the habit of using others." Galileo and Yeats are equally poets in Rorty's sense, and human history is a series of "successive metaphors" introduced by the poet or "shaper of new languages, ...the vanguard of the species."

"Feminism and Pragmatism," the second selection reprinted below, exemplifies the "solidarity" in the title of Rorty's *Contingency, Irony, and Solidarity.* Beginning with Catharine MacKinnon's evocation of a "voice that, unsilenced, might say something that has never been heard," Rorty argues that "only if somebody has a dream, and a voice to describe that dream, does what looked like nature begin to look like culture, what looked like fate begin to look like a moral abomination." Rorty brings to feminism a sense of history and a pragmatic sense of openness, expressed in the statement he quotes from John Dewey: "before choice no evil presents itself as evil. Until it is rejected, it is a competing good." Rorty does not, however, find all feminist voices equally acceptable. He criticizes a hidden essentialism in the contemporary rhetoric of "unmasking hegemony,'" which "presupposes the reality-appearance distinction which opponents of phallogocentrism claim to have set aside." Rorty's "pragmatist feminist" thinks of herself as helping to create women rather than as describing them more accurately.

"Feminism and Pragmatism" also provides a general statement of Rorty's postmodern liberalism. Rorty rejects "radical" views, whether Marxist, feminist, or "conservative," because the idea that "a mistake deep down at the roots" has been made relies on the mistaken "essentialistic" or "metaphysical" idea that there are such roots, and some absolute ground for them to grasp hold of. Rather than searching for foundations, Rorty's liberal looks to the future, like Emerson or James. She is a "Utopian" who gives up "the contrast between superficial appearance and deep reality in favor of the contrast between a painful present and a possibly less painful, dimly-seen, future."

THE CONTINGENCY OF LANGUAGE

RICHARD RORTY

About two hundred years ago, the idea that truth was made rather than found began to take hold of the imagination of Europe. The French Revolution had shown that the whole vocabulary of social relations, and the whole spectrum of social institutions, could be replaced almost overnight. This precedent made utopian politics the rule rather than the exception among intellectuals. Utopian politics sets aside questions about both the will of God and the nature of man and dreams of creating a hitherto unknown form of society.

At about the same time, the Romantic poets were showing what happens when art is thought of no longer as imitation but, rather, as the artist's self-creation. The poets claimed for art the place in culture traditionally held by religion and philosophy, the place which the Enlightenment had claimed for science. The precedent the Romantics set lent initial plausibility to their claim. The actual role of novels, poems, plays, paintings, statues, and buildings in the social movements of the last century and a half has given it still greater plausibility.

By now these two tendencies have joined forces and have achieved cultural hegemony. For most contemporary intellectuals, questions of ends as opposed to means—questions about how to give a sense to one's own life or that of one's community—are questions for art or politics, or both, rather than for religion, philosophy, or science. This development has led to a split within philosophy. Some philosophers have remained faithful to the Enlightenment and have continued to identify themselves with the cause of science. They see the old struggle between science and religion, reason and unreason, as still going on, having now taken the form of a struggle between reason and all those forces within culture which think of truth as made rather than found. These philosophers take science as the paradigmatic human activity, and they insist that natural science discovers truth rather than makes it. They regard "making truth" as a merely metaphorical, and thoroughly misleading, phrase. They think of politics and art as spheres in which the notion of "truth" is out of place. Other philosophers, realizing that the world as it is described by the physical sciences teaches no moral lesson, offers no spiritual comfort, have concluded that science is no more than the handmaiden of technology. These philosophers have ranged themselves alongside the political utopian and the innovative artist.

Whereas the first kind of philosopher contrasts "hard scientific fact" with the "subjective" or with "metaphor," the second kind sees science as one more human activity, rather as the place at which human beings encounter a "hard," nonhuman reality. On this view, great scientists invent descriptions of the world which are useful for purposes of predicting and controlling what happens, just as poets and political thinkers invent other descriptions of it for other purposes. But there is no sense in which *any* of these descriptions is an accurate representation of the way the world is in itself. These philosophers regard the very idea of such a representation as pointless.

Had the first sort of philosopher, the sort whose hero is the natural scientist, always been the only sort, we should probably never have had an autonomous discipline called "philosophy"—a discipline as distinct from the sciences as it is from theology or from the arts. As such a discipline, philosophy is no more than two hundred years old. It owes its existence to attempts by the German idealists to put the sciences in their place and to give a clear sense to the vague idea that human beings make truth rather than find it. Kant wanted to consign science to the realm of second-rate truth—truth about a phenomenal world. Hegel wanted to think of natural science as a description of spirit not yet fully conscious of its own spiritual nature, and thereby to elevate the sort of truth offered by the poet and the political revolutionary to first-rate status.

German idealism, however, was a short-lived and unsatisfactory compromise. For Kant and Hegel went only halfway in their repudiation of the idea that truth is "out there." They were willing to view the world of empirical science as a made world—to see matter as constructed by mind, or as consisting in mind insufficiently conscious of its own mental character. But they persisted in seeing mind, spirit, the depths of the human self, as having an intrinsic nature—one which could be known by a kind of nonempirical super science called philosophy. This meant that only half of truth—the bottom, scientific half—was made. Higher truth, the truth about mind, the province of philosophy, was still a matter of discovery rather than creation.

What was needed, and what the idealists were unable to envisage, was a repudiation of the very idea of anything—mind or matter, self or world—having an intrinsic nature to be expressed or represented. For the idealists confused the idea that nothing has such a nature with the idea that space and time are unreal, that human beings cause the spatiotemporal world to exist.

We need to make a distinction between the claim that the world is out there and the claim that truth is out there. To say that the world is out there, that it is not our creation, is to say, with common sense, that most things in space and time are the effects of causes which do not include human mental states. To say that truth is not out there is simply to say that where there are no sentences there is no truth, that sentences are elements of human languages, and that human languages are human creations.

Truth cannot be out there—cannot exist independently of the human mind—because sentences cannot so exist, or be out there. The world is out there, but descriptions of the world are not. Only descriptions of the world can be true or false. The world on its own—unaided by the describing activities of human beings—cannot.

The suggestion that truth, as well as the world, is out there is a legacy of an age in which the world was seen as the creation of a being who had a language of his own. If we cease to attempt to make sense of the idea of such a nonhuman language, we shall not be tempted to confuse the platitude that the world may cause us to be justified in believing a sentence true with the claim that the world splits itself up, on its own initiative, into sentence-shaped chunks called "facts." But if one clings to the notion of self-subsistent facts, it is easy to start capitalizing the word "truth" and treating it as something identical either with God or with the world as God's project. Then one will say, for example, that Truth is great, and will prevail.

This conflation is facilitated by confining attention to single sentences as opposed to vocabularies. For we often let the world decide the competition between alternative sentences (e.g., between "Red wins" and "Black wins" or between "The butler did it" and "The doctor did it"). In such cases, it is easy to run together the fact that the world contains the causes of our being justified in holding a belief with the claim that some nonlinguistic state of the world is itself an example of truth, or that some such state "makes a belief true" by "corresponding" to it. But it is not so easy when we turn from individual sentences to vocabularies as wholes. When we consider examples of alternative language games—the vocabulary of ancient Athenian politics versus Jefferson's, the moral vocabulary of Saint Paul versus Freud's, the jargon of Newton versus that of Aristotle, the idiom of Blake versus that of Dryden—it is difficult to think of the world as making one of these better than another, of the world as deciding between them. When the notion of "description of the world" is moved from the level of criterion-governed sentences within language games to language games as wholes, games which we do not choose between by reference to criteria, the idea that the world decides which descriptions are true can no longer be given a clear sense. It becomes hard to think that that vocabulary is somehow already out there in the world, waiting for us to discover it. Attention (of the sort fostered by intellectual historians like Thomas Kuhn and Quentin Skinner) to the vocabularies in which sentences are formulated, rather than to individual sentences, makes us realize, for example, that the fact that Newton's vocabulary lets us predict the world more easily than Aristotle's does not mean that the world speaks Newtonian.

The world does not speak. Only we do. The world can, once we have programmed ourselves with a language, cause us to hold beliefs. But it cannot propose a language for us to speak. Only other human beings can do that. The realization that the world does not tell us what language games to play should not, however, lead us to say that a decision about which to play is arbitrary, nor to say that it is the expression of something deep within us. The moral is not that objective criteria for choice of vocabulary are to be replaced with subjective criteria, reason with will or feeling. It is rather that the notions of criteria and choice (including that of "arbitrary" choice) are no longer in point when it comes to changes from one language game to another. Europe did not *decide* to accept the idiom of Romantic poetry, or of socialist politics, or of Galilean mechanics. That sort of shift was no more an act of will than it was a result of argument. Rather, Europe gradually lost the habit of using certain words and gradually acquired the habit of using others.

As Kuhn argues in *The Copernican Revolution,* we did not decide on the basis of some telescopic observations, or on the basis of anything else, that the earth was not the center of the universe, that macroscopic behavior could be explained on the basis of microstructural motion, and that prediction and control should be the principal aim of scientific theorizing. Rather, after a hundred years of inconclusive muddle, the Europeans found themselves speaking in a way which took these interlocked theses for granted. Cultural change of this magnitude does not result from applying criteria (or from "arbitrary decision") any more than individuals become theists or atheists, or shift from one spouse or circle of friends to another, as a result either of applying criteria or of *actes gratuits.* We should not look within ourselves for criteria of decision in such matters any more than we should look to the world.

The temptation to look for criteria is a species of the more general temptation to think of the world, or the human self, as possessing an intrinsic nature, an essence. That is, it is the result of the temptation to privilege some one among the many languages in which we habitually describe the world or ourselves. As long as we think that there is some relation called "fitting the world" or "expressing the real nature of the self" which can be possessed or lacked by vocabularies-as-wholes, we shall continue the traditional philosophical search for a criterion to tell us which vocabularies have this desirable feature. But if we could ever become reconciled to the idea that most of reality is indifferent to our descriptions of it, and that the human self is created by the use of a vocabulary rather than being adequately or inadequately expressed in a vocabulary, then we should at last have assimilated what was true in the Romantic idea that truth is made rather than found. What is true about this claim is just that *languages* are made rather than found, and that truth is a property of linguistic entities, of sentences.[1]

I can sum up by redescribing what, in my view, the revolutionaries and poets of two centuries ago were getting at. What was glimpsed at the end of the eighteenth century was that anything could be made to look good or bad, important or unimportant, useful or useless, by being redescribed. What Hegel describes as the process of spirit gradually becoming self-conscious of its intrinsic nature is better described as the process of European linguistic practices changing at a faster and faster rate. The phenomenon Hegel describes is that of more people offering more radical redescriptions of more things than ever before, of young people going through half a dozen spiritual gestalt-switches before reaching adulthood. What the Romantics expressed as the claim that imagination, rather than reason, is the central human faculty was the realization that a talent for speaking differently, rather than for arguing well, is the chief instrument of cultural change. What political utopians since the French Revolution have sensed is not that an enduring, substratal human nature has been suppressed or repressed by "unnatural" or "irrational" social institutions but rather that changing languages and other social practices may produce human beings of a sort that had never before existed. The German idealists, the French revolutionaries, and the Romantic poets had in common a dim sense that human beings whose language changed so that they no longer spoke of themselves as responsible to nonhuman powers would thereby become a new kind of human beings.

The difficulty faced by a philosopher who, like myself, is sympathetic to this suggestion—one who thinks of himself as auxiliary to the poet rather than to the physicist—is to avoid hinting that this suggestion gets something right, that my sort of philosophy corresponds to the way things really are. For this talk of correspondence brings back just the idea my sort of philosopher wants to get rid of, the idea that the world or the self has an intrinsic nature. From our point of view, explaining the success of science, or the desirability of political liberalism, by talk of "fitting the world" or "expressing human nature" is like explaining why opium makes you sleepy by talking about its dormitive power. To say that Freud's vocabulary gets at the truth about human nature, or Newton's at the truth about the heavens, is not an explanation of anything. It is just an empty compliment—one traditionally paid to writers whose novel jargon we have found useful. To say that there is no such thing as intrinsic nature is not to say that the intrinsic nature of reality has turned out, surprisingly enough, to be extrinsic. It is to say that the term "intrinsic nature" is one which it would pay us not to use, an expression which has caused more trouble than it has been worth. To say that we should drop the idea of truth as out there waiting to be discovered is not to say that we have discovered that, out there, there is no truth.[2] It is to say that our purposes would be served best by ceasing to see truth as a deep matter, as a topic of philosophical interest, or "true" as a term which repays "analysis." "The nature of truth" is an unprofitable topic, resembling in this respect "the nature of man" and "the nature of God," and differing from "the nature of the positron," and "the nature of Oedipal fixation." But this claim about relative profitability, in turn, is just the recommendation that we in fact *say* little about these topics, and see how we get on.

On the view of philosophy which I am offering, philosophers should not be asked for arguments against, for example, the correspondence theory of truth or the idea of the "intrinsic nature of reality." The trouble with arguments against the use of a familiar and time-honored vocabulary is that they are expected to be phrased in that very vocabulary. They are expected to show that central elements in that vocabulary are "inconsistent in their own terms" or that they "deconstruct themselves." But that can *never* be shown. Any argument to the effect that our familiar use of a familiar term is incoherent, or empty, or confused, or vague, or "merely metaphorical" is bound to be inconclusive and question-begging. For such use is, after all, the paradigm of coherent, meaningful, literal, speech. Such arguments are always parasitic upon, and abbreviations for, claims that a better vocabulary is available. Interesting philosophy is rarely an examination of the pros and cons of a thesis. Usually it is, implicitly or explicitly, a contest between an entrenched vocabulary which has become a nuisance and a half-formed new vocabulary which vaguely promises great things.

The latter "method" of philosophy is the same as the "method" of utopian politics or revolutionary science (as opposed to parliamentary politics, or normal science). The method is to redescribe lots and lots of things in new ways, until you have created a pattern of linguistic behavior which will tempt the rising generation to adopt it, thereby causing them to look for appropriate new forms of nonlinguistic behavior, for example, the adoption of new scientific equipment or new social institutions. This sort of philosophy does not work piece by piece, analyzing concept after concept, or testing thesis after thesis. Rather, it works holistically and pragmatically. It says things like "try thinking of it this way"—or more specifically, "try to ignore the apparently futile traditional questions by substituting the following new and possibly interesting questions." It does not pretend to have a better candidate for doing the same old things which we did when we spoke in the old way. Rather, it suggests that we might want to stop doing those things and do something else. But it does not argue for this suggestion on the basis of antecedent criteria common to the old and the new language games. For just insofar as the new language really is new, there will be no such criteria.

Conforming to my own precepts, I am not going to offer arguments against the vocabulary I want to replace. Instead, I am going to try to make the vocabulary I favor look attractive by showing how it may be used to describe a variety of topics. More specifically, in this chapter I shall be describing the work of Donald Davidson in philosophy of language as a manifestation of a willingness to drop the idea of "intrinsic nature," a willingness to face up to the *contingency* of the language we use. In subsequent chapters, I shall try to show how a recognition of that contingency leads to a recognition of the contingency of conscience, and how both recognitions lead to a picture of intellectual and moral progress as a history of increasingly useful metaphors rather than of increasing understanding of how things really are.

I begin, in this first chapter, with the philosophy of language because I want to spell out the consequences of my claims that only sentences can be true, and that human beings make truths by making languages in which to phrase sentences. I shall concentrate on the work of Davidson because he is the philosopher who has done most to explore these consequences.[3] Davidson's treatment of truth ties in with his treatment of language learning and of metaphor to form the first systematic treatment of language which breaks *completely* with the notion of language as something which can be adequate or inadequate to the world or to the self. For Davidson breaks with the notion that language is a *medium*—a medium either of representation or of expression.

I can explain what I mean by a medium by noting that the traditional picture of the human situation has been one in which human beings are not simply networks of beliefs and desires but rather beings which *have* those beliefs and desires. The traditional view is that there is a core self which can look at, decide among, use, and express itself by means of, such beliefs and desires. Further, these beliefs and desires are criticizable not simply by reference to their ability to cohere with one another, but by reference to something exterior to the network within which they are strands. Beliefs are, on this account, criticizable because they fail to correspond to reality. Desires are criticizable because they fail to correspond to the essential nature of the human self—because they are "irrational" or "unnatural." So we have a picture of the essential core of the self on one side of this network of beliefs and desires, and reality on the other side. In this picture, the network is the product of an interaction between the two, alternately expressing the one and representing the other. This is the traditional subject-object picture which idealism tried and failed to replace, and which Nietzsche, Heidegger, Derrida, James, Dewey, Goodman, Sellars, Putnam, Davidson, and others have tried to replace without entangling themselves in the idealists' paradoxes.

One phase of this effort of replacement consisted in an attempt to substitute "language" for "mind" or "consciousness" as the medium out of which beliefs and desires are constructed, the third, mediating, element between self and world. This turn toward language was thought of as a progressive, naturalizing move. It seemed so because it seemed easier to give a causal account of the evolutionary emergence of language-using organisms than of the metaphysical emergence of consciousness out of nonconsciousness. But in itself this substitution is ineffective. For if we stick to the picture of language as a medium, something standing between the self and the nonhuman reality with which the self seeks to be in touch, we have made no progress. We are still using a subject-object picture, and we are still stuck with issues about skepticism, idealism, and realism. For we are still able to ask questions about language of the same sort we asked about consciousness.

These are such questions as: "Does the medium between the self and reality get them together or keep them apart?" "Should we see the medium primarily as a medium of expression—of articulating what lies deep within the self? Or should we see it as primarily a medium of representation—showing the self what lies outside it?" Idealist theories of knowledge and Romantic notions of the imagination can, alas, easily be transposed from the jargon of "consciousness" into that of "language." Realistic and moralistic reactions to such theories can be transposed equally easily. So the seesaw battles between romanticism and moralism, and between idealism and realism, will continue as long as one thinks there is a hope of making sense of the question of whether a given language is "adequate" to a task—either the task of properly expressing the nature of the human species, or the task of properly representing the structure of non-human reality.

We need to get off this seesaw. Davidson helps us do so. For he does not view language as a medium for either expression or representation. So he is able to set aside the idea that both the self and reality have intrinsic natures, natures which are out there waiting to be known. Davidson's view of language is neither reductionist nor expansionist. It does not, as analytical philosophers sometimes have, purport to give reductive definitions of semantical notions like "truth" or "intentionality" or "reference." Nor does it resemble Heidegger's attempt to make language into a kind of divinity, something of which human beings are mere emanations. As Derrida has warned us, such an apotheosis of language is merely a transposed version of the idealists' apotheosis of consciousness.

In avoiding both reductionism and expansionism, Davidson resembles Wittgenstein. Both philosophers treat alternative vocabularies as more like alternative tools than like bits of a jigsaw puzzle. To treat them as pieces of a puzzle is to assume that all vocabularies are dispensable, or reducible to other vocabularies, or capable of being united with all other vocabularies in one grand unified super vocabulary. If we avoid this assumption, we shall not be inclined to ask questions like "What is the place of consciousness in a world of molecules?" "Are colors more mind-dependent than weights?" "What is the place of value in a world of fact?" "What is the place of intentionality in a world of causation?" "What is the relation between the solid table of common sense and the unsolid table of microphysics?" or "What is the relation of language to thought?" We should not try to answer such questions, for doing so leads either to the evident failures of reductionism or to the short-lived successes of expansionism. We should restrict ourselves to questions like "Does our use of these words get in the way of our use of those other words?" This is a question about whether our use of tools is inefficient, not a question about whether our beliefs are contradictory.

"Merely philosophical" questions, like Eddington's question about the two tables, are attempts to stir up a factitious theoretical quarrel between vocabularies which have proved capable of peaceful coexistence. The questions I have recited above are all cases in which philosophers have given their subject a bad name by seeing difficulties nobody else sees. But this is not to say that vocabularies never do get in the way of each other. On the contrary, revolutionary achievements in the arts, in the sciences, and in moral and political thought typically occur when somebody realizes that two or more of our vocabularies are interfering with each other, and proceeds to invent a new vocabulary to replace both. For example, the traditional Aristotelian vocabulary got in the way of the mathematized vocabulary that was being developed in the sixteenth century by students of mechanics. Again, young German theology students of the late eighteenth century— like Hegel and Holderlin—found that the vocabulary in which they worshipped Jesus was getting in the way of the vocabulary in which they worshiped the Greeks. Yet again, the use of Rossetti-like tropes got in the way of the early Yeats's use of Blakean tropes.

The gradual trial-and-error creation of a new, third, vocabulary—the sort of vocabulary developed by people like Galileo, Hegel, or the later Yeats—is not a discovery about how old vocabularies fit together. That is why it cannot be reached by an inferential process—by starting with premises formulated in the old vocabularies. Such creations are not the result of successfully fitting together pieces of a puzzle. They are not discoveries of a reality behind the appearances, of an undistorted view of the whole picture with which to replace myopic views of its parts. The proper analogy is with the invention of new tools to take the place of old tools. To come up with such a vocabulary is more like discarding the lever and the chock because one has envisaged the pulley, or like discarding gesso and tempera because one has now figured out how to size canvas properly.

This Wittgensteinian analogy between vocabularies and tools has one obvious drawback. The craftsman typically knows what job he needs to do before picking or inventing tools with which to do it. By contrast, someone like Galileo, Yeats, or Hegel (a "poet" in my wide sense of the term—the sense of "one who makes things new") is typically unable to make clear exactly what it is that he wants to do before developing the language in which he succeeds in doing it. His new vocabulary makes possible, for the first time, a formulation of its own purpose. It is a tool for doing something which could not have been envisaged prior to the development of a particular set of descriptions, those which it itself helps to provide. But I shall, for the moment, ignore this disanalogy. I want simply to remark that the contrast between the jigsaw-puzzle and the "tool" models of alternative vocabularies reflects the contrast between in Nietzsche's slightly misleading terms—the will truth and the will to self-overcoming. Both are expressions of the contrast between the attempt to represent or express something that was already there and the attempt to make something that never had been dreamed of before.

Davidson spells out the implications of Wittgenstein's treatment of vocabularies as tools by raising explicit doubts about the assumptions underlying traditional pre-Wittgensteinian accounts of language. These accounts have taken for granted that questions like "Is the language we are presently using the 'right' language—is it adequate to its task as a medium of expression or representation?" "Is our language a transparent or an opaque medium?" make sense. Such questions assume there are relations such as "fitting the world" or "being faithful to the true nature of the self" in which language might stand to nonlanguage. This assumption goes along with the assumption that "our language"—the language we speak now, the vocabulary at the disposal of educated inhabitants of the twentieth century—is somehow a unity, a third thing which stands in some determinate relation with two other unities—the self and reality. Both assumptions are natural enough, once we accept the idea that there are nonlinguistic things called "meanings" which it is the task of language to express, as well as the idea that there are nonlinguistic things called "facts" which it is the task of language to represent. Both ideas enshrine the notion of language as medium.

Davidson's polemics against the traditional philosophical uses of the terms "fact" and "meaning," and against what he calls "the scheme-content model" of thought and inquiry, are parts of a larger polemic against the idea that there is a fixed task for language to perform, and an entity called "language" or "the language" or "our language" which may or may not be performing this task efficiently. Davidson's doubt that there is any such entity parallels Gilbert Ryle's and Daniel Dennett's doubts about whether there is anything called "the mind" or "consciousness."[4] Both sets of doubts are doubts about the utility of the notion of a medium between the self and reality—the sort of medium which realists see as transparent and skeptics as opaque.

In a recent paper, nicely entitled "A Nice Derangement of Epitaphs,"[5] Davidson tries to undermine the notion of languages as entities by developing the notion of what he calls "a passing theory" about the noises and inscriptions presently being produced by a fellow human. Think of such a theory as part of a larger "passing theory" about this person's total behavior—a set of guesses about what she will do under what conditions. Such a theory is "passing" because it must constantly be corrected to allow for mumbles, stumbles, malapropisms, metaphors, tics, seizures, psychotic symptoms, egregious stupidity, strokes of genius, and the like. To make things easier, imagine that I am forming such a theory about the current behavior of a native of an exotic culture into which I have unexpectedly parachuted. This strange person, who presumably finds me equally strange, will simultaneously be busy forming a theory about my behavior. If we ever succeed in communicating easily and happily, it will be because her guesses about what I am going to do next, including what noises I am going to make next, and my own expectations about what I shall do or say under certain circumstances, come more or less to coincide, and because the converse is also true. She and I are coping with each other as we might cope with mangoes or boa constrictors—we are trying not to be taken by surprise. To say that we come to speak the same language is to say, as Davidson puts it, that "we tend to converge on passing theories." Davidson's point is that all "two people need, if they are to understand one another through speech, is the ability to converge on passing theories from utterance to utterance."

Davidson's account of linguistic communication dispenses with the picture of language as a third thing intervening between self and reality, and of different languages as barriers between persons or cultures. To say that one's previous language was inappropriate for dealing with some segment of the world (for example, the starry heavens above, or the raging passions within) is just to say that one is now, having learned a new language, able to handle that segment more easily. To say that two communities have trouble getting along because the words they use are so hard to translate into each other is just to say that the linguistic behavior of inhabitants of one community may, like the rest of their behavior, be hard for inhabitants of the other community to predict. As Davidson puts it,

We should realize that we have abandoned not only the ordinary notion of a language, but we have erased the boundary between knowing a language and knowing our way around the world generally. For there are no rules for arriving at passing theories that work.... There is no more chance of regularizing, or teaching, this process than there is of regularizing or teaching the process of creating new theories to cope with new data—for that is what this process involves....

There is no such thing as a language, not if a language is anything like what philosophers, at least, have supposed. There is therefore no such thing to be learned or mastered. We must give up the idea of a clearly defined shared structure which language users master and then apply to cases.... We should give up the attempt to illuminate how we communicate by appeal to conventions.[6]

This line of thought about language is analogous to the Ryle-Dennett view that when we use a mentalistic terminology we are simply using an efficient vocabulary—the vocabulary characteristic of what Dennett calls the "intentional stance"—to predict what an organism is likely to do or say under various sets of circumstances. Davidson is a nonreductive behaviorist about language in the same way that Ryle was a nonreductive behaviorist about mind. Neither has any desire to give equivalents in Behaviorese for talk about beliefs or about reference. But both are saying: Think of the term "mind" or "language" not as the name of a medium between self and reality but simply as a flag which signals the desirability of using a certain vocabulary when trying to cope with certain kinds of organisms. To say that a given organism—or, for that matter, a given machine—has a mind is just to say that, for some purposes, it will pay to think of it as having beliefs and desires. To say that it is a language user is just to say that pairing off the marks and noises it makes with those we make will prove a useful tactic in predicting and controlling its future behavior.

This Wittgensteinian attitude, developed by Ryle and Dennett for minds and by Davidson for languages, naturalizes mind and language by making all questions about the relation of either to the rest of universe *causal* questions, as opposed to questions about adequacy of representation or expression. It makes perfectly good sense to ask how we got from the relative mindlessness of the monkey to the full-fledged mindedness of the human, or from speaking Neanderthal to speaking postmodern, if these are construed as straightforward causal questions. In the former case the answer takes us off into neurology and thence into evolutionary biology. But in the latter case it takes us into intellectual history viewed as the history of metaphor. For my purposes in this book, it is the latter which is important. So I shall spend the rest of this chapter sketching an account of intellectual and moral progress which squares with Davidson's account of language.

To see the history of language, and thus of the arts, the sciences, and the moral sense, as the history of metaphor is to drop the picture of the human mind, or human languages, becoming better and better suited to the purposes for which God or Nature designed them, for example, able to express more and more meanings or to represent more and more facts. The idea that language has a purpose goes once the idea of language as medium goes. A culture which renounced both ideas would be the triumph of those tendencies in modern thought which began two hundred years ago, the tendencies common to German idealism, Romantic poetry, and utopian politics.

A nonteleological view of intellectual history, including the history of science, does for the theory of culture what the Mendelian, mechanistic, account of natural selection did for evolutionary theory. Mendel let us see mind as something which just happened rather than as something which was the point of the whole process. Davidson lets us think of the history of language, and thus of culture, as Darwin taught us to think of the history of a coral reef. Old metaphors are constantly dying off into literalness, and then serving as a platform and foil for new metaphors. This analogy lets us think of "our language"—that is, of the science and culture of twentieth-century Europe—as something that took shape as a result of a great number of sheer contingencies. Our language and our culture are as much a contingency, as much a result of thousands of small mutations finding niches (and millions of others finding no niches), as are the orchids and the anthropoids.

To accept this analogy, we must follow Mary Hesse in thinking of scientific revolutions as "metaphoric redescriptions" of nature rather than insights into the intrinsic nature of nature.[7] Further, we must resist the temptation to think that the redescriptions of reality offered by contemporary physical or biological science are somehow closer to "the things themselves," less "mind-dependent," than the redescriptions of history offered by contemporary culture criticism. We need to see the constellations of causal forces which produced talk of DNA or of the Big Bang as of a piece with the causal forces which produced talk of "secularization" or of "late capitalism."[8] These various constellations are the random factors which have made some things subjects of conversation for us and others not, have made some projects and not others possible and important.

I can develop the contrast between the idea that the history of culture has a *telos*—such as the discovery of truth, or the emancipation of humanity—and the Nietzschean and Davidsonian picture which I am sketching by noting that the latter picture is compatible with a bleakly mechanical description of the relation between human beings and the rest of the universe. For genuine novelty can, after all, occur in a world of blind, contingent, mechanical forces. Think of novelty as the sort of thing which happens when, for example, a cosmic ray scrambles the atoms in a DNA molecule, thus sending things off in the direction of the orchids or the anthropoids. The orchids, when their time came, were no less novel or marvelous for the sheer contingency of this necessary condition of their existence. Analogously, for all we know, or should care, Aristotle's metaphorical use of *ousia,* Saint Paul's metaphorical use of *agapé,* and Newton's metaphorical use of *gravitas,* were the results of cosmic rays scrambling the fine structure of some crucial neurons in their respective brains. Or, more plausibly, they were the result of some odd episodes in infancy—some obsessional kinks left in these brains by idiosyn-cratic traumata. It hardly matters how the trick was done. The results were marvelous. There had never been such things before.

This account of intellectual history chimes with Nietzsche's definition of "truth" as "a mobile army of metaphors." It also chimes with the description I offered earlier of peo-ple like Galileo and Hegel and Yeats, people in whose minds new vocabularies developed, thereby equipping them with tools for doing things which could not even have been envisaged before these tools were available. But in order to accept this picture, we need to see the distinction between the literal and the metaphorical in the way Davidson sees it: not as a distinction between two sorts of meaning, nor as a distinction between two sorts of interpretation, but as a distinction between familiar and unfamiliar uses of noises and marks. The literal uses of noises and marks are the uses we can handle by our old theories about what people will say under various conditions. Their metaphorical use is the sort which makes us get busy developing a new theory.

Davidson puts this point by saying that one should not think of metaphorical expres-sions as having meanings distinct from their literal ones. To have a meaning is to have a place in a language game. Metaphors, by definition, do not. Davidson denies, in his words, "the thesis that associated with a metaphor is a cognitive content that its author wishes to convey and that the interpreter must grasp if he is to get the message."[9] In his view, tossing a metaphor into a conversation is like suddenly breaking off the conversa-tion long enough to make a face, or pulling a photograph out of your pocket and displaying it, or pointing at a feature of the surroundings, or slapping your interlocutor's face, or kissing him. Tossing a metaphor into a text is like using italics, or illustrations, or odd punctuation or formats.

All these are ways of producing effects on your interlocutor or your reader, but not ways of conveying a message. To none of these is it appropriate to respond with "What exactly are you trying to say?" If one had wanted to say something—if one had wanted to utter a sentence with a meaning—one would presumably have done so. But instead one thought that one's aim could be better carried out by other means. That one uses familiar words in unfamiliar ways—rather than slaps, kisses, pictures, gestures, or gri-maces—does not show that what one said must have a meaning. An attempt to state that meaning would be an attempt to find some familiar (that is, literal) use of words—some sentence which already had a place in the language game—and, to claim that one might just as well have *that*. But the unparaphrasability of metaphor is just the unsuit-ability of any such familiar sentence for one's purpose.

Uttering a sentence without a fixed place in a language game is, as the positivists rightly have said, to utter something which is neither true nor false—something which is not, in Ian Hacking's terms, a "truth-value candidate." This is because it is a sentence which one cannot confirm or disconfirm, argue for or against. One can only savor it or spit it out. But this is not to say that it may not, in time, *become* a truth-value candidate. If it is savored rather than spat out, the sentence may be repeated, caught up, bandied about. Then it will gradually require a habitual use, a familiar place in the language game. It will thereby have ceased to be a metaphor—or, if you like, it will have become what most sentences of our language are, a dead metaphor. It will be just one more, literally true or literally false, sentence of the language. That is to say, our theories about the linguistic behavior of our fellows will suffice to let us cope with its utterance in the same unthinking way in which we cope with most of their other utterances.

The Davidsonian claim that metaphors do not have meanings may seem like a typical philosopher's quibble, but it is not.[10] It is part of an attempt to get us to stop thinking of language as a medium. This, in turn, is part of a larger attempt to get rid of the traditional philosophical picture of what it is to be human. The importance of Davidson's point can perhaps best be seen by contrasting his treatment of metaphor with those of the Platonist and the positivist on the one hand and the Romantic on the other. The Platonist and the positivist share a reductionist view of metaphor: They think metaphors are either paraphrasable or useless for the one serious purpose which language has, namely, representing reality. By contrast, the Romantic has an expansionist view: He thinks metaphor is strange, mystic, wonderful. Romantics attribute metaphor to a mysterious faculty called the "imagination," a faculty they suppose to be at the very center of the self, the deep heart's core. Whereas the metaphorical looks irrelevant to Platonists and positivists, the literal looks irrelevant to Romantics. For the former think that the point of language is to represent a hidden reality which lies outside us, and the latter thinks its purpose is to express a hidden reality which lies within us.

Positivist history of culture thus sees language as gradually shaping itself around the contours of the physical world. Romantic history of culture sees language as gradually bringing Spirit to self-consciousness. Nietzschean history of culture, and Davidsonian philosophy of language, see language as we now see evolution, as new forms of life constantly killing off old forms—not to accomplish a higher purpose, but blindly. Whereas the positivist sees Galileo as making a discovery—finally coming up with the words which were needed to fit the world properly, words Aristotle missed—the Davidsonian sees him as having hit upon a tool which happened to work better for certain purposes than any previous tool. Once we found out what could be done with a Galilean vocabulary, nobody was much interested in doing the things which used to be done (and which Thomists thought should still be done) with an Aristotelian vocabulary.

Similarly, whereas the Romantic sees Yeats as having gotten at something which nobody had previously gotten at, expressed something which had long been yearning for expression, the Davidsonian sees him as having hit upon some tools which enabled him to write poems which were not just variations on the poems of his precursors. Once we had Yeats's later poems in hand, we were less interested in reading Rossetti's. What goes for revolutionary, strong scientists and poets goes also for strong philosophers— people like Hegel and Davidson, the sort of philosophers who are interested in dissolving inherited problems rather than in solving them. In this view, substituting dialectic for demonstration as the method of philosophy, or getting rid of the correspondence theory of truth, is not a discovery about the nature of a preexistent entity called "philosophy" or "truth." It is changing the way we talk, and thereby changing what we want to do and what we think we are.

But in a Nietzschean view, one which drops the reality-appearance distinction, to change how we talk is to change what, for our own purposes, we are. To say, with Nietzsche, that God is dead, is to say that we serve no higher purposes. The Nietzschean substitution of self-creation for discovery substitutes a picture of the hungry generations treading each other down for a picture of humanity approaching closer and closer to the light. A culture in which Nietzschean metaphors were literalized would be one which took for granted that philosophical problems are as temporary as poetic problems, that there are no problems which bind the generations together into a single natural kind called "humanity." A sense of human history as the history of successive metaphors would let us see the poet, in the generic sense of the maker of new words, the shaper of new languages, as the vanguard of the species.

I shall try to develop this last point in Chapters 2 and 3 in terms of Harold Bloom's notion of the "strong poet." But I shall end this first chapter by going back to the claim, which has been central to what I have been saying, that the world does not provide us with any criterion of choice between alternative metaphors, that we can only compare languages or metaphors with one another, not with something beyond language called "fact."

The only way to argue for this claim is to do what philosophers like Goodman, Putnam, and Davidson have done: exhibit the sterility of attempts to give a sense to phrases like "the way the world is" or "fitting the facts." Such efforts can be supplemented by the work of philosophers of science such as Kuhn and Hesse. These philosophers explain why there is no way to explain the fact that a Galilean vocabulary enables us to make better predictions than an Aristotelian vocabulary by the claim that the book of nature is written in the language of mathematics.

These sorts of arguments by philosophers of language and of science should be seen against the background of the work of intellectual historians: historians who, like Hans Blumenberg, have tried to trace the similarities and dissimilarities between the Age of Faith and the Age of Reason.[11] These historians have made the point I mentioned earlier: The very idea that the world or the self has an intrinsic nature—one which the physicist or the poet may have glimpsed—is a remnant of the idea that the world is a divine creation, the work of someone who had something in mind, who Himself spoke some language in which He described His own project. Only if we have some such picture in mind, some picture of the universe as either itself a person or as created by a person, can we make sense of the idea that the world has an "intrinsic nature." For the cash value of that phrase is just that some vocabularies are better representations of the world than others, as opposed to being better tools for dealing with the world for one or another purpose.

To drop the idea of languages as representations, and to be thoroughly Wittgensteinian in our approach to language, would be to de-divinize the world. Only if we do that can we fully accept the argument I offered earlier—the argument that since truth is a property of sentences, since sentences are dependent for their existence upon vocabularies, and since vocabularies are made by human beings, so are truths. For as long as we think that "the world" names something we ought to respect as well as cope with, something personlike in that it has a preferred description of itself, we shall insist that any philosophical account of truth save the "intuition" that truth is "out there." This institution amounts to the vague sense that it would be *hybris* on our part to abandon the traditional language of "respect for fact" and "objectivity"—that it would be risky, and blasphemous, not to see the scientist (or the philosopher, or the poet, or *somebody*) as having a priestly function, as putting us in touch with a realm which transcends the human.

On the view I am suggesting, the claim that an "adequate" philosophical doctrine must make room for our intuitions is a reactionary slogan, one which begs the question at hand.[12] For it is essential to my view that we have no prelinguistic consciousness to which language needs to be adequate, no deep sense of how things are which it is the duty of philosophers to spell out in language. What is described as such a consciousness is simply a disposition to use the language of our ancestors, to worship the corpses of their metaphors. Unless we suffer from what Derrida calls "Heideggerian nostalgia," we shall not think of our "intuitions" as more than platitudes, more than the habitual use of a certain repertoire of terms, more than old tools which as yet have no replacements.

I can crudely sum up the story which historians like Blumenberg tell by saying that once upon a time we felt a need to worship something which lay beyond the visible world. Beginning in the seventeenth century we tried to substitute a love of truth for a love of God, treating the world described by science as a quasi divinity. Beginning at the end of the eighteenth century we tried to substitute a love of ourselves for a love of scientific truth, a worship of our own deep spiritual or poetic nature, treated as one more quasi divinity.

The line of thought common to Blumenberg, Nietzsche, Freud, and Davidson suggests that we try to get to the point where we no longer worship *anything*, where we treat *nothing* as a quasi divinity, where we treat *everything*—our language, our conscience, our community—as a product of time and chance. To reach this point would be, in Freud's words, to "treat chance as worthy of determining our fate." In the next chapter I claim that Freud, Nietzsche, and Bloom do for our conscience what Wittgenstein and Davidson do for our language, namely, exhibit its sheer contingency.

Notes

1   I have no criterion of individuation for distinct languages or vocabularies to offer, but I am not sure
    that we need one. Philosophers have used phrases like "in the language L" for a long time without wor-

rying too much about how one can tell where one natural language ends and another begins, nor about when "the scientific vocabulary of the sixteenth century" ends and "the vocabulary of the New Science" begins. Roughly, a break of this sort occurs when we start using "translation" rather than "explanation" in talking about geographical or chronological differences. This will happen whenever we find it handy to start mentioning words rather than using them—to highlight the difference between two sets of human practices by putting quotation marks around elements of those practices.

2 Nietzsche has caused a lot of confusion by inferring from "truth is not a matter of correspondence to reality" to "what we call 'truths' are just useful lies." The same confusion is occasionally found in Derrida, in the inference from "there is no such reality as the metaphysicians have hoped to find" to "what we call 'real' is not really real." Such confusions make Nietzsche and Derrida liable to charges of self-referential inconsistency—to claiming to know what they themselves claim cannot be known.

3 I should remark that Davidson cannot be held responsible for the interpretation I am putting on his views, nor for the further views I extrapolate from his. For an extended statement of that interpretation, see my "Pragmatism, Davidson and Truth," in Ernest Lepore, ed., *Truth and Interpretation: Perspectives on the Philosophy of Donald Davidson* (Oxford: Blackwell, 1984). For Davidson's reaction to this interpretation, see his "After-thoughts" to "A Coherence Theory of Truth and Knowledge," in Alan Malachowski, *Reading Rorty* (Oxford: Blackwell, 1990).

4 For an elaboration of these doubts, see my "Contemporary Philosophy of Mind," *Synthese* 53 (1982): 332–348. For Dennett's doubts about my interpretations of his views, see his "Comments on Rorty," pp. 348–354.

5 This essay can be found in Lepore, ed., *Truth and Interpretation.*

6 "A Nice Derangement of Epitaphs," in Lepore, ed., *Truth and Interpretation,* p. 446. Italics added.

7 See "The Explanatory Function of Metaphor," in Hesse, *Revolutions and Reconstructions in the Philosophy of Science* (Bloomington: Indiana University Press, 1980).

8 This coalescence is resisted in Bernard Williams's discussion of Davidson's and my views in chap. 6 of his *Ethics and the Limits of Philosophy* (Cambridge, MA: Harvard University Press, 1985). For a partial reply to Williams, see my "Is Natural Science a Natural Kind?" in Ernan McMullin, ed., *Construction and Constraint: The Shaping of Scientific Rationality* (Notre Dame, IN: University of Notre Dame Press, 1988).

9 Davidson, "What Metaphors Mean," in his *Inquiries into Truth and Interpretation* (Oxford: Oxford University Press, 1984), p. 262.

10 For a further defense of Davidson against the charge of quibbling, and various other charges, see my "Unfamiliar Noises: Hesse and Davidson on Metaphor," *Proceedings of the Aristotelian Society,* supplementary vol. 61 (1987): 283–296.

11 See Hans Blumenberg, *The Legitimacy of the Modern Age,* trans. Robert Wallace (Cambridge, MA: MIT Press, 1982).

12 For an application of this dictum to a particular case, see my discussion of the appeals to intuition found in Thomas Nagel's view of "subjectivity" and in John Searle's doctrine of "intrinsic intentionality," in "Contemporary Philosophy of Mind." For further criticisms of both, criticisms which harmonize with my own, see Daniel Dennett, "Setting Off on the Right Foot" and "Evolution, Error, and Intentionality," in Dennett, in *The Intentional Stance* (Cambridge, MA: MIT Press, 1987).

FEMINISM AND PRAGMATISM

RICHARD RORTY

When two women ascended to the Supreme Court of Minnesota, Catharine MacKinnon asked: "Will they use the tools of law as women, for all women?" She continued as follows:

> I think that the real feminist issue is not whether biological males or biological females hold positions of power, although it is utterly essential that women be there. And I am not saying that viewpoints have genitals. My issue is what our identifications are, what our loyalties are, who our community is, to whom we are accountable. If it seems as if this is not very concrete, I think it is because we have no idea what women as women would have to say. I'm evoking for women a role that we have yet to make, in the name of a voice that, unsilenced, might say something that has never been heard.[1]

Urging judges to "use the tools of law as women, for all women" alarms universalist philosophers. These are the philosophers who think that moral theory should come up with principles which mention no group smaller than "persons" or "human beings" or "rational agents." Such philosophers would be happier if MacKinnon talked less about accountability to women as women and more about an ideal Minnesota, or an ideal America, one in which all human beings would be treated impartially. Universalists would prefer to think of feminism as Mary Wollstonecraft and Olympe de Gouges did, as a matter of rights which are already recognizable and describable, although not yet granted. This describability, they feel, makes MacKinnon's hope for a voice saying something never heard before unnecessary, overly dramatic, hyperbolic.

Universalist philosophers assume, with Kant, that all the logical space necessary for moral deliberation is now available—that all important truths about right and wrong can not only be stated, but be made plausible, in language already to hand. I take MacKinnon to be siding with historicists like Hegel and Dewey, and to be saying that moral progress depends upon expanding this space. She illustrates the need for such expansion when she notes that present sex-discrimination law assumes that women "have to meet either the male standard for males or the male standard for females.... For purposes of sex discrimination law, to be a woman means either to be like a man or to be like a lady."[2] In my terms, MacKinnon is saying that unless women fit into the logical space prepared for them by current linguistic and other practices, the law does not know how to deal with them. MacKinnon cites the example of a judicial decision that permitted women to be excluded from employment as prison guards, because they are so susceptible to rape. The court, she continues, "took the viewpoint of the reasonable rapist on women's employment opportunities."[3] "The conditions that create women's rapeability as the definition of womanhood were not even seen as susceptible to change."[4]

MacKinnon thinks that such assumptions of unchangeability will only be overcome once we can hear "what women as women would have to say." I take her point to be that assumptions become visible as assumptions only if we can make the contradictories of those assumptions sound plausible. So injustices may not be perceived as injustices, even by those who suffer them, until somebody invents a previously unplayed role. Only if somebody has a dream, and a voice to describe that dream, does what looked like nature begin to look like culture, what looked like fate begin to look like a moral abomination. For until then only the language of the oppressor is available, and most oppressors have had the wit to teach the oppressed a language in which the oppressed will sound crazy— *even to themselves*—if they describe themselves as oppressed.[5]

MacKinnon's point that logical space may need to be expanded before justice can be envisaged, much less done, can be restated in terms of John Rawls's claim that moral theorizing is a matter attaining reflective equilibrium between general principles and particular intuitions—particular reactions of revulsion, horror, satisfaction, or delight to real or imagined situations or actions. MacKinnon sees moral and legal principles, particularly those phrased in terms of equal rights, as impotent to change those reactions.[6] So she sees feminists as needing to alter the data of moral theory rather than needing to formulate principles which fit pre-existent data better. Feminists are trying to get people to feel indifference or satisfaction where they once recoiled, and revulsion and rage where they once felt indifference or resignation.

One way to change instinctive emotional reactions is to provide new language which will facilitate new reactions. By "new language" I mean not just new words but also creative misuses of language—familiar words used in ways which initially sound crazy. Something traditionally regarded as a moral abomination can become an object of general satisfaction, or conversely, as a result of the increased popularity of an alternative description of what is happening. Such popularity extends logical space by making descriptions of situations which used to seem crazy seem sane. Once, for example, it would have sounded crazy to describe homosexual sodomy as a touching expression of devotion, or to describe a woman manipulating the elements of the Eucharist as a figuration of the relation of the Virgin to her Son. But such descriptions are now acquiring popularity. At most times, it sounds crazy to describe the degradation and extirpation of helpless minorities as a purification of the moral and spiritual life of Europe. But at certain periods and places—under the Inquisition, during the Wars of Religion, under the Nazis—it did not.

Universalistic moral philosophers think that the notion of "violation of human rights" provides sufficient conceptual resources to explain why some traditional occasions of revulsion really are moral abominations and others only appear to be. They think of moral progress as an increasing ability to see the reality behind the illusions created by superstition, prejudice, and unreflective custom. The typical universalist is a moral realist, someone who thinks that true moral judgments are *made* true by something out there in the world. Universalists typically take this truth-maker to be the intrinsic features of human beings *qua* human. They think you can sort out the real from the illusory abominations by figuring out which those intrinsic features are, and that all that is required to figure this out is hard, clear, thought.

Historicists, by contrast, think that if "intrinsic" means "ahistorical, untouched by historical change," then the only intrinsic features of human beings are those they share with the brutes—for example, the ability to suffer and inflict pain. Every other feature is up for grabs. Historicists say, with Susan Hurley, that "the existence of certain shared practices, any of which might not have existed, is all that our having determinate reasons... to do anything rests on."[7] So they think that we are not yet in a position to know what human beings are, since we do not yet know what practices human beings may start sharing.[8] Universalists talk as if any rational agent, at any epoch, could somehow have envisaged all the possible morally relevant differences, all the possible moral identities, brought into existence by such shared practices. But for MacKinnon, as for Hegel and Dewey, we know, at most, only those possibilities which history has actualized so far. MacKinnon's central point, as I read her, is that "a woman" is not yet the name of a way of being human—not yet the name of a moral identity, but, at most, the name of a disability.[9]

Taking seriously the idea of as yet unrealized possibilities, and as yet unrecognized moral abominations resulting from failure to envisage those possibilities, requires one to take seriously the suggestion that we do not presently have the logical space necessary for adequate moral deliberation. Only if such suggestions are taken seriously can passages like the one I quoted from MacKinnon be read as prophecy rather than empty hyperbole. But this means revising our conception of moral progress. We have to stop talking about the need to go from distorted to undistorted perception of moral reality, and instead talk about the need to modify our practices so as to take account of new descriptions of what has been going on.

Here is where pragmatist philosophy might be useful to feminist politics. For pragmatism redescribes both intellectual and moral progress by substituting metaphors of evolutionary development for metaphors of progressively less distorted perception. By dropping a representationalist account of knowledge, we pragmatists drop the appearance-reality distinction in favor of a distinction between beliefs which serve some purposes and beliefs which serve other purposes—for example, the purposes of one group and those of another group. We drop the notion of beliefs being made true by reality, as well as the distinction between intrinsic and accidental features of things. So we drop questions about (in Nelson Goodman's phrase) The Way the World Is. We thereby drop the ideas of The Nature of Humanity and of The Moral Law, considered as objects which inquiry is trying to represent accurately, or as objects which make true moral judgments true. So we have to give up the comforting belief that competing groups will always be able to reason together on the basis of plausible and neutral premises.

From a pragmatist angle, neither Christianity nor the Enlightenment nor contemporary feminism are cases of cognitive clarity overcoming cognitive distortion. They are, instead, examples of evolutionary struggle—struggle which is Mendelian rather than Darwinian in character, in that it is guided by no immanent teleology. The history of human social practices is continuous with the history of biological evolution, the only difference being that what Richard Dawkins and Daniel Dennett call "memes" gradually take over the role of Mendel's genes. Memes are things like turns of speech, terms of aesthetic or moral praise, political slogans, proverbs, musical phrases, stereotypical icons, and the like. Memes compete with one another for the available cultural space as genes compete for the available *Lebensraum*.[10] Different batches of both genes and memes are carried by different human social groups, and so the triumph of one such group amounts to the triumph of those genes or memes. But no gene or meme is closer to the purpose of evolution or to the nature of humanity than any other—for evolution has no purpose and humanity no nature. So the moral world does not divide into the intrinsically decent and the intrinsically abominable, but rather into the goods of different groups and different epochs. As Dewey put it, "The worse or evil is a rejected good. In deliberation and before choice no evil presents itself as evil. Until it is rejected, it is a competing good. After rejection, it figures not as a lesser good, but as the bad of that situation."[11] On a Deweyan view, the replacement of one species by another in a given ecological niche, or the enslavement of one human tribe or race by another, or of the human females by the human males, is not an intrinsic evil. The latter is a rejected good, rejected on the basis of the greater good which feminism is presently making imaginable. The claim that this good is greater is like the claim that mammals are preferable to reptiles, or Aryans to Jews; it is an ethnocentric claim made from the point of view of a given cluster of genes or memes. There is no larger entity which stands behind that cluster and makes its claim true (or makes some contradictory claim true).

Pragmatists like myself think that this Deweyan account of moral truth and moral progress comports better with the prophetic tone in contemporary feminism than do universalism and realism. Prophecy, as we see it, is all that non-violent political movements can fall back on when argument fails. Argument for the rights of the oppressed *will* fail just insofar as the only language in which to state relevant premises is one in which the relevant emancipatory premises sound crazy. We pragmatists see universalism and realism as committed to the idea of a reality-tracking faculty called "reason" and an unchanging moral reality to be tracked, and thus unable to make sense of the claim that a new voice is needed. So we commend ourselves to feminists on the ground that we can fit that claim into *our* view of moral progress with relative ease.

We see it as unfortunate that many feminists intermingle pragmatist and realist rhetoric. For example, MacKinnon at one point defines feminism as the belief "that women are human beings in truth but not in social reality."[12] The phrase "in truth" here can only mean "in a reality which is distinct from social reality," one which is as it is whether or not women ever succeed in saying what has never been heard. Such invocations of an ahistoricist realism leave it unclear whether MacKinnon sees women as appealing from a bad social practice to something which transcends social practice, appealing from appearance to reality, or instead sees them as doing the same sort of thing as the early Christians, the early socialists, the Albigensians, and the Nazis did: trying to actualize hitherto undreamt-of possibilities by putting new linguistic and other practices into play, and erecting new social constructs.[13]

Some contemporary feminist philosophers are sympathetic to the latter alternative, because they explicitly reject universalism and realism. They do so because they see both as symptoms of what Derrida has called "phallogocentrism"—what MacKinnon calls "the epistemological stance . . . of which male dominance is the politics."[14] Other such philosophers, however, warn against accepting the criticisms of universalism and realism common to Nietzsche, Heidegger, and Derrida—against finding an ally in what is sometimes called "postmodernism." Sabina Lovibond, for example, cautions against throwing Enlightenment universalism and realism overboard. "How can any one ask me to say goodbye to 'emancipatory metanarratives'", she asks, "when my own emancipation is still such a patchy, hit-or-miss affair?"[15] Lovibond's universalism comes out when she says that "It would be arbitrary to work for sexual equality unless one believed that human society was disfigured by inequality *as such*." Her realism comes out in her claim that feminism has a "background commitment... to the elimination of (self-interested) cognitive distortion."[16]

I share Lovibond's doubts about the apocalyptic tone, and the rhetoric of unmasking, prevalent among people who believe that we are living in a "postmodern" period.[17] But, on all the crucial philosophical issues, I am on the side of Lovibond's postmodernist opponents.[18] I hope that feminists will continue to consider the possibility of dropping realism and universalism, dropping the notion that the subordination of women is *intrinsically* abominable, dropping the claim that there is something called "right" or "justice" or "humanity" which has always been on their side, making their claims true. I agree with those whom Lovibond paraphrases as saying "the Enlightenment rhetoric of 'emancipation', 'autonomy' and the like is complicit in a fantasy of escape from the embodied condition."[19] In particular, it is complicit in the fantasy of escape from an historical situation into an ahistoricist empyrean—one in which moral theory can be pursued, like Euclidean geometry, within an unalterable, unextendable, logical space. Although practical politics will doubtless often require feminists to speak with the universalist vulgar, I think that they might profit from thinking with the pragmatists.

One of the best things about contemporary feminism, it seems to me, is its ability to eschew such Enlightenment fantasies of escape. My favorite passages in MacKinnon are ones in which she says things like "we are not attempting to be objective about it, we're attempting to represent the point of view of women."[20] Feminists are much less inclined than Marxists were to fall back on a comfortable doctrine of immanent teleology. There is a lot of feminist writing which can be read as saying: we are *not* appealing from phallist appearance to non-phallist reality. We are *not* saying that the voice in which women will some day speak will be better at representing reality than present-day masculist discourse. We are not attempting the impossible task of developing a non-hegemonic discourse, one in which truth is no longer connected with power. We are not trying to do away with social constructs in order to find something that is not a social construct. We are just trying to help women out of the traps men have constructed for them, help them get the power they do not presently have, and help them create a moral identity as women.

I have argued in the past that Deweyan pragmatism, when linguistified along the lines suggested by Putnam and Davidson, gives you all that is politically useful in the Nietzsche-Heidegger-Derrida-Foucault tradition. Pragmatism, I claim, offers all the dialectical advantages of postmodernism while avoiding the self-contradictory postmodernist rhetoric of unmasking. I admit that insofar as feminists adopt a Deweyan rhetoric of the sort I have just described, they commit themselves to a lot of apparent paradoxes, and incur the usual charges of relativism, irrationalism, and power-worship.[21] But these disadvantages are, I think, outweighed by the advantages. By describing themselves in Deweyan terms, feminists would free themselves from Lovibond's demand for a general theory of oppression—a way of seeing oppression on the basis of race, class, sexual preference, and gender as so many instances of a general failure to treat equals equally.[22] They would thereby avoid the embarrassments of the universalist claim that the term "human being"—or even the term "woman"—names an unchanging essence, an ahistorical natural kind with a permanent set of intrinsic features. Further, they would no longer need to raise what seem to me unanswerable questions about the accuracy of their representations of "woman's experience." They would instead see themselves as *creating* such an experience by creating a language, a tradition, and an identity.

In the remainder of this paper I want to develop this distinction between expression and creation in more detail. But first I want to insert a cautionary remark about the relative insignificance of philosophical movements as compared to social-political movements. Yoking feminism with pragmatism is like yoking Christianity with Platonism, or socialism with dialectical materialism. In each case, something big and important, a vast social hope, is being yoked with something comparatively small and unimportant, a set of answers to philosophical questions—questions which arise only for people who find philosophical topics intriguing rather than silly. Universalists—of both the bourgeois liberal and the Marxist sort—often claim that such questions are in fact urgent, for political movements *need* philosophical foundations. But we pragmatists cannot say this. We are not in the foundations business. *All* we can do is to offer feminists a few pieces of special-purpose ammunition—for example, some additional replies to charges that their aims are unnatural, their demands irrational, or their claims hyperbolic.

So much for an overview of my reasons for trying to bring feminism and pragmatism together. I want now to enlarge on my claim that a pragmatist feminist will see herself as helping to create women rather than attempting to describe them more accurately. I shall do so by taking up two objections which might be made to what I have been saying. The first is the familiar charge that pragmatism is inherently conservative, biased in favor of the status quo.[23]

The second objection arises from the fact that if you say that women need to be created rather than simply freed, you seem to be saying that in some sense women do not now fully exist. But then there seems no basis for saying that men have done women wrong, since you cannot wrong the non-existent.

Hilary Putnam, the most important contemporary philosopher to call himself a pragmatist, has said that "a statement is true of a situation just in case it would be correct to use the words of which the statement consists in that way in describing the situation." Putting the matter this way immediately suggests the question: correct by whose standards? Putnam's position that "truth and rational acceptability are interdependent notions"[24] makes it hard to see how we might ever appeal from the oppressive conventions of our community to something non-conventional, and thus hard to see how we could ever engage in anything like "radical critique." So it may seem that we pragmatists, in our frenzied efforts to undercut epistemological skepticism by doing away with what Davidson calls "the scheme-content distinction," have also undercut political radicalism.

Pragmatists should reply to this charge by saying that they cannot make sense of an appeal from our community's practices to anything except the practice of a real or imagined alternative community. So when prophetic feminists say that it is not enough to make the practices of our community coherent, that the very *language* of our community must be subjected to radical critique, pragmatists add that such critique can only take the form of imagining a community whose linguistic and other practices are different from our own. Once one grants MacKinnon's point that one can only get so far with an appeal to make present beliefs more coherent by treating women on a par with men, once one sees the need for something more than an appeal to rational acceptability by the standards of the existing community, then such an act of imagination is the only recourse.

This means that one will praise movements of liberation not for the accuracy of their diagnoses but for the imagination and courage of their proposals. The difference between pragmatism and positions such as Marxism, which retain the rhetoric of scientism and realism, can be thought of as the difference between radicalism and utopianism. Radicals think that there is a basic mistake being made, a mistake deep down at the roots. They think that deep thinking is required to get down to this deep level, and that only there, when all the superstructural appearances have been undercut, can things be seen as they really are. Utopians, however, do not think in terms of mistakes or of depth. They abandon the contrast between superficial appearance and deep reality in favor of the contrast between a painful present and a possibly less painful, dimly-seen, future. Pragmatists cannot be radicals, in this sense, but they can be utopians. They do not see philosophy as providing instruments for radical surgery, or microscopes which make precise diagnosis possible.[25] Philosophy's function is rather to clear the road for prophets and poets, to make intellectual life a bit simpler and safer for those who have visions of new communities.[26]

So far I have taken MacKinnon as my example of a feminist with such a vision. But of course she is only one of many. Another is Marilyn Frye, who says, in her powerful book *The Politics of Reality*, that "there probably is really no distinction, in the end, between imagination and courage." For, she continues, it takes courage to overcome "a mortal dread of being outside the field of vision of the arrogant eye." This is the eye of a person who prides himself on spotting the rational unacceptability of what is being said—that is, its incoherence with the rest of the beliefs of those who currently control life-chances and logical space. So feminists must, Frye goes on to say, "dare to rely on ourselves to make meaning and we have to imagine ourselves capable of... weaving the web of meaning which will hold us in some kind of intelligibility."[27] Such courage is indistinguishable from the imagination it takes to hear oneself as the spokesperson of a merely possible community, rather than as a lonely, and perhaps crazed, outcast from an actual one.

MacKinnon and many other feminists use "liberalism" as a name for an inability to have this sort of courage and imagination. "In the liberal mind," MacKinnon says, "the worse and more systematic one's mistreatment is, the more it seems justified. Liberalism... never sees power as power, yet can see as significant only that which power does."[28] The phenomenon she is pointing to certainly exists, but "liberalism" seems to me the wrong name for it. So, of course, does "pragmatism." I think the main reason—apart from some reflexes left over from early Marxist conditioning—why pejorative uses of the terms "liberal" and "pragmatist" are still common among political radicals is that if you say, with Putnam, that "truth does transcend use," you may easily be taken as referring to actual, present use. Again, if you deny that truth is a matter of correspondence to reality, you may easily be taken as holding that a true belief is one that coheres with what most people currently believe. If you think that emancipatory moral or social thought requires penetrating to a presently unglimpsed reality beneath the current appearances, and find pragmatists telling you that there is no such reality, you may easily conclude that a pragmatist cannot help the cause of emancipation.

When, however, we remember that John Dewey—a paradigmatic liberal as well as a paradigmatic pragmatist—spent a great deal of time celebrating the sort of courage and imagination Frye describes, we may be willing to grant that the relation between pragmatism and emancipation is more complex. Dewey said remarkably little about the situation of women, but one of the few things he did say is worth quoting:

> Women have as yet made little contribution to philosophy, but when women who are not mere students of other persons' philosophy set out to write it, we cannot conceive that it will be the same in viewpoint or tenor as that composed from the standpoint of the different masculine experience of things. Institutions, customs of life, breed certain systematized predilections and aversions. The wise man reads historic philosophies to detect in them intellectual formulations of men's habitual purposes and cultivated wants, not to gain insight into the ultimate nature of things or information about the make-up of reality. As far as what is loosely called reality figures in philosophies, we may be sure that it signifies those selected aspects of the world which are chosen because they lend themselves to the support of men's judgment of the worth-while life, and hence are most highly prized. In philosophy, "reality" is a term of value or choice.[29]

Suppose we think, as feminists often do, of "men's habitual purposes and cultivated wants" as "the habitual purposes and cultivated wants of the males, the half of the species which long ago enslaved the other half." This permits us to read Dewey as saying: if you find yourself a slave, do not accept your masters' descriptions of the real; do not work within the boundaries of their moral universe; instead, try to invent a reality of your own by selecting aspects of the world which lend themselves to the support of *your* judgment of the worth-while life."[30]

Dewey's doctrine of the means-end continuum might have led him to add: do not expect to know what sort of life is worth-while right off the bat, for that is one of the things you will constantly change your mind about in the process of selecting a reality. You can neither pick your goals on the basis of a clear and explicit claim about the nature of moral reality, nor derive such a claim from clear and explicit goals. There is no method or procedure to be followed except courageous and imaginative experimentation. Dewey would, I think, have been quick to see the point of Frye's description of her own writing as "a sort of flirtation with meaninglessness—dancing about a region of cognitive gaps and negative semantic spaces, kept aloft only by the rhythm and momentum of my own motion, trying to plumb abysses which are generally agreed not to exist."[31] For meaninglessness is exactly what you have to flirt with when you are in between social, and in particular linguistic, practices—unwilling to take part in an old one but not yet having succeeded in creating a new one.

The import of Dewey's pragmatism for movements such as feminism can be seen if we paraphrase Dewey as follows: do not charge a current social practice or a currently spoken language with being unfaithful to reality, with getting things wrong. Do not criticize it as a result of ideology or prejudice, where these are tacitly contrasted with your own employment of a truth-tracking faculty called "reason" or a neutral method called "disinterested observation." Do not even criticize it as "unjust" if "unjust" is supposed to mean more than "sometimes incoherent even on its own terms." Instead of appealing from the transitory current appearances to the permanent reality, appeal to a still only dimly imagined future practice. Drop the appeal to neutral criteria, and the claim that something large like Nature or Reason or History or the Moral Law is on the side of the oppressed. Instead, just make invidious comparisons between the actual present and a possible, if inchoate, future.[32]

So much for the relations between pragmatism and political radicalism. I have been arguing that the two are compatible and mutually supporting. This is because pragmatism allows for the possibility of expanding logical space, and thereby for an appeal to courage and imagination rather than to putatively neutral criteria. What pragmatism loses when it gives up the claim to have right or reality on its side it gains in ability to acknowledge the presence of what Frye calls "abysses which are generally agreed not to exist." These are situations which give the universalist and the realist trouble—ones in which plenty of assent-commanding descriptions are available, but such that none of these descriptions do what is needed.

I turn now to the paradox I noted earlier: the suggestion that women are only now coming into existence, rather than having been deprived of the ability to express what was deep within them all the time. I take MacKinnon's evocation of a "role that women have yet to make" as a way of suggesting that women are only now beginning to put together a moral identity *as* women. To find one's moral identity in being an X means being able to do the following sort of thing: make your Xness salient in your justification of important uncoerced choices, make your Xness an important part of the story you tell yourself when you need to recover your self-confidence, make your relations with other X's central to your claim to be a responsible person. These are all things men have usually been able to do by reminding themselves that they are, come what may, *men*. They are things which men have made it hard for women to do by reminding themselves that they are women. As Frye puts it, men have assigned themselves the status of "full persons"—people who enjoy what she calls "unqualified participation in the radical 'superiority' of the species,"[33] and withheld this status from women. The result of men constantly, fervently, and publicly thanking God that they are not women has been to make it hard for women to thank God that they are. For a woman to say that she finds her moral identity in being a woman would have sounded, until relatively recently, as weird as for a slave to say that he or she finds his or her moral identity in being a slave.

Most feminists might agree that it was only with the beginnings of the feminist movement that it began to become possible for women to find their moral identities in being women.[34] But most feminists are probably still realist and universalist enough to insist that there is a difference between the claim that one cannot find one's moral identity in being an X and the claim that an X is not yet a full-fledged person, a person to whom injustice has been done by forbidding her to find her moral identity in her X-hood. For the great advantage of realism and universalism over pragmatism is that it permits one to say that women were everything they are now, and *therefore* were entitled to everything they are now trying to get—even when they did not know, and might even have explicitly denied, that they were entitled to it.

For us pragmatists, however, it is not so easy to say that. For we see personhood as a matter of degree, not as an all-or-nothing affair, something evenly distributed around the species. We see it as something that slaves typically have less of than their masters. This is not because there are such things as "natural slaves" but because of the masters' control over the language spoken by the slaves—their ability to make the slave think of his or her pain as fated and even somehow deserved, something to be borne rather than resisted. We cannot countenance the notion of a deep reality which reposes unrecognized beneath the superficial appearances. So we have to take seriously the idea, made familiar by such writers as Charles Taylor, that interpretation goes all the way down: that what a human being is, for moral purposes, is largely a matter of how he or she describes himself or herself. We have to take seriously the idea that what you experience yourself to be is largely a function of what it makes sense to describe yourself as in the languages you are able to use. We have to say that the Deltas and Epsilons of Huxley's *Brave New World,* and the proles of Orwell's *Nineteen Eighty-Four*, were persons only in the sense in which fertilized human ova or human infants are persons—in the sense, namely, that they are capable of being made into persons. So we pragmatists have to identify most of the wrongness of past male oppression with its suppression of past potentiality, rather than in its injustice to past actuality.

In order to say that women are only now in the process of achieving a moral identity as women, I do not need to deny that some women have, in every epoch, had doubts about, and offered alternatives to, the standard, androcentric, descriptions of women. All I need to deny is that women have been able to *forget* the latter descriptions—the ones which make them seem incapable of being full persons. I am denying that women in previous epochs have been able to avoid being torn, split, between the men's description of them and whatever alternative descriptions they have given to themselves. As an example of the sort of thing I have in mind—of the need to name, and thus to begin to bridge, what Frye calls "abysses generally agreed not to exist"—consider Adrienne Rich's description of her situation when young. She was, she says, "split between the girl who wrote poems, who defined herself as writing poems, and the girl who was to define herself by her relationships with men."[35] I want to interpret Rich's individual situation as an allegory of the more general situation in which women found themselves before feminism achieved lift-off—of their inability to stop defining themselves in terms of their relationships with men. To envisage this inability, consider how Rich's situation differed from that of a young man in a similar situation.

Since Byron and Goethe men have thought of writing poems as one of the best ways to create an autonomous self, to avoid having to define oneself in the terms used by one's parents, teachers, employers, and rulers. Since 1820 or thereabouts, a young man has had the option of defining himself as a poet, of finding his moral identity in writing verse. But, Rich tells us, this is not easy for a young woman.

What is the difficulty? It is not that there is any dearth of true descriptions which Rich might have applied to herself. There were no well-formed—that is, generally intelligible—questions to which Rich could not have given true, well-formed answers. But nevertheless there was, she tells us, a split. The various true descriptions which she applied did not fit together into a whole. But, she is implicitly suggesting, a young male poet's descriptions would have fitted together easily. Rich was, in her youth, unable to attain the kind of coherence, the kind of integrity, which we think of as characteristic of full persons. For persons who are capable of the full glory of humanity are capable of seeing themselves steadily and whole. Rather than feel that splits are tearing them apart, they can see tensions between their alternative self-descriptions as, at worst, necessary elements in a harmonious variety-in-unity.

Rich's account of herself as split rings true for, as she shows in her essay on Emily Dickinson and elsewhere, the language-games men have arranged that young women should play force them to treat the men in their lives (or, the absence of men in their lives) as the independent variable and everything else—even their poems—as dependent variables. So insofar as Rich could not tie her poems in with her relationships with men, she had a problem. She was split. She could not be, so to speak, a full-time poet, because a language she could not forget did not let one be both a full-time poet and a full-time female. By contrast, since Byron, the language has let one be a full-time poet and a full-time hero (just as, since Socrates, it has been possible to be a full-time intellectual and a full-time hero).

What might solve Rich's problem? Well, perhaps nowadays it is a little easier for a young woman to define herself by and in her poems than when Rich was young—simply because she may have read books by Rich, Frye, and others. But only a little easier. What would make it *really* easy? Only, I would suggest, the sort of circumstance which made it easy for a young man in the generation after Byron to make his poetic activity the independent variable in the story he told himself about himself. In the previous generation there had been what now looks to us like a band of brothers—Hölderlin and Keats, Byron and Goethe, Shelley and Chamisso. Bliss was it in that dawn to be alive, and to be a young male with poetic gifts was to be able to describe oneself in heroic terms, terms which one could not have used earlier without sounding crazy. That band of brothers rounded an invisible club, a very good club, one which is still giving new members a warm welcome.[36] So young male poets do not face abysses when they attempt self-definition. But, as Rich points out, Emily Dickinson was not allowed into that club.[37]

So, to make things *really* easy for future Dickinsons and Richs, there would have to be a good, well-established club which they could join.

Here, I take it, is where feminist separatism comes in. Rich asks that

> we understand lesbian/feminism in the deepest, most radical sense: as that love for ourselves and other women, that commitment to the freedom of all of us, which transcends the category of "sexual preference" and the issue of civil rights, to become a politics of *asking women's questions,* demanding a world in which the integrity of all women—not a chosen few—shall be honored and validated in every aspect of culture.[38]

Someone who tries to fit what Rich is saying into a map drawn on a universalist and realist grid will have trouble locating any space separate from that covered by "the category of 'sexual preference'" or by "the issue of civil rights." For justice, on this universalist view, is a matter of our providing each other with equal advantages. Nothing, in this vision, *could* transcend civil rights and the realization of those rights by institutional change. So, for example, lesbian separatism is likely to be seen simply as an arrangement by which those with a certain sexual preference can escape stigma until such time as the laws have been extended to protect lesbians' rights and the mores have caught up with the laws.

Frye offers a contrasting view of the function of separatism when she writes:

> *Re* the new being and meaning which are being created now by lesbian-feminists, we *do* have semantic authority, and, collectively, can and do define with effect. I think it is only by maintaining boundaries through controlling concrete access to us that we can enforce on those who are not-us our definitions of ourselves, hence force on them *the fact of our existence* and thence open up the *possibility* of our having semantic authority with them.[39]

I take Frye's point to be, in part, that individuals—even individuals of great courage and imagination—cannot achieve semantic authority, *even semantic authority over themselves,* on their own. To get such authority you have to hear your own statements as part of a hated practice. Otherwise you yourself will never know whether they are more than ravings, never know whether you are a heroine or a maniac. People in search of such authority need to band together and form clubs, exclusive clubs. For if you want to work out a story about who you are—put together a moral identity—which decreases the importance of your relationships to one set of people and increases the importance of your relationships to another set, the physical absence of the first set of people may be just what you need. So feminist separatism may indeed, as Rich says, have little to do with sexual preference or with civil rights, and a lot to do with making things easier for women of the future to define themselves in terms not presently available. These would be terms which made it easy for "women as women" to have what Dewey calls "habitual purposes and cultivated wants"—purposes and wants which, as Rich says, only a chosen few women presently have.

To sum up: I am suggesting that we see the contemporary feminist movement as playing the same role in intellectual and moral progress as was played by, for example, Plato's Academy, the early Christians meeting in the catacombs, the invisible Copernican colleges of the seventeenth century, groups of workingmen gathering to discuss Tom Paine's pamphlets, and lots of other clubs which were formed to try out new ways of speaking, and to gather the moral strength to go out and change the world. For groups build their moral strength by achieving increasing semantic authority over their members, thereby increasing the ability of those members to find their moral identities in their membership of such groups.

When a group forms itself in conscious opposition to those who control the life-chances of its members, and succeeds in achieving semantic authority over its members, the result may be its ruthless suppression—the sort of thing that happened to the Albigensians and which Margaret Atwood has imagined happening to the feminists. But it may also happen that, as the generations succeed one another, the masters, those in control, gradually find their conceptions of the possibilities open to human beings changing. For example, they may gradually begin to think of the options open to their own children as including membership in the group in question. The new language spoken by the separatist group may gradually get woven into the language taught in the schools.

Insofar as this sort of thing happens, eyes become less arrogant and the members of the group cease to be treated as wayward children, or as a bit crazy (the ways in which Emily Dickinson was treated). Instead, they gradually achieve what Frye calls "full personhood" in the eyes of everybody, having first achieved it only in the eyes of fellow-members of their own club. They begin to be treated as full-fledged human beings, rather than being seen, like children or the insane, as degenerate cases—as beings entitled to love and protection, but not to participation in deliberation on serious matters. For to be a full-fledged person in a given society is a matter of double negation: it is *not* to think of oneself as belonging to a group which powerful people in that society thank God they do *not* belong to.

In our society, straight white males of my generation—even earnestly egalitarian straight white males—cannot easily stop themselves from feeling guilty relief that they were not born women or gay or black, any more than they can stop themselves from being glad that they were not born mentally retarded or schizophrenic. This is in part because of a calculation of the obvious socio-economic disadvantages of being so born, but not entirely. It is also the sort of instinctive and ineffable horror which noble children used to feel at the thought of having been born to non-noble parents, even very rich non-noble parents.[40]

At some future point in the development of our society, guilty relief over not having been born a woman may not cross the minds of males, any more than the question "noble or base-born?" now crosses their minds.[41] That would be the point at which both males and females had *forgotten* the traditional androcentric language, just as we have all forgotten about the discussion between base and noble ancestry. But if this future comes to pass, we pragmatists think, it will not be because the females have been revealed to possess something—namely, full human dignity—which everybody, even they themselves, once mistakenly thought they lacked. It will be because the linguistic and other practices of the common culture have come to incorporate some of the practices characteristic of imaginative and courageous outcasts.

The new language which, with luck, will get woven into the language taught to children will not, however, be the language which the outcasts spoke in the old days, before the formation of separatist groups. For that was infected by the language of the masters. It will be, instead, a language gradually put together in separatist groups in the course of a long series of flirtations with meaninglessness. Had there been no stage of separation, there would have been no subsequent stage of assimilation. No prior antithesis, no new synthesis. No carefully nurtured pride in membership in a group which might not have attained self-consciousness were it not for its oppression, no expansion of the range of possible moral identities, and so no evolution of the species. This is what Hegel called the cunning of reason, and what Dewey thought of as the irony of evolution.

Someone who takes the passage I quoted from Dewey seriously will not think of oppressed groups as learning to *recognize* their own full personhood and then gradually, by stripping away veils of prejudice, leading their oppressors to confront reality. For they will not see full personhood as an intrinsic attribute of the oppressed, any more than they see human beings having a central and inviolable core surrounded by culturally-conditioned beliefs and desires—a core for which neither biology nor history can account. To be a pragmatist rather than a realist in one's description of the acquisition of full personhood requires thinking of its acquisition by blacks, gays and women in the same terms as we think of its acquisition by Galilean scientists and Romantic poets. We say that the latter groups invented new moral identities for themselves by getting semantic authority over themselves. As time went by, they succeeded in having the language they had developed become part of the language everybody spoke. Similarly, we have to think of gays, blacks and women inventing themselves rather than discovering themselves, and thus of the larger society as coming to terms with something new.

This means taking Frye's phrase "new *being*" literally, and saying that there were very few female full persons around before feminism got started, in the same sense in which there were very few full-fledged Galilean scientists before the seventeenth century. It was of course *true* in earlier times that women should not have been oppressed, just as it was *true* before Newton said so that gravitational attraction accounted for the movements of the planets.[42] But, despite what Scripture says, truth will not necessarily prevail. "Truth" is not the name of a power which eventually wins through, it is just the nominalization of an approbative adjective. So just as a pragmatist in the philosophy of science cannot use the truth of Galileo's views as an explanation either of his success at prediction or of his gradually increasing fame,[43] so a pragmatist in moral philosophy cannot use the rightness of the feminist cause as an explanation either of its attraction for contemporary women or of its possible future triumph. For such explanations require the notion of a truthtracking faculty, one which latches on to antecedently existing truth-makers. Truth is ahistorical, but that is not because truths are made true by ahistorical entities.

Frye's term "new being" may seem even more unnecessarily hyperbolic than MacKinnon's "new voice," but we pragmatists can take it at face value and realists cannot. As I read Frye, the point is that before feminism began to gather women together into a kind of club, there were female eccentrics like Wollstonecraft and de Gouges, but these were not women who existed as women, in MacKinnon's sense of "as." They were eccentric because they failed to fit into roles which men had contrived for them to fill, and because there were as yet no other roles. For roles require a community—a web of social expectations and habits which define the role in question. The community may be small, but, like a club as opposed to a convocation, or a new species as opposed to a few atypical mutant members of an old species, it only exists insofar as it is self-sustaining and self-reproducing.[44]

To sum up for the last time: prophetic feminists like MacKinnon and Frye foresee a new being not only for women but for society. They foresee a society in which the male-female distinction is no longer of much interest. Feminists who are also pragmatists will not see the formation of such a society as the removal of social constructs and the restoration of the way things were always meant to be. They will see it as the production of a better set of social constructs than the ones presently available, and thus as the creation of a new and better sort of human being.

Notes

1 MacKinnon, "On Exceptionality," in her *Feminism Unmodified: Discourses on Life and Law* (Cambridge, MA: Harvard University Press, 1987), p. 77.

2 *Ibid.*, p. 71. See also Carolyn Whitbeck's point that "the category, lesbian, both in the minds of its male inventors and as used in male-dominated culture is that of a physiological female who is in other respects a stereotypical male." See "Love, Knowledge and Transformation" in *Hypatia Reborn*, ed. Azizah Y. al-Hibri and Margaret A. Simons (Bloomington: Indiana University Press, 1990), p. 220. Compare Marilyn Frye's reference to "that other fine and enduring patriarchal institution, Sex Equality" in *The Politics of Reality* (Trumansburg, NY: The Crossing Press, 1983), p. 108.

3 *Ibid.*, p. 38.

4 *Ibid.*, p. 73.

5 At p. 33, Frye remarks that "For subordination to be permanent and cost effective, it is necessary to create conditions such that the subordinated group acquiesces to some extent in the subordination."

Ideally, these will be conditions such that a member of the subordinate group who does not acquiesce will sound crazy. Frye suggests at p. 112 that a person's sounding crazy is a good indicator that you are oppressing that person. See also MacKinnon, *op. cit.*, p. 105: "Especially when you are part of a subordinated group, your own definition of your injuries is powerfully shaped by your assessment of whether you could get anyone to do anything about it, inducing anything official." E.g., a non-crazy claim to have been raped is one acceptable to those (usually males) in a position to offer support or reprisal. Only where there is a socially-accepted remedy can there have been a real (rather than crazily imagined) injury.

6 When Olympe de Gouges appealed in the name of women to The Declaration of the Rights of Men and Citizens, even the most revolution-minded of her male contemporaries thought she was crazy. When Canadian feminists argued, in the 1920s, that the word "persons" in an act specifying the conditions for being a Senator covered women as well as men, the Supreme Court of Canada decided that the word should not be so construed, because it never had been. (The Judicial Committee of the Privy Council, be it said, later ruled in the feminists' favor.)

7 I am quoting here from Samuel Scheffler's quotation from Hurley in his review of her *Natural Reasons* (Oxford: Oxford University Press, 1989) in the *London Review of Books*. I have not yet been able to locate the page from which Scheffler is quoting.

8 In a recent article on Rawls ("Reason and Feeling in Thinking about Justice," *Ethics* 99, p. 248), Susan Moller Okin points out that thinking in Rawls's original position is not a matter of thinking like a "disembodied nobody" but rather of thinking like lots of different people in turn—thinking from the point of view of "every 'concrete other' whom one might turn out to be." Hurley *(Natural Reasons, p.* 381) makes the same point. The historicity of justice—a historicity which Rawls has acknowledged in his papers of the 1980s—amounts to the fact that history keeps producing new sorts of "concrete others" whom one might turn out to be.

9 See the theme of "woman as partial man" in Whitbeck's "Theories of Sex Difference" in *Women and Values,* ed. Marilyn Pearsall (Belmont, CA: Wadsworth, 1986), pp. 34-50. This theme is developed in fascinating detail in Thomas Laqueur, *Making Sex: Body and Gender from the Greeks to Freud* (Cambridge, MA: Harvard University Press, 1990).

10 Michael Gross and Mary Beth Averill, in their "Evolution and Patriarchal Myths" (in *Discovering Reality,* ed. Sandra Harding and Merrill B. Hintikka) suggest that the term "struggle" is a specifically masculist way of describing evolution and ask, "Why not see nature as bounteous, rather than parsimonious, and admit that opportunity and cooperation are more likely to abet novelty, innovation and creation than are struggle and competition?" (p. 85). The question gives me pause, and I have no clear answer to it. All I have is the hunch that, with memes as with genes, tolerant pluralism will sooner or later, in the absence of interstellar travel, have to come terms with shortage of space for self-expression.

There is a more general point involved here, the one raised by Jo-Ann Pilardi's claim that Hegel, Freud and others "were burdened with a notion of identity which defines it as oppositional, one which was derived from the psychosocial development of male children." See "On the War Path and Beyond" in *Hypatia Reborn* (cited above, p. 12.) Just such a notion of identity is central to my claims in this paper, particularly to the claims about the possible benefits of feminist separatism in the paper's later pages. So I am employing what many feminist writers would consider specifically male assumptions. All I can say in reply is that the notion of identity as oppositional seems to me hard to eliminate from such books as Frye's—and especially from her discussion of feminist anger. Anger and opposition seem to me the root of most moral prophecy, and it is the prophetic aspect of feminism that I am emphasizing in this paper.

11 *Human Nature and Conduct (Middle Works*, vol. 14), p. 193. See also "Outlines of a Critical Theory of Ethics" *(Early Works*, vol. 3, p. 379): "Goodness is remoteness from badness. In one sense, goodness is based upon badness; that is, action is always based upon action good once, but bad if persisted in under changing circumstances."

12 MacKinnon, p. 126.

13 Suppose we define a moral abomination, with Jeffrey Stout, as something which goes against our sense of "the seams of our moral universe," one which crosses lines between, as he puts it, "the categories of our cosmology and our social structure" (Stout, *Ethics After Babel* [Boston: Beacon Press, p. 159]). Then the choice between a realist and pragmatist rhetoric is the choice between saying that moral progress gradually aligns these seams with the *real* seams, and saying that it is a matter of simultaneously reweaving and enlarging a fabric which is not intended to be congruent with an antecedent reality. Giving an example of such a seam, Stout says (p. 153), "The sharper the line between masculine and feminine roles and the greater the importance of that line in determining matters such as the division labor and the rules of inheritance, the more likely it is that sodomy will be abominated." Later he says (p. 158), "The question is not whether homosexuality is intrinsically abominable but rather what, all things considered, we should do with relevant categories of our cosmology and social structure." As with the abominableness of homosexual sodomy, so, we pragmatists think, with the abominableness of absence or presence of patriarchy. In all such cases, up to and including the abominableness of torturing people for the sheer pleasure of watching them writhe, pragmatists think that the question is not about intrinsic properties but about what we should do with the relevant categories—a question which boils down to descriptions we should use of what is going on.

14 MacKinnon, p. 50.

15 "Feminism and Postmodernism," *New Left Review*, Winter 1989, p. 12. For a somewhat more tempered account of the relation of postmodernism to feminism see Kate Soper, "Feminism, Humanism and Postmodernism," *Radical Philosophy* 55 (Summer 1990), pp. 11–17. In their "Social Criticism Without Philosophy: An Encounter Between Feminism and Postmodernism" (in *Universal Abandon?*, ed. Andrew Ross (Minneapolis: University of Minnesota Press, 1988), Nancy Fraser and Linda Nicholson argue that "a robust postmodern-feminist paradigm of social criticism without philosophy is possible" (p. 100). I of course agree, but I am less sure about the need for, and utility of, "social-theoretical analysis of large-scale inequalities" (p. 90) than are Fraser and Nicholson.

   This is because I am less sure than Fraser about the possibility that "the basic institutional framework of [our] society could be unjust" (Fraser, "Solidarity or Singularity?" in *Reading Rorty*, ed. Alan Malachowski [Oxford: Blackwell, 1990], p. 318), and hence about "the utility of a theory that could specify links among apparently discrete social problems via the basic institutional structure" (p. 319). I suspect my differences with Fraser are concrete and political rather than abstract and philosophical. She sees, and I do not see, attractive alternatives (more or less Marxist in shape) to such institutions as private ownership of the means of production and constitutional democracy, attractive alternatives to the traditional social-democratic project of constructing an egalitarian welfare state within the context of these two basic institutions. I am not sure whether our differences are due to Fraser's antifoundationalist theory hope (see note 17 below) or to my own lack of imagination.

16 *Ibid.*, p. 28. See Lovibond's reference at p. 12 to "remaking society along rational, egalitarian lines." The idea that egalitarianism is more rational than elitism, rational in a sense which provides reasons for action *not* based on contingent shared practices, is central to the thinking of most liberals who are also moral realists.

17 A rhetoric of "unmasking hegemony" presupposes the reality-appearance distinction which opponents of phallogocentrism claim to have set aside. Many self-consciously "postmodern" writers seem to me trying to have it both ways—to view masks as going all the way down while still making invidious comparisons between other people's masks and the way things will look when all the masks have been stripped off. These postmodernists continue to indulge the bad habits characteristic of those Marxists who insist that morality is a matter of class interest, and then add that everybody has a moral obligation to identify with the interests of a particular class. Just as "ideology" came to mean little more than "other people's ideas," so "product of hegemonic discourse" has come to mean little more than "product of other people's way of talking." I agree with Stanley Fish that much of what goes under the heading of "post-modernism" exemplifies internally inconsistent "antifoundationalist theory hope." See Fish, *Doing What Comes Naturally: Change, Rhetoric and the Practice of Theory in Literary and Legal Studies* (Durham: Duke University Press, 1989), pp. 346, 437–38.

18 I am not fond of the term "postmodernism" and was a bit startled (as presumably was MacIntyre) to find Lovibond saying that Lyotard, MacIntyre and I are "among the most forceful exponents of the arguments and values which constitute postmodernism within academic philosophy" (p. 5). Still, I recognize the similarities between our positions which lead Lovibond to group the three of us together. Some of these similarities are outlined by Fraser and Nicholson at pp. 85 ff. of the article cited in note 15.

19 *Ibid.*, p. 12.

20 MacKinnon, p. 86. See also pp. 50, 54, for the "postmodernist" suggestion that the quest for objectivity is a specifically masculist one.

21 We pragmatists are often told that we reduce moral disagreement to a mere struggle for power by denying the existence of reason, or human nature, conceived as something which provides a neutral court of appeal. We often rejoin that the need for such a court, the need for something ahistorical which will ratify one's claims, is itself a symptom of power-worship—of the conviction that unless something large and powerful is on one's side, one shouldn't bother trying.

22 Developing this point would take too long. Were more time and space available, I should argue that trying to integrate feminism into a general theory of oppression—a frequent reaction to the charge that feminists are oblivious to racial and economic injustice—is like trying to integrate Galilean physics into a general theory of scientific error. The latter attempt is as familiar as it is fruitless. The conviction that there is an interesting general theory about human beings or their oppression seems to me like the conviction that there is an interesting general theory about truth and our failure to achieve it. For the same reasons that transcendental terms like "true" and "good" are not susceptible of definition, neither error nor oppression has a single neck which a single critical slash might sever.

Maria Lugones is an example of a feminist theorist who sees a need for a general philosophical theory of oppression and liberation. She says, for example, that "the ontological or metaphysical possibility of liberation remains to be argued, explained, uncovered" ("Structure/Antistructure and Agency under Oppression," *Journal of Philosophy* 87 [October 1990], p. 502). I should prefer to stick to merely empirical possibilities of liberation. Although I entirely agree with Lugones about the need to "give up the unified self" (p. 503), I do not see this as a matter of ontology, but merely as a way of putting the familiar point that the same human being can contain different coherent sets of belief and desire—different roles, different personalities, etc.—correlated with the different groups to which he or she belongs or whose power he or she must acknowledge. A more important disagreement between us, perhaps, concerns the desirability of harmonizing one's various roles, self-images, etc., in a single unifying story about oneself. Such unification—the sort of thing which I describe below as overcoming splits— seems to me desirable. Lugones, on the other hand, urges the desirability of "experiencing oneself in the limen" (p. 506).

23 For a good example of this charge, see Jonathan Culler, *Framing the Sign: Criticism and its Institutions* (Oklahoma City: University of Oklahoma Press, 1988), p. 55: "... the humanities must make their way between, on the one hand, a traditional, foundationalist conception of their task and, on the other, the so-called 'new pragmatism' to which some critics of foundationalism have retreated. If philosophy is not a foundationalist discipline, argues Richard Rorty, then it is simply engaged in a conversation; it tells stories, which succeed simply by their success. Since there is no standard or reference point outside the system of one's beliefs to appeal to, critical arguments and theoretical reflections can have no purchase on these beliefs or the practices informed by them. Ironically, then, the claim that philosophers and theoreticians tell stories, which originates as a critique of ideology... becomes a way of protecting a dominant ideology and its professionally successful practitioners from the scrutiny of argument, by deeming that critique can have no leverage against ordinary beliefs, and that theoretical arguments have no consequences. This pragmatism, whose complacency seems altogether appropriate to the Age of Reagan, subsists only by a theoretical argument of the kind it in principle opposes, as an ahistorical 'preformism': what one does must be based on one's beliefs, but since there are no foundations outside the system of one's beliefs, the only thing that could logically make one change a belief is something one already believes."

Culler is right in saying that we pragmatists hold the latter view, but wrong in suggesting that we think that *logical* changes in belief are the only respectable ones. What I have called "creative misuses" of language are *causes* to change one's belief, even if not *reasons* to change them. See the discussion of Davidson on metaphor in various papers in my *Objectivity, Relativism and Truth* (Cambridge: Cambridge University Press, 1991) for more on this cause-reason distinction, and for the claim that most moral and intellectual progress is achieved by non-"logical" changes in belief. Culler is one of the people I had in mind in note 17 above—the people who want to hang on to the primacy of logic (and thus of "theoretical reflection" and "critique") while abandoning logocentrism. I do not think this can be done.

Culler's charge can be found in many other authors, e.g., Joseph Singer, "Should Lawyers Care About Philosophy?", *Duke Law Journal* 1989, p. 1752: "...Rorty...has marginalized the enterprise of philosophy, thereby depriving pragmatism of any critical bite." On my view, pragmatism bites other philosophies, but not social problems as such—and so is as useful to fascists like Mussolini and conservatives like Oakeshott as it is to liberals like Dewey. Singer thinks that I have "identified reason with the status quo" and defined "truth as coextensive with the prevailing values in a society" (p. 1763). These claims are, I think, the result of the same inference as Culler draws in the passage quoted above. Both Singer and

Culler want philosophy to be capable of setting goals, and not to be confined to the merely ancillary role I describe in note 26 below.

24 See Putnam's *Representation and Reality* (Cambridge, MA: MIT Press, 1988), pp. 114-15, for the passages cited. See also Robert Brandom's formulation of "phenomenalism about truth" as the view that "being true is to be understood as being *properly* taken-true (believed)." Brandom says that what is of most interest about the classical pragmatist stories (Peirce, James) is "the dual commitment to a normative account of claiming or believing [Bain's and Peirce's account of belief as a rule for action] that does not lean on a supposedly explanatory antecedent notion of truth, and the suggestion that truth can then be understood phenomenalistically, in terms of features of these independently characterized takings-true." See Brandom, "Pragmatism, Phenomenalism, Truth Talk," *Midwest Studies in Philosophy* 12 (1988), p. 80. Brandom (as well as Davidson and I) would agree with Putnam that "truth does not transcend use" but I think all three of us might be puzzled by Putnam's further claim that "whether an epistemic situation is any good or not depends on whether many different statements are true." This seems to me like saying that whether a person is wealthy or not depends on how much money she has.

25 Joseph Singer, in the article cited in note 23, praises Elizabeth Spelman for "using the tools of philosophy to promote justice," and suggests that one such use is to show that "the categories and forms of discourse we use... have important consequences in channeling our attention in particular directions." Surely it is no disrespect to Spelman's achievement, nor to philosophy, to insist that it takes no special tools, no special philosophical expertise, to make and develop this latter point? The use of notions like "powerful methods" and "precise analytical instruments" in the rhetorics of analytic philosophy and of Marxism constitutes, to my mind, misleading advertising. An unfortunate result of such mystification is that whenever a philosophy professor like Spelman or me does something useful, it is assumed that we were doing something distinctively philosophical, something philosophers are specially trained to do. If we then fail to go on to do something else which needs to be done, we will usually be charged with using an obsolete and inadequate set of philosophical tools.

26 See Dewey's "From Absolutism to Experimentalism" in *The Later Works of John Dewey*, vol. 5 (Carbondale: Southern Illinois University Press, 1984), p. 160: "Meantime a chief task of those who call themselves philosophers is to help get rid of the useless lumber that blocks our highways of thought, and strive to make straight and open the paths that lead to the future." There is a lot of this road-clearing rhetoric in Dewey, rhetoric which is continuous with Locke's description of himself as an under-laborer to those who seemed to him the prophetic spirits of his time—corpuscularian scientists like Newton and Boyle. Both metaphors suggest that the philosophers' job is to drag outdated philosophy out of the way of those who are displaying unusual courage and imagination.

Singer, in the article cited in note 23, says that "Dewey, unlike Rorty, saw the problems of philosophy as inseparable from the problems of collective life," and that "by separating philosophy from justice, Rorty's vision reinforces existing power relations..." (p. 1759). It is true that Dewey often speaks as if social problems and philosophical problems were interlocked, but I should argue that all these passages can best be interpreted in the road-clearing sense I have just suggested. Dewey never, I think, saw pragmatism in the way in which Marxists saw dialectical materialism—as a philosophical key which unlocks the secrets of history or of society.

27 This and the previous quote are from Frye, p. 80.

28 MacKinnon, p. 221. Cp. 137.

29 "Philosophy and Democracy," *The Middle Works of John Dewey*, vol. 11, p. 145.

30 To use an analogy suggested by Charlotte Perkins Gilman's poem "Similar Cases," it is as if one said to the creatures which were eventually to become the mammals: "Do not try to imitate the ways in which those larger and more powered fish cope with their environment. Bather, find ways of doing things which will help you find a new environment." ("Similar Cases" is perhaps most easily available at pp. 363-64 of Ann Lane, *To Herland and Beyond: The Life and Works of Charlotte Perkins Gilman* [New York: Pantheon, 1990]. The point of the poem is that if it were true that, as feminists were often told, "you can't change your nature" we should have had neither biological nor cultural evolution.)

31 *The Politics of Reality,* p. 154.

32 As I suggested earlier, it is easy to bring together Dewey's claim that, in philosophy, "real" is as evaluative a term as "good" with "postmodernist" views—for example, those found in Chris Weedon's book *Feminist Practice and Poststructuralist Theory.* Pretty much the only difference between Weedon's criticism of the philosophical tradition and Dewey's is one which also separates contemporary pragmatists like Putnam and Davidson from Dewey—the use of "language" instead of Dewey's word "experience" as the name of what it is important for the oppressed to reshape. Weedon, like Putnam and Davidson and unlike Dewey, is what Willfrid Sellars called a "psychological nominalist"—someone who believes that all awareness is a linguistic affair. At p. 32 she says "Like Althusserian Marxism, feminist poststructuralism makes the primary assumption that it is language which enables us to think, speak and give meaning to the world around us. Meaning and consciousness do not exist outside language." The difference with Dewey has few consequences, however, since Dewey would have heartily agreed with Weedon (p. 131) that one should not view language "as a transparent tool for expressing facts" but as "the material in which particular, often conflicting versions of facts are constructed."

   The only real advantage to psychological nominalism for feminists, perhaps, is that it replaces hard-to-discuss (I am tempted to say "metaphysical") questions about whether women have a different *experience* than men, or Africans a different experience than Europeans, or about whether the experience of upper-class African women is more like that of lower-class European men than that of upper-class European women, with easier-to-discuss (more evidently empirical) questions about what *language* these various groups of people use to justify their actions, exhibit their deepest hopes and fears, etc. Answers to the latter questions are jumping-off places for practical suggestions about different languages which they might use, or might have used. I share MacKinnon's skepticism about the idea that "viewpoints have genitals" and Sandra Harding's skepticism about the utility of notions like "woman's morality," "woman's experience," and "woman's standpoint." See Harding's "The Curious Coincidence of Feminine and African Moralities: Challenges for Feminist Theory," in *Women and Moral Theory,* ed. Eva Kitray and Diana Meyers (Totowa, NJ: Rowman and Littlefield, 1987), pp. 296-315.

   Although most of the doctrines (e.g., essentialism, Cartesian individualism, moral universalism) which Weedon attributes to "liberal humanism" are doctrines Dewey (a notorious liberal humanist) also targeted, Weedon does not seem able to eschew a longing for what Mary Hawkesworth calls "a successor science which can refute once and for all the distortions of androcentrism." See Hawkesworth, "Knowers, Knowing, Known: Feminist Theory and the Claims of Truth" in *Feminist Theory in Practice and Process,* ed. Micheline R. Malson, et al. (Chicago: University of Chicago Press, 1989), p. 331. But once you put aside universalism, you should neither hope for knock-down refutations nor talk about "distortion." Hawkesworth goes on to criticize Harding for saying that "Feminist analytical categories *should* be unstable at this moment in history" (Harding, "The Instability of the Analytical Categories of Feminist Theory," in the same collection, at p. 19). But prophecy and unstable categories go together, and Harding's claim chimes with many of the passages I have been quoting from Frye. Harding's further claim that "we [feminists] should learn how to regard the instabilities themselves as valuable resources" is one that Dewey would have cheered.

33 Frye, pp. 48-49.

34 I am too ignorant about the history of feminism—about how long and how continuous the feminist tradition has been—to speculate about when things began to change.

35 Rich, *On Lies, Secrets, and Silence: Selected Prose 1966-1978* (New York and London: Norton, 1979), p. 40.

36 The continued attractions of this club in our own cynical century are evidenced by the fact that, even as Bernard Shaw was having Candida make fun of Marchbanks, Joyce had Stephen Dedalus write that he would "forge in the smithy of my soul the uncreated conscience of my race." Joyce was not making fun of Stephen, and even Shaw admitted that Candida "does not know the secret in the poet's heart."

37 "What might, in a male writer—a Thoreau, let us say, or a Christopher Smart or William Blake—seem a legitimate strangeness, a unique intention, has been in one of our two major poets [Dickinson] devalued into a kind of naivete, girlish ignorance, feminine lack of professionalism, just as the poet herself has been made into a sentimental object. ('Most of us are half in love with this dead girl,' confesses Archibald MacLeish. Dickinson was fifty-five when she died.)" (Rich, p. 167).

38 Rich, p. 17.

39 Frye, p. 106n.

40 This is the sort of ineffable horror which creates a sense of moral abomination (at, e.g., inter-caste marriage), and thus furnishes the intuitions which one tries to bring into reflective equilibrium with one's principles. To view moral abominableness as capable of being produced or erased by changing the language taught to the young is the first step toward a non-universalist conception of moral progress.

41 To realize how far away such a future is, consider Eve Kosofsky Sedgwick's point that we shall only do justice to gays when we become as indifferent to whether our children turn out gay or straight as we are to whether they become doctors or lawyers. Surely she is right, and yet how many parents at the present time can even imagine such indifference? For the reasons suggested by Stout (see note 13 above), I suspect that neither sexism nor homophobia can vanish while the other persists.

42 Pragmatists need not deny that true sentences are always true (as I have, unhappily, suggested in the past that they might—notably in my *"Waren die Gesetze Newtons schon vor Newton wahr?" Jahrbuch des Wissenschaftskollegs zu Berlin,* 1987). Stout (*Ethics After Babel,* chapter 11) rightly rebukes me for these suggestions, and says that pragmatists should agree with everybody else that "Slavery is absolutely wrong" has always been true—even in periods when this sentence would have sounded crazy to everybody concerned, even the slaves (who hoped that their fellow-tribespeople would return in force and enslave their present masters). All that pragmatists need is the claim that this sentence is not *made* true by something other than the beliefs which we would use to support it—and, in particular, not by something like The Nature of Human Beings.

43 I have criticized realists' claims to explain predictive success by truth in Part I of my *Objectivity, Relativism and Truth* (Cambridge: Cambridge University Press, 1991). A related point—that the success of a true theory needs just as much historico-sociological explanation as the success of a false one—is made by Barry Barnes and other members of the so-called "Edinburgh school" of sociology of science.

44 It may seem that the view I am offering is the one which Frye rejects under the name of "the institutional theory of personhood"—the theory that, as she puts it, "'person' denotes a social and institutional role and that one may be allowed or forbidden to adopt that role" (p. 49). She says that this view "must be attractive to the phallist, who would fancy the power to create persons." But I do not want to say that men have the power to make full persons out of women by an act of grace, in the way in which sovereigns have the power to make nobles out of commoners. On the contrary, I would insist that men could not do this if they tried, for they are as much caught as are women in the linguistic practices which make it hard for women to be full persons. The utopia I foresee, in which these practices are simply forgotten, is not one which could be attained by an act of condescension on the part of men, any more than an absolute monarch could produce an egalitarian utopia by simultaneously ennobling all her subjects.

NANCY FRASER
(B. 1947)

A professor of philosophy at Northwestern and the author of *Unruly Practices: Power, Discourse and Gender in Contemporary Social Theory* (1985), Nancy Fraser attempts to forge a "democratic-socialist-feminist pragmatism" through critical readings of such writers as Jurgen Habermas, Michel Foucault, Julia Kristeva, Luce Irigary, and Richard Rorty. Agreeing with Rorty's basic "zero degree pragmatism"—an "antiessentialism with respect to fundamental concepts like truth and reason, human nature and morality"—she nevertheless criticizes Rorty for too sharply separating the public and the private, continuing a separation that has had momentous and oppressive consequences for women.

In *Unruly Practices* Fraser attacks Habermas for ignoring the power relations—and specifically the "gender oppression"—within the family, for taking political and economic relations to occur only in the public sphere outside the family. She finds in Rorty a more solitary or "Romantic" conception of "abnormal discourse" and a more social or Kuhnian conception, and also criticizes him for focusing on the former, for developing a selfish, anti-social, and aestheticized conception of creativity. Rorty's conception of theory, she charges, becomes "pure *poiesis*" while politics becomes "pure *techne*." Fraser wants instead "a radical democratic politics in which immanent critique and transfigurative desire mingle with one another." Rather than one great solidarity from which one retreats to one's private inner sphere, she sees the public as a collection of "multiple, competing solidarities," struggling over the determination of "cultural meanings and social identities as well as...more narrowly traditional political stakes like electoral offices and legislation."

Fraser's feminist pragmatist—like Cornel West's "prophetic pragmatist"—is an engaged intellectual who sees social change deriving more from social movements than from extraordinary individuals. Fraser detects in Rorty's new essay on "Feminism and Pragmatism" both an important new turn in his philosophy in which the sharp public/private separation begins to break down, and "an excessive preoccupation...with the figure of the feminist as prophet and outcast." She agrees with Rorty that feminists are engaged in "creating new moral identities and sensibilities rather than in realizing or discovering latent or pre-existing ones," but she is determined to put "a more sociological, institutional, and collective spin on these ideas," thereby "achieving a more consistent and thoroughgoing pragmatism."

FROM IRONY TO PROPHECY TO POLITICS:
A RESPONSE TO RICHARD RORTY

NANCY FRASER

It's a great pleasure to participate in this symposium. Actually, I believe that this is an occasion of considerable historical significance, since it is the first time, to my knowledge, in this era of postwar professionalized American philosophy, that a renowned male philosopher has elected to address the subject of feminism and indeed to make it the subject of a major philosophical address. The importance of this should not be underestimated. In a context in which feminist philosophers are still struggling to win a measure of recognition of the legitimacy of our enterprise—recognition that feminist scholars in disciplines like history, anthropology, and literature already enjoy—Richard Rorty's decision to address the subject of "Feminism and Pragmatism" can only have a salutary effect. It cannot but create more space in the discipline for feminist philosophy and promote a wider hearing for our work. It is even possible for me to fantasize today, as I don't think I could have a year ago, that in the not very distant future a Tanner Lecture on feminist philosophy will be delivered *by* a feminist philosopher and a woman.

Since Professor Rorty is breaking new ground as a male philosopher lecturing on this subject, he has not had the benefit of any role models to help him develop a rhetorical posture or stance. He is not, after all, merely speaking *about* feminism; he is also speaking *to* feminists, so he has had to find a way to address us. When I first read his lecture I had the impression that he was addressing us as a suitor with a marriage proposal; much of his paper is devoted to trying to persuade us that we'd be much better off with him than with his universalist and realist rivals. This reading of Rorty's lecture in terms of the generic conventions of heterosexual courtship had its pleasurable elements, to be sure—the pleasure that comes from being wooed—but it could not but be troubling to a feminist sensibility that, as Rorty himself notes, is in the process of constructing itself as the independent variable instead of always defining itself in relation to a man. Just as I was brooding over how a feminist should respond to a proposal from a powerful male philosopher, it occurred to me that there was another possible way to read his lecture. Perhaps what is being proposed is not at all a traditional heterosexual relationship but precisely the reverse. After all, isn't Rorty, in his characteristically modest way, suggesting that he, the pragmatist philosopher, will be the junior partner in the alliance, that he'll confine himself to the relatively unimportant role of support work, clearing away a few conceptual roadblocks here and there, providing a few handy argumentative tools from his bag of tricks, while we feminists will be out on the main stage of history, doing the truly important work of changing language, changing culture, and changing the world? On this reading Rorty is in effect offering to do the housework so that we can be freed for world-historical activity in the public sphere.

Now, this really does look like an attractive proposition. But many of us have learned the hard way that when men offer to help with housework there are frequently hidden costs. In the case of Rorty's proposal, the hidden cost is the implication that feminists—Marilyn Frye or myself, for example—are not philosophers. Granted, we're something bigger, grander, more important—prophets; but I don't know of any universities with departments of prophecy in which we might be gainfully employed and tenured as prophets. So I can't help but think that the division of labor between pragmatism and feminism that Rorty is proposing is yet another way of putting women on a pedestal.

In my response, I want to examine Rorty's characterization of feminist practice as linguistic innovation in the mode of prophecy. And in order to do that, it helps to look first at the role that the idea of linguistic innovation played in his earlier writing.

In a series of essays written in the mid-to-late 1980s, including those collected in *Contingency, Irony, and Solidarity,* the series in the *London Review of Books,* and others scattered in various scholarly journals, Rorty elaborated what many of us found to be a surprisingly dichotomous view of cultural and discursive space. He mapped his earlier distinction from *Philosophy and the Mirror of Nature* between normal discourse and abnormal discourse onto a new distinction between public life and private life. He cast public life, and by implication politics, as the sphere of utility and solidarity, in which it would be irresponsible to forsake the established language of "the community" for the sublime heights of poetic transgression and originality. In contrast, he cast private life as an aesthetic sphere in which poetic invention could be allowed free rein. In private life, sublimity, irony, and individual self-fashioning were appropriate; the strong poet or ironist could disaffiliate from the community and remake himself by redescribing things, without thereby endangering the practical business of social reform and social-problem-solving.

There are several things worth noting about this conception. First, it made linguistic innovation the prerogative of the private aesthete or strong poet. And it cast that activity as an oedipal agon in which a son struggles to overcome "the anxiety of influence," to outstrip his poetic predecessors or cultural fathers, so as in effect to father himself. Thus, the story has a deeply masculinist subtext, and it is individualistic and aestheticizing. Moreover, once linguistic innovation is cast in these terms, it begins to look politically dangerous. If redescription is essentially an expression of the will to power, then better to keep it safely contained in "the private sphere" lest it endanger the public safety.

What this means, however, is that there was no place in Rorty's essays of the 1980s for linguistic innovation that is collective as opposed to individual and political as opposed to aesthetic. Rather, redescription was cast as the very antithesis of collective action and political practice. With linguistic innovation thus aestheticized, oedipalized, and narcissized, there could be no legitimate cultural politics, no genuinely political struggle for cultural hegemony. There could only be oedipal revolts of genius sons against genius fathers.

This conception took its toll, too, on the shape of the public sphere and on the interpretation of politics in Rorty's essays of this period. The public sphere became a space for normal discourse, where all the logical space needed for moral deliberation was already available and mapped out. Politics became overly communitarian and solidary, a matter of everyone pulling together in a shared discourse to solve a common set of problems. The assumption underlying *this* conception was that there were no deep social cleavages, no pervasive axes of dominance and exploitation that could fracture "the community." Abnormal challenges to the going political vocabulary therefore had no possible foothold and no possible point.

The upshot of this way of mapping cultural space was to effect some significant exclusions. There was no place in Rorty's 1980s framework for political motivations for the invention of new idioms, no place for new idioms invented in order to overcome the enforced silencing or muting of a disadvantaged social group. Similarly, there was no place for collective subjects who engaged in abnormal discourse, no place for social movements that contested dominant discourses. Finally, there was no place for nonstandard interpretations of social needs and collective concerns. Whoever was using a nonhegemonic vocabulary had to be talking about something private. In sum, there was no place in this framework for genuinely innovative political redescriptions rooted in oppositional political solidarities. There was no room for what some of us knew actually to exist: the contemporary feminist movement.

That at least was Rorty's view until yesterday. What to me is the most significant thing about yesterday's lecture is the way all those earlier dichotomies have been scrambled. When Rorty takes up the question of feminism, the oppositions between the public and the private, the community and the individual, the political and the aesthetic are exploded. In feminism, in his account, we meet a discursive practice that involves far-reaching redescriptions of social life and thus has all the marks of the sublime, the abnormal, and the poetic, yet is simultaneously tied to the collective political enterprise of overcoming oppression and restructuring society. Thus, in the case of feminism, the enterprise of remaking oneself through redescription is not opposed to political trans-formation but is rather part and parcel of it.

It seems to me, then, that the effort to think about feminism has had a major impact on the structure of Rorty's thought. It is an instance of the sort of paradigm-breaking transformation that feminists have long said must occur whenever androcentric modes of understanding are forced to confront the problematic of gender. I would summarize the transformation in Rorty's thought via the slogan "From Irony to Politics."

Or at least I would *if* the transformation in question had been fully carried through. In fact, I believe that yesterday's lecture does not yet bring to fruition the full implica-tions of the implied paradigm shift I have been describing. Instead of taking us all the way "From Irony to Politics," Rorty only takes us part of the way, "From Irony to Prophecy."

I am suggesting that we can read a kind of failure of nerve in Rorty's excessive preoc-cupation in this lecture with the figure of the feminist as prophet and outcast, the solitary eccentric or member of a small embattled separatist club, huddled together spinning a web of words as a charm to keep from going crazy. I do not mean to suggest that this image is wholly at odds with my experience. I can remember department meet-ings, even fairly recent ones, at which I have felt exactly this way. And while it was principally radical feminists who have cultivated this self-image—one thinks especially of Mary Daly in addition to the writers cited by Rorty— I think all feminists, including socialist-feminists like myself, have felt this way at times.

However, it is still the case that in 1990 feminists are not a ragtag band or exclusive club of witches and crazies. Rather, we constitute a large heterogeneous social movement with a presence in virtually every corner of American life. So it is quite distorting to pre-sent the feminist enterprise so exclusively in such terms. It is as if the individualistic and aestheticizing qualities that Rorty previously associated with linguistic innovation as pri-vate irony and oedipal poetry have come back in a subterranean way to color his account of feminism, the very phenomenon that seemed capable of exploding those associations.

I would like to suggest an alternative way of characterizing the feminist project and feminist movements, a way that is more consistently pragmatic than Rorty's. For my disagreement with him is a disagreement within pragmatism. I, too, reject moral realism and universalism in favor of the historicist view that feminists are engaged in creating new moral identities and sensibilities rather than in realizing or discovering latent or pre-existing ones. And I, too, see the remaking of language as central to this enterprise.

So my difference with Rorty boils down to my wanting to put a more sociological, institutional, and collective spin on these ideas and to divest his account of its individu-alistic, aestheticizing, and depoliticizing residues. This, as I said, is tantamount to achieving a more consistent and thoroughgoing pragmatism. Whereas Rorty has made the significant but still incomplete move "From Irony to Prophecy," I want to go the rest of the way "From Prophecy to Feminist Politics."

Let me suggest a couple of places where one can go further in this direction than Rorty has gone. First, consider the question of creating a "moral identity for women as women." Rorty accepts the view, held by some radical feminists, that until feminists began creating such an identity, the term "woman" could only name a disability, not a moral identity that anyone would want to claim. Now, as it turns out, this is empirically false. Thanks to feminist scholarship, we now know quite a lot about the cultural construction of womanhood in various periods as a moral identity. One need only think of Victorian ideologies of "the cult of pure womanhood," which were premised on the apparently positive view that women had a more refined moral sensibility than men, but which glorified domesticity and thereby restricted women's activity. Here we have a moral identity in which a superficially flattering characterization of femininity merely adorned a disability. But the story does not end there. On the contrary, the originally disabling notion of women's moral superiority was soon appropriated by some middle-class and elite women and transformed into a springboard and platform for reformist activity in the public sphere on behalf of causes such as abolitionism and women's suffrage. These women in effect redeployed a traditional, confining female moral identity precisely in order to expand their field of action. They thereby turned a disability into an enabling identity, an identity one could want to claim.

This example belies Rorty's claim that women have never spoken or acted "as women" and that there are no traditions of female culture for us to draw on and to reconstruct. That was an early radical feminist view that is now largely discredited. Most feminists today, in contrast, are more willing to entertain another approach, which involves retrieving and revaluing marginalized traditions of women's power and agency that androcentric scholars have neglected and denigrated.

If it turns out that there are usable traditions in which the term "woman" has figured as a positive moral identity, then we will need another way of characterizing the innovation of feminist movements. Perhaps we will want to say that what feminism has accomplished is the transformation of *feminine* moral identities into feminist moral identities. Or perhaps we will say that feminism transformed the term "woman" from an *individual moral* identity into a *collective political* identity, a banner around which we can join in together and behind which we can march.

Rorty is right, in my view, that this is more a matter of creating women than of trying to describe women more accurately. And he is also right that seeing the feminist project in such terms can help avoid an essentialist view of "woman" as an ahistorical natural kind. However, what he does not see is that this also opens the lid of a big can of political worms. Out of all the available candidates, *which* new descriptions will count as "taking the viewpoint of women *as* women"? *Which* women will be empowered to impose their "semantic authority" on the rest of us?

This is no mere academic question but a burning political issue within the feminist movement today. It has turned out that every attempt to specify any content for "the point of view of women as women" has ended up privileging the characteristics or sensibilities of some specific group of women, usually the educated white middle-class heterosexual women who have the cultural capital to generate and disseminate relatively authoritative descriptions. Every attempt, therefore, has been persuasively criticized for failing to constitute a usable political identity for *all* women. So, we have seen a dizzying succession of proposals for defining "the point of view of women as women," followed by an equally dizzying succession of critiques. The upshot of this is that many feminists now reject the very idea that there can be such a thing as a "viewpoint of women *as* women" and are looking for alternative conceptions and models of political affiliation and solidarity. Thus, while the idea of constructing an identity for women "*as* women" was a plausible initial response to the discovery that the supposedly human identities constructed by men were actually androcentric, it has not proved a workable political tool. The reason is that feminism is at base not an exclusive club of prophets, but a mass democratic social movement.

This brings me to a second point at which Rorty's attempt to pragmatize feminism ends up individualizing and depoliticizing it. He is certainly right that only linguistic communities or groups can sustain and regularize new descriptions, but the examples he uses to illustrate the point end up working against it. The club of female poets he imagines can only be a small, elite affair, while the separatist community tends toward inward-directedness as opposed to outward-looking political struggle: it also tends at times, alas, toward an authoritarian stress on "correctness." A better example, I think, is the consciousness-raising group, that small-scale, democratic, collective enterprise of renaming the world that suddenly appeared and spread like wildfire across the American scene in the late 1960s and early-to-mid 1970s. In fact, it was in consciousness-raising groups that many of the most important feminist redescriptions were gestated: "sexism," "sexual harassment," "marital rape," "date rape," "the double shift"—these are perhaps the best feminist examples of the ways in which renaming things facilitates new moral assessments of them and mobilizes new social movements and collectivities. But these were the products less of individual self-fashioning or poetizing than of the collective practice of consciousness-raising. In fact, consciousness-raising represents major linguistic innovation not only at the level of the meanings it has generated, but also at the level of the invention and institutionalization of a new language game or discursive practice. Informed by the democratic aspiration of empowering women to speak for themselves, consciousness-raising helped transform the nature of private life, public life, and their relation to one another.

One could also speak of the institution over the last twenty years in the United States of a feminist counterpublic sphere, a network of bookstores, journals, film and video distribution networks, conferences, festivals, local meeting places, and the like. This concept of counterpublic sphere, with its institutional and sociological dimension and its outward-looking agitational thrust, better captures the political character of the feminist movement than does Rorty's image of the separatist community or club. It also links feminism as a discursive enterprise to the best of the democratic tradition. At best, the feminist counterpublic sphere is a discursive space where "semantic authority" is constructed collectively, critically, and democratically, rather than imposed via prophetic pronouncements from mountaintops.

I can sum up the thrust of my remarks as follows. By teasing out some connections between feminism and pragmatism, Rorty's lecture represents the beginnings of a major new positive development in his own thought. It also represents a potential contribution to feminist theory. But Rorty fails fully to develop the political implications of his insight. We need to continue on the path "From Irony to Prophecy to Politics."

HILARY PUTNAM
(B. 1926)

When Richard Rorty calls Putnam, who is the Walter Beverly Pearson Professor of Modern Mathematics and Mathematical Logic at Harvard, "the most important contemporary philosopher to call himself a pragmatist," he alludes not only to Putnam's leading role in contemporary discussions of mind, language, logic, and knowledge but to his increasing use of the thought of Dewey and James. Putnam's publications include three volumes of collected papers: *Mathematics, Matter and Method* (1975), *Mind, Language, and Reality* (1975), and *Realism and Reason* (1983); and five books with important pragmatist themes: *Reason, Truth, and History* (1981), *The Many Faces of Realism* (1987), *Realism With a Human Face* (1990), *Renewing Philosophy* (1992), and *Words and Life.* (1994).

Central to Putnam's new pragmatism is something resembling what James called "humanism"—expressed in the phrase Putnam appropriates from James: "the trail of the human serpent is over all." In the two sections from his 1987 Carus lectures *The Many Faces of Realism* reprinted below—"Is There Still Anything to Say About Reality and Truth?" and "Reasonableness as a Fact and as a Value"—Putnam defends a view he had once called "internal realism" and now wishes to call "pragmatic realism." Following Kant as well as James, Putnam's pragmatic realism emphasizes the degree to which we are in touch with the world—as much because it resists us as because it bears our imprint.

Putnam calls himself a realist ("with a small 'r'"), but he opposes "metaphysical" or "scientific" realism ("Realism with a big 'R'"), according to which the world is not really colored or solid, but only a swarm of particles whose correct description is given by the language of mathematical physics. "Why," Dewey had asked, "should what gives tragedy, comedy, and poignancy to life, be excluded from things?" Putnam makes no such exclusion, and finds among "the philosophers who in one way or another stand in the Neo-Kantian tradition—James, Husserl, Wittgenstein—[the view that] common-sense tables and chairs and sensations and electrons are *equally real.…*"

Among the "many faces" of Putnam's realism are what may be called "values." In "Reasonableness as a Fact and as a Value," Putnam argues that a statement may be warranted or reasonable to believe "even though we cannot specify an experiment (or data) such that were we to perform it (or were we to collect them) we would be able to confirm or disconfirm the hypothesis to an extent which would command the assent of all educated and unbiased people." We can't do this in science, as Kuhn has taught us, nor in history, nor in morality. We can't produce "an argument to show that Hitler is a bad man *that would convince Hitler himself,*" but that does not show that morality is "all relative"—any more than the fact that there are well-educated creationists who are not convinced by Darwinian theory shows that biology is "all relative."

"What is wrong with relativist views," Putnam writes, "(apart from their horrifying irresponsibility), is that they do not at all correspond to how we think and to how we shall continue to think." Like Wittgenstein, Putnam retains a strong sense of and allegiance to the forms of ordinary human life and to what they show about our bedrock beliefs: "Our *lives* show that we believe that there are more and less warranted beliefs about political contingencies, about historical interpretations, etc." The heart of James's and Dewey's pragmatism, Putnam maintains, lies in their taking such human activity seriously, in "their insistence on the supremacy of the agent point of view. If we find that we must take a certain point of view, use a certain 'conceptual system,' when we are engaged in practical activity, in the widest sense of 'practical activity,' then we must not simultaneously advance the claim that it is not really 'the way things are in themselves.'"

Putnam's thinking about political and social philosophy under the banner of pragmatism is displayed in "A Reconsideration of Deweyan Democracy," the second selection reprinted below. In Putnam's hands as in Rorty's, pragmatism becomes a vigorous and formidable mediator among contemporary positions in social and political philosophy. Putnam's central concern is the Deweyan claim that "democracy is a precondition for the full application of intelligence to solving social problems." In the course of considering this question Putnam presents: (a) a Peircean critique of Alasdair MacIntyre's subjection to "the method of authority" and neglect of experiment; (b) a powerful statement of an argument for democracy based on the work of Jürgen Habermas and Karl Otto Apel; and (c) an exposition of Dewey's empirical—rather than, as in Habermas, "transcendental"—justification for democracy: it is "better than all the other systems which have actually been tried."

Dewey, Putnam reminds us, is no apologist for the *status quo*, but a radical for whom education plays the role that revolution did for Marx. Deweyan education and Deweyan democracy both proceed from the ground up. "The social welfare," Putnam quotes

Dewey as writing, "can be advanced only by means which enlist the positive interest and active energy of those to be benefited or 'improved.'"

Putnam faults Dewey neither for his justification of democracy nor for his transformative philosophy and politics, but rather for his neglect of "individual existential choices." Finding William James more attuned to such issues than Dewey—especially the James of "The Will to Believe" (1897)—Putnam searches for an account of human life that does justice both to our necessary entanglements with others and to our isolation, as "on a mountain pass in the midst of whirling snow and blinding mist."

THE MANY FACES OF REALISM

HILARY PUTNAM

Is There Still Anything to Say About Reality and Truth?

The man on the street, Eddington reminded us, visualizes a table as "solid"—that is, as *mostly* solid matter. But physics has discovered that the table is mostly empty space: that the distance between the particles is immense in relation to the radius of the electron or the nucleus of one of the atoms of which the table consists. One reaction to this state of affairs, the reaction of Wilfrid Sellars,[1] is to deny that there are tables at all as we ordinarily conceive them (although he chooses an ice cube rather than a table as his example). The commonsense conception of ordinary middle-sized material objects such as tables and ice cubes (the "manifest image") is simply *false* in Sellars's view (although not without at least some cognitive value—there are real objects that the "tables" and "ice cubes" of the manifest image "picture," according to Sellars, even if these real objects are not the layman's tables and ice cubes). I don't agree with this view of Sellars's, but I hope he will forgive me if I use it, or the phenomenon of its appearance on the philosophical scene, to highlight certain features of the philosophical debate about "realism."

First of all, this view illustrates the fact that Realism with a capital "R" doesn't always deliver what the innocent expect of it. If there is any appeal of Realism which is wholly legitimate it is the appeal to the commonsense feeling that *of course* there are tables and chairs, and any philosophy that tell us that there really aren't—that there are really only sense data, or only "texts," or whatever, is more than slightly crazy. In appealing to this commonsense feeling, Realism reminds me of the Seducer in the old-fashioned melodrama. In the melodramas of the 1890s the Seducer always promised various things to the Innocent Maiden, which he failed to deliver when the time came. In this case the Realist (the evil Seducer) promises common sense (the Innocent Maiden) that he will rescue her from her enemies (Idealists, Kantians and Neo-Kantians, Pragmatists, and the fearsome self-described "Irrealist" Nelson Goodman) who (the Realist says) want to deprive her of her good old ice cubes and chairs. Faced with this dreadful prospect, the fair Maiden naturally opts for the company of the commonsensical Realist. But when they have traveled together for a little while the "Scientific Realist" breaks the news that what the Maiden is going to get *isn't* her ice cubes and tables and chairs. In fact, all there *really* is—the Scientific Realist tells her over breakfast—is what 'finished science' will say there is—whatever that may be. She is left with a promissory note for She Knows Not What, and the assurance that even if there *aren't* tables and chairs, still there are some *Dinge an sich* that her manifest image (or her "folk physics," as some Scientific Realists put it) "picture." Some will say that the lady has been had.

Thus, it is clear that the name "Realism" can be claimed by or given to at least two very different philosophical attitudes (and, in fact, to many). The philosopher who claims that only scientific objects "really exist" and that much, if not all, of the commonsense world is mere "projection" claims to be a "realist," but so does the philosopher who insists that there *really are* chairs and ice cubes (and some of these ice cubes really are *pink*), and these two attitudes, these two images of the world, can lead to and have led to many different programs for philosophy.

Husserl[2] traces the first line of thought, the line that denies that there "really are" commonsense objects, back to Galileo, and with good reason. The present Western world-view depends, according to Husserl, on a new way of conceiving "external objects"—the way of mathematical physics. An external thing is conceived of as a con-geries of particles (by atomists) or as some kind of extended disturbance (in the seventeenth century, a "vortex," and later a collection of "fields"). Either way, the table in front of me (or the object that I "picture as" a table) is described by "mathematical for-mulas," as Husserl says. And this, he points out, is what above all came into Western thinking with the Galilean revolution: the idea of the "external world" as something whose true description, whose description "in itself," consists of mathematical formulas.

It is important to this way of thinking that certain familiar properties of the table—its size and shape and location—are "real" properties, describable, for example, in the lan-guage of Descartes' analytic geometry. Other properties, however, the so-called "secondary" properties, of which *color* is a chief example, are *not* treated as real properties in the same sense. No "occurrent" (non-dispositional) property of that swarm of mole-cules (or that space-time region) recognized in mathematical physics can be said to be what we all along called its *color*.

What about dispositional properties? It is often claimed that color is simply a function of *reflectancy*, that is, of the disposition of an object (or of the surface of an object) to selec-tively absorb certain wavelengths of incident light and reflect others. But this doesn't really do much for the reality of colors. Not only has recent research shown that this account is much too simple (because changes of reflectancy across edges turn out to play an important role in determining the colors we see), but reflectancy itself does not have one uniform physical explanation. A red star and a red apple and a reddish glass of colored water are red for quite different physical reasons. In fact, there may well be an infinite number of different physical conditions which could result in the disposition to reflect (or emit) red light and absorb light of other wavelengths. A dispositional property whose underlying non-dispositional "explanation" is so very non-uniform is simply incapable of being represented as a mathematical function of the dynamical variables. And these—the dynamical variables—are the parameters that this way of thinking treats as the "characteristics" of "external" objects.

Another problem[3] is that *hues* turn out to be much more subjective than we thought. In fact, any shade on the color chart in the green part of the spectrum will be classed as "standard green" by some subject—even if it lies at the extreme "yellow-green" end or the extreme "blue-green" end.

In sum, no "characteristic" recognized by this way of thinking—no "well-behaved function of the dynamical variables"—corresponds to such a familiar property of objects as *red* or *green*. The idea that there is a property all red objects have in common—the same in all cases—and another property all green objects have in common—the same in all cases—is a kind of illusion, on the view we have come more and more to take for granted since the age of Descartes and Locke.

However, Locke and Descartes did give us a sophisticated substitute for our pre-scientific notion of color; a substitute that has, perhaps, come to seem mere "post-scientific common sense" to most people. This substitute involves the idea of a sense datum (except that, in the seventeenth and eighteenth century vocabulary, sense data were referred to as "ideas" or "impressions"). The red sweater I see is not red in the way I thought it was (there is no "physical magnitude" which is its redness), but it does have a disposition (a Power, in the seventeenth and eighteenth century idiom) to affect me in a certain way—to cause me to have sense data. And these, the sense data, do truly have a simple, uniform, non-dispositional sort of "redness."

This is the famous picture, the dualistic picture of the physical world and its primary qualities, on the one hand, and the mind and its sense data, on the other, that philosophers have been wrangling over since the time of Galileo, as Husserl says. And it is Husserl's idea—as it was the idea of William James, who influenced Husserl—that this picture is disastrous.

But why should we regard it as disastrous? It was once shocking, to be sure, but as I have already said it is by now widely accepted as "post-scientific common sense." What is *really* wrong with this picture?

For one thing, *solidity* is in much the same boat as color. If objects do not have color as they "naively" seem to, no more do they have solidity as they "naively" seem to.[4] It is this that leads Sellars to say that such commonsense objects as ice cubes do not really exist at all. What is our conception of a typical commonsense object if not of something solid (or liquid), which exhibits certain colors? What there really are, in Sellars's scientific metaphysics, are objects of mathematical physics, on the one hand, and "raw feels," on the other. This is precisely the picture I have just described as "disastrous"; it is the picture that denies precisely the common man's kind of realism, his realism about tables and chairs.

The reply to me (the reply a philosopher who accepts the post-Galilean picture will make) is obvious: "You are just nostalgic for an older and simpler world. This picture works; our acceptance of it is an inference to the best explanation. We cannot regard it as an objection to a view that it does not preserve everything that laymen once falsely believed."

If it is an inference to the best explanation, it is a strange one, however. How does the familiar explanation of what happens when I "see something red" go? The light strikes the object (say, a sweater), and is reflected to my eye. There is an image on the retina (Berkeley knew about images on the retina, and so did Descartes, even if the wave aspect of light was not well understood until much later). There are resultant nerve impulses (Descartes knew there was some kind of transmission along the nerves, even if he was wrong about its nature—and it is not clear we know its nature either, since there is again debate about the significance of chemical, as opposed to electrical, transmissions from neuron to neuron). There are events in the brain, some of which we understand thanks to the work of Hubel and Wiesel, David Marr, and others. And then—this is the mysterious part—there is somehow a "sense datum" or a "raw feel." *This* is an *explanation*?

An "explanation" that involves connections of a kind we do not understand at all ("nomological danglers," Herbert Feigl called them[5]) and concerning which we have not even the sketch of a theory is an explanation through something more obscure than the phenomenon to be explained. As has been pointed out by thinkers as different from one another as William James, Husserl, and John Austin, every single part of the sense datum story is supposition—theory—and theory of a most peculiar kind. Yet the epistemological role "sense data" are supposed to play by traditional philosophy required them to be what is "given," to be *what we are absolutely sure of independently of scientific theory*. The kind of scientific realism we have inherited from the seventeenth century has not lost all its prestige even yet, but it has saddled us with a disastrous picture of the world. It is high time we looked for a different picture.

Intrinsic Properties: Dispositions

I want to suggest that the problem with the "Objectivist" picture of the world (to use Husserl's term for this kind of scientific realism) lies deeper than the postulation of "sense data"; sense data are, so to speak, the visible symptoms of a systemic disease, like the pock marks in the case of smallpox. The deep systemic root of the disease, I want to suggest, lies in the notion of an "intrinsic" property, a property something has "in itself," apart from any contribution made by language or the mind.

This notion, and the correlative notion of a property that is merely "appearance," or merely something we "project" onto the object, has proved extremely robust, judging by its appeal to different kinds of philosophers. In spite of their deep disagreements, all the strains of philosophy that accepted the seventeenth-century circle of problems—subjective idealists as well as dualists and materialists—accepted the distinction, even if they disagreed over its application. A subjective idealist would say that there are only sense data (or minds and sense data, in some versions), and that "red" is an intrinsic property of these objects, while persistence (being there even when we don't look) is something we "project"; a dualist or a materialist would say the "external" objects have persistence as an intrinsic property, but red is, in their case, something we "project." But all of these philosophers *have* the distinction. Even Kant, who expresses serious doubts about it in the first Critique (to the point of saying that the notion of a "Ding an sich" *may* be "empty"), makes heavy use of it in the second Critique.

Putting aside the Berkeleyan view (that there aren't really any external objects at all) as an aberrant form of the seventeenth-century view, we may say that the remaining philosophers all accept the account of "redness" and "solidity" that I have been describing; these are not "intrinsic properties" of the external things we ascribe them to, but rather (in the case of external things) dispositions to affect us in certain ways—to produce certain sense data in us, or, the materialist philosophers would say, to produce certain sorts of "states" in our brains and nervous systems. The idea that these properties are "in" the things themselves, as intrinsic properties, is a spontaneous "projection."

The Achilles' Heel of this story is the notion of a disposition. To indicate the problems that arise—they have preoccupied many first-rate philosophical minds, starting with Charles Peirce's—let me introduce a technical term (I shall not introduce much terminology in this lecture, I promise!). A disposition that something has to do something *no matter what*, I shall call a *strict disposition*. A disposition to do something under "normal conditions," I shall call an *"other things being equal" disposition*. Perhaps it would be wise to give examples.

The disposition of bodies with non-zero rest mass to travel at sub-light speeds is a *strict* disposition; it is physically impossible for a body with non-zero rest mass to travel at the speed of light. Of course, the notion of a "strict disposition" presupposes the notion of "physical necessity," as this example illustrates, but this is a notion I am allowing the "scientific realist," at least for the sake of argument. What of the disposition of sugar to dissolve in water?

This is not a strict disposition, since sugar which is placed in water which is already saturated with sugar (or even with other appropriate chemicals) will not dissolve. Is the disposition of sugar to dissolve in *chemically pure water,* then, a strict disposition?

This is also not a strict disposition; the first counterexample I shall mention comes from thermodynamics. Suppose I drop a sugar cube in water and the sugar cube dissolves. Consider sugar which is in water, but in such a way that while the situation is identical with the situation I just produced (the sugar is dissolved in the water) with respect to the position of each particle, and also with respect to the numerical value of the momentum of each particle, all the momentum vectors have the exactly opposite directions from the ones they now have. This is a famous example: what happens in the example is that the sugar, instead of staying dissolved, simply forms a sugar cube which spontaneously leaps out of the water! Since every normal state (every state in which sugar dissolves) can be paired with a state in which it "undissolves," we see that there are infinitely many physically-possible conditions in which sugar "undissolves" instead of staying in solution. Of course, these are all states in which entropy decreases; but that is not impossible, only extremely improbable!

Shall we say, then, that sugar has a strict disposition to dissolve unless the condition is one in which an entropy decrease takes place? No, because if sugar is put in water and there is immediately a flash freeze, the sugar will not dissolve if the freezing takes place fast enough. . . .

The fact is that what we can say is that under *normal* conditions sugar will dissolve if placed in water. And there is no reason to think that all the various abnormal conditions (including bizarre quantum mechanical states, bizarre local fluctuations in the space-time, etc.) under which sugar would not dissolve if placed in water could be summed up in a closed formula in the language of fundamental physics.

This is exactly the problem we previously observed in connection with redness and solidity! If the "intrinsic" properties of "external" things are the ones that we can represent by formulas in the language of fundamental physics, by "suitable functions of the dynamical variables," then *solubility* is also not an "intrinsic" property of any external thing. And, similarly, neither is any "other things being equal" disposition. The Powers, to use the seventeenth-century language, have to be set over against, and carefully distinguished from, the properties the things have "in themselves."

Intrinsic Properties: Intentionality

Well, what of it? Why should we not say that dispositions (or at least "other things being equal" dispositions, such as solubility) are also not "in the things themselves" but rather something we "project" onto those things? Philosophers who talk this way rarely if ever stop to say what *projection* itself is supposed to be. Where in the scheme does the ability of the mind to "project" anything onto anything come in?

Projection is thinking of something as having properties it does not have, but that we can imagine (perhaps because something else we are acquainted with really does have them), without being conscious that this is what we are doing. It is thus a species of *thought*—thought about something. Does the familiar "Objectivist" picture have anything to tell us about thought (or, as philosophers say, about "intentionality," that is, about *aboutness*)?

Descartes certainly intended that it should. His view was that there are two fundamental substances—mind and matter—not one, and, correspondingly there should be two fundamental sciences: physics and psychology. But we have ceased to think of mind as a separate "substance" at all. And a "fundamental science" of psychology which explains the nature of thought (including how thoughts can be true or false, warranted or unwarranted, about something or not about something) never did come into existence, contrary to Descartes' hopes. So to explain the features of the commonsense world, including color, solidity, causality—I include causality because the commonsense notion of "the cause" of something is a "projection" if dispositions are "projections"; it depends on the notion of "normal conditions" in exactly the same way—in terms of a mental operation called "projection" is to explain just about every feature of the commonsense world in terms of *thought*.

But wasn't that what idealists were accused of doing? This is the paradox that I pointed out at the beginning of this lecture. So far as the commonsense world is concerned (the world we experience ourselves as *living* in, which is why Husserl called it the *Lebenswelt,* the effect of what is called "realism" in philosophy is to deny objective reality, to make it all simply *thought.* It is the philosophers who in one way or another stand in the Neo-Kantian tradition—James, Husserl, Wittgenstein—who claim that commonsense tables and chairs and sensations and electrons are *equally real,* and not the metaphysical realists.

Today, some metaphysical realists would say that we don't need a perfected science of psychology to account for thought and intentionality, because the problem is solved by some philosophical theory; while others claim that a perfected "cognitive science" based on the "computer model" will solve the problem for us in the near or distant future. I obviously do not have time to examine these suggestions closely today, but I shall indicate briefly why I believe that none of them will withstand close inspection.

Why Intentionality is so Intractable

The problem, in a nutshell, is that thought itself has come to be treated more and more as a "projection" by the philosophy that traces its pedigree to the seventeenth century. The reason is clear: we have not succeeded in giving the theory that thought is just a primitive property of a mysterious "substance," mind, any content. As Kant pointed out in the first Critique, we have no theory of this substance or its powers and no prospect of having one. If *unlike* the Kant of the first Critique (as I read the *Critique of Pure Reason*), we insist on sticking to the fundamental "Objectivist" assumptions, the only line we can then take is that *mental phenomena must be highly derived physical phenomena in some way,* as Diderot and Hobbes had already proposed. By the "fundamental Objectivist assumptions," I mean (1) the assumption that there is a clear distinction to be drawn between the properties things have "in themselves" and the properties which are "projected by us" and (2) the assumption that the fundamental science—in the singular, since only physics has that status today—tells us what properties things have "in themselves." (Even if we were to assume, with Wilfrid Sellars, that "raw feels"—fundamental sensuous qualities of experience—are not going to be reduced to physics, but are in some way going to be added to fundamental science in some future century, it would not affect the situation much; Sellars does not anticipate that *intentionality* will turn out to be something we have to add to physics in the same way, but rather supposes that a theory of the "use of words" is all that is needed to account for it.) Modern Objectivism has simply become Materialism. And the central problem for Materialism is "explaining the emergence of mind." But if "explaining the emergence of mind" means solving Brentano's problem, that is, saying in *reductive* terms what "thinking there are a lot of cats in the neighborhood" *is*, and what "remembering where Paris is" *is*, etc., why should we now think that's possible? If reducing color or solidity or solubility to fundamental physics has proved impossible, why should this vastly more ambitious reduction program prove tractable?

Starting in the late 1950s, I myself proposed a program in the philosophy of mind that has become widely known under the name "Functionalism." The claim of my "Functionalism" was that thinking beings are *compositionally plastic*—that is, that there is no one physical state or event (i.e., no necessary and sufficient condition expressible by a finite formula in the language of first-order fundamental physics) for being even a *physically possible* (let alone "logically possible" or "metaphysically possible") occurrence of a thought with a given propositional content, or of a feeling of anger, or of a pain, etc. *A fortiori*, propositional attitudes, emotions, feelings, are not *identical* with brain states, or even with more broadly characterized physical states. When I advanced this claim, I pointed out that thinking of a being's mentality, affectivity, etc., as aspects of its *organization to function* allows one to recognize that all sorts of logically possible "systems" or beings could be conscious, exhibit mentality and affect, etc., in exactly the same sense without having the same matter (without even consisting of "matter" in the sense of elementary particles and electromagnetic fields at all). For beings of many different physical (and even "non-physical") constitutions could have the same functional organization. The thing we want insight into is the nature of human (and animal) functional organization, not the nature of a mysterious "substance," on the one hand, or merely additional physiological information on the other.

I also proposed a theory as to what our organization to function is, one I have now given up—this was the theory that our functional organization is that of a Turing machine. I have given this up because I believe that there are good arguments to show that mental states are not only compositionally plastic but also computationally plastic. What I mean by this is that physically possible creatures who believe that there are a lot of cats in the neighborhood, or whatever, may have an indefinite number of different "programs." The hypothesis that there is a necessary and sufficient condition for the presence of a given belief in computational (or computational *cum*—physical) terms is unrealistic in just the way that the theory that there is a necessary and sufficient condition for the presence of a table in phenomenalistic terms is unrealistic. Such a condition would have to be infinitely long, and not constructed according to any effective rule, or even according to a non-effective prescription that we could state without using the very terms to be reduced. I do not believe that even all humans who have the same belief (in different cultures, or with different bodies of knowledge and different conceptual resources) have in common a physical cum computational feature which could be "identified with" that belief. The "intentional level" is simply not reducible to the "computational level" any more than it is to the "physical level."6

If this is right, then the Objectivist will have to conclude that intentionality *too* must be a mere "projection." But how can any philosopher think this suggestion has even the semblance of making sense? As we saw, the very notion of "projection" *presupposes* intentionality!

Strange to say, the idea that thought *is* a mere projection is being defended by a number of philosophers in the United States and England, in spite of its absurdity. The strength of the "Objectivist" tradition is so strong that some philosophers will abandon the deepest intuitions we have about ourselves-in-the-world, rather than ask (as Husserl and Wittgenstein did) whether the whole picture is not a mistake. Thus it is that in the closing decades of the twentieth century we have intelligent philosophers[7] claiming that intentionality itself is something we project by taking a "stance" to some parts of the world (as if "taking a stance" were not itself an intentional notion!), intelligent philosophers claiming that no one really has propositional attitudes (beliefs and desires), that "belief" and "desire" are just notions from a false theory called "folk psychology," and intelligent philosophers claiming there is no such property as "truth" and no such relation as reference, that "is true" is just a phrase we use to "raise the level of language." One of these—Richard Rorty—a thinker of great depth—sees that he is committed to rejecting the intuitions that underlie every kind of realism[8] (and not just metaphysical realism), but most of these thinkers write as if they were *saving* realism (in its Materialist version) by abandoning intentionality! It's as if it were all right to say "I don't deny that there is an external world; I just deny that we *think* about it!" Come to think of it, this is the way Foucault wrote, too. The line between relativism *à la française* and Analytic Philosophy seems to be thinner than anglophone philosophers think! Amusingly enough, the dust-jacket of one of the latest attacks on "folk psychology"[9] bears an enthusiastic blurb in which a reviewer explains the importance of the book inside the dust-jacket by saying that most people believe that there are such things as beliefs!

"The Trail of the Human Serpent is Over All"

If seventeenth-century Objectivism has led twentieth-century philosophy into a blind alley, the solution is neither to fall into extreme relativism, as French philosophy has been doing, nor to deny our commonsense realism. There *are* tables and chairs and ice cubes. There are also electrons and space-time regions and prime numbers and people who are a menace to world peace and moments of beauty and transcendence and many other things. My old-fashioned story of the Seducer and the Innocent Maiden was meant as a double warning; a warning against giving up commonsense realism and, simultaneously, a warning against supposing that the seventeenth-century talk of "external world" and "sense impressions," "intrinsic properties," and "projections," etc., was in any way a Rescuer of our commonsense realism. Realism with a capital "R" is, sad to say, the foe, not the defender, of realism with a small "r."

If this is hard to see, it is because the task of overcoming the seventeenth-century world picture is only begun. I asked—as the title of this lecture—whether there is still anything to say, anything really new to say, about reality and truth. If "new" means "absolutely unprecedented," I suspect the answer is "no." But if we allow that William James might have had something "new" to say—something new to *us*, not just new to his own time—or, at least, might have had a program for philosophy that is, in part, the right program, even if it has not been properly worked out yet (and may never be completely "worked out"); if we allow that Husserl and Wittgenstein and Austin may have shared something of the same program, even if they too, in their different ways, failed to state it properly; then there is still something new, something *unfinished and important* to say about reality and truth. And that is what I believe.

The key to working out the program of preserving commonsense realism while avoiding the absurdities and antinomies of metaphysical realism in all its familiar varieties (Brand X: Materialism; Brand Y: Subjective Idealism; Brand Z: Dualism.......) is something I have called *internal realism*. (I should have called it pragmatic realism!) Internal realism is, at bottom, just the insistence that realism is *not* incompatible with conceptual relativity. One can be *both* a realist *and* a conceptual relativist. Realism (with a small "r") has already been introduced; as was said, it is a view that takes our familiar commonsense scheme, as well as our scientific and artistic and other schemes, at face value, without helping itself to the notion of the thing "in itself." But what is conceptual relativity?

Conceptual relativity sounds like "relativism," but has none of the "there is no truth to be found... 'true' is just a name for what a bunch of people can agree on" implications of "relativism." A simple example will illustrate what I mean. Consider "a world with three individuals" (Carnap often used examples like this when we were doing inductive logic together in the early nineteen-fifties), $x1, x2, x3$. How many *objects* are there in this world?

Well, I *said* "consider a world with just three individuals," didn't I? So mustn't there be three objects? Can there be non-abstract entities which are not "individuals?"

One possible answer is "no." We can identify "individual," "object," "particular," etc., and find no absurdity in a world with just three objects which are independent, unrelated "logical atoms." But there are perfectly good logical doctrines which lead to different results.

Suppose, for example, that like some Polish logicians, I believe that for every two particulars there is an object which is their sum. (This is the basic assumption of "mereology," the calculus of parts and wholes invented by Lezniewski.) If I ignore, for the moment, the so-called "null object," then I will find that the world of "three individuals" (as Carnap might have had it, at least when he was doing inductive logic) actually contains *seven* objects:

WORLD 1	WORLD 2
x1, x2, x3	x1, x2, x3, x1 + x2, x1 + x3, x2 + x3, x1 + x2 + x3
(A world à la Carnap)	("Same" world à la Polish logician)

Some Polish logicians would also say that there is a "null object" which they count as a part of every object. If we accepted this suggestion, and added this individual (call it **O**), then we would say that Carnap's world contains *eight* objects.

Now, the classic metaphysical realist way of dealing with such problems is well-known. It is to say that there is a single world (think of this as a piece of dough) which we can slice into pieces in different ways. But this "cookie cutter" metaphor founders on the question, "What are the "parts" of this dough?" If the answer is that **O, x1, x2, x3, x1 + x2, x1 + x3, x2 + x3, x1 + x2 + x3** are all the different "pieces," then we have not a *neutral* description, but rather a *partisan* description—just the description of the Warsaw logician! And it is no accident that metaphysical realism cannot really recognize the phenomenon of conceptual relativity—for that phenomenon turns on the fact that *the logical primitives themselves, and in particular the notions of object and existence, have a multitude of different uses rather than one absolute "meaning."*

An example, which is historically important, if more complex than the one just given, is the ancient dispute about the ontological status of the Euclidean plane. Imagine a Euclidean plane. Think of the points in the plane. Are these *parts* of the plane, as Leibniz thought? Or are they "mere limits," as Kant said?

If you say, in *this* case, that these are "two ways of slicing the same dough," then you must admit that what is a *part* of space, in one version of the facts, is an abstract entity (say, a set of convergent spheres—although there is not, of course, a *unique* way of construing points as limits) in the other version. But then you will have conceded that which entities are "abstract entities" and which are "concrete objects," at least, is version-relative. Metaphysical realists to this day continue to argue about whether points (space-time points, nowadays, rather than points in the plane or in three-dimensional space) are individuals or properties, particulars or mere limits, etc. My view is that God himself, if he consented to answer the question "Do points really exist or are they mere limits?," would say "I don't know"; not because His omniscience is limited, but because there is a limit to how far questions make sense.

One last point before I leave these examples: *given* a version, the question, "How many objects are there?" has an answer, namely "three" in the case of the first version ("Carnap's World") and "seven" (or "eight") in the case of the second version ("The Polish Logician's World"). Once we make clear how we are using "object" (or "exist"), the question "How many objects exist?" has an answer that is not at all a matter of "convention." That is why I say that this sort of example does not support *radical* cultural relativism. Our concepts may be culturally relative, but it does not follow that the truth or falsity of everything we say using those concepts is simply "decided" by the culture. But the idea that there is an Archimedean point, or a use of "exist" inherent in the world itself, from which the question "How many objects *really* exist?" makes sense, is an illusion.

If this is right, then it may be possible to see how it can be that what is in one sense the "same" world (the two versions are deeply related) can be described as consisting of "tables and chairs" (and these described as colored, possessing dispositional properties, etc.) in one version *and* as consisting of space-time regions, particles and fields, etc., in other versions. To require that all of these *must* be reducible to a single version is to make the mistake of supposing that "Which are the real objects?" is a question that makes sense *independently of our choice of concepts.*

What I am saying is frankly programmatic. Let me close by briefly indicating where the program leads, and what I hope from it.

Many thinkers have argued that the traditional dichotomy between the world "in itself" and the concepts we use to think and talk about it must be given up. To mention only the most recent examples, Davidson has argued that the distinction between "scheme" and "content" cannot be drawn; Goodman has argued that the distinction between "world" and "versions" is untenable; and Quine has defended "ontological relativity." Like the great pragmatists, these thinkers have urged us to reject the spectator point of view in metaphysics and epistemology. Quine has urged us to accept the existence of abstract entities on the ground that these are indispensable in mathematics,[10] and of microparticles and space-time points on the ground that these are indispensible in physics; and what better justification is there for accepting an ontology than its indispensibility in our scientific practice? he asks. Goodman has urged us to take seriously the metaphors that artists use to restructure our worlds, on the ground that these are an indispensable way of understanding our experience. Davidson has rejected the idea that talk of propositional attitudes is "second class," on similar grounds. These thinkers have been somewhat hesitant to forthrightly extend the same approach to our moral images of ourselves and the world. Yet what can giving up the spectator view in philosophy mean if we don't extend the pragmatic approach to the most indispensable "versions" of ourselves and our world that we possess? Like William James (and like my teacher Morton White[11]) I propose to do exactly that. In the remaining lectures, I shall illustrate the standpoint of pragmatic realism in ethics by taking a look at some of our moral images, and particularly at the ones that underlie the central democratic value of equality. Although reality and truth are old, and to superficial appearances "dry," topics, I shall try to convince you in the course of these lectures that it is the persistence of obsolete assumptions about these "dry" topics that sabotages philosophical discussion about all the "exciting" topics, not to say the possibility of doing justice to the reality and mystery of our commonsense world....

Reasonableness as a Fact and as a Value

At the present point, I would not be surprised if many of my hearers felt inclined to say something like this: "The moral images you described in the last lecture are splendid, wonderful, but look! Any serious philosopher will ask how we can *justify* any of this."

In a book I published some years ago,[12] I defended the idea that something can be both a fact and a value—I said that it is a fact, for example, that Yeats was a great poet, and a fact that the Nazis were evil. And then too, it was the question of justification that bothered people. Very often people expressed their worry by asking: "But don't you have to admit that there is much more agreement on scientific results than on ethical values? Doesn't that show that there is a kind of objectivity that scientific results have and that ethical values lack?"

An argument is implicit in the question. We might call it the *argument from non-controversiality.* The idea is that the hallmark of cognitive status is, in some way, the possibility of becoming "public" knowledge, i.e., of becoming non-controversial.

I don't mean to suggest that anyone really thinks that only what is non-controversial is really knowledge. The idea, rather, is that "facts" can be demonstrated "scientifically." If there is controversy over a factual question, that is because we have not yet performed enough experiments, or amassed enough data. What is a fact can "in principle" be established in a way that will command the assent of all "rational persons," where this is often taken to mean all *educated* persons, or all *intelligent* persons. Thus Weber[13] argued that value judgments can only be a matter of "faith"; and he thought this was sufficiently established by pointing out that there were some Western values of whose correctness he could not convince a "Chinese Mandarin." The issue I want to begin with today is this supposed "public" character of fact, the idea that fact can "in principle" be established beyond controversy.

It is not at all clear that this idea is correct even for the "hard sciences." Science has changed its mind in a startling way about the age of the universe, and it may do so again. If establishing something beyond controversy is establishing it *for all time,* as opposed to merely establishing it so that it is the accepted wisdom of one time, then it is far from clear how much fundamental science is, or ever will be, "established beyond controversy." The issue is familiar to philosophers of science from discussions of "convergence," and I do not propose to pursue it here.

One reason that my interlocutor's question cannot be dismissed by pointing out how "controversial" the issue of convergence in theoretical science is, is that the questioner is likely to say that there is convergence with respect to the *observational* results, at least. Here too there are problems, of course. At one time "simultaneous" seemed to be an observation term (in such predictions as "if you do X, the system will simultaneously Y and Z"). But since the acceptance of the Theory of Special Relativity, we are aware of a strong "theoretical" component in the notion of simultaneity. A similar point could be made about other "observational" terms.[14] But my interlocutor would not be putting this question to me if he believed Tom Kuhn's[15] story about the "incommensurability" of even the observational vocabularies of the sciences. So he will just say that even if our *theory* of simultaneity, or whatever, has changed, still there is *something* invariant about the kind of prediction I have just mentioned.

Let me, rather, just *give* my interlocutor his idea that we get convergence, consensus, freedom from controversy, in the hard sciences, at least "in principle." The question which deserves a long hard look is: "What follows?" Does the presence of disputes which cannot be settled in other areas, areas we do not count as "real science," really show that "subjective" or "cognitively meaningless" statements are being made? And (since I have recently been teaching William James) what would be the consequences for our lives of *seriously* answering "yes" to this question? What is the "cash value" of believing that only what can be established beyond controversy has anything to do with "cognition," knowledge, understanding?

It is not small. Consider, for a moment, our *historical* knowledge. I recently had occasion to read a work by a great historian[16] who built a powerful case for the view that "medieval" civilization did not really begin with the fall of Rome. Under the Merovingian kings, this historian argued, the civilization which prevailed was still recognizably "Roman." The drastic changes which created what we still picture as "medieval" civilization—the disappearance of Latin, except among very learned monastics, the ascendance of the North German princes, the complete break with Byzantium, the whole feudal order—came about as a consequence of the rise of Islam, and of the Islamic conquest of Egypt, Roman Africa, and Spain. This is a typical example of a historical reconstruction. We all know that such reconstructions are, as a rule, extremely controversial. Let us imagine that this particular reconstruction continues to be so. What are we to conclude?

If we take seriously the idea that controversiality indicates lack of "cognitive" status, then we would be compelled to believe that this historian has made no "cognitively meaningful" claim—a conclusion which seems absurd on the face of it!

My interlocutor might respond by saying that the principle that what is fact can be established beyond controversy is intended to apply only to fundamental existence claims. If the fundamental existence claims presupposed by an investigation or by a whole discipline have been verified "publicly," then individual hypotheses formulated in terms of the entities and properties whose existence has been thus established do not need to be individually testable to count as cognitively meaningful. (The Logical Empiricists made such a move when they changed from "testability" to "expressibility in an empiricist language" as the "criterion of cognitive significance.")[17] The existence of the Middle Ages, of Merovingians, of Pippin and Charlemagne and the Pope and Byzantium, etc., are non-controversial, he might point out, and this justifies our regarding individual hypotheses about them as cognitively significant.

There are two problems (at least) with this response, however. First of all, the hypothesis in question is a hypothesis about the causes of a whole social framework, a hypothesis about "what happened because," or, alternatively, about what would not have happened if the rise of Islam had not happened. Has the existence of global causal explanations, or of facts about what would not have happened if a certain unrepeatable historical event had not happened, been itself "scientifically" established? It is hard to see how. Indeed, there are philosophers who would regard all such statements as cognitively meaningless. Secondly, as I remarked in the first lecture, the list of objects whose "real existence" has not been established by "hard science" (according to leading philosophers) is impressive indeed—even ice cubes don't make it, according to Sellars! In fact, what science says about the *behavior* of ice cubes is far clearer than whether science says they "really exist."

A different response was offered long ago by Ernest Nagel[18] and also by Reichenbach[19] and other empiricists of his school. According to these philosophers, the inferences made by historians are simply inductive inferences of the same sort that we see in physics. If those inferences do not lead to very high degrees of confirmation (according to these thinkers), that is because social science is still "immature"; we have not yet discovered the laws of social behavior. When we have succeeded in formulating these, then we will be able to determine in a more satisfactory way which of the presently available interpretations of social events are acceptable and which are not.

Today, however, the very belief that there *are* "laws of social behavior" of an exact sort—and the belief that the fate of social science is to come to resemble physics—has become a minority view among social scientists and also among philosophers and methodologists of the social sciences. Certainly this is an empirical claim; if it is false, then historical theories such as the one I took as an example cannot be verified beyond significant controversy in this way.

Reichenbach would not, I think, have been as disturbed as Nagel was by this possibility. My memories of him from the time I was his student lead me to think that he might have said something like this: "Sometimes we have to accept theories which are only weakly confirmed, when all the alternatives are even more improbable. The fact that historical theories do not attain a high degree of probability, and perhaps never will, does not mean that the nature of the inductions that we use to measure that probability is in any way special."

If this view is right, then what is special about "science" is not at all the possibility of establishing the truth of hypotheses more or less conclusively (beyond controversy). This view concedes one of the things it is my concern to argue for: that a hypothesis or a statement may be warranted, may be reasonable to believe, in an objective sense of the words "warrant" and "reasonable," even though we cannot specify an experiment (or data) such that were we to perform it (or were we to collect them) we would be able to confirm or disconfirm the hypothesis to an extent which would command the assent of all educated and unbiased people. According to Reichenbach's view,[20] what is essential about science is its use of "induction," and not at all the possibility of getting the woman on the street (or the educated woman on the street) to believe its results.

My interlocutor might, of course, say that we could settle the controversy about the causes of the characteristic features of "medieval" civilization by *producing a large number of possible worlds just like our own prior to the birth of Mohammed, but in which Mohammed wasn't born, and seeing what happens,* but this would be science fiction rather than methodology. Or, he might say that "some evidence may turn up which we cannot now envisage and which will decide the issue—we may even discover those laws of social science that Ernest Nagel hoped for." But there is all the difference in the world between saying an issue is "settlable in principle" in the sense that one can describe experiments—experiments humanly possible to perform—whose outcome would confirm or disconfirm the hypothesis to a very high degree, and saying "something may turn up." There are, after all, thinkers[21] who hold that most ethical disagreement is an unrecognized by-product of factual disagreement: if people agreed on social and psychological theory, in the widest sense (conceptions of human nature, and society), then, these thinkers claim, they would come to agree on most disputed ethical issues. It is not logically impossible that this view is right; so "in principle" something may turn up that will settle most ethical disagreement. This is not the question that the person who asks whether ethical disagreements could be settled is asking: he is asking whether we can *now* specify findings that would settle ethical controversies.

Sometimes, in fact, he is asking for something even stronger. Robert Nozick reports being asked whether one could give an argument to show that Hitler is a bad man *that would convince Hitler himself.* The only answer to this demand—the demand that what is fact must be provable to every "intelligent" person—is to point out that probably no statement except the Principle of Contradiction—has this property.[22]

Finally, my interlocutor could just bite the bullet and deny that historical hypotheses (such as the one I mentioned) *do* have cognitive status. This is the most interesting move open to him, and there are at least some philosophers and social scientists who are tempted by it. But what would it mean to *seriously* believe such a thing?

The fact is that every cultured person does have an image of the Middle Ages, of the Roman Empire, of the Renaissance, etc. These images are not cast in concrete; since History reached maturity as an intellectual discipline in the nineteenth century, they have been repeatedly revised, and the work of cliometricians and social historians is leading to still further revisions at the present time. Still other innovations in historical method will lead to still other revisions in the future. But, even if my images of the past are not absolutely correct, I regard them as better than nothing. I take the attitude toward them that Reichenbach would have recommended. What would it mean to regard everything I believe about the past except the "bare historical record" *(is there* such a thing?) as *fiction?*

Again, consider *political* opinions, insofar as they deal with "factual" as opposed to "moral" issues. Each of us has many views about "what would happen if" this or that political, or foreign political, or economic, or social policy were implemented, and many views about "what would have happened" if this or that policy *had not* been implemented.

Even if some of our moral views do not depend on these beliefs, most of us are sensitive to consequences in deciding what policies our moral views entail; if one has no beliefs at all about which actions are most likely to avoid war, or to bring peace in the Middle East, or to make jobs, or to provide shelter for the homeless, then how could one have a political position at all? Yet these judgments too resist the kind of settlement that would put them beyond controversy. Even when we predict correctly what the result of a given policy will be, the morals we draw from the success of our prediction are usually hotly disputed. And it is easy to dispute them, for our claims about "what would have happened" if *other* policies had been instituted instead (the ones advocated by our political opponents, in the case in which it was our policy that was carried out and the success we anticipated resulted; the ones we advocated, in case it was the opponent's policy that was carried out) are such complex counterfactual assertions that no way to "prove" or "disprove" them—no way to put them beyond controversy—exists. Again, one *could*, I suppose, take the view that all such views are no more than fictions: and a consequence might be the attitude that "truth" in such matters is to be determined by imposing one's will; the true political philosophy is the one that succeeds in imposing itself, and in resisting attempts to overthrow it.

What is wrong with relativist views (apart from their horrifying irresponsibility) is that they do not at all correspond to how we think and to how we shall continue to think. I remember Donald Davidson's once asking me the rhetorical question: "What is the point of saying that intentional idioms are "second class"[23] if we are going to go on using them?" The question was a good pragmatist question. The heart of pragmatism, it seems to me—of James's and Dewey's pragmatism, if not of Peirce's—was the insistence on the supremacy of the agent point of view. If we find that we must take a certain point of view, use a certain "conceptual system," when we are engaged in practical activity, in the widest sense of "practical activity," then we must not simultaneously advance the claim that it is not really "the way things are in themselves." Although philosophers have traditionally allowed themselves to keep a double set of books in this way, the effect is to perpetuate at least two intellectualist errors: it leads one to debase the notion of *belief* (remember, Pragmatism was inspired by Bain's definition of belief—"of that upon which a man is prepared to act"); and it leads one to indulge in the fiction that there is a God's Eye point of view that we can usefully imagine. Our *lives* show that we believe that there are more and less warranted beliefs about political contingencies, about historical interpretations, etc.

Of course, my prediction that we will continue to talk this way, that we will continue to speak of political analyses and historical theories as more or less warranted, even if controversy continues to be permanent, may be falsified. We may come to think of history and politics as nothing but power struggle, with truth as the reward that goes to the victor's view. But then our culture—everything in our culture that is of value—will be at an end.

This is not, it may seem, an argument. It will be said that I have only pointed out that belief in this sort of scientism—in a scientism which *seriously* holds that everything that cannot be settled beyond controversy is non-cognitive—would have disastrous consequences, and that this does not show the view is false. I plead "guilty." In extenuation, let me say that I have argued elsewhere that Verificationist views (and the rhetorical question that my interlocutor asked was, I think, an expression of a pre-philosophical kind of Verificationism) are self refuting.[24] My purpose today was different. My purpose was to break the grip that a certain picture has on our thinking; the picture of a dualism, a dichotomous division of our thought into two realms, a realm of "facts" which can be established beyond controversy, and a realm of "values" where we are always in hopeless disagreement. What I hope to have reminded all of us of—and I include myself, for we all slip back into the picture at times—is the vast stretches of our thought that do not consist of "value judgments," but which are, on the other hand, just as "controversial" as value judgments. No sane person should believe that something is "subjective" merely because it cannot be settled beyond controversy.

Notes

1 Wilfrid Sellars, *Science, Perception, and Reality* (Atlantic Highlands, NJ: Humanities Press, 1963).

2 Edmund Husserl, *The Crisis of the European Sciences and Transcendental Phenomenology*, trans. David Carr (Evanston: Northwestern University Press, 1970).

3 See C. L. Hardin's "Are Scientific Objects Colored?" in *Mind* 93:22 (October 1964), 491–500.

4 The commonsense notion of "solidity" should not be confused with the physicist's notion of being in "the solid state." For example, a sand dune is in the "solid state" but is not solid in the ordinary sense of the term,while a bottle of milk may be solid, but most of its contents are not in the solid state.

5 Herbert Feigl, "The 'Mental' and the 'Physical,'" in *Minnesota Studies in the Philosophy of Science*, vol. 11, *Concepts, Theories and the Mind–Body Problem*, ed. Feigl, Scriven, and Maxwell (Minneapolis: University of Minnesota Press, 1958), 370–497.

6 This is argued in my *Representation and Reality* (Cambridge, MA: MIT Press, 1989).

7 D. C. Dennett, *Content and Consciousness* (Atlantic Highlands, NJ: Humanities Press, 1969).

8 *Philosophy and the Mirror of Nature* (Princeton: Princeton University Press, 1979).

9 Stephen Stich, *From Folk Psychology to Cognitive Science: The Case Against Belief* (Cambridge, MA: MIT Press, 1983).

10 "On What There Is," reprinted in W. V. O. Quine, *From a Logical Point of View* (Cambridge, MA: Harvard University Press, 1953).

11 White has advocated doing this early and late (Morton White, *Toward Reunion in Philosophy*, Cambridge, MA: Harvard University Press, 1956; *What Is and What Ought to Be Done*, Oxford: Oxford University Press, 1981).

12 *Reason, Truth, and Histor,* (New York: Cambridge University Press, 1981).

13 Cf. Max Weber, *The Methodology of the Social Sciences* (New York: The Free Press [MacMillan]), 1949.

14 For example, the *shape* of an object depends on the velocity of the observer relative to the object, in the Special Theory of Relativity. "Square" is, thus, strictly speaking, a *frame-dependent* term in relativity physics.

This illustrates the fact that no term in the ordinary "observation vocabulary" of the physicist is immune from the possibility of receiving extremely complex kinds of theoretical loading.

15 See Thomas Kuhn, *The Structure of Scientific Revolutions* (Chicago: University of Chicago Press, 1981).

16 Henri Pirenne, *Mohammed and Charlemagne* (translation of his *Mahomet et Charlemagne*) (Totawa, NJ: Barnes and Noble, 1980).

17 See C. G. Hempel's classic paper, "Problems and Changes in the Empiricist Criterion of Meaning," in *Revue International de Philosophie* 4:41–63 (1950), reprinted in L. Linsky, ed., *Semantics and the Philosophy of Language*, pp. 163–85, Urbana: University of Illinois Press, 1952.

18 E.g., Nagel wrote that "There appears to be no good reason for claiming that the general pattern of explanations in historical inquiry... differs from those encountered in the generalizing and the natural science" ("The Logic of Historical Analysis," in H. Feigl and M. Brodbeck, eds., *Readings in the Philosophy of Science*, New York: Appleton–Century Crofts, 1953, 688–700). Immediately after making this statement, Nagel goes on to say that the "explanatory premises in history" include laws "as well as many explicitly (although incompletely) formulated statements of initial conditions." Note that "law" and "initial conditions" are physicists' jargon, and not any historian's way of speaking.

19 E.g., Reichenbach writes that "The argument that sociological happenings are unique and do not repeat themselves breaks down because the same is true for physical happenings. The weather of one day is never the same as that of another day. The condition of one piece of wood is never the same as that of any other piece of wood. The scientist overcomes these difficulties by incorporating the individual cases into a class and looking for laws that control the unique conditions at least in a majority of cases. Why should the social scientist be unable to do the same thing?" *The Rise of Scientific Philosophy* (Berkeley: University of California Press, 1951, 309–310).

20 See, for example, *Experience and Prediction* (Chicago: University of Chicago Press, 1938).

21 Richard Boyd has recently argued this point of view in (unpublished at this writing) lectures at the University of California and elsewhere.

22 For example, the factual statement that the world is more than 6,000 years old does not have the property of being provable to every intelligent person—I recently came across an article by Paul Rosenbloom—the author of the book on advanced mathematical logic that I worked through in my graduate student days—defending his right to believe that God created the world less than 6,000 years ago. Rosenbloom's claim is that God may have created the world at the time traditional Judaism gives as the moment of Creation, but complete with monuments, written records, people with false memories, etc., as in the familiar skeptical hypothesis about "the world coming into existence five minutes ago."

23 The reference was to Quine's claim (in *Word and Object*) that talk of meaning (and in the case of an alien language, even of truth and reference) belongs to our "second class conceptual system"; the one we use when our interests are "heuristic" or practical. The "first class" conceptual system, Quine says, is the conceptual system of physics. This is what describes "the true and ultimate nature of reality".

24 See Hilary Putnam, *Reason, Truth and History* (Cambridge: Cambridge University Press, 1981), 105–113.

A RECONSIDERATION OF DEWEYAN DEMOCRACY

HILARY PUTNAM

I. Introduction

I want to discuss a philosopher whose work at its best illustrates the way in which American pragmatism (at *its* best) avoided both the illusions of metaphysics and the pitfalls of skepticism: John Dewey. While Dewey's output was vast, one concern informed all of it; even what seem to be his purely epistemological writings cannot be understood apart from that concern. That concern is with the meaning and future of democracy. I shall discuss a philosophical justification of democracy that I believe one can find in Dewey's work. I shall call it *the epistemological justification of democracy* and although I shall state it in my own words, I shall deliberately select words which come from Dewey's own philosophical vocabulary.

The claim, then, is this: Democracy is not just a form of social life among other workable forms of social life; it is the precondition for the full application of intelligence to the solution of social problems. The notions from Dewey's vocabulary that I have employed are, of course, *intelligence* (which Dewey contrasts with the traditional philosophical notion of *reason*) and *problem solving*. First, let me say a word about the sense in which such a claim, if supported, can be called a *justification* of a form of social life.

In *Ethics and the Limits of Philosophy*,[1] Bernard Williams draws a very useful distinction between two senses in which one might attempt to justify ethical claims. One is an Utopian sense: One might try to find a justification for ethical claims that would actually convince skeptics or amoralists and persuade them to change their ways. (This is like finding a "proof" that Hitler was a bad man that Hitler himself would have had to accept.) Williams rightly concludes that this is an unrealistic objective.

When the philosopher raised the question of what we shall have to say to the skeptic or amoralist, he should rather have asked what we shall have to say about him. The justification he is looking for is in fact designed for the people who are largely within the ethical world, and the aim of the discourse is not to deal with someone who probably will not listen to it, but to reassure, strengthen, and give insight to those who will.... If, by contrast, the justification is addressed to a community that is already an ethical one, then the politics of ethical discourse, including moral philosophy, are significantly different. The aim is not to control the enemies of the community or its shirkers but, by giving reason to people already disposed to hear it, to help in continually creating a community held together by that same disposition.[2]

Here Williams's conception of moral philosophy seems to be exactly Dewey's conception. Yet Williams ignores not only the historical figure John Dewey, but the very possibility of Dewey's particular justification. Instead, Williams considers just two ways in which ethical claims could "objectively" be justified, and associates these two kinds of justification with Aristotle and Kant, respectively.[3] Even though Williams considers Kantian and Aristotelian strategies of justification to be the only possible ones, he might still have left room for a discussion of Dewey. Some commentators have seen a sense in which Dewey might be an Aristotelian, even though he was much more of an empiricist than Aristotle.[4] But when Williams discusses Aristotelian strategies—strategies of justification based on conceptions of human flourishing—something very strange happens. "Human flourishing" is defined in an entirely individualistic sense. Thus, after repeating the remark that "the answer to Socrates' question [How should one live?] cannot be used by those who (from the perspective of the rest) most need it,"[5] Williams goes on to say:

Still, this does not cast us to the opposite extreme, that the answer is simply meant to keep up the spirits of those within the system, give them more insight, and help them to bring up their children. The answer does that, but not only that. On Aristotle's account a virtuous life would indeed conduce to the well-being of the man who has had a bad upbringing, even if he cannot see it. The fact that he is incurable, and cannot properly understand the diagnosis, does not mean that he is not ill.[6]

An *Aristotelian* justification, in the only sense that Williams considers, is one that can be given to each nondefective human being (each human being who is not "ill"). In short, the only hope for an objective foundation for ethics[7] that Williams considers is what might be called a "medical" justification—an "objective" justification for ethics that would show, in some sense of "ill" that does not beg the question, that the amoral or immoral man is ill. Moreover, the only place that such a justification could originate, according to Williams, is in "some branch of psychology."[8] Williams is skeptical about that possibility, although he says that "[i]t would be silly to try to determine a priori and in a few pages whether there could be such a theory."[9] The aim mentioned earlier, "not to control the enemies of the community or its shirkers but, by giving reason to people already disposed to hear it, to help in continually creating a community held together by that same disposition"[10]—has been radically reinterpreted.

However, when Williams explains why it is unlikely that there will ever be a "branch of psychology" that will provide us with "objective" foundations for ethics, he makes a very interesting remark:

> Any adequate psychology of character will presumably include the truth, in some scientifically presentable form, that many people are horrible because they are unhappy, and conversely: where their unhappiness is not something specially defined in ethical terms, but is simply basic unhappiness—misery, rage, loneliness, despair. That is a well-known and powerful fact; but it is only one in a range of equally everyday facts. Some who are not horrible, and who try hard to be generous and to accommodate others' interests, are miserable, and from their ethical state. They may be victims of a suppressed self-assertion that might once have been acknowledged but now cannot be, still less overcome or redirected. There is also the figure, rarer perhaps than Callicles supposed, but real, who is horrible enough and not miserable at all but, by any ethological standard of the bright eye and the gleaming coat, dangerously flourishing. For people who want to ground the ethical life in psychological health, it is something of a problem that there can be such people at all.[11]

Williams does go on to question whether the latter sort of people really exist, or whether it is simply an illusion that they do. What I want to call your attention to here is not the worry about whether such people really exist, but the reference to "any ethological standard of the bright eye and the gleaming coat."[12] Apparently, an "objective" standard of human flourishing would regard us as if we were tigers (or perhaps squirrels)! Williams describes a standard of human flourishing that ignores everything that Aristotle himself would have regarded as typically human. Dewey, on the other hand, thought of us primarily in terms of our capacity to intelligently initiate action, to talk, and to experiment.

Not only is Dewey's justification a social justification—that is, one addressed to the community as a whole rather than to each member of the community—it is also an *epistemological* justification, and this too is a possibility that Williams ignores. As I stated earlier, the possibility that Williams considers is a "medical" justification; a proof that if you are amoral then you are in some way "ill." If we tried to recast Dewey's justification in such terms, then we would have to say that society which is not democratic is in a certain way ill; but the medical metaphor is, I think, best dropped altogether.

II. The Noble Savage and the Golden Age

Although John Dewey's arguments are largely ignored in contemporary moral and political philosophy, his enterprise—the enterprise of justifying democracy—is alive and well. John Rawls's monumental *A Theory of Justice*,[13] for example, attempts both to produce a rationale for democratic institutions and a standpoint from which to criticize the failures of those institutions. This could also serve as a description of Dewey's project. But there are scholars in disciplines other than philosophy, and to some extent even scholars of philosophy, who consider the very enterprise of justifying democracy a wrong-headed one. One objection comes from anthropologists and other social scientists,[14] although it is by no means limited to them.[15] These relativist social scientists are sometimes also radicals when it comes to their own cultures, but they strongly oppose any attempt by members of liberal democratic cultures to prescribe change for traditional societies. In the most extreme case (the case I have in mind is an essay by a radical economist, Stephen Marglin[16]), they reject the idea that we can criticize traditional societies even for such sexist practices as female circumcision. Marglin defends his point of view in part by defending an extreme relativism,[17] but I think there is something else at work—something which one finds in the arguments of many social scientists who are not nearly as sophisticated as Marglin: Not to be too nice about it, what I think we are seeing is the revival of the myth of the Noble Savage.

Basically, traditional societies are viewed by these thinkers as so superior to our own societies that we have no right to disturb them in any way. To see what is wrong with this view, let us for the moment focus on the case of male chauvinism in traditional societies.

One argument that is often used to justify a relativistic standpoint is virtually identical to an argument that is used by reactionaries in our own culture, and it is surprising that these social scientists fail to see this. At bottom, the idea is that people in traditional societies are "content"—they are not asking for changes and we have no right to say that they should be asking for changes, because in so doing we are simply imposing a morality that comes from a different social world. It is important in discussing this to separate two questions: the question of paternalistic intervention on one hand, and the question of moral judgment, moral argument, and persuasion on the other. It is not part of Dewey's view, for example, that benevolent despots should step in and correct social ills wherever they may exist. It is time to let Dewey speak for himself:

> The conception of community of good may be clarified by reference to attempts of those in fixed positions of superiority to confer good upon others. History shows that there have been benevolent despots who wished to bestow blessings on others. They have not succeeded except when their actions have taken the indirect form of changing the conditions under which those lived who were disadvantageously placed. The same principle holds of reformers and philanthropists when they try to do good to others in ways which leave passive those to be benefited. There is a moral tragedy inherent in efforts to further the common good which prevent the result from being either good

or common—not good, because it is at the expense of the active growth of those to be helped, and not common because these have no share in bringing the result about. The social welfare can be advanced only by means which enlist the positive interest and active energy of those to be benefited or "improved." The traditional notion of the great man, of the hero, works harm. It encourages the idea that some "leader" is to show the way; others are to follow in imitation. It takes time to arouse minds from apathy and lethargy, to get them to thinking for themselves, to share in making plans, to take part in their execution. But without active cooperation both in forming aims and in carrying them out there is no possibility of a common good.[18]

The true paternalists are those who object to *informing* the victims of male chauvinism, or of other forms of oppression, of the injustice of their situation and of the existence of alternatives. Their argument is a thinly disguised utilitarian one. Their conception of the good is basically "satisfaction" in one of the classic utilitarian senses; in effect they are saying that the women (or whoever the oppressed may be) are satisfied, and that the "agitator" who "stirs them up" is the one who is guilty of creating *dissatisfaction.* But Dewey is no utilitarian. (He was a consequentialist, but he was no utilitarian.) The fact that someone feels satisfied with a situation means little if the person has no information or false information concerning either her own capacities or the existence of available alternatives to her present way of life. The real test is not what women who have never heard of feminism say about their situation; indeed, it is hard to see how the situation of a chauvinist woman in India is different from the situation of a chauvinist woman in this country thirty years ago who had never been exposed to feminist ideas. Such women might well have answered a questionnaire by saying that they were satisfied with their lives; but after realizing the falsity of the beliefs on which the acceptance of their lives had been based, the same women not only felt dissatisfied with those lives, but they sometimes felt ashamed of themselves for having allowed such a belief system to be imposed upon them. One of Dewey's fundamental assumptions is that people value growth more than pleasure. To keep the oppressed from learning so that they remain "satisfied" is, in a phrase originated by Peirce, to "block the path of inquiry."

What the radical social scientists are in fact proposing is an "immunizing strategy," a strategy by which the rationales of oppression in other cultures can be protected from criticism. If this is based on the idea that the aspirations to equality and dignity are confined to citizens of Western industrial democracies, then the events of Tien-an-men Square in the spring of 1989 speak a more powerful refutation of that view than any words I could write here.

At the other extreme, at least politically, from the "Noble Savage" argument against attempting to justify democratic institutions is an argument found in the recent writings of Alasdair MacIntyre.[19] MacIntyre gives a sweeping philosophical resumé of the history of Western thought which endorses the idea that one system of ethical beliefs can "rationally defeat" another system and insists that there can be progress in the development of world views. MacIntyre's argument, however, is haunted by the suggestion that such progress fundamentally stopped somewhere between the twelfth and fourteenth centuries, and that we have been retrogressing ever since.

MacIntyre's conception of rationality is based largely on the work of Thomas Kuhn[20] but with certain interesting omissions. Like Kuhn, MacIntyre believes that world views such as Confucianism, or Aristotelianism, or utilitarianism cum empiricism are often incommensurable. At the same time, MacIntyre believes that the adherents of a world view can incorporate elements from another world view, or even in exceptional cases, scrap their world view and go over to another by a kind of wholesale conversion. What makes such a wholesale conversion rational is that the new paradigm dissolves difficulties that the old paradigm is unable to escape either by straightforwardly answering the questions, or by showing why and how they are not genuine questions at all. Moreover, the new paradigm solves problems in a way that an honest adherent of the old paradigm must acknowledge as superior to anything his or her paradigm can supply.[21] Of course, the new paradigm must not at the same time lose the ability to answer what its adherents must admit are genuine questions that the old paradigm could answer.

MacIntyre makes one application[22] of this idea that startled me. According to MacIntyre, the great Scholastic synthesis of Aquinas and his successors was rationally superior, in this sense, to Aristotelian philosophy.[23] What is startling about this is that, according to MacIntyre, a key ingredient which enabled Scholastic philosophy to handle problems and internal difficulties that the Aristotelian system could not solve was the notion of original sin![24]

What makes this startling is that if the new system *could* solve or dissolve problems that the old system could not, it also purchased difficulties that the old system did not face. Christianity took over from Judaism the notion of a Fall, but it interpreted that notion in a way in which traditional Judaism, for the most part, refused to do. The specifically Christian notion of original sin is unintelligible apart from the Christian notion of a Redeemer. That is, no religion would or could hold that we are compelled to sin or that our nature is so fundamentally corrupt that we cannot help sinning, unless it was prepared to provide a Redeemer to help us (or at least *some* of us) out of this predicament. I don't mean that this was the only option open to Christianity as a matter of logic, but it was the only option open to Christianity as a matter of its own history and traditions.

MacIntyre speaks[25] of the great medieval synthesis of Revelation and Greek philosophy which requires both the notions of original sin and of a triune God. If Christianity is to be viewed as the resolution of a set of problems and difficulties that a scientific or metaphysical system may be called upon to explain, dissolve, or reformulate, then surely the question of the *intelligibility* and the *logical coherence* of its fundamental notions must arise. Of course, if we view Christianity in a different way, for example, as Kierkegaard viewed it,[26] as not something that we accept on the basis of reason at all, then the problem does not arise in the same way (or the notion of "intelligibility" becomes a very different one).

The fact is that the methodological conceptions that MacIntyre defends are deeply flawed. I said that MacIntyre leaves certain things out of Kuhn's account of paradigm change in science. What he leaves out, in fact, is simply *experiment.* But the pragmatists recognized the value of experimentation. Dewey, of course, comes from the pragmatist tradition, and while the founder of pragmatism, Charles Sanders Peirce, eventually repudiated both the label "pragmatism" and much that William James and Dewey associated with that word, the two famous articles that Peirce published in *Popular Science Monthly* in 1877 and 1878, "The Fixation of Belief" and "How to Make Our Ideas Clear,"[27] remain the founding documents of the movement to the present day. In the first of those articles, Peirce discusses a methodology closely related to the one that MacIntyre proposes. He calls that the methodology of "What is Agreeable to Reason."[28] Peirce tells us, I think rightly, that what we have learned—learned by trying that method, and trying again and again throughout the long history of our culture—is that it simply does not work. The method of "What is Agreeable to Reason" by itself, without fallibilism, without experimentation, has never been able to lead to the successful discovery of laws of nature, nor has it been able to lead to resolutions of metaphysical disputes that would command the consensus of intelligent men and women. In place of the method of "What is Agreeable to Reason" (and the other failed methods that Peirce calls the methods of "tenacity" and "authority"),[29] Peirce proposes the "scientific method." By employing the scientific method Peirce does not mean following some rule book, say John Stuart Mill's, or Francis Bacon's, or Rudolf Carnap's. What he means is testing one's ideas in practice, and maintaining an attitude of fallibilism toward them. To judge ideas simply on the basis of their ability to resolve difficulties without putting them under strain, without testing them, without trying to falsify them is to proceed prescientifically. Peirce would agree with MacIntyre that rational decision between paradigms requires reflection and discussion. More than any scientific philosopher of his time, Peirce stressed that scientific method is not *just* a matter of experimentation, but experimentation and testing remain crucial in the formation of rational beliefs about matters of fact.

I know that MacIntyre will say that this criticism passes him by. Far from claiming that rationality is just "out there," available to all properly trained human minds, as traditional rationalists did, MacIntyre insists that rationality (but not truth) is relative to one's paradigm.[30] No historical or universalistic account of rationality can be given at all, he insists. And, he argues, rejecting claims to unrevisable possession of truth makes one a fallibilist. The charm of MacIntyre's writing lies precisely in displaying how such a "postmodern" mind can come to such traditional conclusions! But I cannot accept this defense for two reasons. First, although rationality is relative and historical (perhaps *too* relative and historical!), in MacIntyre's view, there is a fixed principle governing rational discussion *between* paradigms, which allows one paradigm to sometimes "rationally defeat" another. It is in the application of *this* principle that MacIntyre is forced back upon what amounts to "What is Agreeable to [MacIntyre's] Reason." The claim that he is only conceding what any "honest" adherent of the defeated paradigm would have to concede is a bit of persiflage that, in a different context, MacIntyre would be the first to see through. Second, fallibilism in the sense of giving up the a priori is not all there is to Peirce's sense of fallibilism. Peirce's fallibilism requires that one see experimentation, in the widest sense of that term, as the decisive element in rational paradigm change. MacIntyre might reply that reliance on experimentation is only rational "relative to" the contemporary scientific paradigm. But if that were his reply, then this is just where MacIntyre and pragmatism decisively part company.

If I am disturbed by the suggestion haunting MacIntyre's writing that we have been retrogressing ever since the late Middle Ages (a suggestion that has been put forward much more blatantly in Allan Bloom's best seller, *The Closing of the American Mind*),[31] it is because the politics which such views can justify are nothing less than appalling. As many historians have reminded us, the Roman Catholic Church practiced torture through much of its long history. There was a total contempt for what are today regarded as human rights (of course, MacIntyre knows this), and there was terrible persecution of religious minorities. As a Jew, I am particularly worried by the possibility that the sufferings that the Church inflicted upon Jews could someday be "justified" as exercises of a paradigm which had "rationally defeated" the Jewish world view.

What the defenders of the Noble Savage and the defenders of the Golden Age have in common is that their doctrines tend to immunize institutionalized oppression from criticism. The immunizing strategies are different, but they have this in common: they give up the idea that it would be good for the victims of oppression to know of alternative ways of life, alternative conceptions of their situation, and to be free to see for themselves which conception is better. Both Noble Savagers and Golden Agers block the path of inquiry.

III. Dewey's Metaphysics (Or Lack Thereof)

From what "premises" does Dewey derive the claim that I imputed to him, that is, that democracy is a precondition for the full application of intelligence to solving social problems? As we shall shortly see, the underlying premises are some very "ordinary" assumptions. Dewey believes (as we all do, when we are not playing the skeptic) that there are better and worse resolutions to human predicaments—to what he calls "problematical situations."[32] He believes that of all the methods for finding better resolutions, the "scientific method" has proved itself superior to Peirce's methods of "tenacity," "authority," and "What is Agreeable to Reason." For Dewey, the scientific method is simply the method of experimental inquiry combined with free and full discussion—which means, in the case of social problems, the maximum use of the capacities of citizens for proposing courses of action, for testing them, and for evaluating the results. And, in my view, that is all that Dewey really needs to assume.

Of course, a conventional analytic metaphysician would not hold this view. In analytic philosophy today, one cannot simply assume that intelligent people are able to distinguish better resolutions to problematical situations from worse resolutions even after experimentation, reflection and discussion; one first must show that better and worse resolutions to problematical situations exist. This is, for example, what bothers Bernard Williams. For Bernard Williams there could only be facts about what forms of social life are better and worse if such facts issued from "some branch of psychology."[33] Lacking such a "branch of psychology" (and Williams thinks it very unlikely there will ever be one), we have no basis for believing that one form of social life can be better than another except in a relativist sense, that is, unless the judgment of better or worse is explicitly made relative to the principles and practices of "some social world or other."[34] For Williams the distinction between facts which are relative in this way and facts which are "absolute" is omnipresent; there can not be "absolute" facts of the kind Dewey thinks intelligent people are able to discover.[35] Dewey, as I read him, would reply that the whole notion of an "absolute" fact is nonsensical.

However, it is a fact that, while at one time analytic philosophy was an antimetaphysical movement (during the period of Logical Positivism), it has recently become the most pro-metaphysical movement. And from a metaphysician's point of view, one can never begin with an epistemological premise that people are able to tell whether A is better or worse than B; one must first show that, in "the absolute conception of the world," there are such possible facts as "better" and "worse." A metaphysical-reductive account of what "good" is must precede any discussion of what is better than what. In my view, Dewey's great contribution was to insist that we neither have nor require a "theory of everything," and to stress that what we need instead is insight into how human beings resolve problematical situations. But again, it is time to let Dewey speak for himself:

> [Philosophy's] primary concern is to clarify, liberate and extend the goods which inhere in the naturally generated functions of experience. It has no call to create a world of "reality" *de novo*, nor to delve into secrets of Being hidden from common sense and science. It has no stock of information or body of knowledge peculiarly its own; if it does not always become ridiculous when it sets up as a rival of science, it is only because a particular philosopher happens to be also, as a human being, a prophetic man of science. Its business is to accept and to utilize for a purpose the best available knowledge of its own time and place. And this purpose is criticism of beliefs, institutions, customs, policies with respect to their bearing upon good. This does not mean their bearing upon *the* good, as something itself attained and formulated in philosophy. For as philosophy has no private score of knowledge or of methods for attaining truth, so it has no private access to good. As it accepts knowledge of facts and principles from those competent in inquiry and discovery, so it accepts the goods that are diffused in human experience. It has no Mosaic or Pauline authority of revelation entrusted to it. But it has the authority of intelligence, of criticism of these common and natural goods.[36]

Here Dewey uses the notion of "intelligence." This notion, however, is not meant to be a metaphysical notion. Dewey contrasts this notion of intelligence with the traditional philosophical notion of reason. Intelligence, for Dewey, is not a transcendental faculty; it is simply the ability to plan conduct, to learn relevant facts, to make experiments, and to profit from the planning, the facts, and the experiments. The notion is admittedly vague, but we do have the ability to determine whether persons are more or less intelligent with respect to the conduct of their activities in particular areas. In a number of places Dewey connects intelligence with the ability for developing new capacities for acting effectively in an environment with what he calls "growth."

IV. Habermas's and Apel's Epistemological Justifications for Democracy

If Deweyan insights and argumentative strategies have been largely ignored by analytic philosophers in recent years, they have in a sense been rediscovered, although with a difference, in recent continental philosophy. Both Jürgen Habermas[37] and Karl-Otto Apel[38] give epistemological justifications for democracy that have a definite relation to Dewey's arguments. I think we can better understand Dewey's view by comparing it with their epistemological justifications for democracy.

Both Habermas and Apel present arguments that are at least in part "transcendental arguments," but the term must be taken with caution. Neither Apel nor Habermas believes in the possibility of a transcendental deduction of a system of categories which will give the a priori structure of the world of experience, in the style of Kant. For Apel and Habermas, "transcendental argument" is simply inquiry into the presuppositions of things that we do—for example, the presuppositions of the activity of arguing about whether something should or should not be done. Their work cannot be simply assimilated to the philosophical work of pragmatists like Dewey (which may be a good reason to compare and contrast it with that work), for it rests on the notion of internal relations between concepts (i.e., the notion of analytic truth). Dewey was extremely leery of such a notion, and he certainly would not have given it a prominent place in any exposition of his views. Moreover, Apel, in particular, seems to view philosophy as consisting entirely of transcendental argument (although Habermas allows both "transcendental" and empirical considerations to play a role), and Dewey would certainly have rejected such a conception.

In Apel's presentation of the argument,[39] the act of stating something has certain formal presuppositions: the speaker implicitly or explicitly claims that what he is saying is true (if the statement is descriptive) or normatively right (if the statement is normative), or possesses still other kinds of validity (in the case of other kinds of statements).[40] The speaker implicitly or explicitly claims to be sincere: "I say that p, but I am not sincere in saying this" is self-defeating, if intended as a "constative" speech act (an act of asserting that p). The speaker implicitly or explicitly claims to be able to give reasons: in most circumstances, "I claim that p, but I can give no reason" will fail in a rational discussion. And there are still other conditions of this kind that need not concern us in this sketch of the position.[41]

Apel and Habermas further explain that the idea of a fully justified statement is that the statement can withstand tests and criticism. This is implicit in the practice of discussing whether or not a given statement really is fully justified. At the same time, they draw on the work of Peirce and the later work of Wittgenstein to argue that the idea of a statement whose complete and final warrant is wholly available to the speaker him or herself—who neither needs nor can profit from the data of others—is an empty and fallacious idea. The idea of a statement which is true (or normatively right) or one which can withstand tests and criticism, is empty unless we allow any statement claimed to be true to be tested by an ongoing community of testers, or at any rate, critics. The upshot is that if I am a participant in a rational discussion (or wish to be, and therefore refrain from pragmatically contradicting my declared intention to participate in such a discussion), then I am committed to the idea of a possible community of inquirers.

So far this may not seem to have anything to do with democracy, although it does concern pragmatist models of inquiry, Wittgenstein's private language argument,[42] and other philosophical models. But what sort of community must the ideal community of inquirers be? A community which is competent to determine what is true and false (or any other sort of validity that can be rationally discussed) must be such that anyone in that community can criticize what is put forward knowing that his or her criticism will be heard and discussed. If some criticisms are simply ignored, then the possibility of an "immunizing strategy" rears its ugly head; we are back at the method of "What is Agreeable to Reason," or worse, the methods of "tenacity" or (still worse) "authority."[43] In short, the community must be one which respects the principles of intellectual freedom and equality.

Although the argument just summarized has clear points of agreement and overlap with Dewey's view, there are strong differences. Habermas and Apel claim to show that the moral obligations fundamental to democratic politics can be derived from the obligation not to perform "pragmatically contradictory" speech-acts. That is, they would claim, each member of the community of inquirers has the obligation to make only statements which are (as far as one knows) true, sincere, and supported by reasons. But such a derivation, even if correct, surely is backward. We are not concerned with the ethical or democratic life only or even primarily because we have to live that way in order to discover and tell the truth, be sincere, and have reasons; rather, being sincere and telling the truth are among the obligations that we sometimes undertake in connection with the ethical life. Moreover, the obligation to discover and to tell the truth is a defeasible obligation. For example, we should not try to discover any more truths about better ways to make bacteriological weapons or nerve gasses. Indeed, if the whole human race could agree not to try to discover any more truths about better ways to make atom bombs, that would be a good thing. I don't mean that it would be a good thing if we stopped doing physics altogether, and I recognize that pursuing pure physics will undoubtedly lead to discoveries that can be used to make weapons. But the fact remains that there is a difference between trying to discover fundamental laws of nature and trying to discover specific engineering applications. Refusing to discover specific engineering applications is, after all, refusing to even try to discover some truths that human beings are capable of discovering and that have bearing on rational arguments. Yet the decision that, for weighty moral reasons, we are better off not knowing certain things is at times perfectly justified. Indeed, someone who thought that we had an obligation to discover the most effective ways to torture people and a further obligation to publicize that knowledge would be a monster.

But this observation seems to undercut much of the force of Habermas's and Apel's arguments. After all, the anti-democratic despot need not be insincere when saying what he or she believes to be the truth. He or she may honestly believe that an authoritarian society is the best society. He or she may refuse to allow that belief to be put to the test because the despot believes that the moral cost of such a test would be much too high. If, for example, the despot is convinced that trying democratic modes of social organization would lead to enormous amounts of suffering, he or she may feel that while not allowing them to be tried, or even discussed, is unfortunate epistemologically, and prevents his or her beliefs from having as much warrant as they might otherwise have, not trying them is not only morally justified, but morally required. The problem with the arguments of Habermas and Apel is that what is required for the optimal pursuit of truth may not be what is required for human flourishing or even for human survival.

Apel's reply to this objection is that when the anti-democratic despot puts forward this argument, then, by the very act of offering an argument, he or she undertakes to listen to reasons on the other side. If this is right, the despot's behavior is pragmatically self-contradictory. But I do not see the force of this reply at all. Avoiding "pragmatic self-contradiction" in this highly sophisticated sense can hardly be the supreme maxim governing human life!

It seems to me that Dewey does have an answer to this kind of objection, but it is not a "transcendental" answer. Dewey believes, and he recognizes that this is an empirical hypothesis, that it is simply not true that democratic societies (and Dewey was a democratic socialist) cannot survive without producing massive unhappiness, or that ordinary people are not capable of making the decisions and taking the responsibilities that they must make and take if democracy is to function effectively. As a matter of empirical fact, the arguments offered by the despot and by all who defend special privilege are rationalizations, that is, they are offered in what is, at bottom, bad faith. I quote:

> All special privilege narrows the outlook of those who possess it, as well as limits the development of those not having it. A very considerable portion of what is regarded as the inherent selfishness of mankind is the product of an inequitable distribution of power—inequitable because it shuts out some from the conditions which direct and evoke their capacities, while it produces a one-sided growth in those who have privilege. Much of the alleged unchangeableness of human nature signifies only that as long as social conditions are static and distribute opportunity unevenly, it is absurd to expect

change in men's desires and aspirations. Special privilege always induces a stand pat and reactionary attitude on the part of those who have it; in the end it usually provokes a blind rage of destruction on the part of those who suffer from it. The intellectual blindness caused by privileged and monopolistic possession is made evident in "rationalization" of the misery and cultural degradation of others which attend its existence. These are asserted to be the fault of those who suffer, to be the consequence of their own improvidence, lack of industry, willful ignorance, etc. There is no favored class in history which has not suffered from distorted ideas and ideals, just as the deprived classes suffered from inertia and underdevelopment.[44]

The critical thrust of this discussion is unmistakable. Democracy may, as Winston Churchill said, be "better than all the other systems which have actually been tried," but it by no means provides full opportunity for the use of "social intelligence" in Dewey's sense. For the use of "social intelligence," as Dewey makes clear, is incompatible, on the one hand, with denying the underprivileged the opportunity to develop and use their capacities, and, on the other hand, with the rationalization of entrenched privilege. Dewey's justification is a critical justification of democracy, one that calls as much for the reform of democracy as for its defense. But what I wish to call attention to here, by contrasting Dewey's argument with Habermas's and Apel's arguments, is its thoroughgoing dependence on empirical hypotheses. For Dewey, the justification of democracy rests at every point on arguments which are not at all transcendental, but which represent the fruit of our collective experience. Deweyan philosophy exemplifies the very methodology for which it argues.

V. Dewey and James

While Dewey's social philosophy seems, as far as it goes, entirely correct, his moral philosophy is less satisfactory when we try to apply it to individual existential choices. To see why, consider the famous example of an existential choice that Sartre employed in *Existentialism and Humanism*.[45] It is World War II, and Pierre has to make an agonizing choice. He has to choose between joining the Resistance, which means leaving his aging mother alone on the farm, or staying and taking care of his mother, but not helping to fight the enemy. Dewey's recommendation to use intelligently guided experimentation in solving ethical problems does not really help in Pierre's case. Pierre is not out to "maximize" the "good," however conceived; he is out to do what is right. Like all consequentialists, Dewey has trouble doing justice to considerations of what is right. This is not to say that Dewey's philosophy never applies to individual existential choices. Some choices are just dumb. But Pierre is not dumb. Neither of the alternatives he is considering is in any way stupid. Yet he cannot just flip a coin.

There are, of course, problems of individual choice which can be handled just as one should handle social problems. If, for example, I cannot decide which school my child should attend, I may decide to experiment. I may send the child to a school with the idea that if it doesn't work out, I can take her out and put her in a different school. But that is not the sort of problem that Pierre faces. Pierre is not free to experiment.

What some philosophers say about such a situation is that the agent should look for a policy such that, if everyone in a similar situation were to act on that policy, the consequences would be for the best. He or she should then act on that policy. Sometimes that is reasonable, but in Pierre's situation it isn't. One of the things that is at stake in Pierre's situation is Pierre's need to decide who Pierre is. Individuality is at stake; and individuality in this sense is not just a "bourgeois value" or an Enlightenment idea. In the Jewish tradition one often quotes the saying of Rabbi Susiah, who said that in the hereafter the Lord would not ask him, "Have you been Abraham?," or "Have you been Moses?," or "Have you been Hillel?," but "Have you been Susiah?" Pierre wants to be Pierre; or as Kierkegaard would say, he wants to become who he already is.[46] And this is not the same thing as wanting to follow the "optimal policy"; or perhaps it is—perhaps the optimal policy in such a case is, in fact, to "become who you are." But doing that is not something that the advice to use "the scientific method" can help you very much with, even if your conception of the scientific method is as generous as Dewey's.

There are various possible future continuations of Pierre's story, no matter what decision he makes. Years afterward, if he survives, Pierre may tell the story of his life (rightly or wrongly) depicting his decision (to join the Resistance or to stay with his mother) as clearly the right decision, with no regrets or doubts, whatever the costs may have turned out to be. Or he may tell his story depicting his decision as the wrong decision, or depicting it as a "moral dilemma" to which there was no correct answer.[47] But part of the problem Pierre faces at the time he makes the decision is that he doesn't even know that he faces a "moral dilemma."

William James somewhere quotes an aphorism of Kierkegaard's (whom he could not have read, since Kierkegaard had not been translated into any language James read) to the effect that "We live forward but we understand backward."[48] That is exactly Pierre's situation. Dewey's advice to consider "consummatory experiences" is of no use in this case, even if we restrict ourselves to consummatory experiences which are intelligently brought about and "appraised." For if Pierre considers only his own consummatory experiences, then he is horrendously selfish, but if he tries to consider all relevant consummatory experiences, then he is involved with a hopelessly vague question. This is often the case when we try to think like consequentialists in real life.

It was precisely this sort of situation that William James was addressing when he wrote the famous essay "The Will to Believe"[49] (which James later said should have been titled "The *Right* to Believe"). Although this essay has received a great deal of hostile criticism, I believe that its logic is, in fact, precise and impeccable, but I will not try to defend that claim here. For James it is crucial for understanding situations like Pierre's that we recognize at least three of their features: that the choice Pierre faces is "forced," that is, these are the only options realistically available to him; that the choice is "vital"—it matters deeply to him; and that it is not possible for Pierre to decide what to do on intellectual grounds. In such a situation—and only in such a situation—James believes that Pierre has the right to believe and to act "running ahead of scientific evidence."[50] The storm of controversy around "The Will to Believe" was largely occasioned by the fact that James took the decision to believe or not to believe in God to be a decision of this kind. Because religious (and even more anti-religious) passions are involved, most of the critics do not even notice that the argument of "The Will to Believe" is applied by James and is meant to apply to all existential decisions.[51] Most critics also have not noticed that it is meant to apply to the individual's choice of a philosophy, including pragmatism itself.[52]

James believed, as Wittgenstein did,[53] that religious belief is neither rational nor irrational but arational. It may, of course, not be a viable option for those who are committed atheists or committed believers. But those for whom it is a viable option may be in a situation completely analogous to the one Sartre imagines (or so James believed). For James, however, the need to "believe ahead of the evidence" is not confined to religious and existential decisions. It plays an essential role in science itself. Although this is hardly controversial nowadays, it was what caused the most controversy when the lecture, "The Will to Believe" was repeated for the graduate students at Harvard University.[54] James's point—which anticipated an idea that historians of science have documented very well in recent years—was that the great innovators in science (as well as their partisans) very often believe their theories despite having very little evidence, and defend them with enormous passion.

The scientific community's acceptance of Einstein's theory of relativity provides a very nice example of James's point. By way of background, let me explain that Max Planck was an early convert to Einstein's theory of special relativity. He played a crucial role in bringing that theory to the attention of elite physicists.[55] At that time, however, Einstein's theory appeared to lead to exactly the same predictions as Poincaré's theory, which also incorporated Lorentz transformations. (In Poincaré's theory there is still an absolute rest that cannot be detected experimentally because of the Lorentz contractions.) According to Gerald Holton, who recently related the story to me, the physicists in Berlin met with Planck on one occasion and drove him to the wall by demanding that he provide an experimental reason for preferring Einstein's theory over Poincaré's. Planck could not do this. Instead he said, "*Es ist mir eigentlich mehr sympatisch*" (it's simply more sympatico). Einstein himself had an equally passionate belief in his own general theory of relativity. When asked what he would have said if the eclipse experiment had turned out the wrong way, Einstein responded, "I would have felt sorry for the Lord God."

James made a point not just about the history of science, although he was quite right about that. His claim—a claim which the logical positivists paradoxically helped to make part of the conventional philosophy of science with their sharp distinction between context of discovery and context of justification—was that science would not progress if scientists never believe or defend theories except on sufficient evidence. When it comes to the institutional decision, the decision made by academically organized science, to accept a theory or not, then it is important to apply the scientific method; in "the context of justification" (although James did not use that jargon) James was all on the side of scrupulous attention to evidence. Even before logical positivism appeared, however, James recognized that there is another moment in scientific procedure—the discovery moment—during which the same constraints cannot be applied.

Perhaps even the positivists might not have gone as far as James. Even the positivists might have said that in the context of discovery it is all right to think of a theory, and propose it for testing without sufficient evidence, but even the individual scientist should not become a believer in his or her theory before it has been fully tested. To this, James would say, in company with many historians and sociologists of science nowadays, that if scientists took that advice, too many good theories would never get tested at all. Enormous numbers of theories are proposed every day, and only a very small number really are eventually tested. The willingness of individuals to "believe ahead of the evidence" thus plays a crucial role in empirical science itself.

The situation with respect to religion is, of course, quite different. Even though the physicist or the molecular biologist who invents a theory, or the advocates who find the theory *"sympatisch,"* may believe the theory ahead of the evidence, the eventual acceptance by the scientific community depends on public confirmation. In the case of religious belief however—*pace* Alasdair MacIntyre—there is never public confirmation. Perhaps the only One who can "verify" that God exists is God Himself.[56] The Pierre case, moreover, is still a third kind of case.[57] In that case, as I already remarked (following an observation by Ruth Anna Putnam[58]), Pierre may come to feel afterward that he made the right choice (although he will hardly be able to "verify" that he did), but there is no guarantee that he will "know" later whether he did. James would say that in each of these cases it is valuable, both from the point of view of the individual and of the public, that there should be individuals who make such choices.

James thought that every single human being must make decisions of the kind that Pierre had to make, even if they are not as dramatic (of course, this was Sartre's point as well). Our best energies, James argued, cannot be set free unless we are willing to make the sort of existential commitment that this example illustrates. Someone who only acts when the "estimated utilities" are favorable does not live a meaningful human life. For instance, even if I choose to devote my life to a calling whose ethical and social value is certain, say, to comforting the dying, helping the mentally ill, curing the sick, or relieving poverty, I still have to decide, not whether it is good that someone should do that thing, but whether it is good that I, Hilary Putnam, do that thing. The answer to that question cannot be a matter of well-established scientific fact, no matter how generously "scientific" is defined.

This existentialist note is unmistakable in the quotation from Fitzjames Stephen[59] with which James ends *The Will to Believe:*

"What do you think of yourself? What do you think of the world?.... These are questions with which all must deal as it seems good to them. They are riddles of the Sphinx, and in some way or other we must deal with them.... In all important transactions of Life we have to take a leap in the dark.... If we decide to leave the riddles unanswered, that is a choice. If we waver in our answer, that too is a choice; but whatever choice we make, we make it at our peril. If a man chooses to turn his back altogether on God and the future, no one can prevent him. No one can show beyond reasonable doubt that he is mistaken. If a man thinks otherwise, and acts as he thinks, I do not see how any one can prove that he is mistaken. If a man thinks otherwise, and acts as he thinks, I do not see how any one can prove that he is mistaken. Each must act as he thinks best, and if he is wrong so much the worse for him. We stand on a mountain pass in the midst of whirling snow and blinding mist, through which we get glimpses now and then of paths which may be deceptive. If we stand still, we shall be frozen to death. If we take the wrong road, we shall be dashed to pieces. We do not certainly know whether there is any right one. What must we do? 'Be strong and of a good courage.' Act for the best, hope for the best, and take what comes.... If death ends all, we cannot meet death better."[60]

The life of Rudolf Carnap is a beautiful example of James's point. No doubt Carnap thought that his entire adult life was based on rational principles, and that at each point he could cogently and rationally justify what he did. This includes his commitment to socialism, as well as his commitment to logical positivism (which he called "the scientific conception of the world" in a famous manifesto[61]). He believed in logical positivism not only for what he considered its intrinsic correctness, but also as a means to "social transformation." Yet those of us who look back on Carnap's life can see that he was making exactly the "leaps in the dark" that Fitzjames Stephen described.

James's existentialism is all the more remarkable because he had not read a single existentialist writer (except Nietzsche, whom he pitied[62] and read without any sensitivity). At the same time, James never failed to see the need for a check on existential commitment. For James, my right to my own existential commitments stops where it infringes upon the similar right of my neighbor. Indeed, James described the principle of tolerance ("our ancient national doctrine of live and let live") as having "a far deeper meaning than our people now seem to imagine it to possess."[63] If reason (or "intelligence") cannot decide what my ultimate commitment should be, it can certainly decide from long and bitter experience that fanaticism is a terrible and destructive force. James always tempered a sympathetic understanding of the need for commitment with a healthy awareness of the horrors of fanaticism.

If Dewey is less sensitive than James to the limits of intelligence as a guide to life, it is perhaps because of Dewey's dualistic conception of human goods. For Dewey there are fundamentally two, and only two, dominant dimensions to human life: the aesthetic dimension and the social dimension, which for Dewey meant the struggle for a better world, a better society, and for the release of human potential. Dewey was criticized for seeing all of life as social action; he could and did always reply that on the contrary, in the last analysis he saw all "consummatory experience" as aesthetic. The trouble with this answer is that a bifurcation of goods into social goods, which are attained through the use of instrumental rationality, and consummatory experiences, which are ultimately aesthetic, too closely resembles a similar positivist or empiricist division of life into the prediction and control of experiences and the enjoyment of experiences. James, I think, succumbs less than Dewey to the temptation to offer a metaphysics of terminal goods.

VI. Conclusion

If, in spite of these criticisms, I still take John Dewey as one of my philosophical heroes, it is because his reflection on democracy never degenerates into mere propaganda for the democratic status quo. It is true that Dewey's optimism about human potential is not something which has been proven right beyond all doubt, nor does Dewey claim that it has. As Dewey emphatically reminds us, however, neither has pessimism about human potential been proven to be right. On the contrary, to the extent that previously oppressed groups have been given the opportunity to develop their capacities, those capacities have always been surprising.

I would like to close by saying a little more about this critical dimension of Dewey's thought. When Dewey speaks of using the scientific method to solve social problems, he does not mean relying on experts who, Dewey emphasizes, could not solve social problems. For one thing, experts belong to privileged classes and are affected by the rationalizations of which Dewey spoke. As an elite, they are accustomed to telling others how to solve their social problems. For Dewey, social problems are not resolved by telling other people what to do. Rather, they are resolved by releasing human energies so that people will be able to act for themselves.[64] Dewey's social philosophy is not simply a restatement of classical liberalism; for, as Dewey says,

> The real fallacy [of classical liberalism] lies in the notion that individuals have such a native or original endowment of rights, powers and wants that all that is required on the side of institutions and laws is to eliminate the obstructions they offer to the "free" play of the natural equipment of individuals. The removal of obstructions did not have a liberating effect upon such individuals as were antecedently possessed of the means, intellectual and economic, to take advantage of the changed social conditions. But it left all others at the mercy of the new social conditions brought about by the freed powers of those advantageously situated. The notion that men are equally free to act if only the same legal arrangements apply equally to all—irrespective of differences in education, in command of capital, and that control of the social environment which is furnished by the institution of property—is a pure absurdity, as facts have demonstrated. Since actual, that is, effective, rights and demands are products of interactions, and are not found in the original and isolated constitution of human nature, whether

moral or psychological, mere elimination of obstructions is not enough. The latter merely liberates force and ability as that happens to be distributed by past accidents of history. This "free" action operates disastrously as far as the many are concerned. The only possible conclusion, both intellectually and practically, is that the attainment of freedom conceived as power to act in accord with choice depends upon positive and constructive changes in social arrangements.[65]

We too often forget that Dewey was a radical. But he was a radical democrat, not a radical scoffer at "bourgeois democracy." For Dewey, our democracy is not something to be spurned, nor is it something with which we should be satisfied. Our democracy is an emblem of what could be. What could be is a society that develops the capacities of all its men and women to think for themselves, to participate in the design and testing of social policies, and to judge the results. Perhaps for Dewey education plays the role that revolution plays in the philosophy of Karl Marx. Not that education is enough. Education is a means by which people can acquire capacities, but they have to be empowered to use those capacities. In the above passage, Dewey lists a number of things that stand in the way of that empowerment. Nevertheless, education is a precondition for democracy if democracy is a precondition for the use of intelligence to solve social problems. The kind of education that Dewey advocated did not consist in a Rousseauistic belief in the native goodness of every child, or in an opposition to discipline in public schools, or in a belief that content need not be taught. As Dewey's writings on education show, he was far more hard-headed and realistic than the "progressive educators" in all of these respects. Dewey did insist, however, that education must not be designed to teach people their place, or to defer to experts, or to accept uncritically a set of opinions. Education must be designed to produce men and women who are capable of learning on their own and of thinking critically. The extent to which we take the commitment to democracy seriously is measured by the extent to which we take the commitment to education seriously. In these days, saying these words fills me with shame for the state of democracy at the end of the twentieth century.

Notes

1 Bernard Williams, *Ethics and the Limits of Philosophy* (London: Fontana), 1985.

2 *Ibid.* 26–27.

3 *Ibid.* 29.

4 See, e.g., James Gouinlock, introduction to *The Moral Writings of John Dewey*, ed. James Gouinlock (New York: Hafner, 1976), xxiii.

5 Williams, 40.

6 *Ibid.*

7 Although Williams also considers the Kantian strategy, he concludes that it is unworkable, and that if any objective justification could be given—which he doubts—it would have to be along Aristotelian lines.

8 Williams, 45.

9 *Ibid.*

10 *Ibid.* 27.

11 *Ibid.* 45–46.

12 *Ibid.* 46.

13 John Rawls, *A Theory of Justice* (Cambridge, MA: Harvard University Press, 1971).

14 See, *e.g.*, Frédérique A. Marglin & Stephen A. Marglin eds., *Dominating Knowledge*, Oxford: Oxford University Press, 1990).

15 See, *e.g.*, Michael Walzer, *Interpretation and Social Criticism* (Cambridge, MA: Harvard University Press, 1987). In his recent work, Walzer seems to be searching for a middle path between relativistic social scientists and moral philosophers like John Rawls.

16 Stephen Marglin, "Towards the Decolonization of the Mind," in *Dominating Knowledge*, 1–29.

17 *Ibid.*

18 John Dewey and J. H. Tufts, *Ethics*, rev. ed. (New York: Holt, 1936.)

19 These arguments are set forth in Alasdair MacIntyre, *After Virtue,* 2nd ed. (Notre Dame, IN: University of Notre Dame Press, 1984), and its successor, Alasdair MacIntyre, *Whose Justice? Which Rationality?* (Notre Dame, IN: University of Notre Dame Press, 1988).

20 Thomas Kuhn, *The Structure of Scientific Revolutions* (Chicago: University of Chicago Press, 1962).

21 Here MacIntyre's thinking resonates more with Stephen Toulmin's than with Kuhn's.

22 MacIntyre, *Whose Justice? Which Rationality,* chapters 9–11.

23 MacIntyre, *After Virtue*, 205.

24 *Ibid.* 181.

25 See *Ibid.* 182.

26 See Søren Kierkegaard, *Concluding Unscientific Postscript*, trans. David F. Swenson (Princeton: Princeton University Press, 1941).

27 Charles Sanders Peirce, "The Fixation of Belief" and "How to Make Our Ideas Clear," reprinted in *Writings of Charles S. Peirce,* ed. Christian J. Kloesl (Bloomington: Indiana University Press, 1986), 3.242–276.

28 Peirce, "Fixation," 256.

29 *Ibid.* 230, 251.

30 MacIntyre, *After Virtue,* 9–10.

31 Allan Bloom, *The Closing of the American Mind* (New York: Simon and Schuster, 1987).

32 John Dewey, *Logic* (New York: Holt, 1938), 280.

33 Williams, 45.

34 *Ibid.* 150.

35 For a discussion of Williams's metaphysical views, see Hilary Putnam, "Objectivity and the Science/Ethics Distinction," in *The Quality of Life*, ed. Martha Nussbaum and Amartya Sen (Oxford: Clarendson Press, 1993).

36 Dewey, *Experience and Nature*, 407–08.

37 See Jürgen Habermas, *The Theory of Communicative Action*, trans. Thomas McCarthy (Boston: Beacon Press, 1984); Habermas, "Wahrheitstheorien," in *Wirklichkeit und Reflexion: Festschrift für W. Schulz*, ed. H. Fahrenbach (Pfüllingen, 1973), 211–65.

38 See Karl-Otto Apel, *Diskurs und Verantwortung: Das Problem des Ubergangs zur Postkonventionellen Moral*, 1985.

39 *Ibid.* Habermas refers to this argument repeatedly in *The Theory of Communicative Action*, but it is not given explicitly at any one place in that book. One can, nevertheless, get a pretty clear view of how Habermas understands the argument from the first Chapter of volume I of that work, and Habermas's own statement of the argument that appears in Habermas, "Wahrheitstheorien."

40 It my be noticed that even though Habermas and Apel are, like Dewey, "cognitivists" in ethics, they accept a dichotomy between normative and descriptive statements that Dewey would have regarded as an untenable dualism.

41 While I would of course agree with these other conditions, I would not attach weight to the claim that they express "internal relations," that is, that they are analytic. But neither would I attach much weight to the fact that they are not (in my view) analytic. The important thing is that they are "necessarily relative to our present body of knowledge." Hilary Putnam, *Philosophical Papers, Volume I: Mathematics, Matter, and Method* (Cambridge: Cambridge University Press), 1976, 237–249. Although American analytic philosophers, who have been disabused of the notion of analyticity by Quine, will be quick to point out that a "paradigm shift" might someday lead us to abandon the very notions of truth and statement making in favor of we–know–not–what "successor notions." Furthermore, they will argue, the fact that we do not as of this time know what it would be like to have such "successor concepts" makes such talk empty, even if the claim that there are not "analytic" truths in this area is correct.

42 Ludwig Wittgenstein, *Philosophical Investigations,* trans. G. E. M. Anscombe New York: Macmillan, 1953, paragraphs 243–326.

43 See Peirce, "The Fixation of Belief," 29.

44 Dewey and Tufts, *Ethics,* 385–86.

45 Jean-Paul Sartre, *Existentialism and Humanism*, trans. P. Mairet (London: Methuen, 1948).

46 Kierkegaard, 116.

47 See also Ruth Anna Putnam, "Weaving Seamless Webs," *Philosophy* 62 (April, 1987), 207–220. Ruth Anna Putnam uses as an example of a "moral dilemma" the predicament of a pacifist who must decide whether and to what extent he or she is willing to participate in the war effort, for example, by serving in a noncombat capacity. As she says, "sometimes only within the frame of a whole life, and sometimes only within the frame of the life of a whole community, can these decisions be evaluated." *Ibid.* 216.

48 William James, *Pragmatism* (Cambridge, MA: Harvard University Press, 1975), 107.

49 William James, "The Will to Believe" (first published in 1897), in *The Will to Believe and Other Essays in Popular Philosophy* (Cambridge, MA: Harvard University Press, 1979).

50 *Ibid.* 29.

51 This conclusion is clear not only from the essay itself, but from many other essays in which James offers similar arguments.

52 See James, *Pragmatism*, 281 ("[W]hether the pragmatic theory of truth is true really, they [the pragmatists] cannot warrant—they can only believe it. To their hearers they can only propose it, as I propose it to my   readers, as something to be verified ambulando, or by the way in which its consequences

may confirm it."); William James, *The Meaning of Truth* (Cambridge, MA: Harvard University Press, 1975).

53 Wittgenstein's views can be found in twenty printed pages of notes taken by some of his students on his lectures on religious belief. Reprinted in Ludwig Wittgenstein, *Lectures and Conversations on Aesthetics, Psychology and Religious Belief*, ed. Cyril Barrett (Oxford: Blackwell, 1966).

54 See Edgar Arthur Singer, Jr., *Modern Thinkers and Present Problems: An Approach to Modern Philosophy Through Its History* (New York: Henry Holt, 1923), 218–20.

55 Planck was also responsible for publishing Einstein's paper in the journal Planck edited.

56 This is not to say that religious belief is unwarranted. I believe that it is "warranted," although not by evidence. This stance is intimately connected with a sense of existential decision.

57 See Sartre.

58 See Ruth Anna Putnam.

59 J. Stephen, *Liberty, Equality, Fraternity* (1874).

60 Quotation from James Fitzjames Stephen in William James, "The Will to Believe," 33.

61 Rudolf Carnap, Hans Hahn, and Otto Neurath, "The Scientific Conception of the World: The Vienna Circle," in *Empiricism and Sociology*, ed. Marie Neurath and Robert S. Cohen (Boston: Reidel, 1973), 300–19.

62 See William James, *Varieties of Religious Experience*, first published in 1902 (Cambridge, MA: Harvard University Press, 1985), 296–7 (referring to "poor Nietzsche").

63 William James, *Talks to Teachers on Psychology and to Students on Some of Life's Ideals,* first published in 1899 (Cambridge, MA: Harvard University Press, 1983), 5. The entire concluding paragraph of the preface, from which this quotation is taken, is a paean to tolerance and an attack on "the pretension of our nation to inflict its inner ideals and institutions *vi et armis* upon Orientals." (James was referring to the Philippines).

64 An example that comes to mind is the energies that were released when Polish workers formed Solidarity.

65 John Dewey, "Philosophies of Freedom," in *Freedom in the Modern World*, ed. Horace Meyer Kallen (New York: Coward–McCann, 1928), 236–71; quoted passage on 249–50.

CORNEL WEST
(B. 1953)

A Professor of Religion and Afro-American Studies at Harvard, West is the author of nine books, including the best-seller *Race Matters* (1993); *The Ethical Dimensions of Marxist Thought* (1991); and *The American Evasion of Philosophy: A Genealogy of Pragmatism* (1989), from which the following selection is taken. West embraces the religious, activist pragmatism found in Emerson and Dewey, viewing it as part of a broader American pragmatic tradition that includes Reinhold Niebuhr, Sidney Hook, Lionel Trilling, W. E. B. Du Bois, Roberto Unger, and Martin Luther King. Maintaining that traditions can be either "smothering" or "liberating," West casts a critical eye on epistemology-centered philosophy, conceiving of philosophy instead "as a historically circumscribed quest for wisdom that puts forward new interpretations of the world based on past traditions in order to promote existential sustenance and political relevance." As director of the Afro-American Studies Department at Princeton, West emphasized "a cosmopolitan core of cultural and historical studies," characterizing Afrocentrism as "a gallant yet misguided attempt" that reinforces "narrow discussions about race" and fails to "link race to the common good" (*The New Yorker*, January. 17, 1994, p. 41).

West's own "prophetic pragmatism" is "a child of Protestant Christianity wedded to left romanticism," with romanticism understood as concerned "with Promethean human powers, the recognition of the contingency of the self and society, and the audacious projection of desires and hopes in the form of regulative emancipatory ideas for which one lives and dies." West's pragmatism belongs to the third of three waves of "left romanticism," the first of which is seen in the American and French Revolutions and in their "exemplary figures" Thomas Jefferson and Jean-Jacques Rousseau. The second wave is manifest in the two "great prophetic and prefigurative North Atlantic figures: Ralph Waldo Emerson and Karl Marx," who "had a profound faith in the capacity of human beings to remake themselves and society in more free and democratic ways." The third wave, proceeding from a sense of "deep disappointment with Marxist-Leninism and Americanism," is represented by John Dewey and the Italian Communist philosopher Antonio Gramsci (1891–1937).

West's pragmatism embodies a call to the realization of ideals—to what Dewey called "reconstruction"—from within a deep sense of tradition, of openness, and of human suffering. West attacks such postmodern thinkers as Michel Foucault for their tendency to downplay human agency by "surreptitiously [ascribing] agency to discourses, disciplines, and techniques." "Foucault rightly wants to safeguard relentless criticism and healthy skepticism," West writes, "yet his rejection of even tentative aims and provisional ends results in existential rebellion or micropolitical revolt rather than concerted political praxis informed by moral vision." Embracing a "tragic" sense of evil and incompletion, West nevertheless affirms "the Niebuhrian strenuous mood, never giving up on new possibilities for human agency... yet situating them in light of Du Bois' social structural analyses that focus on working-class, black, and female insurgency."

PROPHETIC PRAGMATISM:
CULTURAL CRITICISM AND POLITICAL ENGAGEMENT

CORNEL WEST

> At the level of theory the philosophy of praxis cannot be con-
> founded with or reduced to any other philosophy. Its originality lies
> not only in its transcending of previous philosophies but also and
> above all in that it opens up a completely new road, renewing from
> head to toe the whole way of conceiving philosophy itself... the
> whole way of conceiving philosophy has been "historicised," that is
> to say a new way of philosophising which is more concrete and his-
> torical than what went before it has begun to come into existence.
>
> —*Antonio Gramsci*

The move from Rorty's model of fluid conversation to that of the multileveled operations of power leads us back to Ralph Waldo Emerson. Like Friedrich Nietzsche,
Emerson is first and foremost a cultural critic obsessed with ways to generate forms of
power. For Rorty, these forms are understood as activities of conversation for the primary purpose of producing new human self-descriptions. But for Emerson,
conversation is but one minor instance of the myriad of possible transactions for the
enhancement of human powers and personalities. Ironically, Rorty's adoption of
Michael Oakeshott's metaphor of "conversation" reflects the dominant ideal of the very
professionalism he criticizes. This ideal indeed is more a public affair than are Emerson's
preferred ideal transactions, e.g., gardening, walking, reading, and yet it also is more
genteel and bourgeois.

The tradition of pragmatism—the most influential stream in American thought—is
in need of an explicit political mode of cultural criticism that refines and revises
Emerson's concerns with power, provocation, and personality in light of Dewey's stress
on historical consciousness and Du Bois' focus on the plight of the wretched of the
earth. This political mode of cultural criticism must recapture Emerson's sense of
vision—his utopian impulse—yet rechannel it through Dewey's conception of creative
democracy and Du Bois' social structural analysis of the limits of capitalist democracy.
Furthermore, this new kind of cultural criticism—we can call it prophetic pragmatism—must confront candidly the tragic sense found in Hook and Trilling, the religious
version of the Jamesian strenuous mood in Niebuhr, and the tortuous grappling with
the vocation of the intellectual in Mills. Prophetic pragmatism, with its roots in the

American heritage and its hopes for the wretched of the earth, constitutes the best chance of promoting an Emersonian culture of creative democracy by means of critical intelligence and social action.

The first step is to define what an Emersonian culture of creative democracy would look like, or at least give some sense of the process by which it can be created. In retrospect, it is important to note that Emerson's swerve from philosophy was not simply a rejection of the Cartesian and Kantian models of epistemology; it also was an assertion of the primacy of power-laden people's opinion *(doxa)* over value-free philosophers' knowledge *(episteme)*. Emerson's swerve was a democratic leveling of the subordination of common sense to Reason. Emerson realized that when philosophers "substitute Reason for common sense, they tend to view the sense of commoners to be nonsense."[1] Emerson's suspicion of philosophy was not simply that it bewitched thinkers by means of language but, more important, that it had deep antidemocratic consequences. For Emerson, reason, formal thought, foundations, certainty were not only far removed from the dynamism of human experience; they also were human creations that appear as detached abstractions which command their creators and thereby constrain their creators' freedom. This consequence is both antilibertarian and antidemocratic in that human potential and participation are suppressed in the name of philosophic truth and knowledge. Emerson's sensibilities are echoed in our own time by Benjamin Barber:

> In conquering the muddled uncertainties of politics and suborning reasonableness to rationality, they [philosophers] have served the ideal of enlightenment better than they have informed our political judgment.... Rights get philosophically vindicated but only as abstractions that undermine the democratic communities that breathe life into rights; justice is given an unimpeachable credential in epistemology without giving it a firm hold on action or the deliberative processes from which political action stems; talk is revivified as the heart of a political process and then recommended to citizens, but in a form that answers to the constraints not of citizenship but of philosophy; civility is celebrated, but construed as incompatible with the sorts of collective human choice and communal purposes that give civility its political meaning.[2]

To speak then of an Emersonian culture of creative democracy is to speak of a society and culture where politically adjudicated forms of knowledge are produced in which human participation is encouraged and for which human personalities are enhanced. Social experimentation is the basic norm, yet it is operative only when those who must suffer the consequences have effective control over the institutions that yield the consequences, i.e., access to decision-making processes. In this sense, the Emersonian swerve from epistemology is inseparable from an Emersonian culture of creative democracy; that is, there is political motivation and political substance to the American evasion of philosophy.

> Politics is what men do when metaphysics fails... It is the forging of common actuality
> in the absence of abstract independent standards. It entails dynamic, ongoing, common
> deliberation and action and it is feasible only when individuals are transformed by social
> interaction into citizens.[3]

The political motivation of the American evasion of philosophy is not ideological in the vulgar sense; that is, the claim here is not that philosophy is a mere cloak that conceals the material interests of a class or group. Rather, the claim is that once one gives up on the search for foundations and the quest for certainty, human inquiry into truth and knowledge shifts to the social and communal circumstances under which persons can communicate and cooperate in the process of acquiring knowledge. What was once purely epistemological now highlights the values and operations of power requisite for the human production of truth and knowledge.

The political substance of the American evasion of philosophy is that what was the prerogative of philosophers, i.e., rational deliberation, is now that of the people—and the populace deliberating is creative democracy in the making. Needless to say, this view is not a license for eliminating or opposing all professional elites, but it does hold them to account. Similarly, the populace deliberating is neither mob rule nor mass prejudice. Rather, it is the citizenry in action, with its civil consciousness molded by participation in public-interest-centered and individual-rights-regarding democracy.

Prophetic pragmatism makes this political motivation and political substance of the American evasion of philosophy explicit. Like Dewey, it understands pragmatism as a political form of cultural criticism and locates politics in the everyday experiences of ordinary people. Unlike Dewey, prophetic pragmatism promotes a more direct encounter with the Marxist tradition of social analysis. The emancipatory social experimentalism that sits at the center of prophetic pragmatic politics closely resembles the radical democratic elements of Marxist theory, yet its flexibility shuns any dogmatic, a priori, or monistic pronouncements.

The encounter of prophetic pragmatism with Marxist theory can be best illustrated by an examination of the most significant and elaborate effort to put forward a Marxist-informed (though not Marxist) democratic social vision: namely, that found in Roberto Unger's multivolume work *Politics.* Unger is not a prophetic pragmatist—yet there are deep elective affinities between Unger's work and prophetic pragmatism. To put it crudely, both are noteworthy exemplars of third-wave left romanticism.

Roberto Unger and Third-Wave Left Romanticism

Roberto Unger's distinctive contribution to contemporary social thought is to deepen and sharpen in a radical manner John Dewey's notion of social experimentation in light of the crisis of Marxist theory and praxis. Unger's fundamental aim is to free Marxist conceptions of human society-making from evolutionary, deterministic, and economistic encumbrances by means of Deweyan concerns with the plethora of historically specific social arrangements and the often overlooked politics of personal relations between unique and purposeful individuals. The basic result of Unger's fascinating efforts is to stake out new discursive space on the contemporary political and ideological spectrum. Prophetic pragmatism occupies this same space. This space is neither simply left nor liberal, Marxist nor Lockean, anarchist nor Kantian. Rather, Unger's perspective is both post-Marxist and postliberal; that is, it consists of an emancipatory experimentalism that promotes permanent social transformation and perennial self-development for the purposes of ever-increasing democracy and individual freedom. Yet, in contrast to most significant social thinkers, Unger is motivated by explicit religious concerns, such as a kinship with nature as seen in romantic love, or transcendence of nature as manifest in the hope for eternal life. In this way, Unger highlights the radical existential insufficiency of his emancipatory experimentalism, which speaks best to human penultimate matters. For Unger, human ultimate concerns are inseparable from yet not reducible to the never-ending quest for social transformation and self-development.

I shall argue three claims regarding Unger's project. First, I shall suggest that his viewpoint can be best characterized as the most elaborate articulation of a *third-wave left romanticism* now sweeping across significant segments of principally the first-world progressive intelligentsia (or what is left of this progressive intelligentsia!). Second, I will show that this third-wave left romanticism—like prophetic pragmatism—is discursively situated between John Dewey's radical liberal version of socialism and Antonio Gramsci's absolute historicist conception of Marxism. Third, I shall highlight the ways in which this provocative project, though an advance beyond much of contemporary social thought, remains inscribed within a Eurocentric and patriarchal discourse that not simply fails to theoretically consider racial and gender forms of subjugation, but also remains silent on the antiracist and feminist dimensions of concrete progressive political struggles.

The most striking impression one gets from reading Unger's work is his unabashedly pronounced romanticism. By romanticism here, I mean quite simply the preoccupation with Promethean human powers, the recognition of the contingency of the self and society, and the audacious projection of desires and hopes in the form of regulative emancipatory ideals for which one lives and dies. In these postmodern times of cynicism and negativism—after the unimaginable atrocities of Hitler, Stalin, Tito, Mussolini, and Franco, and the often forgotten barbarities committed in Asia, Africa, and Latin America under European and American imperialist auspices; and during the present period of Khomeini, Pinochet, Moi, and Mengistu in the third world, bureaucratic henchmen ruling the second world, and Reagan, Thatcher, Kohl, and Chirac setting the pace in the first world—Unger's romanticism is both refreshing and disturbing.

The ameliorative energies and utopian impulses that inform Unger's work are refreshing in that so many of us now "lack any ready way to imagine transformation."[4] We feel trapped in a world with no realizable oppositional options, no actualizable credible alternatives. This sense of political impotence—"this experience of acquiescence without commitment"[5]—yields three basic forms of politics: sporadic terrorism for impatient, angry, and nihilistic radicals; professional reformism for comfortable, cultivated, and concerned liberals; and evangelical nationalism for frightened, paranoid, and accusatory conservatives. Unger's romantic sense that the future can and should be fundamentally different from and better than the present not only leads him to reject these three predominant kinds of politics, but also impels him to answer in the negative to "the great political question of our day: Is social democracy the best that we can reasonably hope for?"[6] Unger believes we can and must do better.

Yet Unger's third-wave left romanticism is disturbing in that we have witnessed—and are often reminded of—the deleterious consequences and dehumanizing effects of the first two waves of left romanticism in the modern world. The first wave—best seen in the American and French Revolutions—unleashed unprecedented human energies and powers, significantly transformed selves and societies, and directed immense human desires and hopes toward the grand moral and credible political ideals of democracy and freedom, equality, and fraternity. Two exemplary figures of this first wave—Thomas Jefferson and Jean-Jacques Rousseau—would undoubtedly affirm the three basic elements of Unger's conception of human activity: the contextual or conditional quality of all human activity; the possibility of breaking through all contexts of practical or conceptual activity; and the need to distinguish between context-preserving, i.e., routinized, and context-breaking, i.e., transgressive, activities.[7]

Furthermore, both Jefferson and Rousseau would agree with Unger's romantic conception of imagination as a human power that conceives of social reality from the vantage point of change and for the purposes of transformation.[8] In this regard, Unger is deeply within the North Atlantic romantic grain. Why, then, ought we to be disturbed? Despite the great human advances initiated and promoted by first-wave left romanticism, its historical and social embodiments reinforced and reproduced barbaric practices: white supremacist practices associated with African slavery and imperial conquest over indigenous and Mexican peoples; male supremacist practices inscribed in familial relations, cultural mores, and societal restrictions; and excessive business control and influence over the public interest as seen in low wages, laws against unions, and government support of select business endeavors, e.g., railroads. These noteworthy instances of the underside of first-wave left romanticism should be disturbing not because all efforts to change the status quo in a progressive direction are undesirable, but rather because any attempt to valorize historically specific forms of human powers must be cognizant of and cautious concerning who will be subjected to those human powers.

The second wave of left romanticism, following upon the heels of profound disillusionment and dissatisfaction with the American and French Revolutions, is manifest in the two great prophetic and prefigurative North Atlantic figures: Ralph Waldo Emerson and Karl Marx. Both were obsessed with the problem of revolution, that is, the specifying and creating of conditions for the transformation of context-preserving activities into context-breaking ones. Both had a profound faith in the capacity of human beings to remake themselves and society in more free and democratic ways. And both looked toward science—the new cultural authority on knowledge, reality, and truth—as an indispensable instrument for this remaking and betterment.

Emersonian themes of the centrality of the self's morally laden transformative vocation; the necessity of experimentation to achieve the self's aims of self-mastery and kinship with nature; and the importance of self-creation and self-authorization loom large in Unger's work. In fact, the penultimate paragraph of volume 1 of *Politics* reads as if it comes right out of Emerson's *Nature*.

> In their better and saner moments men and women have always wanted to live as the originals that they all feel themselves to be and to cement practical and passionate attachments that respect this truth rather than submerge it. As soon as they have understood their social worlds to be made up and pasted together, they have also wanted to become the co-makers of these worlds. Some modern doctrines tell us that we already live in societies in which we can fully satisfy these desires while others urge us to give them up as unrealistic. But the first piece of advice is hard to believe, and the second is hard to practice.[9]

Similarly, Marxist motifs of the centrality of value-laden political struggle; the necessity for transformation of present-day societies and for control over nature; and, most pointedly, the ability of human powers to reshape human societies against constraints always already in place play fundamental roles in Unger's project. Indeed, the last paragraph of volume 1 of *Politics* invokes the same metaphors, passions, and aims as Marx's *1844 Manuscripts* and *1848 Manifesto*.

> The constraints of society, echoed, reinforced, and amplified by the illusions of social thought, have often led people to bear the stigma of longing under the mask of worldliness and resignation. An anti-naturalistic social theory does not strike down the constraints but it dispels the illusions that prevent us from attacking them. Theoretical insight and prophetic vision have joined ravenous self-interest and heartless conflict to set the fire that is burning in the world, and melting apart the amalgam of faith and superstition, and consuming the power of false necessity.[10]

The second wave of left romanticism is dominated by Emersonian ideas of America and Marxist conceptions of socialism. From roughly the 1860s to the 1940s, human hopes for democracy and freedom, equality, and fraternity around the globe rested on the legacy of either Emerson or Marx. Needless to say, European efforts at nation building and empire consolidating—the major sources of second-wave right romanticism—violently opposed both the Emersonian and the Marxist legacies. Yet by the end of the Second World War, with the defeat of Germany's bid for European and world domination at the hands of the Allied forces led by the United States and Russia, the second wave of left romanticism began to wane. The dominant version of the Marxist legacy—Marxist-Leninist (and at the time led by Stalin)—was believed by more and more left romantics to be repressive, repulsive, and retrograde. And the major mode of the Emersonian legacy—Americanism (led then by Truman and Eisenhower)—was viewed by many left romantics as racist, penurious, and hollow.

The third wave of left romanticism proceeded from a sense of deep disappointment with Marxist-Leninism and Americanism. Exemplary activistic stirrings can be found in the third world or among people of color in the first world—Gandhi in India, Mariatequi in Peru, Nasser in Egypt, and Martin Luther King, Jr., in the United States. Yet principally owing to the tragic facts of survival, myopic leadership, and limited options, most third-world romanticism was diverted from the third wave of left romanticism into the traps of a regimenting Marxist-Leninism or a rapacious Americanism. The major exceptions—Chile under Salvador Allende, Jamaica under Michael Manley, Nicaragua under the Sandinistas—encounter formidable, usually insurmountable, obstacles. Needless to say, similar projects in second-world countries—Hungary in 1956, Czechoslovakia in 1968, Poland in 1970—are tragically and brutally crushed.

The two great figures of the third wave or left romanticism are John Dewey and Antonio Gramsci. Dewey applies the Jeffersonian and Emersonian viewpoints to the concrete historical and social realities of our century. Similarly, Gramsci sharpens and revises the Rousseauistic and Marxist perspectives on these realities. As we observed earlier, in numerous essays, articles, and reviews, and, most important, in his texts *The Public and Its Problems* (1927), *Individualism: Old and New* (1929), *Liberalism and Social Action* (1935), and *Freedom and Culture* (1939), Dewey put forward a powerful interpretation of socialism that builds upon yet goes beyond liberalism. This interpretation highlights a conception of social experimentation which "goes all the way down"; that is, it embraces the idea of fundamental economic, political, cultural, and individual transformation in light of Jeffersonian and Emersonian ideals of accountable power, small-scale associations, and individual liberties. In various fragments, incomplete studies, and political interventions, and in works such as *The Prison Notebooks* (1929–35) and *The Modern Prince,* Gramsci sets forth a penetrating version of Marxism that rests upon yet spills over beyond Leninism. This version focuses on a notion of historical specificity and a conception of hegemony which preclude any deterministic, economistic, or reductionist readings of social phenomena. In this way, Dewey and Gramsci partly set the agenda for any acceptable and viable third wave of left romanticism in our time.

Unger's provocative project occupies the discursive space between Dewey and Gramsci; it is the most detailed delineation of third-wave left romanticism we have. Like prophetic pragmatism, he stands at the intersection of the Jefferson-Emerson-Dewey insights and the Rousseau-Marx-Gramsci formulations. Ironically, as an intellectual with third-world origins and sensibilities (Brazilian) and first-world academic status and orientations (Harvard law professor for almost twenty years), Unger is much more conscious of and concerned with his Rousseau-Marx-Gramsci heritage than with his Jefferson-Emerson-Dewey sentiments. In fact, his major aim is to provide an alternative radicalism—at the levels of method and political and personal praxis—to Marxism in light of his third-world experiences and first-world training.

Unlike Dewey and Gramsci, Unger pays little attention to the burning cultural and political issues in the everyday lives of ordinary people—issues such as religious and nationalist (usually xenophobic) revivals, the declining power of trade unions, escalating racial and sexual violence, pervasive drug addiction and alcoholism, breakdowns in the nuclear family, the cultural and political impact of mass media (TV, radio, and videos), and the exponential increase of suicides and homicides. Unger invokes a politics of personal relations and everyday life, yet he remains rather vague regarding its content.

When I claim that Unger's discourse remains inscribed within a Eurocentric and patriarchal framework, I mean that his texts remain relatively silent—on the conceptual and practical levels—on precisely those issues that promote social motion and politicization among the majority of people in the country. I am not suggesting that Unger write simple pamphlets for the masses, but rather that his fascinating works give more attention to those issues that may serve as the motivating forces for his new brand of left politics. To write a masterful text of social theory and politics that does not so much as mention—God forbid, grapple with—forms of racial and gender subjugation in our time is inexcusable on political and theoretical grounds.[11] To do so is to remain captive to a grand though flawed Eurocentric and patriarchal heritage. More pointedly, it is to miss much of the new possibilities for a realizable left politics. Needless to say, to take seriously issues such as race and gender is far from a guarantee for a credible progressive politics, but to bypass them is to commit the fatal sin of supertheory: to elide the concrete at the expense of systemic coherence and consistency.

In conclusion, Unger's ambitious project warrants our close attention and scrutiny. It articulates many of the motives and ideals of the political project of prophetic pragmatism. It is, by far, the most significant attempt to articulate a third-wave left romanticism that builds on the best of the Jefferson-Emerson-Dewey and Rousseau-Marx-Gramsci legacies. Unfortunately, he remains slightly blinded by some of the theoretical and practical shortsightedness of these grand North Atlantic legacies. Yet Unger would be the first to admit that all prophets are imperfect and that all emancipatory visions and programs are subject to revision and transformation.

The Challenge of Michel Foucault

To praise Unger's project and that of prophetic pragmatism for their third-wave left romanticism is to go against the grain in some progressive circles owing to the influence of Michel Foucault. Foucault is the exemplary antiromantic, suspicious of any talk about wholeness, totality, telos, purpose, or even future.[12] Prophetic pragmatism shares with Foucault a preoccupation with the operation of powers. It also incorporates the genealogical mode of inquiry initiated by the later phase of Foucault's work. In fact, prophetic pragmatism promotes genealogical materialist modes of analysis similar in many respects to those of Foucault.[13] Yet prophetic pragmatism rejects Foucault's antiromanticism for three basic reasons.

First, despite the profound insights and rich illuminations of Foucault's renowned archeologies and genealogies, he remains preoccupied by one particular kind of operation of power, namely, the various modes by which human beings are constituted into subjects.[14] His powerful investigations into modes of inquiry that take the form of disciplinary powers of subjection and objectivization of human beings remain within a general Kantian framework. Foucault still asks questions such as "What are the conditions for the possibility of the constitution of the subject?" Instead of providing a transcendental response or even a historically anthropocentric answer, he gives us a genealogical account of anonymous and autonomous discourses that constitute subjects. In short, Foucault gives a Nietzschean reply to the Kantian question of the constitution of subjects.

> I wanted to see how these problems of constitution could be resolved within a historical framework, instead of referring them back to a constituent object (madness, criminality or whatever). But this historical contextualization needed to be something more than the simple relativisation of the phenomenological subject. I don't believe the problem can be solved by historicizing the subject as posited by the phenomenologists, fabricating a subject that evolves through the course of history. One has to dispense with the constituent subject, to get rid of the subject itself, that's to say, to arrive at an analysis which can account for the constitution of the subject within a historical framework. And this is what I would call genealogy, that is, a form of history which can account for the constitution of knowledges, discourses, domains of objects, etc., without having to make reference to a subject which is either transcendental in relation to the field of events or runs in its empty sameness throughout the course of history.[15]

The irony of this self-description is that while Foucault's work swerves from Kantian, Hegelian, and Marxist ways of accounting for the constitution of subjects, he remains obsessed with providing such an account *by asking the Kantian question*. In fact, he is interested in the operations of power only to the degree to which he can answer this subject-centered question. In his most detailed reflections on his own work, Foucault candidly states,

> I would like to say, first of all, what has been the goal of my work during the last twenty years. It has not been to analyze the phenomena of power, nor to elaborate the foundations of such an analysis.

> My objective, instead, has been to create a history of the different modes by which, in

our culture, human beings have been made subjects....Thus, it is not power but the subject which is the general theme of my research.16

Prophetic pragmatism objects to Foucault's project not because he has no historical sense but rather because it remains truncated by the unhelpful Kantian question he starts with. Dewey and Rorty—as well as Wittgenstein and Heidegger—have shown that a question that begins, "What are the conditions for the possibility of... " is misleading in that the question itself is inextricably tied to a conception of validity that stands above and outside the social practices of human beings. In this regard, Foucault's answer—anonymous and autonomous discourses, disciplines, and techniques—is but the latest addition to the older ones: the dialectical development of modes of production (vulgar Marxisms); workings of the *Weltgeist* (crude Hegelians); or activities of transcendental subjects (academic Kantians).[17] All such answers shun the centrality of dynamic social practices structured and unstructured over time and space.

The second prophetic pragmatist objection is, unsurprisingly, to his reification of discourses, disciplines, and techniques. By downplaying human agency—both individual and collective human actions—Foucault surreptitiously ascribes agency to discourses, disciplines, and techniques. There indeed are multiple unintended consequences and unacknowledged antecedent conditions of human actions that both produce and are produced by institutions and structures. Methodological individualism in social theory, according to which isolated and atomistic individual actions fully account for humans' societies and histories, will not suffice. But the alternative is not the exclusive ascription of agency to impersonal forces, transcendental entities, or anonymous and autonomous discourses. For prophetic pragmatists, human agency remains central—all we have in human societies and histories are structured and unstructured human social practices over time and space. Edward Said perceptively states regarding Foucault:

> Yet despite the extraordinary worldliness of this work, Foucault takes a curiously passive and sterile view not so much of the uses of power, but of how and why power is gained, used, and held onto. This is the most dangerous consequence of his disagreement with Marxism, and its result is the least convincing aspect of his work ... However else power may be a kind of indirect bureaucratic discipline and control, there are ascertainable changes stemming from who holds power and who dominates whom...what one misses in Foucault is something resembling Gramsci's analyses of hegemony, historical blocks, ensembles of relationship done from the perspective of an engaged political worker for whom the fascinated description of exercised power is never a substitute for trying to change power relationships within society.[18]

Foucault is a political intellectual—a "specific" intellectual geared to and affiliated with local struggles rather than a "universal" intellectual representing and speaking for the interests of a class, nation, or group—yet his Kantian questions lead him to downplay human agency, to limit the revisability of discourses and disciplines, and thereby to confine his attention to a specific set of operations of power, i.e., those linked to constituting subjects. For instance, he pays little attention to operations of power in economic modes of production and nation-states.

The last prophetic pragmatist criticism of Foucault's project is that he devalues moral discourse. His fervent anti-utopianism—again in reaction to Hegelian and Marxist teleological utopianisms—rejects all forms of ends and aims for political struggle. Therefore, he replaces reform or revolution with revolt and rebellion. In this way, Foucault tends to reduce left ethics to a bold and defiant Great Refusal addressed to the dominant powers that be. Yet by failing to articulate and elaborate ideals of democracy, equality, and freedom, Foucault provides solely negative conceptions of critique and resistance. He rightly suspects the self-authorizing and self-privileging aims of "universal" intellectuals who put forward such ideals, yet he mistakenly holds that *any attempt* to posit these ideals as guides to political action and social reconstruction must fall prey to new modes of subjection and disciplinary control. Foucault rightly wants to safeguard relentless criticism and healthy skepticism, yet his rejection of even tentative aims and provisional ends results in existential rebellion or micropolitical revolt rather than concerted political praxis informed by moral vision and systemic (though flexible) analyses. In stark contrast, prophetic pragmatists take seriously moral discourse—revisable means and ends of political action, the integrity and character of those engaged, and the precious ideals of participatory democracy and the flowering of the uniqueness of different human individualities.

Therefore, prophetic pragmatists reject Foucault's Kantian question, viewing it as a wheel that turns yet plays no part in the mechanism. Instead, they move directly to strategic and tactical modes of thinking and acting.[19] These modes highlight the operations of powers and the uses of provocation for the development of human personalities. Like Foucault, prophetic pragmatists criticize and resist forms of subjection, as well as types of economic exploitation, state repression, and bureaucratic domination. But these critiques and resistances, unlike his, are unashamedly guided by moral ideals of creative democracy and individuality.

Tragedy, Tradition, and Political Praxis

A major shortcoming of Emersonian pragmatism is its optimistic theodicy. The point here is not so much that Emerson himself had no sense of the tragic but rather that the way he formulated the relation of human powers and fate, human agency and circumstances, human will and constraints made it difficult for him and for subsequent pragmatists to maintain a delicate balance between excessive optimism and exorbitant pessimism regarding human capacities. The early Emerson stands at one pole and the later Trilling at another pole. For prophetic pragmatism only the early Hook and Niebuhr—their work in the early thirties—maintain the desirable balance.

This issue of balance raises a fundamental and long-ignored issue for the progressive tradition: the issue of the complex relations between tragedy and revolution, tradition and progress. Prophetic pragmatism refuses to sidestep this issue. The brutalities and atrocities in human history, the genocidal attempts in this century, and the present-day barbarities require that those who accept the progressive and prophetic designations put forth some conception of the tragic. To pose the issue in this way is, in a sense, question-begging since the very term "tragic" presupposes a variety of religious and secular background notions. Yet prophetic pragmatism is a child of Protestant Christianity wedded to left romanticism. So this question-begging is warranted in that prophetic pragmatism stands in a tradition in which the notion of the "tragic" requires attention.

It is crucial to acknowledge from the start that the "tragic" is a polyvalent notion; it has different meanings depending on its context. For example, the context of Greek tragedy—in which the action of ruling families generates pity and terror in the audience—is a society that shares a collective experience of common metaphysical and social meanings. The context of modern tragedy, on the other hand—in which ordinary individuals struggle against meaninglessness and nothingness—is a fragmented society with collapsing metaphysical meanings. More pointedly, the notion of the "tragic" is bound to the idea of human agency, be the agent a person of rank or a retainer, a prince or a pauper.

> The real key, to the modern separation of tragedy from "mere suffering," is the separation of ethical control and, more critically, human agency, from our understanding of social and political life...The events which are not seen as tragic are deep in the pattern of our own culture: war, famine, work, traffic, politics. To see no ethical content or human agency in such events, or to say that we cannot connect them with general meanings, and especially with permanent and universal meanings, is to admit a strange and particular bankruptcy, which no rhetoric of tragedy can finally hide.[20]

It is no accident that James, Hook, Niebuhr, and Trilling focused on the content and character of heroism when they initially grappled with theodicy and the "tragic." Although they had little or no interest in revolution, their preoccupation with human agency, will, and power resembles that of the Promethean romantics, e.g., Blake, Byron, Shelley. Yet the ideological sources of their conceptions of the "tragic" loom large in their deployment of the term.

James's focus on the individual and his distrust of big institutions and groups led him to envision a moral heroism in which each ameliorative step forward is a kind of victory, each minute battle won a sign that the war is not over, hence still winnable. Hook's early Marxism provided him with a historical sense in which the "tragic" requires a choice between a proven evil, i.e., capitalism, and a possible good, i.e., socialism. As the possible good proved to be more and more evil, the old "proven evil" appeared more and more good. The notion of the "tragic" in Hook underwent a metamorphosis such that all utopian quests were trashed in the name of limits, constraints, and circumstances. The later Trilling is even more extreme, for the mere exertion of will was often seen as symptomatic of the self's utopian quest for the unconditioned.

Niebuhr held the most complex view of the "tragic" in the pragmatist tradition. Even more than the middle Trilling's intriguing ruminations on Keatsian theodicy, Niebuhr's struggle with liberal Protestantism—especially with Richard Rorty's grandfather, Walter Rauschenbusch—forced him to remain on the tightrope between Promethean romanticism and Augustinian pessimism. In fact, Niebuhr never succumbs to either, nor does he ever cease to promote incessant human agency and will against limits and circumstances. In his leftist years, mindful of the novel forms of evil in the new envisioned social order yet fed up with those in the present, he supported the insurgency of exploited workers. In his liberal years, obsessed with the evil structures in the communist world and more and more (though never fully) forgetful of the institutional evil in American society, Niebuhr encourages state actions against the Soviet Union and piecemeal reformist practice within America.

Prophetic pragmatism affirms the Niebuhrian strenuous mood, never giving up on new possibilities for human agency—both individual and collective—in the present, yet situating them in light of Du Bois' social structural analyses that focus on working-class, black, and female insurgency. Following the pioneering work of Hans-Georg Gadamer and Edward Shils, prophetic pragmatism acknowledges the inescapable and inexpungible character of tradition, the burden and buoyancy of that which is transmitted from the past to the present.[21] This process of transmittance is one of socialization and appropriation, of acculturation and construction. Tradition, in this sense, can be both a smothering and a liberating affair, depending on which traditions are being invoked, internalized, and invented.

In this way, the relation of tragedy to revolution (or resistance) is intertwined with that of tradition to progress (or betterment). Prophetic pragmatism, as a form of third-wave left romanticism, tempers its utopian impulse with a profound sense of the tragic character of life and history. This sense of the tragic highlights the irreducible predicament of unique individuals who undergo dread, despair, disillusionment, disease, and death *and* the institutional forms of oppression that dehumanize people. Tragic thought is not confined solely to the plight of the individual; it also applies to social experiences of resistance, revolution, and societal reconstruction. Prophetic pragmatism is a form of tragic thought in that it confronts candidly individual and collective experiences of evil in individuals and institutions—with little expectation of ridding the world of *all* evil. Yet it is a kind of romanticism in that it holds many experiences of evil to be neither inevitable nor necessary but rather the results of human agency, i.e., choices and actions.

This interplay between tragic thought and romantic impulse, inescapable evils and transformable evils makes prophetic pragmatism seem schizophrenic. On the one hand, it appears to affirm a Sisyphean outlook in which human resistance to evil makes no progress. On the other hand, it looks as if it approves a utopian quest for paradise. In fact, prophetic pragmatism denies Sisyphean pessimism and utopian perfectionism. Rather, it promotes the possibility of human progress and the human impossibility of paradise. This progress results from principled and protracted Promethean efforts, yet even such efforts are no guarantee. And all human struggles—including successful ones—against specific forms of evil produce new, though possibly lesser, forms of evil. Human struggle sits at the center of prophetic pragmatism, a struggle guided by a democratic and libertarian vision, sustained by moral courage and existential integrity, and tempered by the recognition of human finitude and frailty. It calls for utopian energies and tragic actions, energies and actions that yield permanent and perennial revolutionary, rebellious, and reformist strategies that oppose the status quos of our day. These strategies are never to become ends-in-themselves, but rather to remain means through which are channeled moral outrage and human desperation in the face of prevailing forms of evil in human societies and in human lives. Such outrage must never cease, and such desperation will never disappear, yet without revolutionary, rebellious, and reformist strategies, credible and effective opposition wanes. Prophetic pragmatism attempts to keep alive the sense of alternative ways of life and of struggle based on the best of the past. In this sense, the praxis of prophetic pragmatism is tragic action with revolutionary intent, usually reformist consequences, and always visionary outlook. It concurs with Raymond Williams's tragic revolutionary perspective:

> The tragic action, in its deepest sense, is not the confirmation of disorder, but its experience, its comprehension and its resolution. In our own time, this action is general, and its common name is revolution. We have to see the evil and the suffering, in the factual disorder that makes revolution necessary, and in the disordered struggle against the disorder. We have to recognize this suffering in a close and immediate experience, and not cover it with names. But we follow the whole action: not only the evil, but the men who have fought against evil; not only the crisis, but the energy released by it, the spirit learned in it. We make the connections, because that is the action of tragedy, and what we learn in suffering is again revolution, because we acknowledge others as men and any such acknowledgement is the beginning of struggle, as the continuing reality of our lives. Then to see revolution in this tragic perspective is the only way to maintain it.[22]

This oppositional consciousness draws its sustenance principally from a tradition of resistance. To keep alive a sense of alternative ways of life and of struggle requires memory of those who prefigured such life and struggle in the past. In this sense, tradition is to be associated not solely with ignorance and intolerance, prejudice and parochialism, dogmatism and docility. Rather, tradition is also to be identified with insight and intelligence, rationality and resistance, critique and contestation. Tradition per se is never a problem, but rather those traditions that have been and are hegemonic over other traditions. All that human beings basically have are traditions—those institutions and practices, values and sensibilities, stories and symbols, ideas and metaphors that shape human identities, attitudes, outlooks, and dispositions. These traditions are dynamic, malleable, and revisable, yet all changes in a tradition are done in light of some old or newly emerging tradition. Innovation presupposes some tradition and inaugurates another tradition. The profound historical consciousness of prophetic pragmatism shuns the Emersonian devaluing of the past. Yet it also highlights those elements of old and new traditions that promote innovation and resistance for the aims of enhancing individuality and expanding democracy. This enhancement and expansion constitute human progress. And all such progress takes place within the contours of clashing traditions. In this way, just as tragic action constitutes resistance to prevailing status quos, the critical treatment and nurturing of a tradition yield human progress. Tragedy can be an impetus rather than an impediment to oppositional activity; tradition may serve as a stimulus rather than a stumbling block to human progress.

Prophetic pragmatism understands the Emersonian swerve from epistemology—and the American evasion of philosophy—not as a wholesale rejection of philosophy but rather as a reconception of philosophy as a form of cultural criticism that attempts to transform linguistic, social, cultural, and political traditions for the purposes of increasing the scope of individual development and democratic operations. Prophetic pragmatism conceives of philosophy as a historically circumscribed quest for wisdom that puts forward new interpretations of the world based on past traditions in order to promote existential sustenance and political relevance. Like Emerson and earlier pragmatists, it views truth as a species of the good, as that which enhances the flourishing of human progress. This does not mean that philosophy ignores the ugly facts and unpleasant realities of life and history. Rather, it highlights these facts and realities precisely because they provoke doubt, curiosity, outrage, or desperation that motivates efforts to overcome them. These efforts take the forms of critique and praxis, forms that attempt to change what is into a better what can be.

Prophetic pragmatism closely resembles and, in some ways, converges with the metaphilosophical perspectives of Antonio Gramsci. Both conceive of philosophical activity as "a cultural battle to transform the popular 'mentality.'"[23] It is not surprising that Gramsci writes:

> What the pragmatists wrote about this question merits re-examination... they felt real needs and "described" them with an exactness that was not far off the mark, even if they did not succeed in posing the problems fully or in providing a solution.[24]

Prophetic pragmatism is inspired by the example of Antonio Gramsci principally because he is the major twentieth-century philosopher of praxis, power, and provocation without devaluing theory, adopting unidimensional conceptions of power, or reducing provocation to Clausewitzian calculations of warfare. Gramsci's work is historically specific, theoretically engaging, and politically activistic in an exemplary manner. His concrete and detailed investigations are grounded in and reflections upon local struggles, yet theoretically sensitive to structural dynamics and international phenomena. He is attuned to the complex linkage of socially constructed identities to human agency while still convinced of the crucial role of the ever-changing forms in class-ridden economic modes of production. Despite his fluid Leninist conception of political organization and mobilization (which downplays the democratic and libertarian values of prophetic pragmatists) and his unswerving allegiance to sophisticated Marxist social theory (which is an indispensable yet ultimately inadequate weapon for prophetic pragmatists), Gramsci exemplifies the critical spirit and oppositional sentiments of prophetic pragmatism.

This is seen most clearly in Gramsci's view of the relation of philosophy to "common sense." For him, the aim of philosophy is not only to become worldly by imposing its elite intellectual views upon people, but to become part of a social movement by nourishing and being nourished by the philosophical views of oppressed people themselves for the aims of social change and personal meaning. Gramsci viewed this mutually critical process in world-historical terms.

> From the disintegration of Hegelianism derives the beginning of a new cultural process, different in character from its predecessors, a process in which practical movement and theoretical thought are united (or are trying to unite through a struggle that is both theoretical and practical).
>
> It is not important that this movement had its origins in mediocre philosophical works or, at best, in works that were not philosophical masterpieces. What matters is that a new way of conceiving the world and man is born and that this conception is no longer reserved to the great intellectuals, to professional philosophers, but tends rather to become a popular, mass phenomenon, with a concretely world-wide character, capable of modifying (even if the result includes hybrid combinations) popular thought and mummified popular culture.
>
> One should not be surprised if this beginning arises from the convergence of various elements, apparently heterogeneous... j. Indeed, it is worth noting that such an overthrow could not but have connections with religion.[25]

Gramsci's bold suggestion here relates elite philosophical activity to the cultures of the oppressed in the name of a common effort for social change. Prophetic pragmatist sensibilities permit (or even encourage) this rejection of the arrogant scientistic self-privileging or haughty secular self-images of many modern philosophers and intellectuals. The point here is not that serious contemporary thinkers should surrender their critical intelligence, but rather that they should not demand that all peoples mimic their version of critical intelligence, especially if common efforts for social change can be strengthened. On this point, even the nuanced secularism of Edward Said—the most significant and salient Gramscian critic on the American intellectual scene today—can be questioned.[26] For Gramsci, ideologies of secularism or religions are less sets of beliefs and values, attitudes and sensibilities and more ways of life and ways of struggle manufactured and mobilized by certain sectors of the population in order to legitimate and preserve their social, political, and intellectual powers. Hence, the universities and churches, schools and synagogues, mass media and mosques become crucial terrain for ideological and political contestation. And philosophers are in no way exempt from this fierce battle even within the "serene" walls and halls of the academy. Similar to the American pragmatist tradition, Gramsci simply suggests that philosophers more consciously posit these battles themselves as objects of investigation and thereby intervene in these battles with intellectual integrity and ideological honesty.

Prophetic pragmatism purports to be not only an oppositional cultural criticism but also a material force for individuality and democracy. By "material force" I simply mean a practice that has some potency and effect or makes a difference in the world. There is—and should be—no such thing as a prophetic pragmatist movement. The translation of philosophic outlook into social motion is not that simple. In fact, it is possible to be a prophetic pragmatist and belong to different political movements, e.g., feminist, Chicano, black, socialist, left-liberal ones. It also is possible to subscribe to prophetic pragmatism and belong to different religious and/or secular traditions. This is so because a prophetic pragmatist commitment to individuality and democracy, historical consciousness and systemic social analyses, and tragic action in an evil-ridden world can take place in—though usually on the margin of—a variety of traditions. The distinctive hallmarks of a prophetic pragmatist are a universal consciousness that promotes an all-embracing democratic and libertarian moral vision, a historical consciousness that acknowledges human finitude and conditionedness, and a critical consciousness which encourages relentless critique and self-criticism for the aims of social change and personal humility.

My own version of prophetic pragmatism is situated within the Christian tradition. Unlike Gramsci, I am religious not simply for political aims but also by personal commitment. To put it crudely, I find existential sustenance in many of the narratives in the biblical scriptures as interpreted by streams in the Christian heritage; and I see political relevance in the biblical focus on the plight of the wretched of the earth. Needless to say, without the addition of modern intepretations of racial and gender equality, tolerance, and democracy, much of the tradition warrants rejection. Yet the Christian epic, stripped of static dogmas and decrepit doctrines, remains a rich source of existential empowerment and political engagement when viewed through modern lenses (indeed the only ones we moderns have!).

Like James, Niebuhr, and to some extent Du Bois, I hold a religious conception of pragmatism. I have dubbed it "prophetic" in that it harks back to the Jewish and Christian tradition of prophets who brought urgent and compassionate critique to bear on the evils of their day. The mark of the prophet is to speak the truth in love with courage—come what may. Prophetic pragmatism proceeds from this impulse. It neither requires a religious foundation nor entails a religious perspective, yet prophetic pragmatism is compatible with certain religious outlooks.

My kind of prophetic pragmatism is located in the Christian tradition for two basic reasons. First, on the existential level, the self-understanding and self-identity that flow from this tradition's insights into the crises and traumas of life are indispensable *for me* to remain sane. It holds at bay the sheer absurdity so evident in life, without erasing or eliding the tragedy of life. Like Kierkegaard, whose reflections on Christian faith were so profound yet often so frustrating, I do not think it possible to put forward rational defenses of one's faith that verify its veracity or even persuade one's critics. Yet it is possible to convey to others the sense of deep emptiness and pervasive meaninglessness one feels if one is not critically aligned with an enabling tradition. One risks not logical inconsistency but actual insanity; the issue is not reason or irrationality but life or death. Of course, the fundamental philosophical question remains whether the Christian gospel is ultimately true.[27] And, as a Christian prophetic pragmatist whose focus is on coping with transient and provisional penultimate matters yet whose hope goes beyond them, I reply in the affirmative, bank my all on it, yet am willing to entertain the possibility in low moments that I may be deluded.

Second, on the political level, the culture of the wretched of the earth is deeply religious. To be in solidarity with them requires not only an acknowledgment of what they are up against but also an appreciation of how they cope with their situation. This appreciation does not require that one be religious; but if one is religious, one has wider access into their life-worlds. This appreciation also does not entail an uncritical acceptance of religious narratives, their interpretations, or, most important, their often oppressive consequences. Yet to be religious permits one to devote one's life to accenting the prophetic and progressive potential within those traditions that shape the everyday practices and deeply held perspectives of most oppressed peoples. What a wonderful privilege and vocation this is!

The prophetic religious person, much like C. Wright Mills's activist intellectual, puts a premium on educating and being educated by struggling peoples, organizing and being organized by resisting groups. This political dimension of prophetic pragmatism as practiced within the Christian tradition impels one to be an organic intellectual, that is, one who revels in the life of the mind yet relates ideas to collective praxis. An organic intellectual, in contrast to traditional intellectuals who often remain comfortably nested in the academy, attempts to be entrenched in and affiliated with organizations, associations, and, possibly, movements of grass-roots folk. Of course, he or she need be neither religious nor linked to religious institutions. Trade unions, community groups, and political formations also suffice. Yet, since the Enlightenment in eighteenth-century Europe, most of the progressive energies among the intelligentsia have shunned religious channels. And in these days of global religious revivals, progressive forces are reaping the whirlwind. Those of us who remain in these religious channels see clearly just how myopic such an antireligious strategy is. The severing of ties to churches, synagogues, temples, and mosques by the left intelligentsia is tantamount to political suicide; it turns the pessimism of many self-deprecating and self-pitying secular progressive intellectuals into a self-fulfilling prophecy. This point was never grasped by C. Wright Mills, though W. E. B. Du Bois understood it well.

Like Gramsci, Du Bois remained intimately linked with oppositional forces in an oppressed community. And in his case, these forces were (and are) often led by prophetic figures of the black Christian tradition. To be a part of the black freedom movement is to rub elbows with some prophetic black preachers and parishioners. And to be a part of the forces of progress in America is to rub up against some of these black freedom fighters.

If prophetic pragmatism is ever to become more than a conversational subject matter for cultural critics in and out of the academy, it must inspire progressive and prophetic social motion. One precondition of this kind of social movement is the emergence of potent prophetic religious practices in churches, synagogues, temples, and mosques. And given the historical weight of such practices in the American past, the probable catalyst for social motion will be the prophetic wing of the black church. Need we remind ourselves that the most significant and successful organic intellectual in twentieth-century America—maybe in American history—was a product of and leader in the prophetic wing of the black church? Rarely has a figure in modern history outside of elected public office linked the life of the mind to social change with such moral persuasiveness and political effectiveness.

The social movement led by Martin Luther King, Jr., represents the best of what the political dimension of prophetic pragmatism is all about. Like Sojourner Truth, Walter Rauschenbusch, Elizabeth Cady Stanton, and Dorothy Day, King was not a prophetic pragmatist. Yet like them he was a prophet, in which role he contributed mightily to the political project of prophetic pragmatism. His all-embracing moral vision facilitated alliances and coalitions across racial, gender, class, and religious lines. His Gandhian method of nonviolent resistance highlighted forms of love, courage, and discipline worthy of a compassionate prophet. And his appropriation and interpretation of American civil religion extended the tradition of American jeremiads, a tradition of public exhortation that joins social criticisms of America to moral renewal and admonishes the country to be true to its founding ideals of freedom, equality, and democracy. King accented the antiracist and anti-imperialist consequences of taking seriously these ideals, thereby linking the struggle for freedom in America to those movements in South Africa, Poland, South Korea, Ethiopia, Chile, and the Soviet Union.

Prophetic pragmatism worships at no ideological altars. It condemns oppression anywhere and everywhere, be it the brutal butchery of third-world dictators, the regimentation and repression of peoples in the Soviet Union and Soviet-bloc countries, or the racism, patriarchy, homophobia, and economic injustice in the first-world capitalist nations. In this way, the precious ideals of individuality and democracy of prophetic pragmatism oppose all those power structures that lack public accountability, be they headed by military generals, bureaucratic party bosses, or corporate tycoons. Nor is prophetic pragmatism confined to any preordained historical agent, such as the working class, black people, or women. Rather, it invites all people of goodwill both here and abroad to fight for an Emersonian culture of creative democracy in which the plight of the wretched of the earth is alleviated.

Prophetic Pragmatism and Postmodernity

Prophetic pragmatism emerges at a particular moment in the history of North Atlantic civilization—the moment of postmodernity. A critical self-inventory of prophetic pragmatism—a historical situating of its emergence and possible development—requires an understanding of this postmodern moment.

Postmodernity can be understood in light of three fundamental historical processes. First, the end of the European Age (1492-1945) shattered European self-confidence and prompted intense self-criticism, even self-contempt. This monumental decentering of Europe produced exemplary intellectual reflections such as the demystifying of European cultural hegemony, the destruction of the Western metaphysical traditions, and the deconstruction of North Atlantic philosophical systems. Second, in the wake of European devastation and decline and upon the eclipse of European domination, the United States of America emerged as the world power with respect to military might, economic prosperity, political direction, and cultural production. Third, the advent of national political independence in Asia and Africa signaled the first stage of the decolonization of the third world.

Much of the current "postmodernism" debate, be it in architecture, literature, painting, photography, criticism, or philosophy, highlights the themes of difference, marginality, otherness, transgression, disruption, and simulation. Unfortunately, most of the treatments of these issues remain narrowly focused on the European and Euro-American predicament. For example, Jean-François Lyotard's celebrated and influential book *The Postmodern Condition* defines postmodernism as a progressive loss of faith in master narratives, e.g., religion, Marxism, liberalism; a rejection of representation in epistemic outlook; and a demand for radical artistic experimentation. For Lyotard, postmodernism becomes a recurring moment within the modern that is performative in character and aesthetic in content. The major sources from which Lyotard borrows—Kant's notion of the sublime and Wittgenstein's idea of language games—are deployed to promote certain modernist practices, namely, nonrepresentational, experimental techniques and viewpoints that shun and shatter quests for wholeness and totality.

Although both Jacques Derrida and Michel Foucault reject the term "postmodernism," their philosophies are widely viewed as major examples of postmodern thought. As with their fellow Frenchman Lyotard, Eurocentric frameworks and modernist loyalties loom large in the work of Derrida and Foucault. Derrida's deconstructionist version of poststructuralism accents the transgressive and disruptive aspects of Nietzsche and Heidegger, Mallarmé and Artaud. As an Algerian Jew in a

French Catholic (and anti-Semitic) society, Derrida attacks the major philosophic traditions of the West in the form of fascinating though ultimately monotonous deconstructions. This version of relentless skepticism toward logical consistency and theoretical coherence, which refuses to entertain or encourage novel reconstructions, may be symptomatic of the relative political impotence of marginal peoples, their inability to creatively transform and build on the ambiguous legacy of the Age of Europe.

Foucault provides rich social and historical substance to contemporary inquiries into the operations of otherness and marginality in his studies on the insane and the incarcerated. But even the "others" he investigates remain within European (usually French) boundaries. His heroes, like those of Derrida, are transgressive modernists such as Nietzsche and Bataille. Needless to say, the prominent opponents of "postmodernism"—Jürgen Habermas from the moderate left and Hilton Kramer from the far right—invoke past European projects, that is, the German Enlightenment and Anglo-American modernism, respectively.

Noteworthy attempts to broaden the "postmodernism" debate from its current focus on architecture and painting to post-World War II American cultural practices and artifacts in general can be seen in the work of William Spanos and the early Paul Bové.[28] In their illuminating neo-Heideggerian readings of American poets like Wallace Stevens, Robert Creeley, and Charles Olson, postmodern formulations of temporality, difference, and heterogeneity are put forward. Yet both Spanos and Bové remain at the level of philosophic outlooks and artistic strategies; that is, they understand postmodernism as a complex set of sensibilities, styles, or worldviews. This observation holds for the pioneering work of Rosalind Krauss.[29]

The significant breakthroughs of Fredric Jameson, Craig Owens, Hal Foster, and Andreas Huyssen are to push the "postmodernism" debate beyond narrow disciplinary boundaries, insulated artistic practices, and vague pronouncements of men and women of letters.[30] Instead of viewing "postmodernism" as a set of styles, sensibilities, or viewpoints, they posit "postmodernism" as a social category, a cultural dominant. They understand "postmodernism" as embracing certain exemplary social and cultural responses to new structural and institutional processes at work in the world.

For example, Jameson views such prevalent social and cultural features as depthlessness, ubiquitous images and simulacra, waning historical consciousness, escalating emotional intensities, schizophrenic subjects, and the breakdown of the distinction between high and low cultures as having been shaped by and as shaping advanced capitalist societies in which commodity production has a hold over all spheres of contemporary life. The important point here is not whether one fully agrees with Jameson's laundry list of postmodern constitutive characteristics or whether one approves of his treatments of individual cultural artifacts. Rather, what is salutary about Jameson's project is that he forces the debate to become more consciously historical, social, political, and ideological. Jameson helps situate the emergence of the "postmodernism" debate in relation to larger developments in society and history by providing a heuristic framework (in his case, a Marxist one) that discloses its broader significance.

Prophetic pragmatism arrives on the scene as a particular American intervention conscious and critical of its roots, and radically historical and political in its outlook. Furthermore, it gives prominence to the plight of those peoples who embody and enact the "postmodern" themes of degraded otherness, subjected alienness, and subaltern marginality, that is, the wretched of the earth (poor peoples of color, women, workers).

Prophetic pragmatism is a deeply American response to the end of the Age of Europe, the emergence of the United States as the world power, and the decolonization of the third world. The response is "American" not simply because it appropriates and promotes the major American tradition of cultural criticism, but also because it is shaped by the immediate American intellectual situation. This situation is not a "closing of the American mind," as nostalgically and tendentiously understood by Allan Bloom's popular work. Rather, it is a complex configuration of the effects on American intellectual life of the decentering of Europe, the centering of the United States, and the decolonizing of Asia and Africa.

The first consequence of these three historical processes for American intellectual life was the emergence of the first major subcultures of non-WASP intellectuals as exemplified in the so-called New York intellectuals, the abstract expressionist group, or the bebop jazz artists. These subcultures constituted a major challenge to an American male WASP cultural elite loyal to an older and eroding European model of culture, that of a genteel tradition. Irving Babbitt's fervent defense of highbrow humanism in the academy and Royal Cortissoz's philistine trashing of modernism outside of the academy represent two distant poles of this declining genteel tradition.

The first significant and salutary blow consisted of the entrance of gifted assimilated Jewish Americans like Lionel Trilling into the higher echelons of the academy, especially the fervently anti-Semitic Ivy League institutions of the forties. This development signified the slow but sure undoing of male WASP cultural harmony and homogeneity. Furthermore, the postwar American economic boom laid the groundwork for expansion, professionalization, and specialization in institutions of higher education, forcing humanistic scholars to forge self-images of rigor and scientific seriousness. New methods that helped create such self-images included the close reading techniques of New Criticism in literature, the logical precision of reasoning in analytic philosophy, and the theoretical jargon of Parsonian structural functionalism in sociology. Only the new programs of American studies in the fifties provided academic space for broad cultural criticism, criticism that often remained rather muted owing to the repressive atmosphere of McCarthyism.

The sixties constitute the watershed period in contemporary American intellectual life. The inclusion of Afro-Americans, Spanish-speaking Americans, Asian Americans, Native Americans, American women, and working-class white men in significant numbers in the academy shattered male WASP cultural pretension and predominance. Accompanied by great fanfare and tremendous turbulence, often at the expense of intellectual seriousness on the part of both defenders and opponents of the status quo, this development revealed the pervasive political character of academic life in America. The sixties did not simply politicize American intellectual life; rather, they repoliticized in an explicit manner what had been political in an implicit manner. The consequent disorienting intellectual polemics and inescapable ideological polarization that tend to reduce complex formulations and traduce genuine conversations have been a lasting legacy of the sixties. It was initiated by the worst of the New Left and has been perfected by the best of the New Right.

Another intellectual legacy of the sixties is the American obsession with theories from continental Europe. These theories internationalized American humanistic discourses, yet also turned American intellectuals away from their own national traditions of thought. Only in historiography did American intellectuals dig deep to recover and revise the understanding of the U.S. past in light of those on its underside. A final legacy was the onslaught of forms of popular culture, such as TV and film, on highbrow literate culture. Academic humanists were rendered marginal to the intellectual life of the country, displaced by journalists usually ill equipped for the task yet eager to speak to an ever-growing middlebrow audience.

The academic inclusion on a grand scale of the students of color, working-class origins, and women produced ideologies of institutional pluralism to mediate between the clashing methods and perspectives in the structurally fragmented humanistic departments and programs. Dissensus reigned and reigns supreme. Pluralism served both to contain and often to conceal unsolvable ideological conflict; yet it also ensured a few slots for ambitious and upwardly mobile young left professors enchanted with their bold oppositional rhetoric even as they remained too anxious to retain their professional-managerial class status to be anything but politically innocuous in larger American society. The influential conservative strategy was to attack this academic inclusion of the "new barbarians" in the name of standards, tradition, and cultural literacy. Ironically, both the right and left critics posit academicism and commercialism as major culprits in American intellectual life.

Prophetic pragmatism is a form of American left thought and action in our postmodern moment. It is deeply indebted to the continental traveling theories such as Marxism, structuralism, and poststructuralism, yet it remains in the American grain. It is rooted in the best of American radicalism but refuses to be simply another polemical position on the ideological spectrum. Prophetic pragmatism calls for reinvigoration of a sane, sober, and sophisticated intellectual life in America and for regeneration of social forces empowering the disadvantaged, degraded, and dejected. It rejects the faddish cynicism and fashionable conservatism rampant in the intelligentsia and general populace. Prophetic pragmatism rests upon the conviction that the American evasion of philosophy is not an evasion of serious thought and moral action. Rather such evasion is a rich and revisable tradition that serves as the occasion for cultural criticism and political engagement in the service of an Emersonian culture of creative democracy.

Notes

1 Benjamin Barber, *The Conquest of Politics: Liberal Philosophy in Democratic Times*, chap. 8.

2 Ibid.

3 Ibid. The best practical outline of the desirable economy I know is in Alec Nove's *The Economics of Feasible Socialism* (London: George Allen and Unwin, 1983), pp. 197–230.

4 Roberto Unger, *Social Theory, Its Situation and Its Task: A Critical Introduction to Politics—A Work in Constructive Social Theory* (Cambridge : Cambridge University Press, 1987), p. 41.

5 Ibid.

6 Ibid., p. 14.

7 Ibid., pp. 18–22.

8 Ibid., p. 43.

9 Ibid., p. 214.

10 Ibid., pp. 214–15.

11 For a preliminary effort in this regard pertaining to race, see Cornel West, "Race and Social Theory: Towards a Genealogical Materialist Analysis," in *American Left Yearbook* 2, ed. Michael Davis et al. (London: Verso, 1987), pp. 74–90.

12 See Foucault's influential essay "Nietzsche, Genealogy, History," *Language, Counter-Memory, Practice,* trans. Donald F. Bouchard and Sherry Simon (Ithaca: Cornell University Press, 1977), pp. 139–64.

13 The best example of Foucault's powerful genealogical investigations is his work *Discipline and Punish: The Birth of the Prison,* trans. Alan Sheridan (New York: Vintage Books, 1979).

14 For a reading of Foucault that highlights this aspect of his work, see John Rajchman, *Michel Foucault: The Freedom of Philosophy* (New York: Columbia University Press, 1985), pp. 103–8.

15 Michel Foucault, "Truth and Power," *Power/Knowledge: Selected Interviews and Other Writings, 1972–1977,* trans. Colin Gordon et al. (New York: Pantheon Books, 1980), p. 117.

16 Michel Foucault, "The Subject and Power, " *Critical Inquiry,* 8, no. 1 (Summer 1982), pp. 777, 778.

17 Rajchman, *Michel Foucault,* p. 103.

18 Edward W. Said, *The World, the Text, and the Critic* (Cambridge: Harvard University Press, 1983), pp. 221, 222.

19 In discussions with Professor Daniel Defert in Paris during the spring of 1987, he informed me that Foucault's letters contain evidence of deep familiarity with American pragmatism (Foucault's neighbor in Tunisia for two years was France's leading interpreter of American philosophy, Gerard Deledalle). Furthermore, Foucault's reading of materials produced by the Black Panther party was instrumental in his turn toward the centrality of the strategic and tactical in genealogical work. My basic claim here is that certain Kantian residues still haunt Foucault's later work.

20 Raymond Williams, *Modern Tragedy* (Stanford: Stanford University Press, 1966), pp. 48–49.

21 Hans-Georg Gadamer, *Truth and Method* (New York: Seabury Press, 1975), pp. 245–341. Edward Shils, *Tradition* (Chicago: University of Chicago Press, 1981).

22 Williams, *Modern Tragedy,* pp. 83–84.

23 Antonio Gramsci, *Selections from the Prison Notebooks,* ed. and trans. Quintin Hoare and Geoffrey Nowell Smith (New York: International Publishers, 1971), p. 348.

24 Ibid., pp. 348, 349.

25 Ibid., p. 417. For an elaboration of this Gramscian viewpoint, see Cornel West, "Religion and the Left," *Prophetic Fragments* (Grand Rapids, MI: Eerdmans, 1988), pp. 13–21.

26 Said, *The World, the Text, and the Critic,* pp. 1–30.

27 For a prophetic pragmatist treatment of this matter, see Cornel West, "The Historicist Turn in Philosophy of Religion," in *Knowing Religiously,* ed. Leroy S. Rouner (Notre Dame, IN: University of Notre Dame Press, 1985), pp. 36–51. See also, Cornel West, "On Leszek Kolakowski's *Religion,"* in *Prophetic Fragments,* pp. 216–21.

28 William Spanos, *Repetitions: Essays on the Postmodern Occasion* (Bloomington: Indiana University Press, 1987); Paul Bové, *Destructive Poetics: Heidegger and Modern American Poetry* (New York: Columbia University Press, 1980). Bové has since become one of the few sophisticated Foucaultian critics in America as seen in *Intellectuals in Power: A Genealogy of Critical Humanism* (New York: Columbia University Press, 1986). See also the essays by Jonathan Arac, Donald Pease, and Joseph Buttigieg in *Criticism without Boundaries: Directions and Crosscurrents in Postmodern Critical Theory,* ed. Joseph Buttigieg (Notre Dame: Notre Dame University Press, 1987).

29 Rosalind E. Krauss, *The Originality of the Avant-Garde and Other Modernist Myths* (Cambridge, MA: MIT Press, 1985).

30 *The Anti-Aesthetic: Essays on Postmodern Culture,* ed. Hal Foster (Port Townsend: Bay Press, 1983); Hal Foster, *Recodings: Art, Spectacle, Cultural Politics;* Andreas Huyssen, *After the Great Divide: Modernism, Mass Culture, Postmodernism* (Bloomington: Indiana University Press, 1986); Fredric Jameson, "Postmodernism, or the Cultural Logic of Late Capitalism," *New Left Review* (July–August 1984), pp.53–92.

IAN HACKING
(B. 1936)

Hacking's three parables center on the problem of objectivity and, with their discussions of Thomas Kuhn, Richard Rorty, and Michel Foucault, operate in the universe of contemporary pragmatism. Yet Hacking—who is a professor of the history and philosophy of science at Toronto and the author of *The Emergence of Probability* (1975), *Scientific Revolutions* (1981), and *Representing and Intervening* (1983)—is no pragmatist, for he is skeptical about the far-reaching relativistic or idealistic claims that are often advanced in the name of pragmatism. Hacking holds that although the progression of science is in part explained by its history and cultural setting (as Kuhn argued in The *Structure of Scientific Revolutions*), there are nevertheless important differences between the social and historical sciences on the one hand and the natural sciences on the other. Hacking puts the difference by saying that although we "remake the world," we "make up people."

For example, as the new science of statistics was applied to data gathering in the early nineteenth century, "we find classifications of over 4,000 different criss-crossing motives for murder. I do not believe that mad people of these sorts, or these motives for murder, in general existed until there came into being the practice of counting them." Whereas certain kinds of people are thus impossible without human culture, electrons will always be, and always have been there—available as it were—no matter what the history of the universe or the culture of those who look for them.

Hacking distinguishes between nominalism and idealism, arguing that Kuhn is a revolutionary nominalist but not an idealist. As a nominalist he believes that there is nothing all things called by a name share, except that they are called by that name; but he does not believe the idealist thesis "that the mind and its ideas determine the structure of our world." Kuhn does believe, according to Hacking, that our categories for describing the world have a history, but thinks nevertheless that the objects we are describing do not. Hacking's position owes much to Peirce, who believed that although our schemes for describing the world are thoroughly human constructions, they are fated—in the long run and if examined by an ideal community of inquirers—to correspond to an independently existing reality.

Hacking's robust sense of realism serves as a corrective to the more idealistic versions of pragmatism in Rorty or Fish or James. Nevertheless, there is no reason a pragmatist cannot be a realist, writers from William James to Hilary Putnam would want to insist. But they must then find some way of meeting the challenge Hacking poses: of explaining why some of our schemes work better than others.

THREE PARABLES

IAN HACKING

I The Green Family

A short time ago I visited the phoenix city of Dresden which, in addition to its collections of European art, is home to a remarkable display of Chinese porcelain. We owe both to the man whom everyone in Saxony calls August der Stark, although technically he is Augustus II (1670–1733), sometime king of Poland, and Friedrich Augustus I, elector of Saxony. He is less admired for his skill as politician and warrior than for his lavish art collections, his prodigious strength and (in some quarters) for having fathered the largest number of children on historical record. August bought any good porcelain he could lay his hands on. His objects are limited in scope, coming mostly from the period of K'ang Hsi, 1662–1722. In 1717 he built a small palace for his china, and in the same year he traded Friedrich Wilhelm I of Prussia a crack regiment of dragoons for 151 vases, still known as the *Dragonenvasen.* Although he did indeed wield his sword, not all that effectually, he was no Prussian. August der Stark chiefly made love, not war. He put his research and development money not into cannon but chemistry, funding the rediscovery of the ancient Chinese secret of porcelain manufacture, so that Meissen in Saxony became the first European porcelain factory. (This was of commercial as well as aesthetic interest, for in those days porcelain was the main manufactured commodity imported into Europe.)

I know little about porcelain. I report without any claim to discernment that in Dresden my eye was especially caught by work in the style called "the green family." New techniques of glazing were developed in one of the great exporting regions. The results were stunningly beautiful. I do not single out August der Stark's pieces as the highpoint of Chinese art. Slightly later work is often more esteemed in the West, and I know well that very much earlier work has a grace and simplicity that moves the spirit more deeply. I use the green family rather as a parable of changing tastes and enduring values.

August der Stark may have loved his china to the point of building a palace for it, but it was dismissed by later cognoscenti as of no more value than a collection of dolls. For a century it languished in a crowded cellar, where on dull days you could only barely make out the looming shapes of some of the larger pieces. One man in particular guarded these obscure treasures, Dr. Gustav Klemm, and he traded duplicate pieces with other dusty curators to expand what would become the noblest collection of this kind of work in Europe. Only towards the end of the nineteenth century was it returned to light. Then it came out to amaze and delight not only scholars but transients such as me. During the last European war the china went into the cellars again, and survived the Dresden massacre. Then all the Dresden collections went to Moscow for care and custody. They returned in 1958 to be housed in the noble rebuilt rooms of the Zwinger palace.

One could use this adventure to tell two opposite stories. One says: here is a typical human tale of wealth, lust, changes in taste, destruction, survival. Only a sequence of accidents created the Chinese export trade of objects suited to a certain European fashion for chinoiserie around 1700, and then brought some characteristic examples under one lavish roof, saw them lapse from public taste, witnessed a revival, a firestorm and a return. It is a mere historical fact that Leibniz (for example) doted on Chinese work, for such was the fashion of his time. Likewise I, more ignorantly, gape at it too, conditioned by present trends. It was not, however, for Wolff, Kant or Hegel to admire. In short there were periods of admiration and times when these pieces were despised, unlit, unloved. It will be like that again, not only in Europe but also in the land of their manufacture. In some years they will be condemned as an example of early subservience to the bourgeoisie of Europe and its colonies (the green family was a big hit with the planter families in Indonesia). In other years it will come out of Chinese cellars and be invested with an entirely different aura. *Evidently there is no intrinsic value in this stuff, it goes up and down in the scale of human admiration as the wind blows.*

Relativists seldom state their position so crassly, but that is roughly what they think. No one pretends that the conclusion, "there is no intrinsic value in this stuff" follows from the events described in my example, but I wish to urge, against that conclusion, a slightly more empirical claim which is, I think, supported by the historical facts. I hold that no matter what dark ages we endure, so long as cellars save for us an adequate body of work by the green family, there will be generations that rediscover it. It will time and again *show itself.* I do not need to be reminded that porcelain will show itself only under certain conditions of wealth, pride, and human eccentricities (such as the bizarre practice of crossing disagreeable borders to wander around a strange institution that we call a museum).

I claim no intrinsic value for the green family to be found in heaven, but only an essentially human value, one tiny instance of an inherently human bundle of values, some of which manifest themselves more strongly at one time, some more strongly at another. Achievements created by humans have a strange persistence that contrasts with fashion. Most of the junk that we create has no such value. A sufficiently broad experience of the older private European collections—where objects are kept more for reasons of historical piety than of taste—assures us that being museumized is almost irrelevant to worth. August's collection is special, as its systematic survival and revival bear witness.

What has this to do with philosophy? The resurgence of historicism in philosophy brings its own relativism. Richard Rorty has captured it, or is thought to have captured it, in his powerful book, *Philosophy and the Mirror of Nature*. I was happily innoculated against that message. Just before *Mirror* appeared, I had been giving a course introducing undergraduates to the philosophers who were contemporaries of the green family and August der Stark. My hero had been Leibniz, and as usual my audience gave me pained looks. But after the last meeting some students gathered around and began with the conventional, "Gee, what a great course." The subsequent remarks were more instructive: "But you could not help it... What with all those great books, I mean like Descartes..." They loved Descartes and his *Meditations*.

I happen to give terrible lectures on Descartes, for I mumble along saying that I do not understand him much. It does not matter. Descartes speaks directly to these young people, who know as little about Descartes and his times as I know about the green family and its time. But just as the green family showed itself to me, directly, so Descartes shows himself to them. My reading list served the function of the Zwinger gallery: it is the porcelain or the reading itself, not the gallery or lecture room, that does the showing. The value of Descartes to these students is completely anachronistic, out of time. Half will have begun with the idea Descartes and Sartre were contemporaries, both being French. Descartes, even more than Sartre, can speak directly to them across the seas of time. Historicism, even Rorty's, forgets that.

A novice needs food, then space, then time, then books, and then an incentive to read, and often that is hardly enough, for just as with the green family, Descartes will have his ups and downs. In London 150 years ago, Spinoza was the rage and Descartes ignored. Neither goes down well in Dresden or Canton today. Both will be much read there in the future, if physical and human conditions permit, or so I say.

As for our more immediate surroundings, any of ten thousand lecture courses would serve as the gallery for Descartes to show himself. It may be my bumbling attempt to locate Descartes in the problematic of his day; it may be Rorty's destruction; or it may be any one of the standard pen-friend-across-the-seas-of-times courses. I give no argument for my conviction, but invite only experience. I mimic G. E. Moore holding up his hand before an audience of jaded skeptics. Most of us are too jaded even to remember the initial way in which Descartes spoke to us. That is the point of my parable. I gave, from my own recent past, a parallel to just that first speaking. I invite readers to invent or recall their own personal parallel. But if you resist, let me point once more: Hegel dominated the formation of Dewey, and perhaps that of Peirce, and also that of the upstarts Moore and Russell who laid waste to him within a few years. Hegel has, however, long lain fallow among those who read and work in English. Yet I need only point to the author of our opening chapter, Charles Taylor (whose expositions have much to do with the new anglophone practice of reading Hegel)[1] to remind you that Hegel is back. The francophone was, a little earlier, even more hindered when attempting to read Hegel, until Jean Hypolyte provided the gallery within which Hegel would once again show himself. But now we even find Michel Foucault, although he may be seen in print as the denier of the substantiality of "the text," willing in conversation to admit with glee, when asked for his reaction to the *Phenomenology of Spirit,* that it is *un beau livre.* As indeed it is. That is what it is for a writer such as Hegel to speak directly, once again, first to the French, and later to us, after decades of oblivion.

II Remaking the World

No one from his generation has had a more dramatic impact on the philosophy of science than T. S. Kuhn. Any discussion of the relation between history and philosophy of science will begin with *The Structure of Scientific Revolutions.* This is odd, because he wrote entirely about natural science, indeed about the physical sciences. There is a time-honoured opinion that history matters to the very content of the human sciences, while it does not matter much to the natural sciences. If Kuhn had succeeded in historicizing our understanding of natural science, his achievement would have been revolutionary. I want to show why he did not succeed, and to give another twist to the old idea about a difference between natural and social science. This is in no sense a criticism of Kuhn. I believe that the totality of the work of this historian places him among the major philosophers of this century. Philosophers usually respond only to *Structure.* His work on experiments, measurement, and the second scientific revolution (all published in *The Essential Tension)* are of comparable importance. His latest historical book, *Black Body Theory and the Quantum Discontinuity, 1894–1912,* is what *Structure* is all about, and it is a notable achievement. Yet it is possible to learn from Kuhn in the most thorough way possible, and still to hold that there is a sense in which he did not succeed, and could not have succeeded, in historicizing natural science.

My distinction comes out at the level of one of the older philosophical disputes. It concerns nominalism. The most extreme version of nominalism says that we make up the categories that we use to describe the world. That is a most mysterious doctrine, which is perhaps why, like solipsism, it is almost never maintained. The problem is that we cannot understand why the world is so tractable to our systems of naming. Must there not be some natural kinds in the world for our invented categories to latch on to? Does not that refute strict nominalism?

I hold that Kuhn has importantly advanced the nominalist cause by giving some account of how at least an important group of "our" categories come into being in the course of scientific revolutions. There is a construction of new systems of classification

going hand in hand with certain interests in describing the world, interests closely connected with the "anomalies" on which a community focuses in times of "crisis." At the
same time this cannot lead us to a *very* strict nominalism, for the anomalies "really" do
have to appear to be resolved in order for a revolutionary achievement to be recognized.
Removal of anomaly is never enough, Kuhn has taught, because all sorts of social conditions are needed for a revolution to "take." But reality has to go some part of the way
—more than a wilder, stricter, nominalism would allow.

My contrast with the social sciences is as follows. In natural science our invention of
categories does not "really" change the way the world works. Even though we create
new phenomena which did not exist before our scientific endeavours, we do so only with
a licence from the world (or so we think). But in social phenomena we may generate
kinds of people and kinds of action as we devise new classifications and categories. My
claim is that we "make up people" in a stronger sense than we "make up" the world. The
difference is, as I say, connected with the ancient question of nominalism. It is also connected with history, because the objects of the social sciences—people and groups of
people—are constituted by an historical process, while the objects of the natural sciences, particular experimental apparatus, are created in time, but, in some sense, they
are not constituted historically.

It must be clear that I am groping for a complex distinction between social and natural
science. Perhaps I should warn against the most superficial distinction of all. It is curious,
even comical, that physical scientists have paid little attention to Kuhn. Science journalists may now fill their articles with the word "paradigm," but it is not a word that
plays any role in reflection about serious research. It is quite the opposite in the social
and psychological sciences. Kuhn's *Structure* had hardly appeared in print when presiden-
tial addresses to annual meetings of the American Psychological Association and the
American Sociological Association avowed their need for paradigms. It has always
seemed to me that Kuhn was a good deal clearer about his use of his famous word than
most of his readers, including presidents of learned societies. When I claim that there is
a sense in which Kuhn has not succeeded in historicizing physical science, it is not
because his terminology has had more of a fad in the social sciences. Quite the contrary:
it may be that the impact of Kuhn on social sciences is a sign of their lack of self-understanding.

Let us first recall philosophical reaction to Kuhn's book. He was accused of a scan-
dalous undermining of rationality. "Normal science" did not seem to have any of the
virtues that a previous generation of positivists ascribed to science. Even worse, revolutionary change was not cumulative, nor did it occur because there was good reason for
making the change, sound evidence for the new post-revolutionary science. Part of the
philosophical guild defended its entrenched rights, and protested that history could
never teach us anything about scientific rationality. The historian might exhibit some
events in the history of science, but the philosopher would always be required to say
whether those events were rational or not.

Thus the first wave of philosophical reaction was on the score of rationality, and people still do debate Kuhn's contribution, if any, to the methodology of science. He himself was a bit bemused by this reception, as is shown by his 1973 lecture, "Objectivity, value judgment, and theory choice." He subscribed to the traditional values after all—theories should be accurate, consistent, broad in scope, simple, and fruitful in new research findings. He insisted that these desiderata were not in general decisive. Moreover, the relative weights given to these considerations vary from research group to research group, from discipline to discipline, and from one era of science to another. Finally, the sheer rough and tumble of research is too messy for there to be any systematic algorithm. Kuhn was, however, no irrationalist demeaning these common-sense values, and I think the rumour of a "rationality crisis" provoked by Kuhn was exaggerated.

Another theme of Kuhn's was less discussed, at first, than rationality: an anti-realism, a strong temptation, it appears, towards idealism. Not only are revolutions "changes in world view"—not a very daring statement, but Kuhn is "tempted" to say that after a revolution one "lives in a different world." Today, some twenty years after the book was published (a period during which Kuhn completed his monumental study of the onset of quantization), he has returned to that theme. People do see the world differently: what better evidence than that they draw it differently! He illustrates this with the first drawings of Volta's electric batteries. When we examine them closely we want to say that the cells cannot have been made like that, for they simply would not work. The voltaic cell, I may add, is no minor invention, but one of the fundamental tools of all science. It came into being in 1800, coinciding with the revival of the wave theory of light, of infrared radiation and much else that had no immediate place in Newtonian Physics. Volta's invention was fundamental because it provided a steady current of electricity, and hence deflected the magnetic compass. Therefore it created a new epoch, that of electromagnetism.

Kuhn's "temptation to speak of living in a different world" suggests that he is an idealist, one who holds, in some way, that the mind and its ideas determine the structure of our world. I think he is no idealist, and urge that we should think not of the post-Kantian realist/idealist dichotomy, but of the older, scholastic, realism/nominalism distinction. Kuhn is not among those who challenge the absolute existence of scientific entities or phenomena, nor among those who query the truth conditions for theoretical propositions. Instead he believes that the classifications, categories and possible descriptions that we deploy are very much of our own devising. But rather than leaving this as a mystery about how human categories come into being, he now makes the creation and adjustment of schemes of classification part of his definition of a revolution:

> What characterizes revolutions is, thus, change in several of the taxonomic categories prerequisite to scientific description and generalization. That change, furthermore, is an adjustment not only of criteria relevant to categorization, but also of the way in which objects and situations are distributed among pre-existing categories.

I read that as a species of nominalism, and name it revolutionary nominalism, because the transitions in systems of categories occur during those revolutionary breaks with the past whose structures Kuhn proposes to describe. It is also, of course, an historicized nominalism, because it gives an historical account (or is it only an historical metaphor?) of the genesis and transformation of systems of naming. It also has the great value of being local rather than global, for although Kuhn includes big events among his revolutions (Lavoisier, Copernicus) he insists that most revolutions apply only within a small community of, say, one hundred main researchers.

Kuhn's revolutionary nominalism invites histories of category change, but it may seem that the objects of the sciences, although described by changing systems of categories, are not themselves historically constituted. Yet what are the objects? Do they include voltaic cells, for example? Do they include such phenomena as the deflection of a magnetic needle by a steady electric current, or Faraday's more ingenious devices, the electric generator and the electric dynamo? These are not eternal items in the inventory of the universe, but came into existence at very specific times. Nor am I content to say that the inventions are dated, while the phenomena and laws of nature that they employ are eternal. I have been urging for some time that one of the chief activities of the experimenter in the physical sciences is quite literally to create phenomena that did not exist before. Moreover most of physical science (as opposed to astronomy) is about phenomena that did not exist until people brought them into being. What physicists have from the 1870s been calling "effects" (the photo-electric effect, the Zeeman effect, the Compton effect, the Josephson effect) are mostly phenomena which do not exist, at least in a pure state, anywhere in unpolluted nature, yet they are arguably what physics is, or has come to be, *about*. A more detailed and more guarded statement of this idea is given in my recent book *Representing and Intervening*. I put it in a more blatant way here to suggest that there is a case (of sorts) for saying that the very objects of physical science are not merely recategorized and rearranged, as Kuhn says, but brought into being by human ingenuity.

If I go to this extreme, is not my proposed distinction between human and natural science in ruins? Is it not the case that the objects of natural science become "historically constituted"? I do not think so. Indeed I have developed a return to serious consideration of experimental science precisely to urge a good many realist, anti-idealist, anti-nominalist conclusions. I claim in the "representing" half of *Representing and Intervening* that in principle no debates at the level of theorizing will settle any of those realism/anti-realism debates in the philosophy of natural science. I urge, in the "intervening" half, that recognition of the facts of experimental life and of changing the world leads powerfully to scientific realism. You will detect one source of my admiration for Brecht's direct materialism that puts "manipulation" rather than "thinking" as the source of realism. My "experimental realism" no more invites nominalism than Brecht's materialism. I think that the physical phenomena that are created by human beings are rather resilient to theoretical change. Kuhn's own example of the voltaic cell serves me well.

Kuhn writes that Volta saw his invention on analogy with the Leyden jar. Volta's description of it is strange, and we cannot credit his drawings, for they build in the wrong analogies. But the thing worked. Current did flow. Once that had been done physics never looked back. Likewise, the photo-electric effect was perhaps first produced in 1829 by Becquerel. Various photo-electric manifestations were induced throughout the nineteenth century. One can construct a Kuhnian argument that the effect was not properly "discovered" until the time of Lenard (1902) or even Einstein and the theory of photons (1905). Certainly once we had the theory we were able to use the phenomena we had begun to create. Automatic doors at supermarkets, and television, were not too far behind. But if (as some have urged) the photon approach needs drastic revision or revolutionary rejection, the supermarket doors will still go on working. Phenomena are resilient to theory. Elementary physics may teach a completely different story about how they work, but work they will. Even if, to re-quote Kuhn, "there is an adjustment not only of criteria relevant to categorization, but also of the way in which objects and situations are distributed among pre-existing categories," the phenomena which we have created will still exist and the inventions will work. We may lose interest in them. We may replace them by more useful or interesting phenomena. We might lose the skills needed to produce a phenomenon (no one can work brass today the way that a nine-teenth-century laboratory assistant could work brass, and I am sure most of the old skills for polishing lenses are now obsolete). I am the last philosopher to forget the radical changes in experimental technology. I still hold that the objects of the physical sciences are largely created by people, *and* that once created, there is no reason except human backsliding why they should not continue to persist.

Thus I claim that Kuhn leads us into a "revolutionary nominalism" which makes nominalism less mysterious by describing the historical processes whereby new cate-gories and distributions of objects come in to being. But I assert that a seemingly more radical step, literal belief in the creation of phenomena, shows why the objects of the sci-ences, although brought into being at moments of time, are not historically constituted. They are phenomena thereafter, regardless of what happens. I call this "experimental realism."

Never shy to add a few more "isms" to our ismically troubled world, I would say that my position is strikingly similar to that evolved by Gaston Bachelard's "applied rational-ism and technical materialism." No other philosopher or historian so assiduously studied the realities of experimental life, nor was anyone less inclined than he to suppose that the mind is unimportant (his applied rationalism). Fifty years ago he was teaching that epistemological breaks occur in science (e.g., "the photo-electric effect represents an absolute discontinuity in the history of the sciences"). At the same time he believed in scientific accumulation and *connaissance approchée*. What we accumulate are *experimental techniques* and *styles of reasoning*. Anglophone philosophy of science has too much debated the question of whether theoretical *knowledge* accumulates. Maybe it does not. So what? Phenomena and reasons accumulate.

Having thus made a slight obeisance towards Bachelard I pass to one of his spiritual descendants, namely, Michel Foucault. I shall try to be aware of one of Addison's warnings in *The Spectator*. "A few general rules, extracted out of the French authors, with a certain cant of words, has sometimes set up an illiterate and heavy writer for a most judicious and formidable critic."[2]

III Making up People

At the end of a recent review of Rorty's *Consequences of Pragmatism*, Bernard Williams first quotes Rorty quoting Foucault, "the being of language continues to shine ever brighter on the horizon." He then goes on to say that unless we keep sense

> that science finds ways out of the cell of words, and if we do not recover the sense that pursuing science is one of our essential experiences of being constrained by the truth, we shall find that the brightness of language on the horizon turns out to be that of the fire in which the supremely bookish hero of Canetti's *Auto Da Fe* immolated himself in his library.

Such games of meta-meta-quoting invite a little burning, but I have two reasons for quoting Williams. The minor one, something of an aside, is that Williams himself may be trapped within the cell of words. The way out of Williams' cell is not to be constrained by the truth but to create phenomena. Only within a theory-dominated verbalistic philosophy of science is "pursuing science one of our essential experiences of being constrained by the truth." Let us take a recent example of an important discovery. The event in question happened three months ago. It bore out some guesses made by Fermi many years before. He thought that there must be a particle, a weak elementary particle or boson W, which was in some sense the "carrier" of weak neutral currents (just as the electron carries ordinary charged currents). Around 1970 people were trying to find W, but then the high energy physics community switched to studying weak neutral currents themselves. They regarded W as a mere hypothetical entity, a figment of our imagination. Only in this decade was the search resumed, at very much higher energy levels than Fermi had thought necessary. Finally, in January 1983, CERN announced it had located W in proton-antiproton decay at 540 GeV. There is a complex history of science story to tell about the shift away from a search for W and then back. There certainly were constraints, but not "constraints of truth." I do not suppose there is a true theory of truth, but there is an instructive one, namely the redundancy theory, which says that "p is true" says no more than p. If something verbal constrained the earlier experimenters, it was a p, not the truth of p. What really constrained research workers was a need for greater energy sources; one had to wait for the next generation in order to create the sought for phenomena involving proton-antiproton decay. There were constraints all over the place, but none of them were constraints of truth, unless by vicious semantic ascent we express the constraints using the redundant word "true."

The redundancy theory of truth is instructive but defective. I refer not to its formal defects, but to its philosophical ones. It makes it seem as if "is true" is merely redundant, but harmless. I think that it does invite semantic ascent, and takes us up the ladder to that cell of words in which philosophers, not excluding Williams, confine themselves. If there is an interesting theory of truth to discuss at the moment, it will lie in Foucault's own "suggestions to be further tested and evaluated":

> "Truth" is to be understood as a system of ordered procedures for the production, regulation, distribution, circulation and operation of statements. "Truth" is linked in a circular relation with systems of power which produce and sustain it, and to effects of power which it induces and which extend it.

We should, if we have a philosophical interest in truth, care about how statements come into being as candidates for being true or false, and as possible objects of knowledge. But even here "truth" is redundant, for we are concerned simply with how statements come into being.

So much by way of aside. What of Williams' critique of Foucault? My second thoughts on *The Order of Things* not withstanding, Williams' remarks seem curiously misplaced. Foucault's books are mostly about practices and how they affect and are affected by the talk in which we embed them. The upshot is less a fascination with words, than with people and institutions, with what we do for people and to people. He does have a noble obsession with what he takes to be oppression: the asylum, the prison, the hospital, public hygiene and forensic medicine. His view of these practices may be entirely wrong. Some say that he has already done untold harm to wretched disturbed people who are released on the streets of the American metropolis because Foucault has convinced doctors that the disturbed ought not to be constrained. But one thing is clear. Without wishing in any way to undervalue the important political activities of Charles Taylor, Foucault, vastly more than anyone else invited to contribute to this volume, has not been locked in a cell of words. Moreover, it is precisely his intellectual work, his philosophical work, that directs our attention away from our talk and on to our practices.

I am not denying that Foucault is verbal. Few people have read his first book, about the surrealist Raymond Roussell. Roussell seems to be the very epitome of the man in the cell of words. One of his books is "How I have written some of my books." He says he would try to find a sentence such that, by changing one letter in one of the words, you change the meaning of each of the words in the sentence, as well as the grammar. (I hope no one at MIT hears of this.) Then you write down the first sentence at the front of your novel, and carry on until you end your book with the second sentence. He wrote a book, "Impressions of Egypt," and then toured Egypt to make sure nothing in the book was true. He came of good stock. His mad rich mother chartered a yacht to make a voyage to India. When she got near the coastline she screwed up her telescope, said, "Now I have seen India" and sailed home. Roussell killed himself. This can all be read at one level as the hyperparisian linguistic obsession. But a caricature, even if lived seriously, may also be read as directing us to the exact opposite.

Whatever be the point of the Roussell phase, let us consider the main sequence of Foucault's work, the madhouse, the clinic, the prison, sexuality, and in general the intermeshing of "knowledge" and "power." I have remarked that Kuhn says nothing about the social sciences or knowledge of human beings. Likewise Foucault says nothing about the physical sciences. His remarks about what we charmingly call the life sciences are chiefly, although not entirely, directed at how we interfere with human lives. I have heard Foucault criticized for being scared of physical science. Let us instead consider the hypothesis that there is something fundamentally correct about the division of labour, Kuhn to the physical sciences, and Foucault to human affairs.

I shall focus on only one thing, making a specific contrast with Kuhn's revolutionary nominalism. The problem with scholastic nominalism, I said, is that it leaves our interaction with, and description of, the world a complete mystery. We can well understand why the word "pencil" nicely sorts out some objects. We manufacture pencils; that is why they exist. Nominalism about human artefacts is no problem. It is nominalism about grass, trees and stars that is the problem. How can our words fit the earth and heavens, if there are not, prior to us, grass, trees and stars? A strict and universal nominalism is a preposterous mystery. What, however, about categories applying to people?

People are alive or dead, tall or short, strong or weak, creative or plodding, foolish or intelligent. These categories arise from the nature of people themselves, although we are by now well aware how "intelligence" can be warped by quotients. But consider the categories so much worked over by Foucault, involving madness, criminality and other kinds of deviancy. Consider even his assertion (which I do not quite believe) about what a soldier was in medieval times, and what he became with the new institutions of discipline and uniform: soldiers themselves became different kinds of people. We may begin to grasp at a different kind of nominalism, which I call *dynamic nominalism*. Categories of people come into existence at the same time as kinds of people come into being to fit those categories, and there is a two-way interaction between these processes.

That is not very sensational, as most of the interesting things about us are what we choose to do, or try not to do, how we behave or misbehave. I subscribe to G.E.M. Anscombe's view in *Intention*, that by and large intentional action is action under a description. So there have to be descriptions. If we can show that descriptions change, some dropping in, some dropping out, then there simply is a change in what we can (as a matter of logic) do or not do. One can reread many of Foucault's books as in part stories about the connection between certain kinds of description coming into being or going out of existence, and certain kinds of people coming into being or going out of existence. More important, one can do this kind of work explicitly oneself. I study the dullest of subjects, nineteenth-century statistics. It turns out to be one aspect of what Foucault calls a "biopolitics of the population," that "gave rise to comprehensive measures, statistical assessments, and interventions aimed at the entire social body or at groups taken as a whole." What do I find at the beginning of the great avalanche of numbers, around 1820? Nothing other than the statistics of deviancy, of madness, suicide, prostitution, vagrancy, crime against the person, crime against property, drunkenness, *les miserables*. These vast arrays of data are called *analyse morale*. We find constant subdivisions and rearrangements of, for example, the mad, as the counting progresses. We find classifications of over 4,000 different criss-crossing motives for murder. I do not believe that mad people of these sorts, or these motives for murder, in general existed until there came into being the practice of counting them.

Constantly new ways of counting people were devised. New slots were created into which people could fall and be counted. Even the decennial censuses in the different states amazingly show that the categories into which people fall change every ten years. This is partly because social change generates new categories of people, but I think the countings were not mere reportings. They were part of an elaborate, well-meaning, indeed innocent creating of new kinds of ways for people to be, and people innocently "chose" to fall into these new categories.

Foucault writes of "two poles of development," one being the biopolitics, the other, an "anatomopolitics of the human body" concerned with the individual, the body and its actions. That is not something I know enough about to make informed judgment. I did follow up one lead, however, and contend that at least one kind of insanity was invented, and then disturbed people to a certain extent chose to be mad in that way. The case is multiple personality. No more than one or two multiples are recorded, per generation, up to 1875. Then there is a host, and this kind of insanity had a quite explicit political role. Pierre Janet, the distinguished psychiatrist, recounts how one Félida X, who attracted much attention in 1875, was of supreme importance. "Her history was the great argument of which the positivist psychologists made use at the time of the heroic struggles against the spiritualist dogmatism of Cousin's school. But for Félida, it is not certain that there would be a professorship of psychology at the Collège de France." Janet held precisely that professorship. After Félida there was a torrent of multiple personalities, which has not quite dried up. Do I mean that there were virtually no multiples before Félida? Is it not just that doctors merely failed to record them? I may be in error, but what I mean is that only after the doctors had done their work was there this syndrome for a disturbed person to adopt. The syndrome bloomed in France, and then moved to America, which is now its home.

I have no idea what such a dynamic nominalism will amount to. Let us however consider its implications for history and philosophy of the human sciences. Like Kuhn's revolutionary nominalism, Foucault's dynamic nominalism is an historicized nominalism. But there is something fundamentally different. History plays an essential role in the constitution of the objects, where the objects are the people and ways in which they behave. Despite my radical doctrine about the experimental creation of phenomena, I hold the common-sense view that the photo-electric effect is timeless at least to this extent: if one does do certain things, certain phenomena will appear. They never did appear until our century. We made them. But what happens is constrained by "the world." The categories created by what Foucault calls anatomopolitics and biopolitics, and the "intermediary cluster of relations" between the two politics, are constituted in an essentially historical setting. Yet it is these very categories in terms of which the human sciences venture to describe us. Moreover, they bring into being new categories which, in part, bring into being new kinds of people. We remake the world, but we make up people. Just before the warning about heavy writing and of French cant, with which I closed Parable II, Addison wrote, "it is very certain that an author, who has not learned the art of distinguishing words and things and of ranging his thoughts and setting them in proper lights, whatever notions he may have, will lose himself in confusion and obscurity." I think that we shall lose ourselves in confusion and obscurity for some time yet, in the so-called social and human sciences, because in those domains the distinction between word and thing is constantly blurred. It is precisely experimental methods that I take to be essential to the physical sciences and which, I claim, make Kuhn's historicized revolutionary nominalism fall short of a strict nominalism. The experimental methods of the human sciences are something else. The lack of a sharp distinction between word and thing is at the root of Wittgenstein's famous concluding remark, that in psychology (and the like) "there are experimental methods and *conceptual confusion."* Here Foucault's "archaeology" may yet prove useful, not in order to "display the shape of the flybottle" but at least to grasp the interrelations of "power" and "knowledge" that literally constitute us as human beings. That would be the strongest impact of history upon philosophy. But until we can do that job better, it will have to remain one more parable, deliberately open, like all parables, to far too many interpretations.

Notes

1 Editor's note: Hacking's parables were first published in *Philosophy in History*, ed. Richard Rorty, Q. Skinner, and J. Schneewind (see p. 322 for details). Taylor's contribution is entitled "Philosophy and its History."

2 *Spectator* 291 (Saturday, 2 Feb.): 1711–12

STANLEY FISH
(B. 1938)

A Professor of English at Duke and Executive Director of the Duke University Press, Stanley Fish highlights the role of interpretation in literary criticism. The justification of an interpretation, he maintains, is a matter more of "interpretive practices" or communities than of the "text" as it is in itself. Even those who allegedly eschew it are involved in interpretation. The "move" of "letting the text speak for itself" is just a means of passing off one's own interpretation by saying that "those other fellows may be interested in displaying their ingenuity, but I am simply a servant of the text." Fish attacks critics' attempts to give uninterpreted "descriptions" of literary works much as Rorty employs Wilfrid Sellars's attack on "The Myth of the Given" to argue that interpretation of the world "goes all the way down."

Fish recounts the story of a student who confided that "she could go into any classroom, no matter what the subject of the course, and win approval for running one of a number of well-defined interpretive routines": viewing the text "as an instance of the tension between nature and culture" or a site of "large mythological oppositions," taking "the true subject of the text as its own composition" or claiming "that in the guise of fashioning a narrative the speaker was fragmenting and displacing his own anxieties and fears." To the question contained in the title of the book from which the following essay is drawn—*Is There a Text in This Class?* —Fish is answering: Yes, there is a text, but "the text is always a function of interpretation," and "interpretation is the only game in town."

But what, it may be asked, is being interpreted? In Fish's essay the word "forests" is cited in support of differing interpretations of Blake's "The Tyger." According to one, the "tall straight forms" the word "forest" suggests "the orderliness of the tiger's stripes"; according to the other, "forest" is uniformly used by Blake in association with the "natural, 'fallen' world." According to the first interpretation the tiger is holy, according to the second, the tiger is evil. Yet as Fish himself states, "the same word is being cited in support of a quite different interpretation." Is this word, "forests"—and its meaning as a "dense growth of trees and underbrush"—not constant in the two interpretations? Isn't this word—with its multifarious meanings—part of the text the critic must confront?

Fish resists any position that would ground interpretations in something independent of human institutions and customs. In response to those who would say that the multiple interpretations Fish finds are all "in the text," or "supported" by the text, Fish sets out and criticizes a "pluralist" position akin to those taken by James or Putnam: "a pluralist is committed to saying that there is something in the text which rules out some readings and allows others (even though no *one* reading can ever capture the text's 'inexhaustible richness and complexity'). His best evidence is that in practice 'we all in fact' do reject unacceptable readings and that more often than not we agree on the readings that are to be rejected." (This statement resembles Putnam's remarks in *The Many Faces of Realism* about "what our lives show," and Rorty's statement, derived from Sellars, that immorality is "the sort of thing *we* don't do.") The problem with pluralism, as Fish sees it, is that there is no uninterpreted text by reference to which acceptable readings are to be distinguished from unacceptable ones: if "the text is always a function of interpretation, then the text cannot be the location of the core of agreement by means of which we reject interpretations." That core Fish finds not "*in* the text" but only in "the ways of *producing* the text" within "literary institutions."

WHAT MAKES AN INTERPRETATION ACCEPTABLE?

STANLEY FISH

Last time I ended by suggesting that the fact of agreement, rather than being a proof of the stability of objects, is a testimony to the power of an interpretive community to constitute the objects upon which its members (also and simultaneously constituted) can then agree. This account of agreement has the additional advantage of providing what the objectivist argument cannot supply, a coherent account of *disagreement*. To someone who believes in determinate meaning, disagreement can only be a theological error. The truth lies plainly in view, available to anyone who has the eyes to see; but some readers choose not to see it and perversely substitute their own meanings for the meanings that texts obviously bear. Nowhere is there an explanation of this waywardness (original sin would seem to be the only relevant model), or of the origin of these idiosyncratic meanings (I have been arguing that there could be none), or of the reason why some readers seem to be exempt from the general infirmity. There is simply the conviction that the facts exist in their own self-evident shape and that disagreements are to be resolved by referring the respective parties to the facts as they really are. In the view that I have been urging, however, disagreements cannot be resolved by reference to the facts, because the facts emerge only in the context of some point of view. It follows, then, that disagreements must occur between those who hold (or are held by) different points of view, and what is at stake in a disagreement is the right to specify what the facts can hereafter be said to be. Disagreements are not settled by the facts, but are the means by which the facts are settled. Of course, no such settling is final, and in the (almost certain) event that the dispute is opened again, the category of the facts "as they really are" will be reconstituted in still another shape.

Nowhere is this process more conveniently on display than in literary criticism, where everyone's claim is that his interpretation more perfectly accords with the facts, but where everyone's purpose is to persuade the rest of us to the version of the facts he espouses by persuading us to the interpretive principles in the light of which those facts will seem indisputable. The recent critical fortunes of William Blake's "The Tyger" provide a nice example. In 1954 Kathleen Raine published an influential essay entitled "Who Made the Tyger" in which she argued that because the tiger is for Blake "the beast that sustains its own life at the expense of its fellow-creatures" it is a "symbol of... predacious selfhood," and that therefore the answer to the poem's final question—" "Did he who made the Lamb make thee"—"is, beyond all possible doubt, No."[1] In short, the tiger is unambiguously and obviously evil. Raine supports her reading by pointing to two bodies of evidence, certain cabbalistic writings which, she avers, "beyond doubt... inspired 'The Tyger,'" and evidence from the poem itself. She pays particular attention to the word "forests" as it appears in line 2, "In the forests of the night": "Never... is the word 'forest' used by Blake in any context in which it does not refer to the natural, 'fallen' world" (p. 48).

The direction of argument here is from the word "forests" to the support it is said to provide for a particular interpretation. Ten years later, however, that same word is being cited in support of a quite different interpretation. While Raine assumes that the lamb is for Blake a symbol of Christ-like self-sacrifice, E. D. Hirsch believes that Blake's intention was "to satirize the singlemindedness of the Lamb": "There can be no doubt," he declares, "that *The Tyger* is a poem that celebrates the holiness of tigerness."[2] In his reading the "ferocity and destructiveness" of the tiger are transfigured and one of the things they are transfigured by is the word "forests": "'*Forests*'... suggests tall straight forms, a world that for all its terror has the orderliness of the tiger's stripes or Blake's perfectly balanced verses" (p. 247).

What we have here then are two critics with opposing interpretations, each of whom claims the same word as internal and confirming evidence. Clearly they cannot both be right, but just as clearly there is no basis for deciding between them. One cannot appeal to the text, because the text has become an extension of the interpretive disagreement that divides them; and, in fact, the text as it is variously characterized is a *consequence* of the interpretation for which it is supposedly evidence. It is not that the meaning of the word "forests" points in the direction of one interpretation or the other; rather, in the light of an already assumed interpretation, the word will be seen to *obviously* have one meaning or another. Nor can the question be settled by turning to the context—say the cabbalistic writings cited by Raine—for that too will only be a context for an already assumed interpretation. If Raine had not already decided that the answer to the poem's final question is "beyond all possible doubt, No," the cabbalistic texts, with their distinction between supreme and inferior deities, would never have suggested themselves to her as Blake's source. The rhetoric of critical argument, as it is usually conducted in our journals, depends upon a distinction between interpretations on the one hand and the textual and contextual facts that will either support or disconfirm them on the other; but as the example of Blake's "Tyger" shows, text, context, and interpretation all emerge together, as a consequence of a gesture (the declaration of belief) that is irreducibly interpretive. It follows, then, that when one interpretation wins out over another, it is not because the first has been shown to be in accordance with the facts but because it is from the perspective of its assumptions that the facts are now being specified. It is these assumptions, and not the facts they make possible, that are at stake in any critical dispute.

Hirsch and Raine seem to be aware of this, at least subliminally; for whenever their respective assumptions surface they are asserted with a vehemence that is finally defensive: "The answer to the question…is beyond all possible doubt, No." "There can be no doubt that *The Tyger* is…a poem that celebrates the holiness of tigerness." If there were a doubt, if the interpretation with which each critic begins were not firmly in place, the account of the poem that follows from that interpretation could not get under way. One could not cite as an "obvious" fact that "forests" is a fallen word or, alternatively, that it "suggests tall and straight forms." Whenever a critic prefaces an assertion with a phrase like "without doubt" or "there can be no doubt," you can be sure that you are within hailing distance of the interpretive principles which produce the facts that he presents as obvious.

In the years since 1964 other interpretations of the poem have been put forward, and they follow a predictable course. Some echo either Raine or Hirsch by arguing that the tiger is either good or evil; others assert that the tiger is *both* good and evil, or beyond good and evil; still others protest that the questions posed in the poem are rhetorical and are therefore not meant to be answered ("It is quite evident that the critics are not trying to understand the poem at all. If they were, they would not attempt to answer its questions.")[3] It is only a matter of time before the focus turns from the questions to their asker and to the possibility that the speaker of the poem is not Blake but a limited persona ("Surely the point … is that Blake sees further or deeper than his *persona*").[4] It then becomes possible to assert that "we don't know who the speaker of 'The Tyger' is," and that therefore the poem "is a maze of questions in which the reader is forced to wander confusedly."[5] In this reading the poem itself becomes rather "tigerish" and one is not at all surprised when the original question—"*Who* made the Tiger?"—is given its quintessentially new-critical answer: the tiger is the poem itself and Blake, the consummate artist who smiles "his work to see," is its creator.[6] As one obvious and indisputable interpretation supplants another, it brings with it a new set of obvious and indisputable facts. Of course each new reading is elaborated in the name of the poem itself, but the poem itself is always a function of the interpretive perspective from which the critic "discovers" it.

A committed pluralist might find in the previous paragraph a confirmation of his own position. After all, while "The Tyger" is obviously open to more than one interpretation, it is not open to an infinite number of interpretations. There may be disagreements as to whether the tiger is good or evil, or whether the speaker is Blake or a persona, and so on, but no one is suggesting that the poem is an allegory of the digestive processes or that it predicts the Second World War, and its limited plurality is simply a testimony to the capacity of a great work of art to generate multiple readings. The point is one that Wayne Booth makes when he asks, "Are we *right* to rule out at least some readings?"[7] and then answers his own question with a resounding yes. It would be my answer too; but the real question is what gives us the right so to be right. A pluralist is committed to saying that there is something in the text which rules out some readings and allows others (even though no *one* reading can ever capture the text's "inexhaustible richness and complexity"). His best evidence is that in practice "we all in fact" do reject unacceptable readings and that more often than not we agree on the readings that are to be rejected. Booth tells us, for example, that he has never found a reader of *Pride and Prejudice* "who sees no jokes against Mr. Collins" when he gives his reasons for wanting to marry Elizabeth Bennet and only belatedly, in fifth position, cites the "violence" of his affection.[8] From this and other examples Booth concludes that there are justified limits to what we can legitimately do with a text, for "surely we could not go on disputing at all if a core of agreement did not exist." Again, I agree, but if, as I have argued, the text is always a function of interpretation, then the text cannot be the location of the core of agreement by means of which we reject interpretations. We seem to be at an impasse: on the one hand there would seem to be no basis for labeling an interpretation unacceptable, but on the other we do it all the time.

This, however, is an impasse only if one assumes that the activity of interpretation is itself unconstrained; but in fact the shape of that activity is determined by the literary institution which at any one time will authorize only a finite number of interpretative strategies. Thus, while there is no core of agreement *in* the text, there is a core of agreement (although one subject to change) concerning the ways of *producing* the text. Nowhere is this set of acceptable ways written down, but it is a part of everyone's knowledge of what it means to be operating within the literary institution as it is now constituted. A student of mine recently demonstrated this knowledge when, with an air of giving away a trade secret, she confided that she could go into any classroom, no matter what the subject of the course, and win approval for running one of a number of well-defined interpretive routines: she could view the assigned text as an instance of the tension between nature and culture; she could look in the text for evidence of large mythological oppositions; she could argue that the true subject of the text was its own composition, or that in the guise of fashioning a narrative the speaker was fragmenting and displacing his own anxieties and fears. She could not, however, at least at Johns Hopkins University today, argue that the text was a prophetic message inspired by the ghost of her Aunt Tilly.

My student's understanding of what she could and could not get away with, of the unwritten rules of the literary game, is shared by everyone who plays that game, by those who write and judge articles for publication in learned journals, by those who read and listen to papers at professional meetings, by those who seek and award tenure in innumerable departments of English and comparative literature, by the armies of graduate students for whom knowledge of the rules is the real mark of professional initiation. This does not mean that these rules and the practices they authorize are either monolithic or stable. Within the literary community there are subcommunities (what will excite the editors of *Diacritics* is likely to distress the editors of *Studies in Philology*), and within any community the boundaries of the acceptable are continually being redrawn. In a classroom whose authority figures include David Bleich and Norman Holland, a student might very well relate a text to her memories of a favorite aunt, while in other classrooms, dominated by the spirit of Brooks and Warren, any such activity would immediately be dismissed as nonliterary, as something that isn't done.

The point is that while there is always a category of things that are not done (it is simply the reverse or flip side of the category of things that *are* done), the membership in that category is continually changing. It changes laterally as one moves from subcommunity to subcommunity, and it changes through time when once interdicted interpretive strategies are admitted into the ranks of the acceptable. Twenty years ago one of the things that literary critics didn't do was talk about the reader, at least in a way that made his experience the focus of the critical act. The prohibition on such talk was largely the result of Wimsatt's and Beardsley's famous essay "The Affective Fallacy," which argued that the variability of readers renders any investigation of their responses ad-hoc and relativistic: "The poem itself," the authors complained, "as an object of specifically critical judgment, tends to disappear."[9] So influential was this essay that it was possible for a reviewer to dismiss a book merely by finding in it evidence that the affective fallacy had been committed. The use of a juridical terminology is not accidental; this was in a very real sense a *legal* finding of activity in violation of understood and institutionalized decorums. Today, however, the affective fallacy, no longer a fallacy but a methodology, is committed all the time, and its practitioners have behind them the full and authorizing weight of a fully articulated institutional apparatus. The "reader in literature" is regularly the subject of forums and workshops at the convention of the Modern Language Association; there is a reader newsletter which reports on the multitudinous labors of a reader industry; any list of currently active schools of literary criticism includes the school of "reader response," and two major university presses have published collections of essays designed both to display the variety of reader-centered criticism (the emergence of factions within a once interdicted activity is a sure sign of its having achieved the status of an orthodoxy) and to detail its history. None of this of course means that a reader-centered criticism is now invulnerable to challenge or attack, merely that it is now recognized as a competing literary strategy that cannot be dismissed simply by being named. It is acceptable not because everyone accepts it but because those who do not are now obliged to argue against it.

The promotion of reader-response criticism to the category of things that are done (even if it is not being done by everyone) brings with it a whole new set of facts to which its practitioners can now refer. These include patterns of expectation and disappointment, reversals of direction, traps, invitations to premature conclusions, textual gaps, delayed revelations, temptations, all of which are related to a corresponding set of authors' intentions, of strategies designed to educate the reader or humiliate him or confound him or, in the more sophisticated versions of the mode, to make him enact in his responses the very subject matter of the poem. These facts and intentions emerge when the text is interrogated by a series of related questions—What is the reader doing? What is being done to him? For what purpose?—questions that follow necessarily from the assumption that the text is not a spatial object but the occasion for a temporal experience. It is in the course of answering such questions that a reader-response critic elaborates "the structure of the reading experience," a structure which is not so much discovered by the interrogation but demanded by it. (If you begin by assuming that readers do something and the something they do has meaning, you will never fail to discover a pattern of reader activities that appears obviously to be meaningful.) As that structure emerges (under the pressure of interrogation) it takes the form of a "reading," and insofar as the procedures which produced it are recognized by the literary community as something that some of its members do, that reading will have the status of a competing interpretation. Of course it is still the case, as Booth insists, that we are "right to rule out at least some readings," but there is now one less reading or kind of reading that can be ruled out, because there is now one more interpretive procedure that has been accorded a place in the literary institution.

The fact that it remains easy to think of a reading that most of us would dismiss out of hand does not mean that the text excludes it but that there is as yet no elaborated interpretive procedure for producing that text. That is why the examples of critics like Wayne Booth seem to have so much force; rather than looking back, as I have, to now familiar strategies that were once alien and strange sounding, they look forward to strategies that have not yet emerged. Norman Holland's analysis of Faulkner's "A Rose for Emily" is a case in point. Holland is arguing for a kind of psychoanalytic pluralism. The text, he declares, is "at most a matrix of psychological possibilities for its readers," but, he insists, "only some possibilities...truly fit the matrix": "One would not say, for example, that a reader of... 'A Rose for Emily' who thought the 'tableau' [of Emily and her father in the doorway] described an Eskimo was really responding to the story at all—only pursuing some mysterious inner exploration."[10]

Holland is making two arguments: first, that anyone who proposes an Eskimo reading of "A Rose for Emily" will not find a hearing in the literary community. And that, I think, is right. ("We are right to rule out at least some readings.") His second argument is that the unacceptability of the Eskimo reading is a function of the text, of what he calls its "sharable promptuary" (p. 287), the public "store of structured language" (p. 287) that sets limits to the interpretations the words can accommodate. And that, I think, is wrong. The Eskimo reading is unacceptable because there is at present no interpretive strategy for producing it, no way of "looking" or reading (and remember, all acts of looking or reading are "ways") that would result in the emergence of obviously Eskimo meanings. This does not mean, however, that no such strategy could ever come into play, and it is not difficult to imagine the circumstances under which it would establish itself. One such circumstance would be the discovery of a letter in which Faulkner confides that he has always believed himself to be an Eskimo changeling. (The example is absurd only if one forgets Yeat's "Vision" or Blake's Swedenborgianism or James Miller's recent elaboration of a homosexual reading of "The Waste Land"). Immediately the workers in the Faulkner industry would begin to reinterpret the canon in the light of this newly revealed "belief" and the work of reinterpretation would involve the elaboration of a symbolic or allusive system (not unlike mythological or typological criticism) whose application would immediately transform the text into one informed everywhere by Eskimo meanings. It might seem that I am admitting that there is a text to be transformed, but the object of transformation would be the text (or texts) given by whatever interpretive strategies the Eskimo strategy was in the process of dislodging or expanding. The result would be that whereas we now have a Freudian "A Rose for Emily," a mythological "A Rose for Emily," a Christological "A Rose for Emily," a regional "A Rose for Emily," a sociological "A Rose for Emily," a linguistic "A Rose for Emily," we would in addition have an Eskimo "A Rose for Emily," existing in some relation of compatibility or incompatibility with the others.

Again the point is that while there are always mechanisms for ruling out readings, their source is not the text but the presently recognized interpretive strategies for producing the text. It follows, then, that no reading, however outlandish it might appear, is inherently an impossible one. Consider, for another example, Booth's report that he has never found a reader who sees no jokes against Mr. Collins, and his conclusion that the text of *Pride and Prejudice* enforces or signals an ironic reading. First of all, the fact that he hasn't yet found such a reader does not mean that one does not exist, and we can even construct his profile; he would be someone for whom the reasons in Mr. Collins's list correspond to a deeply held set of values, exactly the opposite of the set of values that must be assumed if the passage is to be seen as obviously ironic. Presumably no one who has sat in Professor Booth's classes holds that set of values or is allowed to hold them (students always know what they are expected to believe) and it is unlikely that anyone who is now working in the Austen industry begins with an assumption other than the assumption that the novelist is a master ironist. It is precisely for this reason that the time is ripe for the "discovery" by an enterprising scholar of a nonironic Austen, and one can even predict the course such a discovery would take. It would begin with the uncovering of new evidence (a letter, a lost manuscript, a contemporary response) and proceed to the conclusion that Austen's intentions have been misconstrued by generations of literary critics. She was not in fact satirizing the narrow and circumscribed life of a country gentry; rather, she was celebrating that life and its tireless elaboration of a social fabric, complete with values, rituals, and self-perpetuating goals (marriage, the preservation of great houses, and so on). This view, or something very much like it, is already implicit in much of the criticism, and it would only be a matter of extending it to local matters of interpretation, and specifically to Mr. Collins's list of reasons which might now be seen as reflecting a proper ranking of the values and obligations necessary to the maintenance of a way of life.

Of course any such reading would meet resistance; its opponents could point for example to the narrator's unequivocal condemnation of Mr. Collins; but there are always ways in the literary institution of handling this or any other objection. One need only introduce (if it has not already been introduced) the notion of the fallible narrator in any of its various forms (the dupe, the moral prig, the naif in need of education), and the "unequivocal condemnation" would take its place in a structure designed to glorify Mr. Collins and everything he stands for. Still, no matter how many objections were met and explained away, the basic resistance on the part of many scholars to this revisionist reading would remain, and for a time at least *Pride and Prejudice* would have acquired the status of the fourth book of *Gulliver's Travels,* a work whose very shape changes in the light of two radically opposed interpretive assumptions.

Again, I am aware that this argument is a tour-de-force and will continue to seem so as long as the revolution it projects has not occurred. The reading of *Pride and Prejudice,* however, is not meant to be persuasive. I only wanted to describe the conditions under which it might *become* persuasive and to point out that those conditions are not unimaginable given the procedures within the literary institution by which interpretations are proposed and established. Any interpretation could be elaborated by someone in command of those procedures (someone who knows what "will do" as a literary argument), even my own "absurd" reading of "The Tyger" as an allegory of the digestive processes. Here the task is easy because according to the critical consensus there is no belief so bizarre that Blake could not have been committed to it, and it would be no trick at all to find some elaborate system of alimentary significances (Pythagorean? Swedenborgian? Cabbalistic?) which he could be presumed to have known. One might then decide that the poem was the first-person lament of someone who had violated a dietary prohibition against eating tiger meat, and finds that forbidden food burning brightly in his stomach, making its fiery way through the forests of the intestinal tract, beating and hammering like some devil-wielded anvil. In his distress he can do nothing but rail at the tiger and at the mischance that led him to mistake its meat for the meat of some purified animal: "Did he who made the Lamb make thee?" The poem ends as it began, with the speaker still paying the price of his sin and wondering at the inscrutable purposes of a deity who would lead his creatures into digestive temptation. Anyone who thinks that this time I have gone too far might do very well to consult some recent numbers of *Blake Studies.*

In fact, my examples are very serious, and they are serious in part because they are so ridiculous. The fact that they *are* ridiculous, or are at least perceived to be so, is evidence that we are never without canons of acceptability; we are always "right to rule out at least some readings." But the fact that we can imagine conditions under which they would *not* seem ridiculous, and that readings once considered ridiculous are now respectable and even orthodox, is evidence that the canons of acceptability can change. Moreover, that change is not random but orderly and, to some extent, predictable. A new interpretive strategy always makes its way in some relationship of opposition to the old, which has often marked out a negative space (of things that aren't done) from which it can emerge into respectability. Thus, when Wimsatt and Beardsley declare that "the Affective Fallacy is a confusion between the poem and its *results*, what it *is* and what it *does*," the way is open for an affective critic to argue, as I did, that a poem *is* what it does. And when the possibility of a reader-centered criticism seems threatened by the variability of readers, that threat will be countered either by denying the variability (Stephen Booth, Michael Riffaterre) or by controlling it (Wolfgang Iser, Louise Rosenblatt) or by embracing it and making it into a principle of value (David Bleich, Walter Slatoff).

Rhetorically the new position announces itself as a break from the old, but in fact it is radically dependent on the old, because it is only in the context of some differential relationship that it can be perceived as new or, for that matter, perceived at all. No one would bother to assert that Mr. Collins is the hero of *Pride and Prejudice* (even as an example intended to be absurd) were that position not already occupied in the criticism by Elizabeth and Darcy; for then the assertion would have no force; there would be nothing in relation to which it could be surprising. Neither would there be any point in arguing that Blake's tiger is both good and evil if there were not already readings in which he was declared to be one or the other. And if anyone is ever to argue that he is both old and young, someone will first have to argue that he is *either* old or young, for only when his age has become a question will there be any value in a refusal to answer it. Nor is it the case that the moral status of the tiger (as opposed to its age, or nationality, or intelligence) is an issue raised by the poem itself; it becomes an issue because a question is put to the poem (is the tiger good or evil?) and once that question (it could have been another) is answered, the way is open to answering it differently, or declining to answer it, or to declaring that the absence of an answer is the poem's "real point."

The discovery of the "real point" is always what is claimed whenever a new interpretation is advanced, but the claim makes sense only in relation to a point (or points) that had previously been considered the real one. This means that the space in which a critic works has been marked out for him by his predecessors, even though he is obliged by the conventions of the institution to dislodge them. It is only by their prevenience or prepossession that there is something for him to say; that is, it is only because something has already been said that he can now say something different. This dependency, the reverse of the anxiety of influence, is reflected in the unwritten requirement that an interpretation present itself as remedying a deficiency in the interpretations that have come before it. (If it did not do this, what claim would it have on our attention?) Nor can this be just any old deficiency; it will not do, for example, to fault your predecessors for failing to notice that a poem is free of split infinitives or dangling participles. The lack an interpretation supplies must be related to the criteria by which the literary community recognizes and evaluates the objects of its professional attention. As things stand now, text-book grammaticality is not one of those criteria, and therefore the demonstration of its presence in a poem will not reflect credit either on the poem or on the critic who offers it.

Credit *will* accrue to the critic when he bestows the *proper* credit on the poem, when he demonstrates that it possesses one or more of the qualities that are understood to distinguish poems from other verbal productions. In the context of the "new" criticism, under many of whose assumptions we still labor, those qualities include unity, complexity, and universality, and it is the perceived failure of previous commentators to celebrate their presence in a poem that gives a critic the right (or so he will claim) to advance a new interpretation. The unfolding of that interpretation will thus proceed under two constraints: not only must what one says about a work be related to what has already been said (even if the relation is one of reversal) but as a consequence of saying it the work must be shown to possess in a greater degree than had hitherto been recognized the qualities that properly belong to literary productions, whether they be unity and complexity, or unparaphrasability, or metaphoric richness, or indeterminacy and undecidability. In short, the new interpretation must not only claim to tell the truth about the work (in a dependent opposition to the falsehood or partial truths told by its predecessors) but it must claim to make the work better. (The usual phrase is "enhance our appreciation of.") Indeed, these claims are finally inseparable since it is assumed that the truth about a work will be what penetrates to the essence of its literary value.

This assumption, along with several others, is conveniently on display in the opening paragraph of the preface to Stephen Booth's *An Essay on Shakespeare's Sonnets:*[11]

> The history of criticism opens so many possibilities for an essay on Shakespeare's sonnets that I must warn a prospective reader about what this work does and doesn't do. To begin with the negative, I have not solved or tried to solve any of the puzzles of Shakespeare's sonnets. I do not attempt to identify Mr. W. H . or the dark lady. I do not speculate on the occasions that may have evoked particular sonnets. I do not attempt to date them. I offer neither a reorganization of the sequence, nor a defense of the quarto order. What I have tried to do is find out what about the sonnets has made them so highly valued by the vast majority of critics and general readers.

This brief paragraph can serve as an illustration of almost everything I have been saying. First of all, Booth self-consciously locates and defines his position in a differential opposition to the positions he would dislodge. He will not, he tells us, do what any of his predecessors have done; he will do something else, and indeed if it were not something else there would be no reason for him to be doing it. The reason he gives for doing it is that what his predecessors have done is misleading or beside the point. The point is the location of the source of the sonnets' value ("what about the sonnets has made them so highly valued") and his contention (not stated but strongly implied) is that those who have come before him have been looking in the wrong places, in the historical identity of the sequence's characters, in the possibility of recovering the biographical conditions of composition, and in the determination of an authoritative ordering and organization. He, however, will look in the right place and thereby produce an account of the sonnets that does them the justice they so richly deserve.

Thus, in only a few sentences Booth manages to claim for his interpretation everything that certifies it as acceptable within the conventions of literary criticism: he locates a deficiency in previous interpretations and proposes to remedy it: the remedy will take the form of producing a more satisfactory account of the work; and as a result the literary credentials of the work—what makes it of enduring value— will be more securely established, as they are when Booth is able to point in the closing paragraph of his book to Shakespeare's "remarkable achievement." By thus validating Shakespeare's achievement, Booth also validates his own credentials as a literary critic, as someone who knows what claims and demonstrations mark him as a competent member of the institution.

What makes Stephen Booth so interesting (although not at all atypical) is that one of his claims is to have freed himself and the sonnets from that very institution and its practices. "I do not," he declares, "intentionally give any interpretations of the sonnets I discuss. I mean to describe them, not to explain them." The irony is that even as Booth is declaring himself out of the game, he is performing one of its most familiar moves. The move has several versions, and Booth is here availing himself of two: (1) the "external-internal," performed when a critic dismisses his predecessors for being insufficiently literary ("but that has nothing to do with its qualities *as a poem*"); and (2) the "back-to-the-text," performed when the critical history of a work is deplored as so much dross, as an obscuring encrustation ("we are in danger of substituting the criticism for the poem"). The latter is the more powerful version of the move because it trades on the assumption, still basic to the profession's sense of its activities, that the function of literary criticism is to let the text speak for itself. It is thus a move drenched in humility, although it is often performed with righteousness: those other fellows may be interested in displaying their ingenuity, but I am simply a servant of the text and wish only to make it more available to its readers (who happen also to be my readers).

The basic gesture, then, is to disavow interpretation in favor of simply presenting the text: but it is actually a gesture in which one set of interpretive principles is replaced by another that happens to claim for itself the virtue of not being an interpretation at all. The claim, however, is an impossible one since in order "simply to present" the text, one must at the very least describe it ("I mean to describe them") and description can occur only within a stipulative understanding of what there is to be described, an understanding that will produce the object of its attention. Thus, when Booth rejects the assumptions of those who have tried to solve the puzzles of the sonnets in favor of "the assumption that the source of our pleasure in them must be the line by line experience of reading them," he is not avoiding interpretation but proposing a change in the terms within which it will occur. Specifically, he proposes that the focus of attention, and therefore of description, shift from the poem conceived as a spatial object which *contains* meanings to the poem conceived as a temporal experience in the course of which mean- ings become momentarily available, before disappearing under the pressure of other meanings, which are in their turn superseded, contradicted, qualified, or simply forgot- ten. It is only if a reader agrees to this change, that is, agrees to accept Booth's revisionary stipulation as to where the value and the significance of a poem are to be located, that the facts to which his subsequent analyses point will be seen to be facts at all. The descrip- tion which Booth offers in place of an interpretation turns out to be as much of an interpretive construct as the interpretations he rejects.

Nor could it be otherwise. Strictly speaking, getting "back-to-the-text" is not a move one can perform, because the text one gets back to will be the text demanded by some other interpretation and that interpretation will be presiding over its production. This is not to say, however, that the "back-to-the-text" move is ineffectual. The fact that it is not something one can do in no way diminishes the effectiveness of claiming to do it. As a rhetorical ploy, the announcement that one is returning to the text will be powerful so long as the assumption that criticism is secondary to the text and must not be allowed to overwhelm it remains unchallenged. Certainly, Booth does not challenge it: indeed, he relies on it and invokes it even as he relies on and invokes many other assumptions that someone else might want to dispute: the assumption that what distinguishes liter- ary from ordinary language is its invulnerability to paraphrase; the assumption that a poem should not mean, but be; the assumption that the more complex a work is, the more propositions it holds in tension and equilibrium, the better it is. It would not be at all unfair to label these assumptions "conservative" and to point out that in holding to them Booth undermines his radical credentials. But it would also be beside the point, which is not that Booth isn't truly radical but that he *couldn't* be. Nor could anyone else. The challenge he mounts to some of the conventions of literary study (the convention of the poem as artifact, the convention of meaningfulness) would not even be *recognized* as a challenge if others of those conventions were not firmly in place and, for the time being at least, unquestioned. A wholesale challenge would be impossible because there would be no terms in which it could be made; that is, in order to be wholesale, it would have to be made in terms wholly outside the institution; but if that were the case, it would be unintelligible because it is only within the institution that the facts of literary study—texts, authors, periods, genres—become available. In short, the price intelligi- bility exacts (a price Booth pays here) is implication in the very structure of assumptions and goals from which one desires to be free.

So it would seem, finally, that there are no moves that are not moves in the game, and this includes even the move by which one claims no longer to be a player. Indeed, by a logic peculiar to the institution, one of the standard ways of practicing literary criticism is to announce that you are avoiding it. This is so because at the heart of the institution is the wish to deny that its activities have any consequences. The critic is taught to think of himself as a transmitter of the best that had been thought and said by others, and his greatest fear is that he will stand charged of having substituted his own meanings for the meanings of which he is supposedly the guardian; his greatest fear is that he be found guilty of having interpreted. That is why we have the spectacle of commentators who, like Stephen Booth, adopt a stance of aggressive humility and, in the manner of someone who rises to speak at a temperance meeting, declare that they will never interpret again but will instead do something else ("I mean to describe them"). What I have been saying is that whatever they do, it will only be interpretation in another guise because, like it or not, interpretation is the only game in town.

Notes

1 *Encounter*, June, 1954, p. 50.

2 *Innocence and Experience* (New Haven: Yale University Press, 1964), pp. 245, 248.

3 Philip Hobsbaum, "A Rhetorical Question Answered: Blake's *Tyger* and its Critics," *Neophilologus* 48: 2 (1964), p. 154.

4 Warren Stevenson, "'The Tyger' as Artefact," *Blake Studies* 2: 1 (1969–70), p. 9.

5 L. J. Swingle, "Answers to Blake's 'Tyger': A Matter of Reason or of Choice," *Concerning Poetry* 2 (1970), 67.

6 Stevenson, "'The Tyger' as Artefact," p. 15.

7 "Preserving the Exemplar," *Critical Inquiry* 3: 3 (Spring, 1977), p. 413.

8 Ibid., p. 412.

9 *The Verbal Icon* (Lexington: University of Kentucky Press, 1954), p. 21.

10 *5 Readers Reading* (New Haven: Yale University Press, 1975), p. 12.

11 New Haven: Yale University Press, 1969.

RICHARD POIRIER

(B. 1925)

A professor of English at Rutgers, the editor of *Raritan*, and author of *The Performing Self* (1971), *The Renewal of Literature: Emersonian Reflections* (1987), and *Poetry and Pragmatism* (1992), Poirier seeks in pragmatism a position equally distant from what he calls "the loud mouth of contemporary criticism," from T. S. Eliot's "wasteland ethos" and from the "grim prognoses" of contemporary deconstruction. "Literature," he writes, "exists only when it is being read by someone, which is not often, not for long, and not by very many." A pragmatist approach to literature acknowledges that it is not God but human beings who speak through language, that past writing can be a burden as well as an inspiration, and that we nevertheless can exert "authority" over our inherited language, turning it in our own directions. "The stability of words," Poirier maintains, "is achieved only in their fluid relations to other words, and…these are set in motion by the person using the words." Drawing on Emerson's statement in "The Poet" that all language is "fluxional," "vehicular," and "transitive," tracing James's preoccupation with human agency amidst a world of transitions, finding in Robert Frost "a space of expectation rather than deferral," Poirier argues that an "Emersonian pragmatist" line extends through Emerson and William James to Robert Frost, Gertrude Stein, and Wallace Stevens.

James wrote in *The Principles of Psychology* of the "halo or penumbra" of thought, of "psychic transitions… not to be glimpsed except in flight," and of his desire for the "reinstatement of the vague to its proper place in our mental life." Taking his title for the chapter of *Poetry and Pragmatism* reprinted below from James's statement, Poirier explores Jamesian appreciations of vagueness not only in James's *Psychology* but in his *Pragmatism*, in such poetry as Frost's "For Once, Then, Something," and in Stevens's statement that "words, above everything else, are, in poetry, sounds."

Holding that "James's pragmatism looks back to the two American writers he most admired—Emerson with his transitions, Whitman with his lolling about," Poirier maintains that central to pragmatism's approach is a certain casualness, a "laid-back, rather quiet way of imagining and responding to cultural crises" such as the "death of God." We find this approach today in the informality of Hilary Putnam's writings and particularly in Richard Rorty's insouciant, offhanded tone as he takes leave of or undermines traditional philosophical projects. Poirier's pragmatist slogan—"Keep cool but care"—might well have been uttered by one of Rorty's "liberal ironists," who, aware of the "contingency and fragility of their final vocabularies," nevertheless continue to rely on them.

THE REINSTATEMENT OF THE VAGUE

RICHARD POIRIER

While making a case for itself, Emersonian pragmatism, like other isms, depends on certain key, repeated terms. But to a wholly unusual degree it never allows any one of these terms to arrive at a precise or static definition. Their use is conducive less to clarification than to vagueness, as has already been shown with words like "action" and "turning," or "power" and "work," or "nature" and "privacy," along with words having to do with speaking, with trying in public to sound authentically like yourself. While some delimited understanding of these is necessarily assumed as a starting point, the dictionary will be of little help in determining how they function; they are no less figurative in the philosophic writings under consideration than are corollary uses in the poetry; they are constantly being troped within sentences that insist that readers, too, must involve themselves in the salutary activity of troping.

Why salutary? Because though troping involves only words, it might also, as an activity, make us less easily intimidated by them, by terminologies inherited from the historical past or currently employed in the directives of public policy. It might like any art prevent a society from "becoming too assertively, too hopelessly, itself," as Kenneth Burke phrased the possibility some sixty years ago in *Counter-Statement*. It might help us confront the authority, along with its ideological or gendered assumptions, invisibly structured into the customary orderings of sentences and paragraphs.

Thus, we have already heard James, in "What Pragmatism Means," enjoin us to "set [each word] at work within the stream of your experience." The word will then be recognized "less as a solution... than as a program for more work." Though this is a worthy enough injunction, it is compounded of terminological blurrings that could easily make anyone unsure of just how and where to carry it out. It would be helpful to know, for example, where this stream of experience is located before we begin to set a word at work within it. Is the stream in us? Or is it shared with others? Are we on it, or is it next to us? In any case, how is one to identify the stream as peculiar to oneself—and how are its movements to be traced without the use of words, words that will inevitably mediate and thus contaminate or redirect the stream's flow? What, besides, can be meant by the word "work"? In the next sentence all he can promise is that if we set the word "at work within the stream," we will discover "a program for more work." But this work will produce nothing beyond an "indication"—an "indication of the way existing realities might be *changed*."

The italicizing of the word "changed" is one of several signs of James's anxiety lest we wonder what the urgency and effort really accomplish after all. The blurring and vagueness in his formulations are a rhetorical effort to persuade us, and himself, that the "work" will indeed amount to more than a poetic exercise of troping or changing. In fact, however, we cannot even begin to know beyond that where any change is to occur or who will be helped by it. Will it, for example, benefit the millions who haven't the capacity or opportunity to read James's sentences? The change, as he describes it, can at most be a change in some word or other, some word which has, to begin with, a very tentative hold on the "realities" to which he refers. As I see it, he offers here a prescription and a promise only for the writing of poetry and prose. And while these may on occasion change the perception of reality by a particular reader, James's rhetoric, like Emerson's, is obviously hinting at more consequential rewards.

I mean to suggest that James's language is no less "superfluous," in the various senses attached to that word, than is the language of the poets I have allied with him; it is subject to the same degree of metaphorical proliferation, slippage, and excess. James's predecessor Emerson is the more "superfluous" of the two, offering a surplus of meaning in the face of always incipient impoverishment, but James's writing is also "extravagant" and "extra–vagant," writing in which language moves out of bounds, toward the margin, until it becomes loose and vague. Emerson intends to go, as it were, beyond us, and for the reason that, like James—though in a style far more calculated, conscientious, and entangled—he admits that he is writing for the future and into the future. However, he came increasingly to acknowledge that this future might forever elude all the human generations, as is poignantly suggested by those verbs of postponement that lift up even as they deflate the final sentence of "Experience": "the true romance which the world exists to realize, will be the transformation of genius into practical power." Don't hold your breath, is what he is saying. If pragmatism works, then it works the way poetry does—by effecting a change of language, a change carried out entirely *within* language, and for the benefit of those destined to inherit the language. Pragmatism, as I understand it, is not essentially addressed to—indeed it shies away from—historical crises, real or concocted.

This relative indifference to crises, to any cultural apocalypse, helps explain, I suspect, why writers of an Emersonian pragmatist disposition were, for the most part, ignored or regarded as insular and pleasantly irrelevant during the period from about 1920 to 1960. This was a period when the wasteland ethos, with its admixtures of Anglo-Catholicism and Southern Agrarianism, dominated the American literary-academic scene, far more, it should be remembered, than it did the English one. Frost, Stein, and Stevens, not to mention their nineteenth-century predecessors, were generally patronized by the higher criticism for having failed—and what a creditable failure it was!—to subscribe to Eliot's rhetoric about the twentieth century, this "immense panorama of futility and anarchy which is contemporary history," as he described it in the 1923 essay *"Ulysses, Order and Myth."* Frost seems obviously to have had such a characterization in mind when, in 1935, he dryly remarked in a letter to *The Amherst Student,* an undergraduate newspaper, "It is immodest of a man to think of himself as going down before the worst forces ever mobilized by God."

I have already made detailed arguments in *The Renewal of Literature* against the literary and cultural distortions brought on by the acceptance as historical reality of Eliot's idiosyncratic mythologies of twentieth-century crisis and of a consequent obligation, as he saw it, to write a "difficult" and "allusive" poetry like Eliot's own. The Emersonian pragmatist counterview is that there cannot be a crisis of authority which is not also the occasion for celebration and release. As they would have it, the past, including the literature of the past, proves that crisis and celebration are a mixture inherent in human nature. Human consciousness, so their account of it would run, is itself an invention which mediates both the imagination of freedom and the everhaunting sense that freedom is what we have sacrificed to consciousness. The invention of consciousness is simultaneous with the invention of language, which, in turn, measures both the restraint upon and the expression of human freedom. For all practical purposes, human beings are constituted by language; they exist in it, and also by means of it. "It is very unhappy, but too late to be helped," Emerson calmly remarks in "Experience," "the discovery we have made, that we exist. That discovery is called the Fall of Man. Ever afterwards, we suspect our instruments."

Complaints about these "instruments"—what Santayana calls "the kindly infidelities of language"—can be heard as far back as the debate in Plato's dialogue of Cratylus and on through Augustine, Bacon, and Locke. What worries even while it excites Emersonian pragmatists is the actual *inadequacy* of language to the task of representing reality. This becomes a determining factor in their understanding of the work required by writing and by reading. Even before Emerson, such concerns were voiced in America by Jonathan Edwards,[1] along with his resolution of them, and after Emerson in Stevens's suave acceptance of the fact, as in his poem "The Creations of Sound," that "speech is not dirty silence / Clarified. It is silence made still dirtier."

A question that inevitably needs to be asked is why an age-old skepticism about language should have become so pronounced, should so frequently emerge as the inferable subject of Emersonian pragmatist writing. Perhaps more important still is the question of why, nonetheless, the tone of that writing hints at so few of the grim cultural prognoses heard not only in Eliot but in more recent complaints that language is a prison-house, an instrument of repression that destroys individual identity even as it bestows it.

Having posed these questions, let me try to answer them. For Emersonian pragmatists, as I read them, language becomes the surrogate for all other forms of institutional and systematic power; it becomes a substitute for what Emerson calls Fate, and an evidence of the unappeasable human need to blame *something* for our always being less than we intend to become. The geographical literalization of the European mythology of a New World, which Myra Jehlen has convincingly traced out, induced in American writers the conviction that the North American continent is blessedly free of those institutional corruptions that will forever infect the old. And yet, in many cases, an occupational hazard of being an American writer simultaneously compelled another conviction: that language itself remained the one unavoidable cultural inheritance, the one forever demanding Old World institution, that could not be dispensed with. However, a felt need to dispense with it became, for those of an Emersonian inclination, unremitting, not to be assuaged even when you might leave your study, divest yourself of books and of family, and all by yourself go, as Emerson notoriously says he did, to the bare common in Concord, there to become for a brief moment a transparent eyeball. Why even then was it not possible to escape from language? Because it remained the necessary medium by which to talk about efforts to get out of it or beyond it. Language thus came to embody whatever it was that stood in the way of transparency, of the desire—closer to realization on this allegedly bare common of a New World than anywhere else—for an unimpeded expression of human power.

It could be said, then, that insofar as America is represented by Emersonian pragmatists it has always been what is called postmodernist. That is, Emerson's America is a place that from the outset recognized the contingency of all institutions and recognized language as a form of knowledge that was also a form of repressive power. But where Emersonian pragmatism veers away from this postmodernism is in its belief that language, and therefore thinking, can be changed by an individual's acts of imagination and by an individual's manipulation of words. Pragmatism, especially the Emersonian-Jamesian version, seems to me essentially a poetic theory, and while it could therefore be said to evade philosophy (as Cornel West and Harold Bloom, on other grounds, say that it does) I think this is to take a too circumscribed view of what it means to write philosophy. I would tilt the issue somewhat differently, by arguing that Emerson and, to a lesser extent, James refuse systematically to inveigh against the conceptual terminologies to which they are opposed because they know that in working out any such oppositions they would inevitably end up contriving only another terminology, and one no less abstract and potentially just as oppressive. They might get credit for staging a revolution in philosophy, but it would in their eyes be little more than a coup d'etat, wherein some "power-bringing words" would be deposed only so as to allow others to appear on the balcony.

Quite prudently, therefore, they elected to stick with already familiar and nonprofessional forms of language. They did so on the assumption that what James says of beliefs is even more the case with words—that "at any time," as he maintains in "Pragmatism's Conception of Truth," they "are themselves parts of the sum total of the world's experience, and become matter, therefore, for the next day's funding operations." Familiar, homey words cannot, then, be dispensed with; they can, however, be reshaped, especially by alterations in any written syntax designed to catch those tones or sounds of speech that can substantially inflect or even reverse the meanings normally assigned to the words. We must learn once again to hear sounds already deeply embedded in the caves of the human mouth and of the human ear. Such sounds have been relegated by philosophers and intellectualists to the inessential, to the fringes of human discourse, and it is time, James concludes, to restore them to centrality. Thus, to paraphrase a passage of his, instead of focusing on ideas as signaled by nouns in sentences or by images in a poem, there is to be a compensatory emphasis given to transitives—verbs, adverbs, prepositions, conjunctions, and the like—to all the words which are usually assigned the lowly task of moving us toward the substantives and, once that has been accomplished, retiring to the kitchen. Or, to change the figure, rather than complaining, with that failed Jesuit Stephen Dedalus, about "the aquacity of language," you should, with Pater, Stephen's rejected angel, welcome it, remembering that, before Pater, Emerson had advised that "all symbols are fluxional."[2]

This image of flow is picked up in James's various images of streams. The implication is that the stability of words is achieved only in their fluid relations to other words, and that these are set in motion by the person using the words. So that however much can be learned from deconstructive readings about the instabilities of language, Emersonian pragmatists go beyond that to show how words may be kept in motion by human agency, and that their significance is to be found *in* that more or less calculated motion. Because we assent to the fact that instability adheres to language, we become aware, however, that any exertions of authority over it, even when so tentative as these, can be only temporary and sporadic.

The best way to recognize these exertions, these evidences of human presence, is by learning to listen for them, in prose all as attentively as in poetry. We should listen to writing the way we listen caringly to one another in conversation, often catching more from the sounds we hear in the movements of sentences, or fragments of sentences, than from the actual words. This sort of listening is what Frost had in mind in those letters of 1913 and 1914 in which he takes credit for inventing a theory he called "sentence sounds" or "the sound of sense." We often guess what is being meant, he claims, writing to John Bartlett on July 4, 1913, not from words but from "the abstract sound of sense," as "from voices behind a door that cuts off the words." Or later, again to Bartlett, on February 22, 1914, "a sentence is a sound in itself on which other sounds called words may be strung." In what follows, I prefer, with Frost, to talk about "sound" rather than about "voice," because the idea of voice tends to suggest that the human presence in *words* is more emphatic than anything allowed by sounds. Though the sounds I will be describing may be casual and crafty, that does not keep them from being very often prelinguistic.

I think that the incentive, perhaps the actual source of Frost's theory of sound is to be found in a passage in the chapter of James's *Principles of Psychology* entitled "The Stream of Thought":

> The truth is that large tracts of human speech are nothing but *signs of direction* in thought, of which direction we nevertheless have an acutely discriminative sense, though no definite sensorial image plays any part in it whatsoever. Sensorial images are stable psychic facts; we can hold them still and look at them as long as we like. These bare images of logical movement, on the contrary, are psychic transitions, always on the wing, so to speak, and not to be glimpsed except in flight. Their function is to lead from one set of images to another. As they pass, we feel both the waxing and the waning images in a way altogether peculiar and a way quite different from the way of their full presence. If we try to hold fast the feeling of direction, the full presence comes and the feeling of direction is lost. The blank verbal scheme of the logical movement gives us the fleeting sense of the movement as we read it, quite as well as does a rational sentence awakening definite imaginations by its words.

James's wariness about what he calls "full presence," as expressed in the penultimate sentence, is a version of Emerson's in "Self-Reliance," where a self in continuous transition is preferred to any self in repose; and James's approval in the last sentence of what he calls "the blank verbal scheme," looks ahead to Frost's Fourth of July letter to Bartlett, in which he refers to "the abstract vitality of our speech." It is, he says, "pure sound." Soon after this passage in "The Stream of Thought," and still more clearly anticipatory of Frost's theories, James remarks that "a reader incapable of understanding four ideas of the book he is reading aloud, can nevertheless read it with the most delicately modulated expression of intelligence." He then proceeds, and the italics are his, to talk about *"feelings of tendency"*—an echo of the phrase *"signs of direction"* used earlier—and says that these are "often so vague that we are unable to name them at all." It is at this point that he delivers the sentence from which I take the title of this chapter: "It is, in short, the reinstatement of the vague to its proper place in our mental life which I am so anxious to press on the attention."

Poetry has of course always depended upon vagueness as an effect of figuration, rhythm, rhyme, and meter. These are among the contrivances that have traditionally differentiated the rhetoric of poetry from the rhetoric of philosophy or physics. I am arguing, however, that the virtue and necessity of vagueness is brought forward by Emersonian pragmatists as an intellectual and poetic necessity, so that what has always been true of poetry and of poetic language is by them made generally so. This vagueness is a function of sound, of the way the inflected sound of words is manipulated so as to take the edge off words themselves, to blur and refract them. The sounds we will be attending to allow for the most easygoing sort of utterance, like the ambling dialogue of Melanctha and Jeff in Gertrude Stein's *Three Lives*.[3] It is as if the voice is idling, apparently not headed anywhere in particular. The sounds are often untranslatable into rational discourse, or are at least badly served by it. They insinuate an identity for the speaker without asserting one, since assertion depends for credence on dominant mythologies of self, particularly masculine mythologies. Shakespeare, a most androgynous writer, is in his plays obsessed with sound in the way in which I intend to use the term, not only because he meant his plays to be heard rather than read but because the idea of sound as a sign of barely enunciated presence is central to his thematics. *Antony and Cleopatra,* for instance, is essentially about two people who compete to be heard all through the play, even in his death scene at her tomb. "Let me speak a little," he says, still attempting a farewell address suitable to a Roman emperor. "No," she replies, "let me speak."

In citing Shakespeare I repeat my contention that the deconstructive drifts so natural to language can most conveniently (but not only) be traced in canonical texts, where they are exploited to the full. A canonical text, I would say, is generally one that does not want to clarify itself; a journalistic text is generally one, that does. But this distinction must not be taken to mean that the deconstructive movements of language are unique to literature. If they were, how then would they be so audible to fans of Groucho Marx or Jackie Gleason's *The Honeymooners* or in the everyday talk of people closely allied in neighborhoods, in workplaces, and the like? Such ordinary people—and everyone is ordinary some good part of the time—are in fact immensely sophisticated about the mediating and mediated nature of words and phrases. Most of us talk all day and say nothing worth repeating or repeatable. "What did you two talk about?" "Oh, nothing!" It has mostly been sound, efforts to create the gel of human relationships, even as the gel is forever melting away.

Insensitivity to such ordinary uses of language is, I think, most conspicuous just where it should not be, for human as well as for scholarly reasons. I mean among profession-alist members of literature departments who increasingly want to demonstrate that the study of literature has created a field of knowledge little different from a science, with its own chronologies of discovery and progress, and its own technical jargon, which has now become all by itself a subject of study. Literary language is indeed very different from ordinary language, but only as a matter of degree. The fallacy of thinking other-wise shows in a well-known remark by Paul de Man in *Blindness and Insight:* "the statement about language, that sign and meaning can never coincide, is what is precisely taken for granted in the kind of language we call literary. Literature, *unlike everyday language,* begins on the far side of this knowledge; it is the only form of language free from the fallacy of unmediated expression" (my emphasis).

De Man seems to me altogether mistaken in this instance. Of course literature can be said to know that it is mediated expression; so, however, can one's customary salutations in the morning. My platoon in the army consisted of fifteen or so teenagers; most had never finished high school; but when one would say to another "you son of a bitch" he would do so on the confident assumption that every one of his associates knew all about "the fallacy of unmediated expression." It matters not at all that no one of them would have been capable of manufacturing that phrase. Anyone who responded "don't you talk about my mother that way"—and only a few ever did—would have been put down as a numbskull. Obviously, "son of a bitch" is a phrase used all the time to mean anything except what it says, anything from "you're terrific" to "how about that!" Persons who use the phrase are not identifying themselves with the words, but wholly with the performance, with the tonal pitch that can be given to the words. That tone can indeed enunciate the charge that "your mother is a bitch," at which point the language game is usually over, and violence may ensue.

The "performing self" is a title I used as far back as 1971. In part I meant by it then, and mean by it now, a self that responds with a native guile to the deconstructive tendency in language. It responds less by assertion than by inflection. Counteraction would be too strong a word to describe the process. Indeed, the sounds in question would normally assist deconstructive movement. What I am proposing, however, is that the sounds are deployed so as actually to reverse that movement even while allowing it. We all hear these sounds every day, in the flow of familiar, sometimes scarcely audible phrases and words. They call little attention to themselves; they belong so naturally to the rhythm of human speech that everyone takes them for granted: "how about that"; "do you think so?"; "really?"; "well, I guess"; "sometimes I just don't know"; "maybe so"; all kinds of grunts and groans. Words like these tend to disappear on utterance, and are discounted. But in letting them pass unnoticed, it is likely that in our exchanges with one another we unintentionally suppress large areas of feeling and thinking.

In 1890, William James, in his first and greatest book, *Principles of Psychology,* made an argument against such suppression, even while its persistence led him to conclude early in the chapter on "The Stream of Thought" that "language works against our perception of the truth." This claim does not refer so much to words themselves. His stricture could scarcely exist without words; his and our perception of truth depend on them. He is referring rather to our habitual way of ordering them, to the way words "work" in sentences and paragraphs. It is in this, and not in trivial experiments with automatic writing, that his influence on Gertrude Stein shows to positive advantage. A bit later, for example, he says that "so inveterate has our habit become of recognizing the existence of the substantive parts" of the stream of experience that "language almost refuses to lend itself to any other use." That is, the structure of most sentences inclines us toward its conclusive terms or key words. He calls these "resting places," and he says their "peculiarity is that they can be held before the mind for an indefinite time, and contemplated without changing." Sound bites in political advertising depend upon using words in this way, with scarcely edifying results.

A convenient example of a substantive in poetry is the word "wall" in the opening line of Frost's poem "Mending Wall":

Something there is that doesn't love a wall,
That sends the frozen-ground-swell under it,
And spills the upper boulders in the sun;
And makes gaps even two can pass abreast.
The work of hunters is another thing:
I have come after them and made repair
Where they have left not one stone on a stone,
But they would have the rabbit out of hiding,
To please the yelping dogs. The gaps I mean,
No one has seen them made or heard them made,
But at spring mending-time we find them there.
I let my neighbor know beyond the hill;
And on a day we meet to walk the line
And set the wall between us once again.
We keep the wall between us as we go.
To each the boulders that have fallen to each.
And some are loaves and some so nearly balls
We have to use a spell to make them balance:
'Stay where you are until our backs are turned!'
We wear our fingers rough with handling them.
Oh, just another kind of outdoor game,
One on a side. It comes to little more:
There where it is we do not need the wall:
He is all pine and I am apple orchard.
My apple trees will never get across
And eat the cones under his pines, I tell him.
He only says, 'Good fences make good neighbors.'
Spring is the mischief in me, and I wonder
If I could put a notion in his head:
'Why do they make good neighbors? Isn't it
Where there are cows? But here there are no cows.
Before I built a wall I'd ask to know
What I was walling in or walling out,
And to whom I was like to give offense.
Something there is that doesn't love a wall,
That wants it down.' I could say, 'Elves' to him,
But it's not elves exactly, and I'd rather
He said it for himself. I see him there
Bringing a stone grasped firmly by the top
In each hand, like an old-stone savage armed.
He moves in darkness as it seems to me,

Not of woods only and the shade of trees.
He will not go behind his father's saying,
And he likes having thought of it so well
He says again, 'Good fences make good neighbors.'

Given the title of the poem, the first line seems naturally to focus on the idea of
"walls" or "fences." Correspondingly, people tend to remember as its most famous line
a cluster of substantives: "Good fences make good neighbors," wherein one substantive
is said to generate the other. Like Emerson, however, Frost uses aphorisms—and this is
clearly one of them—less to settle arguments than to muddy them. He resorts to a sort
of shuffle, a movement that manages to scramble surrounding efforts at clarification.
For example, the opening line begins as a series of dispersements—"something there is
that doesn't love"—before it hits a blank "wall." "Something," "something there is"—
these vague conjecturals can be heard throughout his poems. They have been heard
before in "Mowing," where the speaker speculates of the whispering scythe that "per-
haps" it was whispering *"something* about the heat of the *sun,* | *Something, perhaps,* about the
lack of sound— | And that was why it whispered and did not speak" (my emphases). Or
there is "For Once, Then, Something." Its very title indicates a willingness to celebrate
not a gift of meaning but only an inconclusive promise of it.

Others taunt me with having knelt at well-curbs
Always wrong to the light, so never seeing
Deeper down in the well than where the water
Gives me back in a shining surface picture
Me myself in the summer heaven godlike
Looking out of a wreath of fern and cloud puffs.
Once, when trying with chin against a well-curb,
I discerned, as I thought, beyond the picture,
Through the picture, a something white, uncertain,
Something more of the depths—and then I lost it.
Water came to rebuke the too clear water.
One drop fell from a fern, and lo, a ripple
Shook whatever it was lay there at bottom,
Blurred it, blotted it out. What was that whiteness?
Truth? A pebble of quartz? For once, then, something.

The spot he discerns at the bottom of a well is not "truth"; it is not, like the whiteness
in *Moby-Dick,* a visionary possibility; it does not claim to be a metaphor. It is called only
"something." There are enticements to significance here; there are, however, no entitle-
ments. It is by that particular phrase—"For once, then, something"—that one is held to
so strict an accounting. The phrase refuses to surrender its vagueness to any one of a

variety of competing emphases, which can fall on the word "once" or on the word "something" or, by different prolongations of voice, on *"then."* In its central image—the picturing of a human face in water—the poem enters into a dialogue with a procession of other works by other writers wherein individual identity gets elevated above its own reflected image so that it may then gaze down on itself as if it were, absurdly, looking into the source of life's mystery. For Frost, who probably knew more Greek and Latin than any of his poetic contemporaries, the echoes of Narcissus would go back to Ovid, and in English to Spenser and Milton, as John Hollander points out in *Melodious Guile* with respect to a similar image in Frost's "Spring Pools." Frost, an avid reader of Milton, knew the scene in Book 4 of *Paradise Lost* where Eve first discovers her image in a pool; "As I bent down to look, just opposite, / A shape within the wat'ry gleam appeared / Bending to look on me." The recurrence of this figuration in Frost is, however, uniquely comic, casual, shrugging. "Looking out of a wreath of fern and cloud puffs," he is clowning on Michelangelo's Sistine ceiling, and even though "that whiteness" evokes Melville's white whale, there is no hint here of the foreboding reference at the beginning of *Moby-Dick* to "that story of Narcissus" and "that same image we ourselves see in all rivers and oceans. It is the image of the ungraspable phantom of life." Coming closer to Frost's casualness, though with none of its self-mockery, is Whitman in "Crossing Brooklyn Ferry," reporting that he "Saw the reflection of the summer sky in the water, / Had my eyes dazzled by the shimmering track of beams, / Look'd at the fine centrifugal spokes of light round the shape of my head in the sunlit water."

More than his predecessors, Frost is playing around with the idea of reflection both as mirroring and—though less evidently than in "Spring Pools"—with reflection as thinking or discernment. Both kinds of reflection are "blurred" and "blotted" out by the simplest accident of water dropping on water. This figuration of blotting comes directly, I think, from Shelley's "To Jane: The Recollection," where reflections in a pool and in a mind suffer exactly the same fate as they do in Frost. But in Shelley the image is far more down-spirited than it is in Frost, who instead displays some of the quick impatience heard in "The Murders in the Rue Morgue," when Poe remarks that "there is such a thing as being too profound. Truth is not always in a well." Perhaps the closest approximation of Frost's attitude here occurs in *The Will to Believe,* where, in the chapter called "The Sentiment of Rationality," James says that "The bottom of being is left logically opaque to us, as something which we simply come upon and find, and about which (if we wish to act) we should pause and wonder as little as possible." The opacity of the self in James and Frost provides no pretext for Melvillean bewilderments about "the ungraspable phantom of life." It is an occasion for easygoing self-caricature.

Sounds for Frost are the more significant when barely audible. In human speech this means that the sounds are so close to the uncalculated casualness of down-home talk as to incline us actually to inattention. The mysteries lurking in the vocabulary begin to get to you only when you force yourself to listen closely, and yet you trust so much in the sound that you barely listen at all. The implication is that we are brought together not by a shared commitment to explicitly defined values; we are brought together instead in a shared confidence that we are all somehow accommodated to what Stephen Dedalus in *Ulysses* calls "the ineluctable modality of the visible." That is, we really do not know what is there or cannot agree on what it is; and yet we assent, or so our most elementary idioms seem to indicate, to the fact that in life and in poetry there is "something" or only "something, perhaps." The value of such verbal sound is that, as pragmatism recommends, it points toward future realization, toward the existence of things which it cannot verbally re-present.

I have been suggesting all along that barriers to clarity can in themselves be modes of communication, expressions of human bonding.[4] The metaphors as well as the sounds of "Mending Wall" suggest as much, and the allegory of the poem allows for no distinction between language in poetry and language in daily life. "A curious formalization of the common speech" is John Peale Bishop's way of describing some similar if more pronounced achievements in Gertrude Stein. Frost is a great poet not in spite of his desire to be a popular one, as is sometimes suggested, but because of it. The desire is rooted in a perception of the mediated and poetic potentials of ordinary idioms. All of us live all the time with the fact that while the language of daily life creates structures we can believe in, it just as beneficially creates gaps in those structures, gaps in what it only pretends already to have settled.

Deconstructive and linguistic theories announce much the same conclusion with an air of discovery Frost would have found amusing. Like Emerson or James, Stein or Stevens, he thinks of the self pragmatically—it is "something which we come upon and find." Since that finding may quickly dissolve, we must be ready to move on to new findings. A deconstructionist argues that when a word is used as the sign of a thing it creates a sense of the thing's absence more than of its presence. This means, as if any good poet or sensible person has ever thought otherwise, that the word is not the thing it represents. Language, so the argument goes, can create an abyss—a Frostean gap with a vengeance—and writing is constructed on that abyss. Emersonian pragmatists like Frost or Stevens scarcely deny this, but for them the evidence of a gap or an abyss is an invitation simply to get moving and keep moving, to make a transition. (Harold Bloom's word "crossing" roughly approximates what I mean by transition, but is used to describe movements more abrupt and assertive than those I have in mind.)[5] A transition can patch over a gap with very indistinct and loose phrasings, the kind people habitually use without expecting that the phrases will do more than keep them in touch with themselves and others, all very noncommittally.

One virtue of the kind of sound I am describing is, then, that it can create spaces or gaps in ascertained structures of meaning and that it can do so in such a way as simultaneously to create trust and reassurance instead of human separation. The sounds invite us to live with others in a space of expectation rather than deferral, the space of "something, perhaps." That is the less than easy significance of "Mending Wall" insofar as it is a poem about the making of neighbors. And yet to be consistent with these sounds—

not, again, any assertion the words make, but the *sound* of them—the poem never does or can directly yield all the significances I want to find in it. If Frost's "sound of sense" is to work as he said it could—through a door or a wall, so that particular words are inaudible—then some of that sense must remain obscure, untranslatable, and forever incipient, like Jamesian truth itself. The sound of the opening line of the poem, "Something there is that doesn't love a wall," creates a mystery, or what the poem itself calls a "gap." This gap is not filled by summary bits of wisdom, like "good fences make good neighbors," a line given, it should be remembered, to "an old-stone savage armed," as if aphorisms are crude weaponry. No, good neighbors are made by phrases whose incompleteness is the very sign of neighborliness: "something there is." Anyone can go along with that. The word "something" partakes mildly of the "mischief" attributed to the emergent energies of spring, when the frozen ground swell "makes gaps even two can pass abreast." It is the sort of "mischief" which creates chances for companionability; this "something" doesn't love walls; its love is given instead to the "gaps" in walls wherein people may join.

To rephrase the poem in Jamesian terms, the "old-stone savage" can be called a believer in "substantives," like walls; the speaker of the poem, while not an enemy of substantives—it is he, after all, who invites his neighbor to join in mending the wall— puts his faith more in what James calls "transitives," in whatever moves things from static positions, be it the forces of spring or the activity of hunters. Naturally, he also wants to provoke motions of mind, and sets out therefore to challenge other people's verbal formulas, less by rejecting them outright than by tactful indirection: "I wonder / If I could put a notion in his head," or "I'd rather / He said it for himself."

In *Principles of Psychology* James complains, in effect, that sentences and paragraphs are usually structured so as to muffle the tonal modulations of speech, especially when these find their way into writing. While the pertinent passage in "The Stream of Thought" has become fairly well known, many of its own modulations have gone unheeded. It is usually read simply as a prescription for change, when instead it describes a situation which James knows probably cannot be changed: "We ought to say a feeling of *and,* a feeling of *if,* a feeling of *but,* and a feeling of *by,* quite as readily as we say a feeling of *blue* or a feeling of *cold.* Yet we do not: so inveterate has our habit become of recognizing the existence of the substantive parts alone, that language almost refuses to lend itself to any other use." He had just observed that "There is not a conjunction or a preposition, and hardly an adverbial phrase, syntactic form, or inflection of voice, in human speech, that does not express some shading or other of relation which we at some moment actually feel to exist between the larger objects of our thought....the relations are numberless, and no existing language is capable of doing justice to all their shades." His strongest objection is reserved for a prevalent error in thinking which supposes that "where there is *no* name"—where there is only "something"—then "no entity can exist." And he concludes with a passage that is apt to make any of us feel guilty about the way we use language day by day: "All *dumb* or anonymous psychic states have, owing to this error, been coolly suppressed; or, if recognized at all, have been named after the substantive perception they led to, as thoughts 'about' this object or 'about' that, the stolid word *about* engulfing all their delicate idiosyncrasies in its monotonous sound."

James is partial to transitives and conjunctives, to fragments that decentralize any grammatical or "textual" structure and that loosen the gravitational pull of substantives. Even before *Principles of Psychology,* his writing looks for a grammar that will do the work of what he later called radical empiricism. The grammar would make us aware that the relations between things are as important to experience as are the things themselves. It is necessary to stay loose. His ideal grammar leads to his politics, and not the other way round. The grammar he proposes is already anti-imperialist, anti-patriarchal, while never becoming directly focused on political or social structures. It is at least implicitly feminist, anticipating a passage in Gertrude Stein's extremely difficult *Patriarchal Poetry:*[6]

Reject rejoice rejuvenate rejuvenate rejoice
reject rejoice rejuvenate reject rejuvenate
reject rejoice.

Both in *Pragmatism* and in *The Meaning of Truth,* the rejection of logocentrisms, and the rejuvenations that go with them, are articulated within confines having essentially to do with language use. In his preface to the latter book he argues that because "parts of experience hold together from next to next by relations that are themselves parts of experience," the "directly apprehended universe needs…no extraneous trans-empirical connective support, but possesses in its own right a concatenated or continuous structure." A structure so imagined need not ask for "a higher unifying agency" like God, since its power derives from its own internal movements. To repeat Emerson in "Self-Reliance," "power ceases in the instant of repose; it resides in the moment of transition from a past to a new state."

James's pragmatism looks back to the two American writers he most admired—Emerson with his transitions, Whitman with his lolling about—and forward to Frost, Stevens, and Stein. All three, along with Emerson and Whitman, find in casual forms of speech a way to play against the power of concepts or epistemic formations, and yet each of them insists that the sounds thus produced have a value in and by themselves. Individualism, as they represent it, is quietly eccentric; it refuses to adopt the tone demanded of it by "the situation." It can withhold itself from the over-defining appeals of ideologies, meanings, images, ideas that are making the rounds at any given moment. Such individualism can keep in touch with an idea without letting itself be possessed by it; it makes its presence felt, especially in the company of the more articulately opinionated, by a lot of Jamesian *ands* and *buts,* Frostean *somethings* and *anythings,* by Stein's elaborately patterned repetitions and the many *as ifs*[7] that frequent the poems of Stevens as well as Frost—not needing any help, by the way, from Hans Vaihinger, whose

Philosophy of As If, published in German in 1911, was not available in English until 1924. The great human repertoire of muttering and murmuring gives irreducible tonal evidences of *someone* there who, in however tattered a shape, remains free floating of any fixed point. Such a presence cannot be deconstructed because the evidences of its self-definition are the sounds also of its self-abandonment as it moves on to other sounds or, as I am tempted to say, to "moving" sounds.

The American writers I have been discussing have made the value of sound explicitly a subject of their work, and explicitly a resource for eccentricity. They suggest that the individual voice has in fact little else to depend on beyond the sounds it makes and, decidedly, those it refuses to make. When, to recall an instance in "Self-Reliance," Emerson says that once anyone has "spoken with *eclat,* he is a committed person," he means, perhaps recalling some advice he had received earlier from his formidable aunt, Mary Moody Emerson,[8] that articulate speech will have made him a prisoner, "clapped into jail by his consciousness." The word *eclat* carries the root meaning of *splinter.* By speaking emphatically you shatter and scatter, you lose rather than express your identity. This fear of the appropriating power of social discourse suggests that the American contingent anticipates an alliance with Nietzsche, Foucault, and Derrida, all differences among them allowed. And yet, it should be apparent by now that in pressing their case the Americans simply *sound* different. They sound altogether less rhetorically embattled, less culturally ambitious than do any of these European cousins.

Literary and cultural narratives that purport to account for the last two hundred years have uniformly neglected this central aspect of the Emersonian pragmatist contribution. I refer, again, to its laid-back, rather quiet way—if under an Emersonian more than a Melvillean dispensation—of imagining and responding to cultural crises. Those who write most confidently about some dubious sequence from a putative modernism to a putative postmodernism leave the American contingent from Emerson to William James on to Frost, Stein, and Stevens off the calendar altogether, as I have already suggested, choosing to locate the lines of force and development only among Continental figures.

Let me give an illustration. It has to do with the death of God, presumably in the late nineteenth century, and with the supposition that this brought about a unique depreciation in the authority of words and, necessarily, of the Word. However persuasive this argument sounds, it must be asked whether the death of God is to be imagined as a shocking discovery in some particular period, and therefore a good excuse for modernist literary anxiety with its anguish about the arbitrariness of language, or whether, instead, it has been a recurrent event to which at least some people have always been habituated and about which they can therefore talk with a certain calm. When Nietzsche announced the death of God in 1881 in *The Gay Science,* he had been assiduously reading Emerson. Indeed, he probably found his title for this book in a lecture called "Prospects," where Emerson says, of another European writer, "I am sorry to read the observation of M. De Tocqueville that a cloud always hangs on an American's brow. Least of all is it to be pardoned in the literary and speculative class. I hate the builders of dungeons in the air." (This is a figure Stevens would have admired, and an echo of it can in fact be heard in *Notes Toward a Supreme Fiction,* where he refers to "the celestial ennui of apartments / That sends us back to the first idea.") "We read," Emerson continues, "another commission in the cipher of nature: we were made for another office, professors of the Joyous Science."

Nietzsche could not have read an entry in the as yet unpublished Journals where Emerson refers, in July 1835, nearly fifty years before *The Gay Science,* to the death of God. I am not making the jingoistic claim that Emerson's obituary came first, especially since neither he nor Nietzsche has priority on that score. I point rather, and always, to the particular tone of voice in the writing, the particular sound in this case with which Emerson expresses the idea. He sounds as if it is something not at all remarkable, as if everyone already knows about it. The tone is easygoing, even jocular: "It seems as if every body was insane on one side & the Bible makes them as crazy as Bentham or Spurzheim or politics. The ethical doctrines of these theosophists are true & exalting, but straightway they run upon their Divine Transformation, the Death of God &c & become horn mad." Later, in 1868 (thirteen years before Nietzsche's), there is another such announcement, in a tone no less easygoing. This time it comes from William James. He writes to Oliver Wendell Holmes, in a letter from Dresden dated May 15, that "If God is dead or at least irrelevant, ditto everything pertaining to the 'Beyond.'" This looks ahead to "the remotest cleanliness of a heaven / That has expelled us and our images" in Stevens's *Notes,* even as it looks back to Emerson. James's "ditto" is a match for Emerson's "&c," and in both instances it is implied that you've heard all this before; you know the rest of the story.

The idea does indeed go far back. Most likely, Emerson would have remembered that at the beginning of the Christian era Plutarch, in "Why Oracles Cease to Give an Answer," reports that "great Pan is dead." Echoing this, while paraphrasing a passage in Jean Paul of 1796–97, Nerval says "God is dead! Heaven is empty—Weep, children, you no longer have a father." It is not necessary to know any of this beforehand, however, in order to recognize from the tone of Emerson and James that they took the idea to be a familiar one long before Nietzsche proposed it. How else could it have become so macabre a joke in Emily Dickinson, who imagines us finding ourselves on the right hand of God, only to discover that he no longer has one:

Those—dying then,
Knew where they went—
They went to God's Right Hand—
That Hand is amputated now
And God cannot be found—

The abdication of Belief
Makes the Behavior small—

Better an ignis fautus
Than no illume at all—

Historians of ideas can only be as good as their hearing. The best clue for determining how long an idea has been around is the way it is spoken about. Phrasing and pitch of voice will indicate, better than anything else, how familiar an idea has become in a given culture, its relative importance, and the possible reasons why it might, until its time had come, have been ignored. In this instance, the sounds made by Emerson, Dickinson and James, like some of the many comic rumblings in Stevens ("The death of one god is the death of all. / Let purple Phoebus lie in umber harvest, / Let Phoebus slumber and die in autumn umber") all indicate that God's reported demise is not as alarming or catastrophic for them as for others who are given to wastelandings. Keep cool but care, as a character in Pynchon advises. Emersonian pragmatists and pragmatist poets concern themselves more with God's aborning than with Gods aborting, and while Stevens's declaration that "the solar chariot is junk" protests too much, he means, more positively, that the disappearance of God permits a less obstructed chance actually to see the sun—which Emerson said most people do not see at all.

As some of the fragments quoted from Stevens might suggest—"the death of one God is the death of all" or "the solar chariot is junk"—his tone on this matter can be rather blustering, more defensively assertive than it is in Frost or James or even Emerson; far more so than in Stein. Of all of them he is the one most given to the extremes of oscillation between deprivation and creative ebullience, often in the same poem. Some of this probably registers those oscillations of sexual potency which are sometimes his inferable subject. But from testimony in his letters it appears to have had as much to do with feelings of spiritual emptiness and with doubts as to whether or not he could summon the creative energies required to dispel those feelings. Even while losing his early belief in the Christian God, he still maintained allegiances to Christian institutions, and there is evidence that at the end of his life he accepted instruction and baptism in the Roman Catholic faith. A comparable decision is unimaginable for Frost. With the death of the Christian God, Stevens was not to be satisfied, as Frost was, by Jamesian hypotheses. If God has become a fiction then the only substitute for something so grand must be other supreme fictions, those of his own devising. As Milton Bates observes in *Wallace Stevens: A Mythology of Self,* he preferred fictions known to be untrue, and therefore liberating, to hypotheses which are simply unverified. "The final belief," according to an adage in *Opus Posthumous,* "is to believe in a fiction, which you know to be a fiction, there being nothing else. The exquisite truth is to know that it is a fiction and that you believe in it willingly."

When he gets round to discussing sound in poetry, it is with a rhetoric that magnifies its importance and its implications far beyond anything allowed by Frost with his "sound of sense" or by James with his desire to "reinstate" the vague, the inarticulate, the nameless "to their proper place in our mental life." Sound for Stevens becomes a supreme fiction, one that by implication has maintained its power more than have gods no longer with us. "And what about the sound of words?" he asks in the essay "The Noble Rider and the Sound of Words":

> What about nobility, of which the fortunes were to be a kind of test of the value of the poet? I do not know of anything that will appear to have suffered more from the passage of time than the music of poetry and that has suffered less. The deepening need for words to express our thoughts and feelings which, we are sure, are all the truth that we shall ever experience, having no illusions, makes us listen to words when we hear them, loving them and feeling them, makes us search the sound of them, for a finality, a perfection, an unalterable vibration, which it is only within the power of the acutest poet to give them. Those of us who may have been thinking of the path of poetry, those who understand that words are thoughts and not only our own thoughts but the thoughts of men and women ignorant of what it is that they are thinking, must be conscious of this: that above everything else, poetry is words; and that words, above everything else, are, in poetry, sounds.

Stevens's prose, as much as his poetry, asks for a good deal of pondering. It would be wrong to conclude, for example, that "the sound of words" is here given a position once occupied by God, as if it could ever achieve "a finality, a perfection, an unalterable vibration" traditionally ascribed to the unmoved mover. He is not proposing any Eliotic desire for a place of rest or fixity. Instead, he deifies the *activities* by which a sense of these things and a feeling for them might, on occasion and very rarely, be produced. This is within the power, he says, of only the "acutest poet"—"acutest" in the root sense of leaving a Jamesian mark—and it produces a corresponding activity in us only because we are aware of a "deepening need." The need—inferentially for anything that might have the attributes of God—explains the imperative phrasing of "makes us listen... makes us search the sound" of words for the truth of "thoughts and feelings, which...are all the truth that we shall ever experience." Truth is not otherwise available. And yet, even to ask that "the sound of words" yield an "unalterable vibration" is to be far more ambitious for poetry than is Frost in "The Figure a Poem Makes," when he asks only that it yield "a momentary stay against confusion." It is also to invite the kind of despair about poetic creation more frequently heard in Stevens.

An especially beautiful example is the first section of "The Rock," entitled "Seventy Years Later":

It is an illusion that we were ever alive,
Lived in the houses of mothers, arranged ourselves
By our own motions in a freedom of air.

Regard the freedom of seventy years ago.
It is no longer air. The houses still stand,
Though they are rigid in rigid emptiness.

Even our shadows, their shadows, no longer remain.
The lives these lived in the mind are at an end.
They never were ... The sounds of the guitar

Were not and are not. Absurd. The words spoken
Were not and are not. It is not to be believed.
The meeting at noon at the edge of the field seems like

An invention, an embrace between one desperate clod
And another in a fantastic consciousness,
In a queer assertion of humanity:

A theorem proposed between the two—
Two figures in a nature of the sun,
In the sun's design of its own happiness,

As if nothingness contained a métier,
A vital assumption, an impermanence
In its permanent cold, an illusion so desired

That the green leaves came and covered the high rock,
That the lilacs came and bloomed, like a blindness cleaned,
Exclaiming bright sight, as it was satisfied,

In a birth of sight. The blooming and the musk
Were being alive, an incessant being alive,
A particular of being, that gross universe.

There is a disturbing mixture here of directness with exploratory uncertainty, of forth-
rightness with confusion, a compulsion to speak along with a fear that there may be
nothing to say. The personal laying bare finds itself in a vocabulary and syntax opaque
even for Stevens, suggesting that a burden of obscurity is revealed to him in the very
process of the poem's delivery to us. The aged poet is haunted by echoes of his earlier
poetry and by the unreality of his life as that poetry now represents it to him. It could be
said, to recall the passage just discussed from "The Noble Rider and the Sound of
Words," that the recollected images no longer produce for him any semblances of reality or feeling because they lack the "unalterable vibration" of great poetry or the
"finality and perfection" that would have assured them a kind of permanence. In effect,
he is saying that his life of poetry is a failure. The mood recalls, as does this whole section
of "The Rock," the opening paragraphs of Emerson's "Experience."

Partway through, he begins to react against this despairing view, though in so agitated a fashion as to suggest no ascertainable hope for recuperation. The past is and was an "invention," a "theorem," and his experiences now seem to have been "fantastic" and "queer." He has at this point begun to talk less about his poems in particular than about the spirit of poetry itself and to envision a creativity in which anyone, poet or not, may participate. The power evoked is impersonal, not exclusive to a specific time or place, not derivative of nature, much less God, who does not belong in the poem at all. The power depends for its credibility simply on the human need to believe in it, the belief being extemporized out of despair and attached to mere "blooming and musk." We are once again at the "bare rock" of Emerson's "Experience."[9] The phrase "As if nothingness contained a métier" is doubly oxymoronic, both in Stevens's familiar use of "as if" and because of the obvious fact that "nothingness" contains nothing. To what can this "métier" refer, if not to a Jamesian will to believe *something,* to believe at least in the work of knowing? These conjectural movements do not validate the personal intensities or images of the past which the poet has tried to hold on to. Instead, they validate the possibilities for new invention, for making "descriptions," as James phrases it in "Pragmatism and Humanism," that may in themselves be "important additions to reality."

A lot depends in this reading on how one hears the phrase "it is not to be believed," along with the word "absurd." Harold Bloom's reading of this seems to me the inevitable one, as when he refers to their "bewildered, quasi-protesting urgency." So much so that the words are divested of anything so arch as the punning J. Hillis Miller finds in them. Like the words "something" or "anything" their meaning is entirely tonal. They do not make an argument beyond giving evidence of a human presence that refuses to be silenced; they are an impatient rejection of defeat amidst so many signs of defeat. Yeats's "Lapis Lazuli" is crossed here with Wordsworth's "Resolution and Independence."

One of Stevens's problems is that "human life," embodied in the poet and the figure he meets at the edge of the field, are not and could not, given their consciousness of loss and death, ever aspire to "an incessant being alive." Such being belongs only to "life" as a principle generally conceived, to something like James's "stream of life," or to the river of rivers in Connecticut, to recall Stevens's very late, very great poem of that name. It is a kind of life the two are able to invent as against the encroachments, on their own individual lives, of inevitable oblivion. "Two figures" could refer to lovers or to a husband and wife, of course, as Bloom supposes when he says that the poem represents a "humanizing struggle to imagine love." "Two figures" refers, still more agitatedly, I think, to the poet and his daemon, as in the dedicatory poem to *Notes Toward a Supreme Fiction,* where the pronoun "you," while apparently referring to Henry Church, refers instead to Stevens's muse. As already suggested, the word "two" ought not to encourage any mathematical pun on "surd" in "absurd." That would be far too contrived, too lucid, forced, and logical within the much greater thrust of anguish and exasperation in the poem. "Absurd" belongs quite desperately only to this speaker and cannot be taken from him by rummagings in the *OED.* Go with the sound, as one must do in equally confusing and resounding passages of Shakespeare, like those famous speeches in *Macbeth*, also responsive to the brutality of loss and time, the speeches beginning "tomorrow and tomorrow" and "pity, like a naked new-born babe / Striding the blast."

Such poetry eludes clarification; it exists in sounds that are right only for the occasion and are not to be abstracted in the service of other occasions. In that sense, Hillis Miller's reading of this part of the poem, in his chapter on Stevens in *The Linguistic Moment*, is antithetical to my own. It is a working out of some incipient possibilities in the language that seem to me already forsworn by more compellingly emotive and dramatic ones. Apropos the word "absurd" he writes:

> *Absurd:* from *ab,* away, an intensive here, and *surdus,* deaf, inaudible, insufferable to the ear.... A *surd* in mathematics is a sum containing one or more irrational roots of numbers. The square root of two is an irrational number. There is a square root of two, but it is not any number that can be said, rationally. A *surd* in phonetics is a voiceless sound, that is to say, a sound with no base in the vibration of the vocal chords. The original root of the word *surd, swer,* means to buzz or whisper, as in *susurration* or *swirl,* which I used above. The Latin *surdus* was chosen in medieval mathematics to translate an Arabic term that was itself a translation of the Greek *alogos:* speechless, wordless, inexpressible, irrational, groundless.[10]

By depriving "absurd" of voice and place—it could have the meanings Miller ascribes to it if it were relocated anywhere in the poem—this account makes the word "absurd" into an abstracted elucidation of the poet's disappearance, when it is instead an assertion, however merely guttural, of his refusal to disappear. The word is not to be taken as an analytic comment on the now soundless guitar; rather, it is in itself a human sound dredged up in opposition to the silencing of the guitar and of his bequest to poetry. And then, after saying further that the words of his poetry also "were not and are not," he makes yet another and similar counterassertion, "it is not to be believed." What then *is* to be believed? Again, only what he calls an "invention," a fiction, a product of the struggling will to believe in something beyond even human love or poetry.

As will have been noticed, perhaps, I have not been content merely to interpret this poem or to argue with other accounts of it. I am using the poem as an allegory of the kind of pragmatist reading that seems to me, quite aside from Wallace Stevens, important to human conduct. I want my readings of Stevens and of Frost or, on other occasions, of Stein, to be coherent with an American pragmatist heritage that goes back to Emerson, a philosophical heritage that is unique for the privileges it accords to casual, extemporized, ordinary idiom, to uses of language that translate into little more than sound. The sounds reveal human presences that barely manage, and only then by virtue of their unobtrusiveness, to frustrate any excluding, incipiently deconstructive forces that lurk in the more obdurate or, as James might say, intellectualist uses of words. Of course this heritage is also, to some extent, my own concoction, derived from an intense reading of Emerson, to whom I feel a deep personal obligation, and from an interpretation of James which makes him, though he never volunteers, into a philosopher of language. That is, I am doing what I feel temperamentally called upon to do, as is every other responsible reader.

Reading is nothing if it is not personal. It ought to get down ultimately to a struggle between what you want to make of a text and what it wants to make of itself and of you. The stakes do not seem to me much higher than that, even when a reader wants to show how a text carries within itself the enabling and sometimes discrediting structures of a surrounding political and oppressively gendered culture. Having over twenty years ago, especially in *The Performing Self,* paid my respects to the politics embedded in literary structures—a respect each generation must pay on its own terms—I am now bothered by something quite different, which can be called, perhaps crudely, the loud mouth of contemporary criticism. It can be traced back to the headiness of Eliot's modernism, as in his grandiose views of his own and of Joyce's practices, and it is evident in calls since then to speak loudly while carrying so delicate a stick as a novel or a poem. And while there is some healthy skepticism currently at work in criticism, especially as directed against literature's claims to transcendence or the incorporation of values, that skepticism needs also to be directed at the language of criticism itself and at *its* claims to large significance.[11] Literature, including criticism, exists in time, but fortunately it does not exist all of the time. Literature exists only when it is being read by someone, which is not often, not for long, and not by very many. Maybe it is at most a stalling for time. I guess I admire Frost a bit more than Stevens, though such choices are tiresome, because he admits without any wringing of hands that a poem is only "a momentary stay against confusion." It is not he who says "only," since for him the moment is quite enough. I must say "only," however, because, in the profession to which I belong, momentariness is obviously too little to satisfy those who clamor, at the expense of literature, for so much more.

Notes

1 See the discussion of Edwards and language in Perry Miller, *Errand into the Wilderness* (Cambridge: Harvard University Press, 1956), 177–183.

2 Some of the resemblances between Paterian and Emersonian pragmatist aesthetics are explored in my "Pater, Joyce, Eliot," *James Joyce Quarterly* 26:1 (1988), 21–35.

3 The influence of William James on Stein, and specifically on "Melanctha," is extensively discussed in Lisa Ruddick, *Reading Gertrude Stein: Body, Text, Gnosis* (Ithaca: Cornell University Press, 1990). See especially the sections entitled "'Melanctha' and the Psychology of William James," pp. 13–25 and "The Style of 'Melanctha': Stein's Resistance to James," pp. 33–41. In her valuable study of Stein, Harriet Chessman discovers the influence of Emerson in "Melanctha" as well as of James. Harriet Scott Chessman, *The Public Is Invited to Dance* (Stanford: Stanford University Press, 1989), 41–53, 156–161. See also Steven Myer, "Stein and

Emerson," *Raritan Quarterly,* 10:2 (1990), 87–115.

4 In an essay on the *Federalist* papers, John Burt makes the point that the founding of the Republic depended, to some measure, on a tacit agreement not to clarify differences or divergent interests, but to resort to phrasings vague enough that contending parties, even in future disputes not then predictable, could depend on enough flexibility in constitutional and legislative language to accommodate opposing interests. See John Burt, "Tyranny and the Public Sphere in *The Federalist," Raritan Quarterly,* forthcoming.

5 In particular, see the discussions of "crossing" in what Bloom calls a "crisis poem," in his *Wallace Stevens: The Poems of Our Climate* (Ithaca: Cornell University Press, 1976), 2.

6 See the informative reference to this passage in Catharine Stimpson's *Where the Meanings Are: Feminism and Cultural Spaces* (New York: Methuen, 1988), 117–118. Stimpson points out that Stein's note after the passage—"Not as if it was tried"—has at least two meanings: "no one has really done this before; if you are going to do this, do it as if no one really had before; i.e., begin again." The passage from *Patriarchal Poetry* can be found in *The Yale Gertrude Stein,* ed. Richard Kostelanetz (New Haven: Yale University Press, 1980), III.

7 Apropos the implications in Stevens of the phrase "as if," see Helen Vendler's essay "'The Qualified Assertions of Wallace Stevens," in *The Act of Mind,* ed. Roy Harvey Pearce and J. Hillis Miller (Baltimore: Johns Hopkins University Press, 1965), 163–78.

8 The word *eclat* is used with negative connotations in a letter to him in 1822, a year after his graduation from Harvard, written by his aunt, Mary Moody Emerson (he liked to call her "Father Mum"). Replying to his complaint that he had been having difficulty with his writing, she remarked that "there is a time approaching that I dread worse than this sweet stagnation, when your muse shall be dragged into eclat." Mary Moody Emerson's use of the term was pointed out to me by Joe Thomas, and can be found in George Tolman, *Mary Moody Emerson,* p. 21. This monograph, a 1902 address by Tolman to the Concord Antiquarian Society, was privately printed in 1929.

9 Matthew Lewis, while a student in a seminar of mine at Rutgers, discovered some correspondences between this first section of "The Rock" and a passage in James's *The Will to Believe.* The echoes are so striking—as are the echoes in James of Emerson's "rock" in "Experience"—that I quote in full the two paragraphs. They are from the chapter called "The Moral Philosopher and the Moral Life" in *The Will to Believe* (Cambridge: Harvard University Press, 1979), 150: "Were all other things, gods and men and starry heavens, blotted out from this universe, and were there left but one rock with two loving souls upon it, that rock would have as thoroughly moral a constitution as any possible world which the eternities and immensities could harbor. It would be a tragic constitution, because the rock's inhabitants would die. But while they lived, there would be real good things and real bad things in the universe; there would be obligations, claims, and expectations; obediences, refusals, and disappointments; compunctions and longings for harmony to come again, and inward peace of conscience when it was restored; there would, in short, be a moral life, whose active energy would have no limit but the intensity of interest in each other with which the hero and heroine might be endowed.

"We, on this terrestrial globe, so far as the visible facts go, are just like the inhabitants of such a rock. Whether a God exist, or whether no God exist, in yon blue heaven above us bent, we form at any rate an ethical republic here below. And the first reflection which this leads to is that ethics have as genuine and real a foothold in a universe where the highest consciousness is human, as in a universe where there is a

God as well. 'The religion of humanity' affords a basis for ethics as well as theism does. Whether the purely human system can gratify the philosopher's demand as well as the other is a different question, which we ourselves must answer ere we close."

10 J. Hillis Miller, *The Linguistic Moment* (Princeton University Press, 1985), 394.

11 Though he has a somewhat different target in mind, Edward Said voices an objection similar to mine against what he calls "these tremendous conflations, inflations, exaggerations" that can occur in the practice of criticism. His 1989 Wellek Lectures in Critical Theory, delivered at the University of California at Irvine, offer some brilliant dissections of the processes by which the artistic productions of particular groups and of particular historical moments are made to seem universally applicable to all times, persons, and cultures. The lectures were published as *Musical Elaborations* (Columbia University Press, 1991). See p. 52 and all of chap. 2, "On the Transgressive Elements in Music," pp. 34–72. See also in this regard Eric Hobsbawm and Terence Ranger, eds., *The Invention of Tradition* (Cambridge University Press, 1984), and specifically Hobsbawm's "Introduction: Inventing Tradition."

STANLEY CAVELL
(B. 1926)

In "The Availability of Wittgenstein's Philosophy" (1962), Harvard philosopher Stanley Cavell wrote of Wittgenstein's concern with breaking the control of "modes of thought and sensibility whose origins are unseen or unremembered…. Because the breaking of such control is a constant purpose of the later Wittgenstein, his writing is deeply practical and negative, the way Freud's is." Cavell came to see this concern, and a form of "deeply practical" writing, as central to the American philosophical tradition—first in Thoreau, the subject of his *The Senses of Walden* (1972), and later in Emerson, to whom Cavell has devoted increasing attention, in the essays published in the expanded edition of *The Senses of Walden* (1981), *In Quest of the Ordinary* (1989), *This New Yet Unapproachable America* (1989) and *Conditions Handsome and Unhandsome* (1990).

Although Cavell does not think of himself as a pragmatist in the tradition of James and Dewey, he is the best current guide to the thought of a philosopher now understood (by such writers as Richard Poirier and Cornel West) to be a founder of pragmatism. As with such contemporary pragmatists as Putnam and Rorty, Cavell's writing is steeped in the philosophy of Wittgenstein, and even more than theirs in the philosophy of Heidegger. Like Wittgenstein or Dewey or Heidegger, Cavell thinks of philosophy as something that helps us move past such "fixated conflicts" as those between "solipsism and realism," "the private and the public," or "subjectivity and objectivity." Like these thinkers also, Cavell writes with the sense—as in "Thinking of Emerson" (1979), reprinted below—that we have "not yet learned true thinking."

Cavell thinks of Emerson in the company of an important range of Western philosophers: Kant, Nietzsche, Heidegger, even John Dewey. What is wrong with empiricism,

Cavell takes Emerson and Dewey to be suggesting, is not its reliance on experience but its paltry idea of experience. A revised empiricism would allow for the epistemological role of moods, a subject Emerson and Heidegger (and also William James) give prominent places in their discussions not only of psychology but of metaphysics and epistemology. "The idea," Cavell writes, "is roughly that moods must be taken as having at least as sound a role in advising us of reality as sense-experience has...." The world we encounter through our mood-laden experience is both separate from and in some way intimate with us, a point Cavell finds Emerson making in such essays as "Experience" and "Circles": "We are in a state of 'romance' with the universe (to use a word from the last sentence of 'Experience'); we do not possess it, but our life is to return to it, in ever-widening circles."

Emerson is above all the philosopher of self-reliance, but it is not easy to say what this means: what either "self" or "reliance" means in Emerson's essays. Cavell develops an interpretation of the Emersonian self (and of Emersonian philosophy) that places it close to pragmatism: the Emersonian self practices "onward thinking," an idea Cavell finds echoed and reinterpreted in Heidegger's idea that thinking is "a matter essentially of getting ourselves 'on the way.'" Movement is necessary because there are no absolute resting places or foundations. We find ourselves, as Emerson says at the beginning of "Experience," "on a stair: there are stairs below us, which we seem to have ascended; there are stairs above us...which go upward and out of sight." Emerson, Cavell tells us in *This New Yet Unapproachable America*, reinterprets philosophical grounding as "lasting," and thinking as "knowing how to go on, being on the way." Emerson, as much as Peirce or Wittgenstein or Dewey, portrays a world of temporary or partial—if not for that reason unsatisfactory—closures or consummations on the one hand; but also a radical openness—James's word was "wildness"—on the other. Cavell, thinking of Emerson in *This New Yet Unapproachable America*, writes: "At each step, or level, explanation comes to an end; there is no level to which all explanations come, at which all end. An American might see this as taking the open road. The philosopher as the hobo of thought."

THINKING OF EMERSON

STANLEY CAVELL

INTRODUCTORY NOTE: For a program arranged by the Division on Philosophical Approaches to Literature at the annual convention of the Modern Language Association in New York, December 1978, Professor Leo Marx invented and chaired a meeting on Emerson whose panelists were asked by him to respond to a passage from my book *The Senses of Walden* that runs this way:

> Study of *Walden* would perhaps not have become such an obsession with me had it not presented itself as a response to questions with which I was already obsessed: Why has America never expressed itself philosophically? Or has it—in the metaphysical riot of its greatest literature? Has the impulse to philosophical speculation been absorbed, or exhausted, by speculation in territory, as in such thoughts as Manifest Destiny? Or are such questions not really intelligible? They are, at any rate, disturbingly like the questions that were asked about American literature before it established itself. In rereading *Walden*, twenty years after first reading it, I seemed to find a book of sufficient intellectual scope and consistency to have established or inspired a tradition of thinking.

My response is the following essay, not quite all of which was read at the meeting. I am grateful to Leo Marx for prompting me to go further with these thoughts, and to Jay Cantor for reading the original draft and pressing me for certain clarifications. A conversation with John McNees was decisive for me in arriving at certain formulations about philosophical prose in its relation to the idea of dialogue and hence to an idea of thinking. I should in this regard also like to refer to an essay by Morse Peckham which appears as the introduction to a facsimile edition of the first printing of Emerson's *Essays* and *Essays: Second Series* (Columbus, 1969). I dedicate the present essay to the members, in the fall of 1978, of a graduate seminar at Harvard on the later writings of Heidegger.

Thinking of Emerson, I can understand my book on *Walden* as something of an embarrassment, but something of an encouragement as well, since if what it suggests about the lack of a tradition of thinking in America is right, e.g., about how Emerson and Thoreau deaden one another's words, then my concentration on understanding Thoreau was bound to leave Emerson out. He kept sounding to me like secondhand Thoreau.

The most significant shortcoming among the places my book mentions Emerson is its accusing him of "misconceiving" Kant's critical enterprise, comparing Emerson unfavorably in this regard with Thoreau. I had been impressed by Thoreau's sentence running "The universe constantly and obediently answers to our conceptions" as in effect an elegant summary of the *Critique of Pure Reason.* When I requote that sentence later in the book, I take it beyond its Kantian precincts, adding that the universe answers whether our conceptions are mean or magnanimous, scientific or magical, faithful or treacherous, thus suggesting that there are more ways of making a habitable world—or more layers to it—than Kant's twelve concepts of the understanding accommodate. But I make no effort to justify this idea of a "world" beyond claiming implicitly that as I used the word I was making sense. The idea is roughly that moods must be taken as having at least as sound a role in advising us of reality as sense-experience has; that, for example, coloring the world, attributing to it the qualities "mean" or "magnanimous," may be no less objective or subjective than coloring an apple, attributing to it the colors red or green. Or perhaps we should say: sense-experience is to objects what moods are to the world. The only philosopher I knew who had made an effort to formulate a kind of epistemology of moods, to find their revelations of what we call the world as sure as the revelations of what we call understanding, was the Heidegger of *Being and Time.* But it was hard to claim support there without committing oneself to more machinery than one had any business for.

Now I see that I might, even ought to, have seen Emerson ahead of me, since, for example, his essay on "Experience" is about the epistemology, or say the logic, of moods. I understand the moral of that essay as contained in its late prayerful remark, "But far be from me the despair which prejudges the law by a paltry empiricism." That is, what is wrong with empiricism is not its reliance on experience but its paltry idea of experience. (This is the kind of criticism of classical empiricism leveled by John Dewey—for example, in "An Empirical Survey of Empiricisms"—who praised Emerson but so far as I know never took him up philosophically.) But I hear Kant working throughout Emerson's essay on "Experience," with his formulation of the question, "Is metaphysics possible?" and his line of answer: Genuine knowledge of (what we call) the world is for us, but it cannot extend beyond (what we call) experience. To which I take Emerson to be replying: Well and good, but then you had better be very careful what it is you understand by experience, for that might be limited in advance by the conceptual limitations you impose upon it, limited by what we know of human existence, i.e., by our limited experience of it. When, for example, you get around to telling us what we may hope for, I must know that you have experienced hope, or else I will surmise that you have not, which is to say precisely that your experience is of despair.

Emerson's "Experience" even contains a little argument, a little more explicitly with Kant, about the nature of experience in its relation to, or revelation of, the natural world. "The secret of the illusoriness [of life] is in the necessity of a succession of moods or objects. Gladly we would anchor, but the anchorage is quicksand. This onward trick of nature is too strong for us: *Pero si muove.*" In the section of the *Critique of Pure Reason* entitled "Analogies of Experience," one of the last before turning to an investigation of transcendental illusion, Kant is at pains to distinguish within experience the *"subjective succession* of apprehension from the *objective succession* of appearances."* The anchor he uses to keep subjectivity and objectivity from sinking one another is, as you would expect, gripped in transcendental ground, which is always, for Kant, a question of locating necessity properly, in this case the necessity, or rules, of succession in experience. (It is curious, speaking of anchoring, that one of Kant's two examples in this specific regard is that of seeing a ship move downstream.) The acceptance of Galileo's—and Western science's—chilling crisis with the Church over the motion of the earth recalls Kant's claim to have accomplished a Copernican Revolution in metaphysics; that is, understanding the configurations of the world as a function of the configurations of our own nature. Now I construe Emerson's implicit argument in the passage cited as follows. The succession of moods is not tractable by the distinction between subjectivity and objectivity Kant proposes for experience. *This* onward trick of nature is too much for us; the given bases of the self are quicksand. The fact that we are taken over by this succession, this onwardness, means that you can think of it as at once a succession of moods (inner matters) and a succession of objects (outer matters). This very evanescence of the world proves its existence to me; it *is* what vanishes from me. I guess this is not realism exactly; but it is not solipsism either.

I believe Emerson may encourage the idea of himself as a solipsist or subjectivist, for example, in such a remark, late in the same essay, as "Thus inevitably does the universe wear our color." But whether you take this to be subjective or objective depends upon whether you take the successive colors or moods of the universe to be subjective or objective. My claim is that Emerson is out to destroy the ground on which such a problem takes itself seriously, I mean interprets itself as a metaphysical fixture. The universe is as separate from me, but as intimately part of me, as one on whose behalf I contest, and who therefore wears my color. We are in a state of "romance" with the universe (to use a word from the last sentence of the essay); we do not possess it, but our life is to return to it, in ever-widening circles, "onward and onward," but with as directed a goal as any quest can have; in the present case, until "the soul attains her due sphericity." Until then, encircled, straitened, you can say the soul is solipsistic; surely it is, to use another critical term of Emerson's, partial. This no doubt implies that we do not have a universe as it is in itself. But this implication is nothing: we do not have selves in themselves either. The universe *is* what constantly and obediently answers to our conceptions. It is what *can* be all the ways we know it to be, which is to say, all the ways we can be. In "Circles" we are told: "Whilst the eternal generation of circles proceeds, the eternal generator abides. That central life... contains all its circles." The universe contains all the colors it wears. That it has no more than I can give it is a fact of what Emerson calls my poverty. (Other philosophers may speak of the emptiness of the self.)

The Kantian ring of the idea of the universe as inevitably wearing our color is, notwithstanding, pertinent. Its implication is that the way specifically Kant understands the generation of the universe keeps it solipsistic, still something partial, something of our, of my, making. Emerson's most explicit reversal of Kant lies in his picturing the intellectual hemisphere of knowledge as passive or receptive and the intuitive or instinctual hemisphere as active or spontaneous. Whereas for Kant the basis of the *Critique of Pure Reason* is that "concepts are based on the spontaneity of thought, sensible intuitions on the receptivity of impressions." Briefly, there is no intellectual intuition. I will come back to this.

But immediately, to imagine that Emerson could challenge the basis of the argument of the *Critique of Pure Reason,* I would have to imagine him to be a philosopher—would I not? I would have, that is to say, to imagine his writing—to take it—in such a way that it does not misconceive Kant but undertakes to engage him in dispute. I like what Matthew Arnold has to say about Emerson, but we ought no longer to be as sure as Arnold was that the great philosophical writer is one who builds a system; hence that Emerson is not such a writer on the ground that he was not such a builder. We are by now too aware of the philosophical *attacks* on system or theory to place the emphasis in defining philosophy on a product of philosophy rather than on the process of philosophizing. We are more prepared to understand as philosophy a mode of thought that undertakes to bring philosophy to an end, as, say, Nietzsche and Wittgenstein attempt to do, not to mention, in their various ways, Bacon, Montaigne, Descartes, Pascal, Marx, Kierkegaard, Carnap, Heidegger, or Austin, and in certain respects Kant and Hegel. Ending philosophy looks to be a commitment of each of the major modern philosophers; so it is hardly to be wondered at that some of them do not quite know whether what they are writing is philosophy. Wittgenstein said that what he did replaced philosophy. Heidegger said in his later period that what he was doing was thinking, or learning thinking, and that philosophy is the greatest enemy of true thinking. But to understand the attack on philosophy as itself philosophy, or undertaken in the name, or rather in the place, of philosophy, we must of course understand the attack as nevertheless internal to the act of philosophizing, accepting that autonomy. Church and State and the Academy and Poetry and the City may each suppress philosophy, but they cannot, without its complicity, replace it.

Can Emerson be understood as wishing to replace philosophy? But isn't that wish really what accounts for the poignancy, or dialectic, of Emerson's call, the year Thoreau graduated college, not for a thinker but for Man Thinking? The American Scholar is to think no longer partially, as a man following a task delegated by a society of which he is a victim, but as leading a life in which thinking is of the essence, as a man whose wholeness, say whose autonomy, is in command of the autonomy of thinking. The hitch of course is that there is no such human being. "Man in history, men in the world today are bugs, spawn" ("The American Scholar"). But the catch is that we aspire to this man, to the metamorphosis, to the human—hence that we can be guided and raised by the cheer of thinking. In claiming the office of the scholar "to cheer, to raise, and to guide men" as well as demanding that "whatsoever new verdict Reason from her inviolable seat pronounces on the passing men and events of today—this [the scholar] shall hear and promulgate," Emerson evidently requires the replacing of theology as well as of philosophy in his kind of building, his edification. We might think of this as internalizing the unended quarrel between philosophy and theology.

Whatever ways I go on to develop such thoughts are bound to be affected by the coincidence that during the months in which I was trying to get Emerson's tune into my ear, free of Thoreau's, I was also beginning to study the writing of the later Heidegger. This study was precipitated at last by a footnote of the editor of a collection of Heidegger essays, in which *The Senses of Walden* is described as in part forming an explication of Heidegger's notion of poetic dwelling (James G. Hart, in *The Piety of Thinking*). Having now read such an essay of Heidegger's as "Building Dwelling Thinking," I am sufficiently startled by the similarities to find the differences of interest and to start wondering about an account of both. I am thinking not so much of my similarities with Heidegger (I had after all profited from *Being and Time,* and it may be that that book leads more naturally to Heidegger's later work than is, I gather, sometimes supposed) but of Heidegger's with Thoreau, at least with my picture of Thoreau. The relation to Emerson was still unexpected, and hence even more startling. The title of the Heidegger collection I referred to is from a sentence of his that says: "For questioning is the piety of thinking." In the right mood, if you lay beside this a sentence of Emerson's from "Intellect" that says, "Always our thinking is a pious reception," you might well pause a moment. And if one starts digging to test how deep the connection might run, I find that one can become quite alarmed.

The principal text of Heidegger's to test here is translated as *What Is Called Thinking?* Here is a work that can be said to internalize the quarrel between philosophy and theology; that calls for a new existence from the human in relation to Being in order that its task of thinking be accomplished; a work based on the poignancy, or dialectic, of thinking about our having not yet learned true thinking, thinking as the receiving or letting be of something, as opposed to the positing or putting together of something, as this is pictured most systematically in Kant's ideas of representation and synthesis, and most radically in Nietzsche's will to power; that attempts to draw clear of Kant's subjectivity, and of the revenge upon time that Nietzsche understood us as taking. A climactic moment in Heidegger's descent into the origins of words is his understanding of the ety-mological entwining of thinking with the word for thanking, leading for example to an unfolding of ideas in which a certain progress of thinking is understood as a form of thanking, and originally a thanking for the gift of thinking, which means for the recep-tion of being human. Here, if one can consider this to be something like philosophy, is something like a philosophical site within which to explore the crux in our relation to Emerson of his power of affirmation, or of his weakness for it.

We have surely known, since at least Newton Arvin (in "The House of Pain") collected the chorus of charges against Emerson to the effect that he lacked a knowledge of evil or of the sense of the tragic, that this missed Emerson's drift, that his task was elsewhere. Arvin insists, appropriately, that what Emerson gives us, what inspires us in him, "when we have cleared our minds of the cant of pessimism, is perhaps the fullest and most authentic expression in modern literature of the more-than-tragic emotion of thank-fulness" *(Emerson: A Collection of Critical Essays,* ed. Konvitz and Whicher). But we might have surmised from Nietzsche's love of Emerson that no sane or mere man could have convincingly conceived "all things [to be] friendly and sacred, all events holy, all men divine" who was not aware that we may be undone by the pain of the world we make and may not make again. The more recent cant of pleasure or playfulness is no less hard to put up with. Yet a more-than-tragic emotion of thankfulness is still not the drift, or not the point. The point is the achievement not of affirmation but of what Emerson calls "the sacred affirmative" ("The Preacher"), the thing Nietzsche calls "the sacred Yes" ("Three Metamorphoses" in *Zarathustra),* the heart for a new creation. This is not an effort to move beyond tragedy—this has taken care of itself; but to move beyond nihilism, or beyond the curse of the charge of human depravity and its consequent con-demnation of us to despair; a charge which is itself, Emerson in effect declares, the only depravity ("New England Reformers").

(I may interject here that the idea of thinking as reception, which began this path of reasoning, seems to me to be a sound intuition, specifically to forward the correct answer to skepticism [which Emerson meant it to do]. The answer does not consist in denying the conclusion of skepticism but in reconceiving its truth. It is true that we do not know the existence of the world with certainty; our relation to its existence is deeper—one in which it is accepted, that is to say, received. My favorite way of putting this is to say that existence is to be acknowledged.)

So the similarity of Emerson with Heidegger can be seen as mediated by Nietzsche; and this will raise more questions than it can answer. As to the question of what may look like the direction of influence, I am not claiming that Heidegger authenticates the think-ing of Emerson and Thoreau; the contrary is, for me, fully as true, that Emerson and Thoreau may authorize our interest in Heidegger. Then further questions will concern the relation of the thinking of each of these writers to their respective traditions of poetry. To the figure of Holderlin, Heidegger is indebted not alone for lessons of thought but for lessons in reading, and I suppose for the lesson that these are not different, or rather that there is ground upon which thinking and reading and philosophy and poetry meet and part. Emerson's implication in the history of the major line of American poetry is something that Harold Bloom has most concretely and I dare say most unforgettably given to us to think through. Emerson's and Thoreau's relation to poetry is inherently their interest in their own writing: they are their own Hölderlins. I do not mean their interest in what we may call their poems, but their interest in the fact that what they are building is writing, that their writing is, as it realizes itself daily under their hands, sentence by shunning sentence, the accomplishment of inhabitation, the making it happen, the poetry of it. Their prose is a battle, using a remark of Nietzsche's, not to become poetry; a battle specifically to remain in conversation with itself, answerable to itself. (So they do write dialogues, and not monologues, after all.)

Such writing takes the same mode of relating to itself as reading and thinking do, the mode of the self's relation to itself, call it self-reliance. Then whatever is required in possessing a self will be required in thinking and reading and writing. This possessing is not—it is the reverse of—possessive; I have implied that in being an act of creation, it is the exercise not of power but of reception. Then the question is: On what terms is the self received?

The answer I give for Emerson here is a theme of his thinking that further stands it with the later Heidegger's, the thing Emerson calls "onward thinking," the thing Heidegger means in taking thinking as a matter essentially of getting ourselves "on the way."

At the beginning of "Circles" Emerson tells us he means (having already deduced one moral in considering the circular or compensatory character of every human action) to trace a further analogy (or, read a further sense; or, deduce a further moral) from the emblem of the form of a circle. Since the time of "The American Scholar" he has told us that "science is nothing but the finding of analogy," and this seems a fair enough idea of thinking. In "Circles" he invites us to think about the fact, or what the fact symbolizes, that every action admits of being outdone, that around every circle another circle can take its place. I should like to extend the invitation to think about how he pictures us as moving from one circle to another, something he sometimes thinks of as expanding, sometimes as rising. I note that there is an ambiguity in his thoughts here as between what he calls the *generating* and what he calls the *drawing* of the new circle, an ambiguity between the picturing of new circles as forming continuously or discontinuously. I will not try to resolve this ambiguity now but I will take it that the essential way of envisioning our growth, from the inside, is as discontinuous. Then my questions are: How does Emerson picture us as crossing, or rather leaping, the span from one circumference to another? What is the motive, the means of motion, of this movement? How do we go on? (In Wittgenstein's *Philosophical Investigations,* knowing how to go on, as well as knowing when to stop, is exactly the measure of our knowing, or learning, in certain of its main regions or modes—for example, in the knowledge we have of our words. Onward thinking, on the way, knowing how to go on, are of course inflections or images of the religious idea of The Way, inflections which specifically deny that there is a place at which our ways end. Were philosophy to concede such a place, one knowable in advance of its setting out, philosophy would cede its own autonomy.)

You may imagine the answer to the question how we move as having to do with power. But power seems to be the result of rising, not the cause. ("Every new prospect is power" ["Circles"].) I take Emerson's answer to be what he means by "abandonment" (ibid.). The idea of abandonment contains what the preacher in Emerson calls "enthusiasm" or the New Englander in him calls "forgetting ourselves" (ibid.), together with what he calls leaving or relief or quitting or release or shunning or allowing or deliverance, which is freedom (as in "Leave your theory as Joseph his coat in the hand of the harlot, and flee" ["Self-Reliance"]), together further with something he means by trusting or suffering (as in the image of the traveler—the conscious intellect, the intellect alone—"who has lost his way, [throwing] his reins on the horse's neck, and [trusting] to the instinct of the animal to find his road" ["The Poet"]). (Perhaps it helps if you think, as he goes on to say, that what carries us through this world is a divine animal. To spell it out, the human is the rational divine animal. It's a thought—one, by the way, which Heidegger would deny.)

This idea of abandonment gives us a way to grasp the act Emerson pictures as "[writing] on the lintels of the door-post, Whim" ("Self-Reliance"). He says he would do this after he has said that he shuns father and mother and wife and brother when his genius calls him; and he follows it by expressing the hope that it is somewhat better than whim at last. (Something has happened; it is up to us to name it, or not to. Something is wrestling us for our blessing.) Whether his writing on the lintels—his writing as such, I gather—is thought of as having the constancy of the contents of a mezuzah or the emergency of the passover blood, either way he is taking upon himself the mark of God, and of departure. His perception of the moment is taken in hope, as something to be proven only on the way, *by the* way. This departure, such setting out, is, in our poverty, what hope consists in, all there is to hope for; it is the abandoning of despair, which is otherwise our condition. (Quiet desperation Thoreau will call it; Emerson had said, silent melancholy.) Hence he may speak of perception as "not Whimsical, but fatal" (ibid.), preeminently, here, the perception of what we may call whim. Our fatality, the determination of our fate, of whether we may hope, goes by our marking the path of whim. We hope it is better than whim at last, as we hope we may at last seem something better than blasphemers; but it is our poverty not to be final but always to be leaving (abandoning whatever we have and have known): to be initial, medial, American. What the ground of the fixated conflict between solipsism and realism should give way to—or between subjectivity and objectivity, or the private and the public, or the inner and the outer—is the task of onwardness. In Heidegger: "The *thanc* means man's inmost mind, the heart, the heart's core, that innermost essence of man which reaches outward most fully and to the outermost limits" *(What Is Called Thinking?)*. In Emerson: "To believe your own thought, to believe that what is true for you in your private heart, is true for all men—that is genius. Speak your latent conviction and it shall be the universal sense; for always the inmost becomes the outmost" ("Self-Reliance"). The substantive disagreement with Heidegger, shared by Emerson and Thoreau, is that the achievement of the human requires not inhabitation and settlement but abandonment, leaving. Then everything depends upon your realization of abandonment. For the significance of leaving lies in its discovery that you have settled something, that you have felt enthusiastically what there is to abandon yourself to, that you can treat the others there are as those to whom the inhabitation of the world can now be left.

SELECTED BIBLIOGRAPHY

Alexander, Thomas M. *John Dewey's Theory of Art, Experience, and Nature: The Horizons of Feeling*. Albany: State University of New York Press, 1987.

Apel, Karl-Otto. *Charles Sanders Peirce: From Pragmatism to Pragmaticism*. Trans. John M. Krois. Amherst: University of Massachusetts Press, 1981.

Barzun, Jacques. *A Stroll With William James*. New York: Harper and Row, 1983.

Bernstein, Richard. *John Dewey*. New York: Washington Square Press, 1966.

——. *Praxis and Action: Contemporary Philosophies of Human Activity*. Philadelphia: University of Pennsylvania Press, 1971.

——. *Beyond Objectivism and Relativism: Science, Hermeneutics, and Praxis*. Philadelphia: University of Pennsylvania Press, 1983.

——. "One Step Forward, Two Steps Backward: Richard Rorty on Liberal Democracy and Philosophy." *Political Theory* 15 (1987).

Bloom, Harold. *A Map of Misreading*. New York: Oxford University Press, 1975.

——. *Agon: Towards a Theory of Revisionism*. New York. Oxford University Press, 1982.

Brandom, Robert. "Pragmatism, Phenomenalism, Truth Talk." *Midwest Studies in Philosophy* 12, 1988.

——. *Making It Explicit*. Cambridge, MA: Harvard University Press, 1994.

Brint, Michael, and William Weaver, eds. *Pragmatism in Law and Society*. Boulder, CO: Westview Press, 1991.

Cavell, Stanley. *Must We Mean What We Say?* Cambridge: Cambridge University Press, 1976.

——. *The Senses of Walden, An Expanded Edition*. San Francisco: North Point Press, 1979.

——. *In Quest of the Ordinary*. Chicago: University of Chicago Press, 1988.

——. *This New Yet Unapproachable America*. Albuquerque, NM: Living Batch Books, 1979.

——. *Conditions Handsome and Unhandsome*. Chicago: University of Chicago Press, 1990.

Conkin, Paul K. *Puritans and Pragmatists: Eight Eminent American Thinkers*. New York: Dodd, Mead, 1968.

Coughlan, Neil. *Young John Dewey*. Chicago: University of Chicago Press, 1975.

Corrington, Robert S. *An Introduction to C. S. Peirce: Philosopher, Semiotician, and Ecstatic Naturalist*. Lanham, MD: Rowman and Littlefield, 1993.

Davidson, Donald. *Essays on Actions and Events*. New York: Oxford University Press, 1985.

——. *Inquiries into Truth and Interpretation*. New York: Oxford University Press, 1985.

——. "A Nice Derangement of Epitaphs." In *Truth and Interpretation: Perspectives on the Philosophy of Donald Davidson*, ed. Ernest Lepore. New York: Blackwell, 1986, pp. 433–46.

Dewey, John. *The Early Works of John Dewey*. Carbondale, IL: Southern Illinois University Press, 1969–72.

——. *The Middle Works of John Dewey*. Carbondale, IL: Southern Illinois University Press, 1976–83.

——. *The Later Works of John Dewey*. Carbondale, IL: Southern Illinois University Press, 1981–

——. *The Philosophy of John Dewey*. Ed. John J. McDermott. Chicago: University of Chicago Press, 1973.

Ellison, Julie, *Emerson's Romantic Style*. Princeton: Princeton University Press, 1984.

Elshtain, Jean Bethke. "Don't Be Cruel: Reflections on Rortyan Liberalism." *Irony: Essays in Self Betrayal*, ed. Daniel W. Conway and John E. Seary. New York: St. Martin's Press, 1992, pp. 199–218.

Emerson, Ralph Waldo. *The Collected Works of Ralph Waldo Emerson*. Ed. Robert E. Spiller, et al. Cambridge, MA: Harvard University Press, 1971–.

——. *Selected Essays*. Ed. Larzer Ziff, New York: Penguin, 1982.

Fish, Stanley. *Is There a Text in This Class?* Cambridge, MA: Harvard University Press, 1978.

——. *Doing What Comes Naturally: Change, Rhetoric and the Practice of Theory in Literary and Legal Studies*. Durham: Duke University Press, 1989.

Foucault, Michel. *Madness and Civilization: A History of Insanity in the Age of Reason*. New York, Random House, 1973.

——. *Language, Counter-Memory, Practice*. Trans. Donald F. Bouchard and Sherry Simon. Ithaca: Cornell University Press, 1977.

——. *Discipline and Punish: The Birth of the Prison*. Trans. Alan Sheridan. New York: Vintage Books, 1979.

——. *Power/Knowledge: Selected Interviews and Other Writings, 1972-1977*. Trans. Colin Gordon et al. New York: Pantheon Books, 1980.

Fraser, Nancy. *Unruly Practices: Power, Discourse and Gender in Contemporary Social Theory*. Minneapolis: University of Minnesota Press, 1985.

Goodman, Nelson. "The Way The World Is." In *Problems and Projects*. Ed. Nelson Goodman. Indianapolis: Bobbs Merrill, 1972, pp. 24-32.

——. *Ways of Worldmaking*. Indianapolis, IN: Hackett, 1978.

Goodman, Russell B. *American Philosophy and the Romantic Tradition*. Cambridge: Cambridge University Press, 1990.

——. "What Wittgenstein Learned from William James." *History of Philosophy Quarterly*, July 1994, pp. 339–54.

Gunn, Giles. *The Culture of Criticism and the Criticism of Culture*. New York: Oxford University Press, 1987.

——. *Thinking Across the American Grain: Ideology, Intellect, and the New Pragmatism*. Chicago: University of Chicago Press, 1992.

Habermas, Jürgen. *Knowledge and Human Interests*. Boston: Beacon Press, 1971.

——. *The Theory of Communicative Action*. Trans. Thomas McCarthy. Boston: Beacon Press, 1984.

Haack, Susan. *Evidence and Inquiry*. Oxford, UK, and Cambridge, MA: Blackwell, 1993.

——."'We Pragmatists....' :Peirce and Rorty in Conversation." *Synthese* (forthcoming).

——. "Pragmatism." In *Companion to Philosophy*, ed. N. Bunnin and E. James. Oxford: Blackwell (forthcoming).

Hacking, Ian. *Representing and Intervening*. Cambridge: Cambridge University Press, 1983.

——. "Five Parables." In *Philosophy in History*, ed. Richard Rorty, J. B. Schneewind, and Quentin Skinner, Cambridge: Cambridge University Press, 1984.

Hausman, Carl R., *C. S. Peirce's Evolutionary Philosophy*. Cambridge: Cambridge University Press, 1993.

Heidegger, Martin. *Being and Time*, Oxford: Blackwell, 1967.

——. *Basic Writings*. Ed. David Farrell Krell. New York: Harper and Row, 1977.

Hempel, Carl G. "Problems and Changes in the Empiricist Criterion of Meaning." In *Revue International de Philosophie* 4:41–63 (1950). Reprinted in *Semantics and the Philosophy of Language,* ed. L. Linsky. Urbana: University of Illinois Press, 1952, pp. 163–85.

Hook, Sidney. *John Dewey: An Intellectual Portrait*. Westport, CT: Greenwood Press, 1971.

Hookway, Christopher. *Peirce*. New York: Routledge, 1985.

Jacobson, David. *Emerson's Pragmatic Vision*. University Park: The Pennsylvania State University Press, 1993.

James, William. *Pragmatism: A New Name For Some Old Ways of Thinking*. 1907. Reprint Cambridge, MA: Harvard University Press, 1975.

——. *Essays in Radical Empiricism*. 1912. Reprint, Cambridge, MA: Harvard University Press, 1976.

——. *The Meaning of Truth*. 1909. Reprint, Cambridge, MA: Harvard University Press, 1975.

——. *A Pluralistic Universe.* 1909. Reprint, Cambridge, MA: Harvard University Press, 1977.

——. *The Will to Believe and Other Essays in Popular Philosophy.* 1897. Reprint, Cambridge, MA: Harvard University Press, 1979.

——. *The Principles of Psychology*. 1890. Reprint, Cambridge, MA: Harvard University Press, 1981.

——. *Talks to Teachers on Psychology and to Students on Some of Life's Ideals.* 1899. Reprint, Cambridge, MA: Harvard University Press, 1983.

——. *Varieties of Religious Experience*. 1902. Reprint, Cambridge, MA: Harvard University Press, 1985.

——. *Writings 1902–1910*. New York: The Library of America, 1987.

Kant, Immanuel. *Immanuel Kant's Critique of Pure Reason*. Trans. Norman Kemp Smith. London: Macmillan, 1963.

Kolenda, Konstantin, ed. *Person and Community in American Philosophy*. Houston: Rice University Press, 1981.

Kuhn, Thomas S. *The Structure of Scientific Revolutions*. Chicago and London: University of Chicago Press, 1962.

Kuklick, Bruce. *Churchmen and Philosophers*. New Haven: Yale University Press, 1985.

Levinson, Henry Samuel. *The Religious Investigations of William James*. Chapel Hill: University of North Carolina Press, 1981.

Lewis, Clarence Irving. *Mind and the World Order*. New York and Chicago: Scribner's and Sons, 1929.

——. *An Analysis of Knowledge and Valuation*. La Salle, IL: Open Court, 1946.

Lovejoy, Arthur. *The Thirteen Pragmatisms*. Baltimore: Johns Hopkins University Press, 1963, pp. 1–29.

Lyotard, Jean-François. *The Postmodern Condition: A Report on Knowledge*. Trans. Geoff Bennington and Brian Massumi. Minneapolis: University of Minnesota Press, 1984.

MacIntyre, Alasdair. *After Virtue.* 2d ed. Notre Dame, IN: University of Notre Dame Press, 1984.

——. *Whose Justice? Which Rationality?* Notre Dame, IN: University of Notre Dame Press, 1988.

MacKinnon, Catharine. "On Exceptionality." In *Feminism Unmodified: Discourses on Life and Law.* Cambridge, MA: Harvard University Press, 1987.

Malachowski, Alan. *Reading Rorty.* Oxford: Blackwell, 1990.

McCarthy, Thomas. *The Critical Theory of Jürgen Habermas.* Cambridge and London: MIT Press, 1981.

McCumber, John. "Reconnecting Rorty: The Situation of Discourse in Richard Rorty's *Contingency, Irony, and Solidarity.*" *Diacritics,* Summer 1990, pp. 2–19.

McDermott, John. *Streams of Experience.* Amherst: University of Massachusetts Press, 1986.

Mitchell, W. J. T., ed. *Against Theory: Literary Studies and the New Pragmatism.* Chicago and London: University of Chicago Press, 1982.

Murphy, John P. *Pragmatism: From Peirce to Davidson.* Boulder, CO: Westview, 1990.

Myers, Gerald. *William James: His Life and Thought.* New Haven: Yale University Press, 1986.

Okrent, Mark. *Heidegger's Pragmatism.* Ithaca: Cornell University Press, 1988.

Peirce, Charles Sanders. *Collected Papers of Charles Sanders Peirce.* Ed. Charles Hartshorne and Paul Weiss. Cambridge, MA: The Belknap Press of Harvard University Press, 1965.

Perry, Ralph Barton. *The Thought and Character of William James.* Boston: Little. Brown. 1935.

Poirier. Richard. *The Renewal of Literature: Emersonian Reflections.* New York: Random House, 1987.

———. *Poetry and Pragmatism.* Cambridge, MA: Harvard University Press, 1992.

Posnock, Ross. *The Trial of Curiosity.* New York: Oxford University Press, 1991.

Putnam, Hilary. *Mathematics, Matter, and Method.* Cambridge: Cambridge University Press, 1975.

———. *Reason, Truth, and History.* Cambridge: Cambridge University Press, 1981.

———. *Realism and Reason.* Cambridge: Cambridge University Press, 1983.

———. *The Many Faces of Realism.* La Salle, IL: Open Court, 1987.

———. *Representation and Reality.* Cambridge, MA: MIT Press, 1989.

———. *Realism with a Human Face.* Cambridge, MA: Harvard University Press, 1990.

———. "A Reconsideration of Deweyan Democracy." *Southern California Law Review,* 63 (1990), pp. 1671–1697.

———. *Renewing Philosophy.* Cambridge, MA: Harvard University Press, 1992.

———. *Words and Life.* Cambridge, MA: Harvard University Press, 1994.

Quine, Willard Van Orman. "Two Dogmas of Empiricism." In W. V. O. Quine, *From a Logical Point of View.* (Cambridge, MA: Harvard University Press, 1953), pp. 20–46.

———. *Word and Object.* Cambridge, MA: MIT Press, 1960.

Robinson, David M. *Emerson and the Conduct of Life: Pragmatism and Cultural Purpose in the Later Work.* Cambridge: Cambridge University Press, 1993.

Rorty, Richard. *Philosophy and the Mirror of Nature.* Princeton: Princeton University Press, 1979.

———. *Consequences of Pragmatism.* Minneapolis: University of Minnesota Press, 1982.

———. *Contingency, Irony, and Solidarity.* Cambridge: Cambridge University Press, 1989.

———. *Objectivity, Relativism and Truth.* Cambridge: Cambridge University Press, 1991.

———. *Essays on Heidegger and Others.* Cambridge: Cambridge University Press, 1991.

———. "Feminism and Pragmatism." *Michigan Quarterly Review,* 1991.

———. "Trotsky and the Wild Orchids." *Common Knowledge,* 1.3, 1992, pp. 140–53.

———. "Putnam and the Relativist Menace." *Journal of Philosophy,* vol. 90, no. 9 (1993), pp. 443–61.

Said, Edward W. *The World, the Text, and the Critic.* Cambridge, MA: Harvard University Press, 1983.

———. *Musical Elaborations.* New York: Columbia University Press, 1991.

Seigfried, Charlene Haddock, ed. *Hypatia,* 8: 2 (Spring. 1993). Special issue on "Feminism and Pragmatism".

Sellars, Wilfrid. *Science, Perception, and Reality.* Atlantic Highlands, NJ: Humanities Press, 1963.

Sleeper, R. W. *The Necessity of Pragmatism: John Dewey's Conception of Philosophy.* New Haven: Yale University Press, 1986.

Thayer, H. S. *Meaning and Action: A Critical History of Pragmatism.* Indianapolis, IN: Hackett, 1981.

Tiles, J. E. *Dewey.* New York: Routledge, 1989.

Unger, Roberto. *Social Theory, Its Situation and Its Task: A Critical Introduction to Politics—A Work in Constructive Social Theory.* Cambridge: Cambridge University Press, 1987.

West, Cornel. *The American Evasion of Philosophy: A Genealogy of Pragmatism.* Madison, WI: University of Wisconsin Press, 1987.

———. "Race and Social Theory: Towards a Genealogical Materialist Analysis," In *American Left Yearbook* 2. Ed. Michael Davis, et al. London: Verso, 1987, pp. 74–90.

———. *Race Matters.* Boston: Beacon Press, 1993.

———. *Keeping Faith.* New York: Routledge, 1994.

White, Morton. *Toward Reunion in Philosophy.* Cambridge, MA: Harvard University Press, 1956.

Williams, Bernard. *Ethics and the Limits of Philosophy.* Cambridge, MA: Harvard University Press, 1985.

Wilshire, Bruce. *William James and Phenomenology.* Bloomington, IN: Indiana University Press, 1968.

Wittgenstein, Ludwig. *Philosophical Investigations.* Trans. G. E. M. Anscombe, New York: Macmillan, 1953.

———. *On Certainty.* Ed. G. E. M. Anscombe and G. H. von Wright. Trans. Denis Paul and G. E. M. Anscombe.Oxford: Blackwell, 1969.

Westbrook, Robert B. *John Dewey and American Democracy.* Ithaca and London: Cornell University Press, 1991.

CONTRIBUTORS

STANLEY CAVELL, Walter M. Cabot Professor of Aesthetics and the General Theory of Value, Harvard University

STANLEY FISH, Professor of English, Duke University

NANCY FRASER, Professor of Philosophy, Northwestern University

RUSSELL B. GOODMAN, Professor of Philosophy, University of New Mexico

IAN HACKING, Professor of the History and Philosophy of Science, University of Toronto

RICHARD POIRIER, Professor of English, Rutgers University

HILARY PUTNAM, Walter Beverly Pearson Professor of Modern Mathematics and Mathematical Logic, Harvard University

RICHARD RORTY, University Professor of Humanities, University of Virginia

CORNEL WEST, Professor of Religion and Afro-American Studies, Harvard University

INDEX